MARK'S STORY OF JESUS, MESSIAH FOR ALL NATIONS

Dewey M. Mulholland

MARK'S STORY OF JESUS, MESSIAH FOR ALL NATIONS

Dewey M. Mulholland

Wipf & Stock
PUBLISHERS
Eugene, Oregon

Mark's Story of Jesus, Messiah for All Nations
By Dewey M. Mulholland

ISBN: 1-57910-251-4

Printed by WIPF & STOCK Publishers, 1999.
199 W. 8th Avenue, Suite 3
Eugene, Oregon 97401
www.wipfandstock.com

DEDICATION

To
EDITH

My Companion "in the way" with Jesus

TABLE OF CONTENTS

PREFACE

For almost forty years I had the privilege of introducing students to inductive study of the Gospel according to Mark, first in the underdeveloped Northeast of Brazil and then in the nation's capital, Brasília. More recently, I enjoyed similar opportunities with seminary students in the Netherlands and Mozambique.

I was nurtured on the Holy Scriptures from birth. I am ever grateful for the influence of Dad's faithful expository preaching and of Mother's gentle example of a person who loved God and others above herself. In 1944 Lorne Sanny of the Navigators led me into personal Bible study. My interest in Mark began eleven years later under the stimulating teaching of Dr. Rebecca Price who introduced me to the enriching study of biblical narratives. Dr. Daniel P. Fuller's disciplined approach fostered in me a desire to examine each literary unit and its contribution to the book as an integrated whole.

I have had the privilege of sowing the seed of the Word of God in fertile soil that has reproduced many times over. In response to my questions designed to force them to probe into the biblical text, my students gained insights of their own. They began to ask of the text questions arising from their own culture. Frequently answers could not be found in commentaries written in the traditions of Western culture. So together we sought answers relevant to their world. In the process, they taught me much about the TWO-THIRDS WORLD and brought me new insights about the meaning of Scripture. Perhaps this volume will repay a little of the debt I owe them.

I was too busy with teaching and seminary administration to give much thought to writing a commentary on Mark's Gospel, although many students encouraged me to write. Although many scholars are publishing studies on Mark, it soon became evident that most were writing from within an Euro-American worldview. Not one of them addressed some questions Brazilian students frequently ask, such as: "Is John the Baptist's appearance in fulfillment of prophecies concerning Elijah (Mk 9.13) a case of reincarnation?"

So when Dr. Russell Shedd asked me to write the commentary on Mark's Gospel for the *Série Cultura Bíblica* (published in Brazil under the title Marcos: Introdução e Comentário), I accepted. Although I touched on some critical questions, I did not write for the specialists but for readers in general who want to understand the gospel and its relevance to their daily lives. I sought to address those things that concern men and women in the TWO-THIRDS WORLD. I readily acknowledge that, even after 43 years in Brazil, my North American cultural background influences my comments. Hopefully, my shortcomings will encourage sons and daughters of other cultures to write for their own contexts. That will be a distinct contribution to Mark's desire (and mine) that the gospel be understood and lived by people in all nations.

I have made some revisions for the English edition and included excursus and additional material for pastors, teachers and knowledgeable lay persons who desire more. I encourage my readers to interact with the text and to make it pertinent to their culture and their own personal needs.

I thank God for revealing himself through Jesus Christ, the living Word, and through the Bible, the written Word. I am grateful to CB International and to Brazilian Baptists for giving me the opportunity to teach the Scriptures in Brazil. I readily acknowledge my indebtedness to authors whose books have enriched my life and research. Some of their works have been so incorporated into my thinking that credit is not always given in the text. I am grateful for their forgiving me in accord with Mark 11.25. I consulted commentaries written in Portuguese and Spanish and, to help those interested in further study, gave preference to reference works available in Portuguese (e.g., Collin Brown's Dictionary of New Testament Theology instead of Gerhard Kittel's ten-volume work which is unavailable in Portuguese).

I gladly express my deep gratitude to all who have helped in making this book possible. Above all others, I thank my wife, Edith, for her encouragement and suggestions as well as her patience when my chores went undone. With love and gratitude for our over fifty years together, I dedicate this book to her. Our daughter, Ann Mulholland Wozniak, rearranged her priorities in order to work through the whole text. Her suggestions and corrections were invaluable. Colleagues in the Faculdade Teológica Batista de Brasília made helpful suggestions about portions of the text. I alone, however, bear responsibility for the final product.

Dewey M. Mulholland

Please send your comments to the author:
Dewey Mulholland
2379 Garfias Dr.
Pasadena, CA 91104
e-mail address: DeweyEdith@earthlink.com
telephone: 626-791-8343

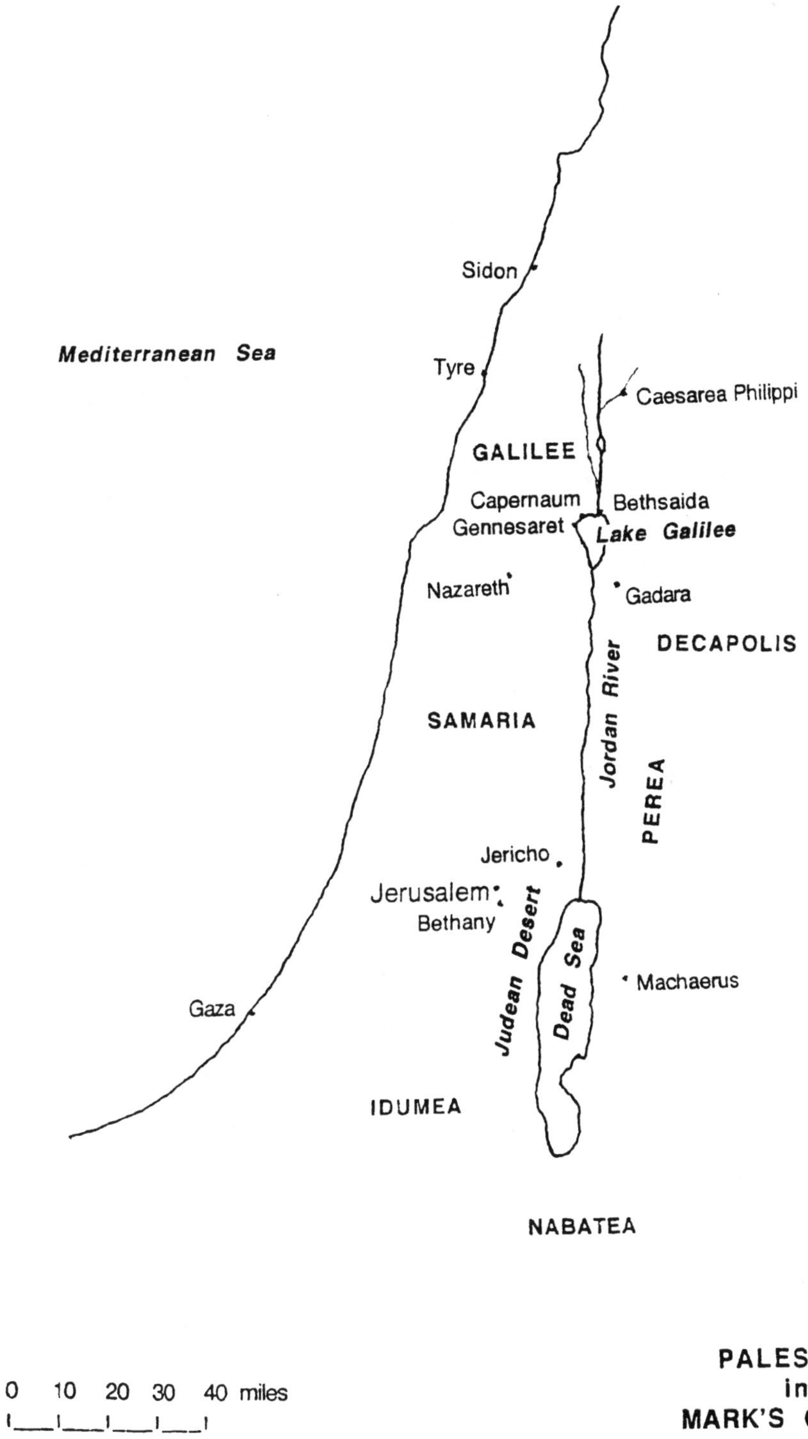

PALESTINE
in
MARK'S GOSPEL

INTRODUCTION

Jesus is the Christ, the Son of God. His life and death, his words and deeds have changed forever the course of human life. He has established the basis of hope for the future. This good news is presented to us in a short book known as "the Gospel according to Mark," probably the oldest of the written accounts about him that we possess.

On the surface, the Gospel of Mark appears to be a simple recounting of incidents in the life and ministry of Jesus. By his skillful portrayal of those episodes, however, the author forcefully introduces a truly human Jesus who is at the same time God among men and women. By competent selection and strategic placement of his material, he integrates theology with the realities of life. His vivid character portrayals draw readers into experiencing those events first-hand, for persons everywhere share the struggles of Jesus' contemporaries. By depicting how God's rule became a reality with the coming of Jesus, he challenges humankind to radical discipleship.

This Gospel offers us an excellent opportunity to contemplate the person of Jesus Christ. Through him, we learn what God is like, what he expects of men and women and what he has done to make that expectation possible. Moreover, Jesus invites each one of us to follow him and thus enjoy here and now the privileges and responsibilities of living in the Kingdom of God.

The Occasion, Author and Date of the Gospel

We would find it helpful if the Gospel explicitly identified its author, his purposes, the date of composition and other details. In the absence of such data, students of the Gospel search for information implicit within the text and for external evidences in their attempts to understand the background and origin of the text. Each approaches such an investigation with his or her own presuppositions. Within these parameters, I present in these introductory pages what I believe to be a credible hypothesis of the origin of the Gospel of Mark.

As those who had been with Jesus were approaching the end of their earthly sojourn, it became imperative that the story of Jesus' life and teachings be recorded for future generations. Beyond its importance as an historical document, this account could introduce men and women to Jesus and lead them to acknowledge him as the Christ, the Son of God. By portraying the disciples' struggles to understand and follow Jesus in the way of the cross, this narrative could also be an effective guide to a life of obedience to God.

The author of this Gospel responds to these needs by writing for people at different levels of understanding. As an evangelist, he seeks radical commitment to Jesus on the part of his readers. He also writes as a pastor mindful of the struggling communities of believers.

During the middle of the first century A.D., Rome was a bustling city of well over a million people. It drew men and women from every province of the far-flung frontiers of the Empire and beyond. They brought with them their own customs, languages and religions.

Christians also came, bringing their new faith in Jesus Christ. They shared the gospel with all, regardless of ethnic origin, social status or economic class. But the diverse ethnic and religious backgrounds of the new believers threatened authentic Christianity. New converts incorporated elements from their religious heritages into Christian doctrine. Their behavior often offended the moral codes of other believers.

Relationships between Jewish and Gentile believers became especially difficult, as synagogue leaders vigorously denounced Jews who rejected their ancient traditions. Incipient persecution by Roman authorities was on the increase as allegiance to Caesar collided with loyalty to Jesus Christ and his Kingdom.

Suffering from internal tensions and under attack by outside forces, the Christian community in Rome needed help. As he composes the Gospel of Mark, the author seeks to minister to those believers.

The house of Mary was a rendezvous for the first Christians in Jerusalem (Ac 12.12; this is possibly the same house mentioned in Ac 1.13). There, her son John (who was called Mark) had ample opportunity to become acquainted with leaders of the early church. He was probably converted through Peter's ministry (1Pe 5.13) and discipled by this apostle and by his relative, Barnabas (Ac 12.25).

On the first missionary journey, Barnabas and Saul took John Mark along as a **huperetes** (Ac 13.5). Normally translated as "helper" or "minister", in Luke 1.2 this same Greek word refers to recognized authorities on Jesus' words and deeds. Among the Jews of that time, some superior pupils were selected to be **huperetes**. They were trained to memorize, interpret and transmit their oral tradition.[1] According to the unanimous testimony of the early church, Mark received the gospel from Peter. Willard M. Swartley[2] suggests "Peter, an apostolic eyewitness, personally trained Mark to be a **huperetes**." In this capacity, Mark "ministered" to Saul of Tarsus (Paul) on the journey into Asia Minor (47-49 A.D.) by filling in the gaps in Saul's knowledge of Jesus' words and deeds.

The Acts of the Apostles does not tell why John Mark "left and returned to Jerusalem" (13.13). Perhaps his training under Peter made him uneasy about Paul's acceptance of Gentiles without requiring circumcision and so Mark rushed off to discuss the problem with his mentor. After the decision on this question by the Jerusalem Council (Ac 15), Barnabas wanted Mark to rejoin the team (15.36-40). They went their separate ways, however, for a sharp disagreement arose between Paul and Barnabas.

Following this report, the book of the Acts omits any further reference to Mark (or to Peter, for that matter). Mark reappears in the Epistles (60-65 A.D.). He and Paul are reconciled and are together in Rome. Mark is Paul's fellow worker and a comfort to him. Commended by Paul to the church in Colosse (Col 4.10-11; Phm 24), Mark presumably visits those believers. Later, Paul asks Timothy to bring Mark to him in Rome, for "he is useful to me in my ministry" (2Ti 4.11).

Markan and Pauline theology evidence a close relationship. For example, both emphasize the centrality of the cross of Christ and his humiliation as the path to his glorification. Both seek to bring harmony in the Christian community composed of Jewish and Gentile believers without softening their denunciation of Jewish legalism. The place of the Mosaic Law in the Christian community, the hostility of civil and religious leaders against Jesus and his followers, and the fulfillment of God's purposes as revealed in the Old Testament are also themes common to both Mark and Paul's writings.

In contrast to Paul's propositional approach, Mark expresses his theology in narratives of Jesus' life. In this way, he invites his readers to identify their experiences with gospel events and to grow in their knowledge of God and how he works. His accounts of Jesus' sufferings, for example, provide bases for self-denial as a part of discipleship (cf 8.34). As William Lane (23) rightly observes, "a careful reading of the Gospel will serve to introduce the author as a theologian of the first rank who never forgot that his primary intention was the strengthening of the people of God in a time of fiery ordeal."

Peter also spent his last years in Rome and was martyred there about the same time as Paul. Mark had been with him in the beginning in Jerusalem; now, he is in daily association with Peter at the end of the apostle's life. Mark's vivid narratives and distinctive use of pronouns reflect the influence of Peter's eyewitness testimony. Through Mark's narrative, Peter even relates details of his own failures to understand the significance of Jesus' ministry and death. His full understanding only came after the resurrection, when Jesus opened the minds of his followers so they could understand the Scriptures (Lk 24.27,45; Ac 1.3). Under the guidance of the Holy Spirit (Jn 16.12ff; cf 2Ti 3.16f; 2Pe 1.20f), Mark drew heavily upon Peter's personal experiences with Jesus and his presentation of the gospel.

According to tradition, Mark had served Christ in various parts of the Roman Empire. A Jew well acquainted with the Law and the Prophets, the traditions and customs of the Jews, he had the joy of leading Gentiles into the family of God. He experienced the heartaches of hostility between Jewish and Gentile believers as he sought to heal the schisms between them. He ministered to followers of Jesus who had experienced imprisonment, to congregations that had lost their leaders, been mutilated by persecution and crippled by inward divisions. Through these experiences, Mark gained knowledge that would be very useful in writing a gospel that could help churches in their struggles.

John Mark was uniquely equipped to write the Gospel attributed to him. As a result of his early association with Jerusalem Christian leaders and his life-long relationship with Peter, Mark had become an authority on the life and deeds of Jesus. With Paul, his theological perception became relevant to the Christian mission among the nations. Beyond his experiences as a colleague of both Peter and Paul, Mark acquired through his own ministries pastoral ability and cross-cultural experiences invaluable in serving the Christians in Rome.

Dates proposed for the appearance of this Gospel in its final form range from the year 39 to well after the destruction of Jerusalem in 70 A.D.[3] It is outside the scope of this introduction to examine those proposals here. It seems reasonable that John Mark began writing his Gospel in Rome with the collaboration of Peter and Paul and that he concluded it after their martyrdom (65 A.D.) but before the Jewish wars exploded (67-70 A.D.).

In composing his Gospel, Mark was mindful of the needs of the Gentile believers. He supplied translations of Aramaic expressions (3.17; 5.41; 7.11,34; 15.22) and explanations of some Jewish customs (7.3f; 15.42). At the same time, he left many allusions to the Old Testament unexplained, evincing the Jewish roots of the Christian faith.

Mark also sought to strengthen the faith of his Jewish readers. His constant use of the Old Testament reminded them that they were God's special people, chosen to share their rich inheritance with the nations. In Jesus, they saw God's compassion and merciful forgiveness. Mark emphasized that Jesus is the Suffering Servant who fulfilled the role of the true Messiah in accord with the Prophets. He gave them hope in the midst of their sufferings. He taught them the elements of true worship, free from the legalism, nationalism and ritualism centered in Jerusalem. Mark knew that the early church must be built upon the truth of the new covenant. God's family could not compromise the Good News and still fulfill its God-given mission.

Mark's close relationship with his first readers explains several things that puzzle modern readers. He felt no need to declare explicitly his authorship: his intended readers knew he was writing Jesus' story. The personal anecdote of the young man who fled away naked would suffice as his signature (14.51-52). His readers knew the Holy Spirit had been given as foretold by John the Baptist (Mk 1.8). There was no need to write about Jesus' post-resurrection appearances, for they knew Jesus had arisen bodily from the grave (as declared in 16.6).

Mark's writing flows out of his pastoral concern for his readers. He encourages them to become growing disciples by applying to themselves all that Jesus sought to teach the Twelve. He is convinced that true knowledge of Jesus' nature, character and ministry are necessary for healthy individual and community life. He bears in mind his readers' dilemmas and opportunities. He wants them to understand the proper significance of the gospel and to follow Jesus whatever the cost. By presenting Jesus' own ministry among Gentiles, Mark encourages Jewish believers to embrace Gentile believers as joint-heirs of God's grace. This unity is essential to authentic disciples and vibrant churches. By presenting Jesus' teachings in such a way as to attend to the existential needs of those first readers in their social context, he serves as a model for all those who seek to present the gospel with relevance for their contemporaries.

Mark is keenly interested in the spread of the gospel to all nations. His Gospel is designed to lead unbelievers to faith in Christ and to prepare believers to live and proclaim the Good News. This is consistent with his emphasis upon discipleship. His method is twofold. First he unfolds the message clearly and fully, and then he exhorts all disciples to follow Jesus in the mission he began, namely, taking the Good News to Jews and Gentiles alike. As Mark emphasizes, Jesus is the Messiah for all nations.

This Gospel has a universal appeal,[4] substantiating Mark's conviction that the story of Jesus is essential for all humanity.

The Genre of the Gospel and its Interpretation

Although the Gospel of Mark was well received when it first appeared, the other Gospels soon gained favor in the early church. After receiving little attention for centuries, Mark was re-examined as the earliest gospel account. (The context will indicate when we use "Mark" in reference to "the Gospel according to Mark" or to the author himself.) Some nineteenth-century scholars sought "the historical Jesus," convinced that the early church had created "the divine Christ of faith." In the 1920s, form critics, led by R. Bultmann and M. Dibelius, labeled Matthew and Mark as "principally collectors of tradition, editors" and their Gospels as unquestionably "unliterary writings."[5] In their opinion, the Gospels consist of collections of stories that had been told and retold by preachers and teachers. Their stories are useful in providing information about the faith of the early Christian community but provide no basis for a life of Jesus. As a result, form critics focused on the formation of the individual units in the Gospels.

Around mid-century, investigation moved a step toward a reintegration of the text. Redaction critics such as W. Marxsen emphasized the need to see the writers of the gospels "as creative artists guided by their theological concepts and community problems."[6] In their investigation of how the individual units, stories and sayings in the gospels where put together, however, they failed to see how the units are related to one another to form a continuous narrative in which each episode is understood in its relationship to the whole.

The purpose of the gospel is to change lives. Some critics, however, changed the Gospels. While appreciative of some insights gained from form and redaction criticism, a number of scholars objected to those who felt free to deny, alter or ignore the text to suit their own presuppositions. Others noted that some writers uncritically adopted rationalistic presuppositions (such as the evolutionary development of religions). Thomas J. Weeden, Sr., expressed his lack of confidence "in the ability of redaction criticism to reconstruct the precise content and contextual parameters of the pre-Markan tradition or traditions."[7] After years of studying questions of tradition and redaction, Norman Perrin concluded that these are relatively unimportant in the interpretation of Mark: "what matters is the *function* of the text concerned in the Gospel as a whole."[8]

While some form and redaction studies have contributed to New Testament studies, the attempt to discover and analyze the preliterary parts has had the effect of dissolving the whole. When the text is viewed as having a literary form similar to that of a fine stamp collection, the result is a disintegration of the Gospels. When Mark is read on his own terms, readers recognize that he was an exceptionally capable and artful writer. Greek is obviously not his mother tongue, but, as Kee concludes (64), his linguistic simplicity "must not lead the interpreter to infer a simplicity of thought patterns."

A new era began around 1970 with the growth of literary criticism. Kealy (198) calls it "Mark Restored." Many scholars now regard Mark's Gospel as a composition produced by a creative author. They see that what is needed is a synthetic approach which avoids atomizing the narrative. Without disregarding perceptions gained from other methodologies, they analyze the whole as a unified narrative. In a continuing process, the parts are examined in relation to the whole and the whole in relation to the parts. They realize that "the first task of exegesis and biblical theology is to interpret the Gospels as they stand."[9]

Each Gospel account has distinctive features that reflect the richness of its sources tuned to the need of its original readers. For this reason, the Evangelists vary in reporting the same saying of Jesus (e.g., compare Mk 10.18 with its parallel in Mt 19.17). From the material at hand, each author carefully selected episodes which show who Jesus is and organized them in such a way as to challenge his readers to radical discipleship. Their decisions were made deliberately under the guidance of the Holy Spirit.

Mark does not describe things as a modern historian, nor does he always quote Jesus word-for-word as required of a court reporter. Yet he presents Jesus and his teachings accurately in ways which would convey their meaning clearly with the most relevance for his readers. He omitted some things we may desire to know. That doesn't mean he didn't know them; they may have been extraneous to his purposes or already known by his first readers. When the text is understood as the purposeful composition of a theologian who carefully selected his material and creatively composed it according to his purposes, many alleged contradictions turn out to be illusory.

In its overall plan, the Gospel of Mark progresses chronologically, from Jesus' baptism by John to his crucifixion and resurrection. The general lines of Jesus' travels can be traced as he moves about Galilee and then journeys on to Jerusalem. Since God's saving activity takes place in historical events, Mark presents his Gospel in the form of an historical narrative. The wealth of graphic detail is evidence of its historical trustworthiness.

However, neither chronology nor geography governs every detail in the general sequence of his narrative. The author felt free to weave in events from other times or places if they would clarify his current theme. As an example, once opposition from religious leaders began (2.1-12), Mark develops that subject in five encounters that end in plans to kill Jesus (3.6). He carefully composes this literary unit in order to make his theological point. To present Jesus' person and why he died is more important than the sequence of events. This does not suggest that Mark invented incidents or sayings of Jesus. There is no indication that he ever did that. His creativity appears in his ability to make his material meaningful to his readers in accord with his purpose.

The author's paramount purpose is aligned with God's purpose in revealing himself: he desires that every reader know God. This includes more than thinking rightly about God. It means knowing him first hand. It entails personal involvement with him, wanting what he wants and wanting to be what he wants one to be. To know him is a great incentive to love, worship and be led by him. Knowledge of God's nature and deeds gives perspective to one's view of self and releases one to realize his or her God-given potential. Mark seeks to achieve this purpose by presenting the person of Jesus Christ who does not just show God's will in action but is the revelation of God himself. He is convinced that it is only through God's Son that a person comes to know the Father. To go through life without knowing God is the greatest of tragedies; to know him is the loftiest endeavor to which anyone can aspire.

Although Mark himself cites the Old Testament only twice (in 1.2-3 and 15.24), his Gospel includes hundreds of allusions and quotations drawn especially from the Pentateuch, the Psalms and the Prophets (including something from every chapter of Daniel). Quotations are blended together, deriving vital significance from their synthesis (e.g., 1.11; 13.24; 14.62). While often denouncing the oral traditions, Jesus lived according to the Scriptures and encouraged his followers to trust in them.

As Rhoads and Michie point out, the author uses sophisticated literary techniques to communicate his message. He employs repetition, cycles, chiasmus, and two- and three-step progressions. He juxtaposes thoughts in order to underline comparisons and contrasts. Mark's use of dialogue and irony draw the reader into the events as a participant. He often embeds stories within stories to interpret the narrative to the reader; sometimes he uses parallelism to comment or enhance meaning. Mark skillfully builds meaning into terms introduced unostentatiously. In an effort to avoid false connotations, he takes special care with titles referring to Jesus. These and other literary characteristics will be considered where they appear in the narrative itself.

Mark is not content to convey knowledge; he desires that each one repent and believe (cf 1.15). He skillfully invites us to identify our own lives and struggles with those of the disciples. He calls attention to their failures so that we might avoid those pitfalls. He illustrates authentic discipleship by portraying men and women who receive Jesus' word with understanding.

Although he never uses the word **ekklesia** ("church"), Mark presents the believer as a member of God's family. He establishes guidelines on the nature and ministry of "the house of prayer" and its leaders. He consciously clarifies the relevance of Jesus' life and death to the needs of the early church. He desires to encourage and change the Christian community. He lays upon it the responsibility to call all persons to repentance and to disciple each one who believes. He understands the theological needs of struggling Christians in a hostile world. He also writes as a pastor mindful of the interpersonal relationships of the struggling communities of believers. His concern extends to Christian leaders, implying that Jesus will reproach them if they fall into pitfalls similar to those he censured among Jewish religious leaders.

Because the Gospel is a close-knit whole, the reader needs to see the whole to understand correctly any part of it. Unfortunately, we normally read the Gospels piece-meal and interpret them with little regard for either the immediate context or the book as a whole. The Gospel of Mark demands a holistic approach, for we can understand a particular passage only when we account for its function within the narrative as a whole. This writer seeks to study Mark as a coherent account, concentrating on the text itself with its demands to take seriously its countless direct and indirect references to the Old Testament.

Prominent Themes in Mark

Mark brought together many episodes in the life and ministry of Jesus and wove them together creatively into a new and exciting whole. The result is a unified, cohesive narrative, with Jesus Christ as central among the many themes that recur as in a great symphony throughout the Gospel. The manifold splendor of the Son of God who is fully human is unveiled through Jesus' life, death and resurrection. He not only demonstrates God's will in action--he reveals God himself, for he is God incarnate, living among men and women in the midst of the human predicament. In warm tones and with a pastoral concern, Mark develops discipleship as a secondary theme. This is inseparable from the dominant theme of Jesus, for through the unique significance of who Jesus is, God calls men, women and children of all nations and enthnicities to radical discipleship and to harmonious life together as members of his family.

Within this two-fold emphasis, the author presents several other themes; each makes a unique contribution to the unity of the whole narrative. Prominent among them is the Kingdom of God, a reality that is already present among men and women but not yet consummated. It spreads among the nations without fanfare; its final, universal triumph is hailed with the clash of celestial symbols.

Resonant pastoral tones swell, fade and swell again. Dissonance resounds as God's kingdom engages in conflict with self-centered humanity and with both religious and political powers, cosmic in dimension, human and Satanic in origin. Harmony seems rejected as the paradoxical themes of revelation and hiddenness, power and weakness, first and last, and triumph through suffering, build up in preparation for an impossible climax. The King is crowned with thorns. Rejected by his own, he is acclaimed by one who crucified him. The rebellion of sinful humans accomplishes God's eternal purposes. And the smitten Shepherd rises again to lead his scattered sheep to fish for men.

As one can never forget experiencing Handel's "Hallelujah Chorus", neither can one forget Mark's symphony of paradoxes. Only by living within the story can we sense its true beauty and significance. As we see and hear, touch, taste and smell what is happening right along with the persons portrayed, we will begin to feel its heartbeat and experience some of the significance and joy of what it means to follow Jesus.

I encourage each one to study the Markan text before reading my comments about it. Make the Bible itself the center of your studies. First of all, read and re-read the text to discover as accurately as you can *what it says*. The second step in direct Bible study is to find out *what it meant for the original readers*. Only then are you in a position to ask, "*what does God want of me in the light of this passage?*" Don't neglect this last step, for Bible study is concluded only when it is applied to life. Read the Gospel to know God, for Jesus reveals God's personality in daily relationships with humans. The Bible was not written just to transmit information; it was written to change lives. My "suggestions for reflection and action" at the end of the commentary are given in the hope of encouraging you in this endeavor.

An Overview of the Gospel of Mark

In studying the Scriptures, we ignore the traditional division of the text into chapters and verses, for it is generally artificial and sometimes prejudicial. Our task requires us to seek to discover the Biblical writer's own arrangement of his material, for he communicates through the relationships of his literary units as well as through words. The skillful structure underlying Mark's Gospel increasingly impresses scholars. It is not a simple addition of components but an integrated whole. From the beginning, the author builds his narrative to the climax by skillfully employing the literary techniques mentioned above.

Paul S. Minear (43) included an outline in his commentary, with the candid confession that "this is not Mark's outline, but ours." While I cannot claim it is Mark's outline, my "Overview" includes what I perceive to be his organization of his Gospel. This commentary is structured accordingly. It helps me understand his Gospel. I hope it will help you, too.

Mark had come to know Jesus as the Son of God. He did not create the story; he was a recipient of God's grace who experienced life under God's rule. As Minear (19) accurately perceives, the author writes "as a slave of Jesus Christ, compelled by love to tell the story of his Master," with the desire that others might experience, as he had, what God has done for the world through his Son.

I also write as a follower of Jesus Christ, with the earnest hope that these studies, imperfect as they are, might encourage you to follow Jesus in radical discipleship.

---

[1]Some peoples today transmit their history in a similar fashion. For example, in his book entitled Roots, the late African-American Alex Haley describes his encounter in Gabon with the African responsible for preserving orally the history of his tribe.

[2]Mark, the Way for all Nations, 29

[3]In his letter to John A.T. Robinson (quoted in Seán P. Kealy 4), C.H. Dodd criticized scholars who advocate late dates for the New Testament, saying that "this late dating is quite arbitrary, even wanton, the offspring not of any argument that can be presented, but rather of the critic's prejudice that if he appears to assent to the traditional position of the early Church he will be thought no better than a stick-in-the-mud."

[4]Now translated into more than 1,500 languages and dialects, Mark is the most widely translated book in the world, and in the words of Professor Reynolds Price (in his Preface to David Rhoads and Donald Michie's Mark as Story, page xi), "the most enduringly powerful narrative in the history of Western civilization, perhaps in the history of the world."

[5]These words of Dibelius are quoted by Howard Clark Kee, p 5. C.H. Turner called Mark "a naive and non-logical composition" (D. E. Nineham 215) while others found in Mark a plot similar to that of a dictionary.

[6]Kealy 160.

[7]Werner H. Kelber Passion 130.

[8]Kelber Passion 90, italics are Perrin's.

[9]George Eldon Ladd Presence 308

An Overview of

THE GOSPEL ACCORDING TO MARK

The Gospel of Jesus Christ	Knowledge initially hidden from humanity ↓ Jesus Christ is the Son of God, anointed by the Spirit, loved by the Father, tempted by Satan	WHO IS JESUS? - - > The Son of Man speaks and acts with authority			WHERE IS HE GOING? - - > WHY? - - > The Son of Man gives his life in weakness		
DIVISIONS	Prologue	Jesus' Authority			Jesus on the Way to the Cross	Jesus and the Temple	Jesus' Suffering, Death & Resurrection
		Affirmed & contested	Its Source & Nature	Its Expansion			
references	1.1 – 1.13	1.14 – 3.6	3.7 – 6.6a	6.6b – 8.26	8.27 – 10.52	11.1 – 13.37	14.1 – 16.8
GEOGRAPHY	Jordan River & Desert	Galilee	Galilee & Decapolis	Galilee & surrounding Gentile areas	From Caesarea Philippi to Jerusalem	Jerusalem and Bethany	Jerusalem
DISCIPLESHIP		Jesus calls 4 to follow him	He appoints 12	He sends them out	His disciples must also deny self	His house of prayer is for all nations	He renews call to scattered disciples

- PART 1 -
PREPARATION
1.1-13

With six well-chosen nouns, the author entitles his work "The beginning of the gospel of Jesus Christ, the Son of God." He will infuse these words with vital and enduring significance as he portrays the life of Jesus among men and women in Palestine. Foretold by God's prophets and dramatically announced by his messenger John, Jesus is anointed by the Holy Spirit and a voice from heaven calls him "my Son". His appearance sets off conflict with Satan. These facts substantiate the declaration that Jesus Christ is the Son of God.

In his brief introduction, the author describes the preparation of people for the coming of Jesus and the preparation of Jesus for his ministry. By giving his readers privileged information, he prepares us so that we might live "the gospel of Jesus Christ, the Son of God." These verses form the background of this Gospel. All the rest should be read in their light.

A. THE TITLE OF THIS GOSPEL, 1.1

The Greek term **euaggélion** ("gospel") had a joyful ring, for it was associated the proclamation of a political communiqué or military victory that resulted in benefits for many people. Against this background, "gospel" alerts readers to the announcement of an historic event that will bring beneficial results for humanity.

Beyond this, the word has prophetic significance for those acquainted with the Old Testament. It recalls God's promise of good news (Isa 61.1f), raising hope that through his anointed servant the Spirit of the Sovereign Lord will proclaim the liberation of the oppressed (cf Lk 4.17ff). It brings assurance that God is present (Isa 40.9) and in control (Isa 52.7).

The New Testament itself never employs **euaggélion** to indicate a book. Around 150 A.D., Justin Martyr first used the term in reference to a book which presents the person of Jesus Christ. In this sense, "the four Gospels" commonly refers to the first books of the New Testament.

The word "gospel" has acquired an addition meaning, also not found in the New Testament. It refers to a specific literary style that does not fall into the other categories of composition. "Gospel genre" includes biographic elements but it does not constitute a biography of Jesus. It relates historical and geographic data, but from them we can neither reconstruct an exact chronology of Jesus' life nor trace on a map every step of his itinerary. It is a narrative with different scenes woven into a unified story that is coherent and complete in itself. A gospel is more than a narrative, however, for its events are interpreted from God's perspective. It is a theological narrative.

The Gospel according to Mark is distinct from all previous literary documents. It is probably the first example of the type of composition known as "gospel".

The author did not invent the good news; he reports it as one convinced of its veracity. He writes as a committed disciple, desirous that. we, too, might follow Jesus as disciples. He presents the good news about Jesus in such a way that we, the readers throughout the centuries, can identify ourselves with the participants in the narrative.

The good news relates to **Jesus** in two ways: it is the good news about Jesus and at the same time, it is the good news that proceeds from him. The gospel presents Jesus and it is Jesus who proclaims the gospel. He himself is the essence of the message that he preaches. In the midst of the diverse scenes and personalities presented in the unfolding of the book, Jesus is always central. The good news is the person of Jesus himself.

The name "Jesus" was used in Israel from the time of Joshua (which is the Hebraic form of the same name) and signifies "The LORD (**YHWH**) is salvation" (Mt 1.21). The designation **Christ** is the

Greek translation of the Hebrew "Messiah," signifying "the anointed one." At the very beginning of his Gospel, Mark joins the two terms: **Jesus Christ**. After this declaration that Jesus is the Christ, the word "Christ" appears only a few times in Mark (8.29; 9.41; 12.35; 13.21; 14.61; 15.32), probably to minimize false expectations connected with the Messiah at that time.

The last affirmation in Mark's title closes the door to the possibility that Jesus Christ might be only a man among other men. The gospel originates in God (1.14); Jesus Christ is the **Son of God**. This is affirmed several times, in ways and places that underscore its importance. Jesus is called the Son of God by God himself (near the beginning, 1.11, and near the middle of the book, 9.7) and by a man, the centurion in charge of the crucifixion (near the end of the book, 15.39). The organization of this Gospel revolves around these references to Jesus as the Son of God.

Mark does not present the birth of Jesus (as do Matthew and Luke), for he purposes to show that Jesus is the Son of God. His presentation is different from the other Evangelists, though all affirm that Jesus is really God incarnate, the Son of God. All four insist that in contemplation of the Son, we have a unique opportunity to know God the Father - his nature, his deeds and his desires for us.

In addition to these direct affirmations in Mark's Gospel, Jesus' divine sonship is implicit in several of his own declarations (8.38; 12.6; 13.32; 14.36, 62) and in the High Priest's inquiry (14.61). When evil spirits make similar declarations, Jesus demands that they be silent (3.11; 5.7). While Mark highlights the phrase "Son of God" by placing it so strategically at the beginning of his narrative, he goes on to emphasize Jesus' humanity as no other Gospel does. As we accompany the unfolding of this narrative, we will understand better both the human and divine connotations of the declaration "Jesus Christ, the Son of God."

The first phrase of the title, "the *beginning* of the gospel," could refer to the Old Testament promises (1.2-3), to John the Baptist's appearance (1.4-8) or to the whole Prologue (1.2-13), for each of these is, in a sense, a "beginning of the gospel." Mark, however, seems to present the whole composition as "the beginning of the gospel," for it is a story which continued with the proclamation of the gospel by the apostles and continues today "wherever the gospel is preached" (14.9). This is the new book of Genesis (both begin with "the beginning"), for, in Minear's words (46), it reports "the Beginning of the Beginning" of the creation of a new humanity for a new cosmos (13.24-27). The gospel of Jesus Christ, the Son of God, certainly had a beginning in time and space. By God's grace, however, it has no terminal point, for it leads to eternal life in the age to come (10.30).

In his title, Mark implies the general plan of his Gospel, divided into two steps: Jesus, the Christ (chapters 1 to 8), the Son of God (8 to 16). The center of the book (8.27-31) constitutes the transition from the first to the second part. At the close of the first step, Peter confesses that Jesus is the Christ; as the second part draws to a close, the centurion confesses that Jesus is the Son of God. In the first, Jesus demonstrates his authority by his words and deeds; in the second, the emphasis falls on Jesus' suffering in filial obedience to God. In the first, he serves in power; in the second, in weakness. Here, as throughout the New Testament, the salvation that God so graciously offers the world is bound up in his Son Jesus Christ.

The author will now unfold the dramatic story of "the beginning of the gospel of Jesus Christ, the Son of God," a story that offers a new beginning for those who heed Jesus' invitation, "Follow me."

• Most scholars agree that the words "Son of God" were a part of the original text but were accidentally omitted in some ancient manuscripts.

B. THE PROLOGUE, 1.2-13

Here the author presents the human and the supernatural preparation for Jesus' ministry. In accord with the prophetic message, John appears, preparing multitudes for the coming of the Lord. Jesus identifies himself with sinners through his baptism, at which time God declares that Jesus is his beloved Son in whom he is well pleased. The Holy Spirit anoints Jesus and drives him out into the desert to be tempted by Satan.

In contrast to public knowledge of John's mission, the people were unaware of God's special activity here. The author transmits this privileged information to his readers in order that they might know Jesus as God's Son.

1. John's Proclamation, 1.2-8

God had promised to redeem his people. For centuries, however, he sent no prophet to Israel. In spite of this, some still awaited good news. This hope resurges with the appearing of a prophet called John, and many openly repent in preparation for the arrival of the Promised One.

In the midst of this reawakened expectation, Jesus comes in fulfillment of the prophecies. His baptism in the Jordan River and his temptation in the desert are not what one would expect, considering the previous declaration that Jesus Christ is the Son of God. The events surrounding Jesus' baptism, however, are unique. Although they are presented with great simplicity, they are dramatic, full of surprises.

The Prologue is composed of three paragraphs, all related to preparation. The first (vv. 2-8) tells how John prepares the people to prepare for the Promised One. With Jesus' appearance and baptism in the second paragraph (vv. 9-11), John's role is fulfilled and he disappears from the narrative. God the Father and the Holy Spirit prepare Jesus for his ministry, thus confirming that it is he in whom the promises will be fulfilled. In the third paragraph (vv. 12-13), under the guidance of the Holy Spirit, Jesus is tempted and his adversary identified.

Even though Jesus is the center of all that takes place throughout this section, he is "passive:" he is being prepared by others for his ministry that begins in 1.14.

These verses move from the past with its expectations founded on God's promises, to the present in which John calls upon the people to repent, to the near future in which God acts through his Promised One.

1.2-3 - In the past, God had spoken (Heb 1.1), nurturing hope among his people. The good news is rooted in these Old Testament promises and is understood in their light. The events in the following narrative took place in fulfillment of God's established plan as announced by his prophets. Referring to the prophet Isaiah (v. 2), Mark emphasizes that God (who had spoken in the past) is now about to accomplish the salvation promised to his people. The Scriptures are worthy of confidence.

Hope springs up specifically in relation to the prophecies quoted, for they are fulfilled in the appearance of John and Jesus. Let us identify the people indicated in the quotations: the Lord God spoke to the Messiah, saying, "I send my messenger John ahead of you, to prepare your way. In the desert, my messenger will call upon the people of Israel to prepare the way for the Lord."

In his quotation, Mark follows the common practice of his time, that of bringing together two or three Old Testament passages. He ties Exodus 23.20, as expressed in Malachi 3.1, to Isaiah 40.3. The promise given in Exodus refers to God's action in Israel's flight from Egypt, while Isaiah looks to the future. Both awaken the expectation dormant for centuries. Together they say this: God is about to act. Consequently, Jesus the Lord appears (v. 9).

v. 2 - Jesus showed special appreciation of the prophet Isaiah. Throughout, Mark includes many quotations and allusions to Isaiah. As a good narrator, he focuses attention on the key prophet without losing his readers in secondary details.
• Composite quotations were considered legitimate by first-century Jews and are used frequently in Mark (e.g., 1.2-3; 1.11; 7.7; 11.17; 14.62) and in the Pauline Epistles. They enrich the significance of the original declarations. The parallel passages do not include Mark's quotation in verse 2b.
• In the Old Testament contexts of these quotations, the "way" refers to the pilgrimage through the desert to "the place I have prepared" (Ex 23.20b). Used twice here in the beginning of Mark, "way" (**hodos**) implies that the ministries of John and of Jesus lead to the Kingdom of God (Swartley New Way 158). In 8.27-10.52, the "way" dramatizes discipleship as following Jesus "in the way" of the Kingdom, that is, the way of the cross.
v. 3 - The Greek words **eremos**, **eremia** and **eremos topos** are translated "desert", "wilderness", "lonely place" and "open country." They indicate an "uninhabited place," not an arid desert (cf 6.31; 8.4).

1.4-6 - God's messenger John comes, preaching in the desert, just as was promised. The desert recalls Israel's experience when, freed from slavery in Egypt, God disciplined them in preparation for entering the Promised Land. Now God is initiating a new exodus. Separating themselves from the ease of institutionalized religious life, multitudes gather in the desert to hear John.

Although no prophetic voice has been heard for centuries, the faithful continue to wait for God to fulfill his promises. They believe that a prophet will appear in the last days, in preparation for the day of the Lord. He will be a faithful emissary from God, with the same message as the true prophets in Israel's history. This hope is nurtured by the Lord's words through Malachi (4.5-6), "I will send you the prophet Elijah before that great and dreadful day of the Lord comes," a day of judgment and of salvation. This prophet will announce the fulfillment of the ancient prophecies.

Nowhere does Mark describe Jesus' appearance, although he is the central figure in the Gospel. However, he purposely describes John's clothing and food (v. 6) in terms that remind us of Elijah's garment of hair and a leather belt (2Ki 1.8, Zec 13.4). In this way, Mark presents the first evidence of the link between John the Baptist and Elijah (6.15; 8.28; 9.11-13; see also 9.4; 15.35-36). John is the promised forerunner, a prophet of great eschatological importance who proclaims, "Prepare the way for the Lord, make straight paths for him."

This message is directed to the whole nation as necessary preparation for the coming of the Lord. There is a massive turnout by those who live in Judea and in Jerusalem (1.5; cf 3.8.), even though they must undertake the difficult journey to hear him in the desert. Many respond to his message which entails three inseparable responses: repentance (a new attitude of the heart and mind) accompanied by confession (an audible demonstration of repentance) and baptism (a visible representation of repentance). John offers no life of ease; he requires much from his hearers (even as, later, Jesus calls men and women to radical discipleship, 8.34-38).

John's call to repentance presupposes that reconciliation with God is indispensable in order to overcome the separation caused by sin. Repentance (**metanoia**) means a deliberate change of attitudes resulting in a change of behavior. Repentant persons neither flee from the reality of their sinfulness nor seek excuses for their sins. They confess their sins openly before God (cf Lk 18.13) and affirm their desire to live according to God's will. Genuine sorrow for sin leads to conversion that involves a complete turn-around. Although this pilgrimage begins in the sadness of a broken spirit, it leads to the enjoyment of the good news of forgiveness, for God does not despise a contrite heart (Ps 51.17).

Calling upon Jews, as individuals and as a nation, to return to God, John preaches immersion (**baptizon**) as an expression of repentance. Just as Gentiles were baptized upon their conversion to Judaism, Jews who confess that they have lived alienated from God (i.e., like Gentiles) are baptized. Just as John's message prepared the way for the promised salvation, the forgiveness he preached prepared the way for the full forgiveness available exclusively through Jesus Christ. Yet it is not the rite of baptism which brings forgiveness; rather, baptism is "the expression of the repentance that results in the forgiveness of sins" (George E. Ladd Theology 40).

v. 5 - John preaches near the Jordan River, east of Jericho, in an uninhabited area with an uninviting physical environment. People from Jerusalem descend approximately 5,000 feet in 15 miles, travelling through a dangerous area (cf Lk 10.30) to reach the Jordan Valley. Those coming from Judea travel even farther. John also baptized at Aenon near Salim (Jn 3.23), over thirty miles to the north.

• Confession is made to God himself, for sins are transgressions against him (cf Ps 51.4). Confession to a priest was not practiced in Judaism nor in the apostolic church. James 5.16 ("confess your sins to each other.") teaches *mutual* confession by fellow believers. Confession to a priest was introduced in the church only in the fifth century. The Fourth Lateran Council (in the year 1215) decreed that all those under the jurisdiction of the Pope must confess to a priest at least once a year.

The call to repentance is not limited to John's message to Israel. It is a continuous element in the proclamation of the Kingdom of God, for it was preached by Jesus (1.15), the disciples (6.12) and the apostles (Ac 2.38; 20.21; 26.20). It characterizes most of the letters to the 7 Churches of Asia (Rev 2-3).

• Until recently, the relationship between baptism as practiced by orthodox Jews, Jewish sects, John and by the early church was not clear. Recent archaeological discoveries show that Jewish baptism (**miqveh**) dictated complete immersion. If John had preached something completely strange to the Scriptures or to rabbinical teaching, the Jews would not have accepted him. Most likely, then, Jewish practice led to the immersion practiced by John and by the early church.

In Qumran, baptisms were constantly repeated in a closed community. In contrast, the baptism of John was given only once, to Jews from all parts of Palestine who repented of their sins. The Qumran community claimed it fulfilled the prophecy of Isaiah 40.3, but the four Gospels attribute this role to John.

In Jesus' day, baptism with water indicated God's preparation of his people for the coming of the Kingdom. It anticipated the messianic baptism with the Spirit, with assurance of forgiveness, cleansing and a place in the Kingdom.

1.7-8 - John's call to repentance indicates that something extremely important is about to happen. In his only words quoted in Mark's Gospel, John declares that Someone more powerful is about to appear. He exalts the person of Jesus, the central figure in his own ministry and in the Gospel itself. Both John and Jesus are servants of God and ministers in his plan of redemption; but, as John himself points out, Jesus is greater in power, in dignity and in ministry.

John is the greatest of the prophets (Mt 11.11), but Jesus is of a different order of greatness. He is God's Son, filled and led by the Holy Spirit (1.10-12). Being greater in power, Jesus enters a strong man's house and frees his captives (3.27). He is the eschatological liberator who will come with great power and glory (13.26)

John is humble in spite of the importance of his mission. In those days, disciples served their masters in every way that slaves served their lords, except to untie their sandals. This task was even beneath Hebrew slaves. John, however, is unworthy even to untie the thongs of the sandals of the Coming One, his Lord of unsurpassing dignity.

Jesus' ministry is also more powerful. Although he is nicknamed "the Baptist" because of his emphasis, John makes it clear that his baptism is limited. It is preparatory for the One who will come. Full cleansing will come through the baptism with the Holy Spirit which Jesus will minister (cf. Ac 1.5). As Morna B. Hooker (75) says, John is "an enigmatic figure, who belongs neither to the old order of the prophets (for he fulfills them) nor to the new order of the gospel (for he is its herald). His role is that of witness and forerunner."

This first mention of the Holy Spirit in this Gospel further identifies Jesus with the promised salvation by associating him with the pouring out of the Spirit (Joel 2.28-29; Eze 36.26-27). Soon to be anointed by the Spirit (1.10), Jesus will bestow the Spirit on others.

In verses 2-8, Mark establishes that John's coming marks the first and indispensable step in fulfilling the ancient promises of salvation. John prepares the way for the Lord. The people, through their repentance and baptism, prepare themselves to receive the Messiah. The scene is set for the Lord to appear. Then, as Mark states in verse 9, "Jesus came."

v. 8 - The preposition **en** means "with," expressing instrumentality rather than sphere.

• "The contrast is primarily between the persons of John and Jesus, not between John's baptism and Christian baptism" (C.E.B. Cranfield 49).

• Mark does not record the fulfillment of the promise that Jesus would baptize with the Spirit because his first readers knew he did. Paul taught his converts that, upon conversion, every believer is baptized with the Spirit and incorporated into the body of Christ (1Co 12.13; Ro 5.5; 8.9).

2. Jesus Is Baptized, 1.9-11

According to the prophets (1.2-3), the messenger was sent to prepare the way for the Lord. As John fulfills this mission, Jesus appears.

Mark does not report anything about Jesus' birth; he has already identified Jesus as the Son of God. He simply states that "Jesus came from Nazareth in Galilee," placing the fulfillment of God's promise within the scope of history. He is not just relating "spiritual truths"; these are events that occurred in certain times and places. Jesus comes from Nazareth, a small, insignificant town in Galilee (Jn 1.46). By closing his Gospel with reference to "Jesus of Nazareth" (16.6), Mark ties his narrative together into a closely-knit literary unity. At the same time, he identifies the resurrected Jesus with God's humble servant from Galilee.

Jesus undertakes this trip of over 100 miles for the specific purpose of being baptized by John in the Jordan River. Considering the contrasts between John and Jesus (vv. 2-8), it seems strange that Jesus, who will baptize with the Spirit, seeks to be baptized with water.

Stranger yet is the fact that Jesus submits himself to "baptism of repentance for the forgiveness of sins" (1.4). Are readers to conclude that Jesus, like the others who are baptized by John, is a repentant sinner? This cannot be, however; for we learned in the Prologue that Jesus is the Christ, the Son of God (v. 1), the Promised One (vv. 2-3) who is the Giver of the Holy Spirit (v. 8). Beyond those evidences, the very God and his Spirit celebrate the baptism of Jesus, bearing witness to his uniqueness. According to these evidences, Jesus is not a sinner. He is the beloved Son with whom the Father is well pleased (v. 11)!

Jesus, the One who baptizes with the Spirit, is baptized with water. Just as John stands between the old and the new covenants, Jesus is the intermediary between God and humanity, representing each before the other. As Man, he takes upon himself God's judgment on sin--that is, judgment upon the sins of others, for he himself has no sin (cf 2Co 5.21).

By his baptism, then, Jesus takes his first step in identifying himself with sinners. He will show his solidarity with humanity in other ways as the story unfolds. But how can God who is holy and separated from the contamination of sin sanction his Son identifying himself with sinners? The text does not answer this question immediately; it clearly affirms, however, that God approves of this relationship.

As Jesus comes out of the water, he sees heaven being ripped open. He perceives that God is bridging the gap that separates heaven and earth. This must be the answer to the prophet's desire for the salvation of Israel, in which he appeals to God to "rend the heavens and come down" (Isa 64.1; see comments on 15.38).

The beginning of the gospel (1.1) reminds us of the beginning of creation (Ge 1.1-2) when the Spirit of God hovered over the face of the waters. Just as a dove descends, hovers and rests, the Spirit comes over Jesus in the beginning of the new creation. He not only hovers over Jesus but comes to rest permanently on him (cf Isa 11.2; 61.1 with Lk 4.18; Jn 1.32-34).

Unlike references to the Spirit *coming upon* Old Testament leaders, Mark says that the Spirit enters *into* (**eis**) Jesus. As God's Spirit-filled and Spirit-led Son, Jesus acts with the authority and power of God. All that follows should be understood in the context of Jesus as uniquely led and empowered by the Holy Spirit. Jesus' words and deeds present concrete examples of what it means to live under the direction of the Spirit, for he was the archetypal "man of the Spirit."

The simplicity of Mark's narrative stands out in marked contrast to the majesty of the event portrayed: a voice from heaven says, "You are my Son, whom I love; with you I am well pleased." God, whose voice has been silent for centuries, speaks to Jesus his Son in intimate family terms that express his complete, unrestricted approval. His pronouncement weaves together several passages of Scripture in such a way as to enrich their original significance. "You are my Son" recalls Psalm 2.7, initially spoken in reference to the kings of Israel. "My Son whom I love" reflects God's instructions to Abraham: "Take your son, your only son Isaac, whom you love" (Ge 22.2; Mk 9.7, 12.6). In Jewish thought, the sacrifice of Isaac was understood as the basis of the sacrifices offered in the Temple in Jerusalem. The beloved son Isaac was ready to die in obedience to his father. This then suggests that Jesus, God's beloved Son, will fulfill all that is implicit in Isaac's experience on Moriah (Ge 22).

In addition, God's words to Jesus recall Isaiah 42.1: "Here is my servant, whom I uphold, my chosen one in whom I delight; I will put my Spirit upon him and he will bring justice to the nations." The allusion to Jesus, Son of God, as king is coherent; but kings are not servants nor are servants kings. This paradox, however, forms the heart of the gospel, an irony that confounded those who accompanied Jesus during his life and continues to be a stumbling block even today. However, as Hugh Anderson (79) says, through this composite quotation "Jesus is designated as the kingly Messiah whose task is radically reinterpreted in terms of the mission of the suffering Servant of God."

The phrase "You are my Son" describes more than just Jesus' deeds; it refers primarily to his *being*. Jesus' role as the suffering servant has redemptive significance because of *who Jesus is* in relationship to God. He is the Son of God; his deeds, words and authority come from his unity with the Father. We come to know God the Father through his Son.

These few words present an unparalleled revelation of the relationship between God and Jesus. They provide a key to the incomparable magnificence of Jesus and offer valuable insight into his ministry. God had not been pleased with his people (Mal 1.10) and for centuries had not revealed himself to them. Now, however, he speaks, expressing his delight in Jesus, his Son. He approves of Jesus' baptism, for he is the obedient Son who identifies himself with sinners and is ready to die because he desires to do God's will above all else. Jesus is destined to reign over God's Kingdom; he is the Suffering Servant, anointed by the Spirit and chosen by the Father. He will govern as the Servant of the Lord.

Jesus experiences the three things that, according to Jewish tradition, would signal the dawning of God's eschatological kingdom: the heavens are torn open, the Spirit descends upon him, and a voice from heaven speaks to him. The concurrence of these three events at his baptism indicates that the Kingdom is about to dawn (cf 1.14-15), with Jesus as the inaugurator.

Although apparently Jesus is baptized in the presence of many others, Mark implies that only God the Father, Son and Holy Spirit are cognizant of what took place between them on this occasion. It seems as though the Triune God holds a private "family" celebration to commemorate this significant event. For the men and women present at his baptism, Jesus' identity remains a secret to become known as his ministry unfolds. Paradoxically, he will reveal that he is the Son of God through his weakness that culminates in his crucifixion. Meanwhile, he is incognito as the Son of God.

Through these first verses, the narrator provides us, his readers, with invaluable information that will enable us to understand what the first disciples understood slowly and painfully.

v. 10 - Mark significantly employs the verb "tear apart" only twice (here; see its use in 15.38). The word is frequently associated with cataclysmic events (Ex 14.21; Is 48.21; Zec 14.4).

• Pious Jews understood that the Spirit's hovering over the waters (Ge 1.2) was related to eschatological redemption, according to the Dead Sea "Fragment of the Messianic Vision." The author of this manuscript prophesied that the Messiah would bring a new creation in which the Spirit would hover over the saints similar to his hovering over the waters.

• In Ps 55.6, 68.13, 74.19 and Hos 11.11, the dove signifies the faithful ones in Israel. In this sense, Jesus is designated the firstborn (Ro 8.29) in whom God forms his new people. In Hosea 11.1, God called his son (Israel) out of Egypt (to the desert). Israel, however, turned from God. In the new Exodus, Jesus is driven into the desert. In contrast to Israel, Jesus is faithful to God (James R. Edwards 47f, 55).

• The Spirit's descent on Jesus was not the promised baptism with the Spirit, because, as John foretold, Jesus himself will minister that baptism.

v. 11 - Mark records only two times in which God himself speaks (1.11 e 9.7). On both occasions, he speaks of Jesus as "my Son whom I love."

• In the Old Testament, God anointed the one he chose to be king. Like David (cf 1Sa 16.13 with 2Sa 5), however, Jesus did not assume the throne immediately. Only much later is he acclaimed as King.

• Jesus does not *become* the Son of God at his baptism; he already *is* the Son. The words of the Father indicate his Sonship rather than institute his Sonship. What is instituted here is his service to the Father as the Messiah. The baptism of Jesus defines the uniqueness of the Father-Son relationship.
• In his Prologue, Mark lays the foundation for understanding the relationship between Jesus and the Holy Spirit. Jesus is led by (1.12) and indwelt by the Holy Spirit (3.29-30). He gives the Holy Spirit to others (1.8), exemplified in 13.11. Mark narrates concrete experiences in which Jesus demonstrates in his daily life and ministry the presence and power of the Holy Spirit. Jewish culture preferred to communicate concepts by narrating concrete facts rather than through abstract ideas.

3. Jesus Is Tempted By Satan, 1.12-13

The reader might expect that the Holy Spirit would immediately present Jesus as God's beloved Son publicly for all humanity to acclaim his power and worship him. Much to the contrary, the Spirit impels Jesus into the wilderness, to engage in a test of strength with Satan who has usurped control of this world (Eph 2.2, 6.12).

The Spirit initiates this struggle immediately following Jesus' anointing (1.9-11), for he must be tested before he can proclaim that "the Kingdom of God is near" (1.14-15). God tests with the desire to approve; it is a part of divine discipline (cf Heb 5.8; 12.6). On the other hand, Satan tests with hostility, intent on conquering Jesus by turning him aside from the mission received from his Father.

Jesus' temptation is not a mere formality: as Hebrews 4.15 says, he "has been tempted in every way, just as we are" (cf Heb 2.14-18). This is evidence of his participating in our humanity. His temptation is distinct, however, for it bears cosmic consequences. In his battle with Satan, the Son of Man starts down the lonely path that leads to more trials and death before his resurrection and glory (cf 8.31).

The number forty recalls Israel's forty years of testing in the desert (Nu 32.13f; Ps 95.10). There they also experienced divine provision in the desert. So now Jesus both undergoes temptation and is served by angels in his wilderness experience. According to Isaiah 40.3 and Mark 1.2-3, the Messiah comes from the desert.

Although Mark does not announce Satan's defeat, he implies that Jesus breaks Satan's power and guarantees his complete victory (as he himself foresees in 8.38; 13.26; 14.62). This account, however, does not imply that Satan leaves Jesus. The temptation constitutes but the first of Jesus' several encounters with the Devil. Evil spirits continue the struggle against him throughout his life. The Adversary intensifies the battle in Gethsemane and at Calvary (14.36; 15.34,37). The conflict will end, however, with the final overthrow and perpetual imprisonment of the Adversary (Rev 20.10).

The angels serve him during these forty days of temptation (just as celestial beings now worship Jesus; Heb 1.6). Possibly the reference to Jesus' presence with the animals alludes to the restoration of Eden (Isa 11.6-8; 65.25; Hos 2.18) with the reversal of the enmity which arose in the universe as a result of the Fall (Ge 3.15). In the final victory over Satan, all of creation will be liberated from its bondage (Ro 8.19-23).

In the midst of abundance, with animals subject to his dominion, Adam fell to temptation in his desire to be like God. Surrounded by scarcity and the hostility of the desert, Jesus prevailed as a man. As Eduard Schweizer declares (43), "he, like Adam, was led by God into temptation immediately after his commissioning; but, unlike Adam, Jesus withstood his temptations and thereby restored paradise."

This conflict with Satan forms part of the background of Jesus' ministry.

v. 12 - As a temporal adverb, "at once" here calls attention to the urgency of Jesus' mission. As a conjunction, it joins ideas, e.g., the close connection between his baptism and temptation. "Immediately" is used over 40 times in Mark.
• "To drive out" implies strong action. In Mark, 11 of its 17 occurrences refer to "driving out" evil spirits.
v. 13 - The number forty in Israel's history is also recorded in Ex 34.28; 1Ki 19.8; Ge 7.12; Jdg 13.1.
• Though testing, Jesus proves that he is "without blemish," thereby satisfying a requirement for sin offerings (Lev 1.3; 4.3; Heb 4.15). In both Testaments, the people of God proved their faith as they passed through trials (e.g., Abraham, in Ro 4.18; Job, in Jas 5.11). Jesus' disciples are also frequently tested, without forewarning (e.g., 4.40; 6.37,50; 8.32f; 14.38).

* * * *

In these opening verses, the author relates Jesus' preparation for the ministry he is soon to undertake. Simultaneously, he gives us, his readers, valuable "inside information" which will aid us in understanding the significance of the whole narrative.

The Prologue presents many of the principal persons and themes of the whole story. We are introduced to the triune God, relationships between Father, Son and Holy Spirit and their active involvement with humanity. We are alerted to the conflict with Satan. We hear the testimonies of God's messengers, climaxed by God's own declaration as to who Jesus is. We are given the opportunity to see Jesus from God's viewpoint. Human participation, however, is limited to John as God's messenger and to people who respond to his message.

These thirteen verses offer us bases for understanding what the participants yet to be introduced learned inductively as, little by little, they pieced together the evidences. As we contemplate Jesus, our understanding of who he is and his relevance to our lives will also become progressively clear, just as it did for men and women of that time who had ears to hear and eyes to see.

- PART 2 -
JESUS AUTHORITY AFFIRMED AND CONTESTED 1.14 - 3.6

In the person of Jesus, God invites men and women to live under his direction as members of his Kingdom. In simple, direct and personal terms, this life is described by the phrase "following Jesus."

We will see Jesus in the midst of the people of his day, approachable and sensitive to their needs. We will be impressed and sometimes shaken by his words. We will observe his authority over natural and supernatural forces. Meanwhile, we will wonder, if he is God's Anointed Son (as declared in 1.1,11), why does he not declare his identity openly and establish God's Kingdom immediately? If the evil spirits know who he is, why does Jesus prohibit them from broadcasting it? Why do the religious leaders reject him? Paradoxes such as these confront us with the basic question: "Who exactly is Jesus?"

In the Prologue, we were introduced to Jesus from God's viewpoint. We now learn how men and women see him. Preparations (1.2-13) have been concluded; now Jesus begins his ministry. With authority, he proclaims the dawning of the Kingdom of God and the requirements for those who desire to enter it. As we accompany four men who answer Jesus' call, we have an opportunity to witness various manifestations of his authority. By following him for twenty-four hours, we begin to know him. We see how he relates to his contemporaries. We gain some basic ideas about God's rule among men and women.

Mark describes the peaks and valleys of the disciples' walk with Jesus. Each of the three major divisions of the first half of the Gospel emphasizes a new phase in Jesus' call to discipleship. The first two divisions (1.14-3.6; 3.7-6.6a) end with reports of people who reject Jesus. By the conclusion of the third division (6.6b-8.26), there is an obvious similarity between the blind man and the disciples who still do not see clearly who Jesus is. They still lack something essential to an accurate identification of Jesus.

Fulfilling their role as protectors of Israel's traditions, the religious leaders mix with the crowds in order to investigate this popular leader. In five paragraphs skillfully formed around five questions (2.1-3.6), Mark traces their growing negative reaction to Jesus. They move from critical thoughts about him to accusing him openly of breaking their sacred laws concerning the Sabbath. They conclude their inquiries with plans to kill Jesus.

Throughout the narrative, Jesus is the central figure; others are always seen in relationship to him. His acts awaken interest, his words provoke responses. No one can remain neutral. By presenting Jesus in this way, the author succeeds in doing more than just relating historical events. He invites his readers to answer personally the questions, "Who is Jesus?" and "Am I living under God's direction?"

A. JESUS AFFIRMS HIS AUTHORITY, 1.14-45

In Jesus, God approaches men and women, offering to those who repent and believe the gospel the opportunity to live under his rule. Four fishermen respond to Jesus' invitation and follow him without hesitation. They observe his authority in teaching and healing in a variety of situations in which many people seek Jesus.

1. Jesus Announces The Good News From God, 1.14-15

This paragraph can be considered as a conclusion to the Prologue (1.2-13) since it reinforces the temporal relationship between these two preachers of repentance, Jesus and John. To a greater degree, however, it prefaces Jesus' ministry centered in Galilee. John is removed from the scene. He will not reappear personally in this Gospel although his past ministry will continue to influence attitudes towards Jesus.

With these two verses, Mark succinctly presents the background of Jesus' proclamation of the gospel (v. 14) and a summary of "the good news of God" (v. 15). Jesus' message holds the key to understanding what follows.

1.14 - Since John had faithfully prepared the way for Jesus' coming, we might expect that God would promote him from the desert to a place of honor. Instead, that servant of the Lord is delivered up to prison. John's experience gives us a foretaste of what is in store for Jesus and his disciples. The forerunner in preaching repentance is also the first to be imprisoned. According to Jesus' later predictions, he himself (8.31; 9.31; 10.33-34) and his followers (13.9) will also be turned over to people opposed to the gospel.

By stating the time and place, the author makes it clear that Jesus' ministry is a matter of historical record. "After John was imprisoned" marks the time; Galilee identifies the region that will dominate half of the book (1.14-8.26). As the book closes (16.7), the resurrected Jesus directs his disciples to follow him from Jerusalem to Galilee.

In his first words recorded by Mark (1.15), Jesus proclaims (**kerusso**) the gospel, an activity which characterizes his ministry (e.g., 1.39; 4.1,3-8; 6.6b) and constitutes one of the principal responsibilities of his followers (3.14; 6.12).

1.15 - For a long time, Jesus' contemporaries have been waiting restlessly, yearning for freedom from oppression. The present evil world offered them no hope. Rather, they focused their hope on a future Messianic kingdom when God would fulfill their national aspirations, drive out the foreign conquerors and redeem Israel to enjoy a new order of justice and peace, free from the corruption they knew so well. John the Baptist's preaching has kindled hope that divine intervention is near. As a result, many people have been prepared for the arrival of the Promised One, convinced that God is about to fulfill his promises to his people.

Into this milieu, Jesus appears, proclaiming the essence of the good news of God (verse 15):

"The time has come; the Kingdom of God is near.
Repent and believe the good news!"

This message contains two clauses with verbs in the indicative mood and two in the imperative. With the indicatives, Jesus asserts the existence of certain God-created realities which demand (the imperatives) certain responses from those who hear (or read).

Jesus declares that "the time (**ho kairos**) has come." This is a special time, distinct from all others. The time for waiting is over, for God is now actively engaged in fulfilling that which he has promised. The time has come for him to break into human history and establish his kingly rule.

Jesus' proclamation that "the kingdom of God is dawning" eclipses John's call to "prepare the way for the Lord." The era of the ancient prophets closes with John's imprisonment; the time of "the One who is to come" has already arrived. In other words, John the Baptist's preaching kindled *expectation* of the Kingdom, whereas Jesus inaugurates its *fulfillment* . In the person of Jesus, God invades history to redeem those alienated from him. Since Jesus is God's Son, beloved by the Father and anointed by the Spirit (as readers learned in 1.1-11), he not only proclaims the good news: *he himself* is the focus of the gospel. His coming signals the inauguration of the kingdom of God. This is the thrust of these two declarations with verbs in the indicative mood.

God's initiative demands a commitment on the part of men and women, for God does not build his Kingdom independently of human involvement. No one can receive his Kingdom passively, as some Jewish sects taught. "Repent and believe the good news!" With these two verbs in the imperative mood, Jesus defines the response God demands from men and women who desire to belong to his Kingdom. Those who hear (or read) the good news are to seize it aggressively. Neither repentance nor faith, however, is a once-for-all gesture; both attitudes and actions are essential and continuing responses if a follower of Jesus is to receive the multiple benefits of God's dynamic presence.

The repentant humbly recognize before God that they fall short of doing what is right and confess that they are not the masters of their own destiny. They recognize their innate unworthiness and confess the falseness of their motives and actions. When they perceive that their greatest delights are not in God or in doing what pleases him, they call out for the mercy of God who "opposes the proud but gives grace to the humble" (1Pe 5.5; cf Lk 18.9-14).

The proclamation of the gospel confronts men and women with the holy God and with their own sinfulness. This encounter should not lead persons to despair because of their sins, but to repentance (cf Isa 6.1-5), for God receives sinners (cf Mk 2.15-17; Lk 15.2) and forgives their sins (cf 2.5-10). Through Jesus Christ he offers men and women the opportunity to realize their potential.

Beyond John's emphasis upon repentance (1.4,5), Jesus stresses faith. As a result of belief in Jesus' pronouncement, a new relationship is created with God. Believers count on God and embrace what he promises in the gospel. Historically, the words **pisteuo** ("to believe") and **pistis** ("faith") signified the faithfulness between partners in an agreement and the trustworthiness of their promises. In the gospel, these terms gain special importance and refer specifically to recognizing and trusting what God has done and promised in his Son.

True belief in the good news results in obedience, as illustrated by the four fishermen (1.16-20). "Faith" in Mark's Gospel is not an abstract idea but life under God's rule. It becomes clear then that the good news from God confronts each person with the decision to either submit to God's lordship or to continue controlling his or her own life.

Although Jesus declares that the Kingdom of God is a present reality, he does not fulfill some of his contemporaries' expectations. For example, they were convinced that God would judge the Gentiles. Jesus, however, serves them (e.g. 7.24-8.9) and accepts them into the Kingdom (e.g., 11.17; 13.10, 27; 14.9). He does not expel the oppressive Roman authorities from the Jewish homeland.

How can one reconcile the presence of God's rule with the continuation of injustices and death? As a matter of fact, the type of kingdom Israel hoped for has not come, nor have all the Old Testament prophecies been entirely fulfilled. In the person of Jesus, however, the Kingdom of God, though veiled, is *already* present, inviting women and men to accept God's dynamic rule with its responsibilities and privileges. God's kingly rule, however, is *not yet* consummated; "at present we do not see everything subject to him" (Heb 2.8). It began with Jesus' first advent. Its fulfillment is in progress, its hiddenness is temporary (cf 4.22), and its full manifestation awaits his Second Advent.

With the coming of Jesus, God's dynamic reign invaded the present age without transforming it into the age to come. Because believers (then and now) live in the interval between the *beginning* of the Kingdom and its *consummation*, they experience the tension of living in two worlds. They find it difficult to live according to the ethics of God's new era in a world dominated by evil. Nevertheless, they rejoice in the privilege of participating here and now in the life and salvation that will reach fullness in the coming age, in the world as God wants it.

Jesus' proclamation (1.15) underlies the rest of the Gospel story. Mark will present case studies which demonstrate the radical commitment which God's rule demands of those who believe in the gospel. We will see individuals who experience the dynamic presence of God in their everyday lives. We will have opportunities to observe that following Jesus is to live under God's kingly rule. In this way, we will see how we, too, can enjoy the privileges and fulfill the responsibilities of those who live under God's dominion.

v. 14 - **Paradidomi** ("to deliver up"), employed 20 times in Mark, begins with John "delivered up to prison" and ends with Jesus "delivered to death" (9.31; 14.10; 15.15).

• "The good news of God" signifies that it originated with God himself. The expression is used in Ro 1.1; 15.16; 2Co 11.7; 1Th 2.2, 8, 9; 1Pe 4.17.

v. 15 - Greek has two different words to indicate time. **Chronos** means simply a period of time; **kairos**, a special time. "One of the chief eschatological terms in the Bible, **kairos** is supremely God's time" (Bratcher and Nida 37). Jesus is proclaiming that this is a decisive moment in God's purposes.

• To avoid connotations foreign to the gospel, the Greek **basileia** ("kingdom") is expressed by phrases such as the rule of God, God's dominion, his sovereignty, God's kingly rule, the dynamic presence of God.
• "The Kingdom of God" and "the Kingdom of heaven" are linguistic variations of the same concept. Jews frequently substituted an appropriate term to avoid using a divine name. Matthew preserves the idiomatic Semitic expression whereas the other Evangelists employ "the Kingdom of God." In Matthew 19.23-24 the two phrases are used as synonyms.
• For centuries, Roman Catholic scholars followed Augustine's teaching that the Kingdom of God is to be identified with the Church. As Ladd says (Theology 58), however, "the church is the people of the Kingdom but cannot be identified with the Kingdom."
• Some translate **eggizo** as "the Kingdom is near;" others, "the Kingdom has arrived." Literally, this eschatological expression says "has drawn nigh." Its meaning in this context is determined in part by considerations other than purely grammatical ones. Taken with Mark 9.1 and 14.25 (the Kingdom is coming), we conclude that "the Kingdom is *already* here *but not yet* consummated.
• **Metanoia** (repentance, cf 1.4-6) signifies the renunciation of sin and is accompanied by a turning to God (i.e., conversion). It means much more than regretting the past, feeling distaste for sin and resolving to live right. It demands a change of mind (**nous**), as Paul describes in Ro 12.1,2. It involves a conversion with a complete reorientation of one's personality. The repentant person purposes to live under God's direction from now on. God's Kingdom is unique; it alone is formed by a call to repentance.

Persons who "do penance" seek to *merit* forgiveness by doing good; according to the Scriptures, however, the repentant cast themselves upon God's *mercy*. Unfortunately, the misleading phrase "doing penance" is found in some translations, even though the Greek text clearly says "repent."
• Rabbis in the first century and some present religions teach "the merit of faith," that is, that the act of believing is a meritorious work that contributes to forgiveness. The Apostle Paul, however, insists that God accepts sinners on the basis of faith, apart from any claim to merit (cf Ro 4.6; Mk 7.1-13).
• In contemporary preaching, "making a decision" and "believing" are frequently stressed, with little mention of the repentance emphasized in the New Testament. This omission attracts those who desire a religion without moral demands but constitutes an offense against the holy God of Scripture.
• The verb **pisteuo** is used in Mk 5.36, 9.23, 24, 42, 11.23, 24, 31, 13.21, 15.32; its corresponding noun, **pistis**, in 2.5; 4.40; 5.34; 10.52; 11.11.
• Although we readers know from Mark 1.1-11 that Jesus is the Son of God, Jesus' contemporaries do not know this when he first appears in Galilee. Through his words and deeds, without coercion, Jesus gives sufficient evidence for them to recognize that he is God's Son. As Cranfield (158) says, "God's self-revelation is veiled, in order that men may be left sufficient room in which to make a personal decision."
• Before the crucifixion, the good news was an invitation to commit oneself to the reality of God's dynamic rule through Jesus. After Jesus' resurrection, the gospel signifies the Christian message in its entirety.

2. Jesus Introduces Men And Women To God's Reign, 1.16-45

The essence of Jesus' message and the response it demands from men and women are preserved for us in verse 15. The author now illustrates the meaning of Jesus' message in the lives of men and women who meet him.

Upon hearing the command, "Follow me," many people would ask, "Who are you, that I should follow you?" and "Where are you going and why?" Those who accompanied Jesus gradually acquired partial answers to these questions, but the breakthrough awaited the closing scenes of the Gospel.

From the declarations by the author (1.1) and the voice from heaven (1.11; cf 9.7), however, readers remember that Jesus is the Messiah (Christ), God's beloved Son. So we seek the answer to questions such as: "What is he like and how does he relate to our lives?" Since he confronts us with God himself, we have an excellent opportunity to learn what God is like and what he is up to in this world.

As we look in on Jesus' encounters with individuals, we are drawn into the story. We discover that Jesus is not only a historical figure who lived 2000 years ago. He continues to live among us, seeking men, women and children. We begin to realize that he is also calling us to "repent and believe," offering us the privilege of "following him," with a promise of being fashioned anew through his handiwork. We are confronted with the need to answer personally the question, "Am I following Jesus?" If so, "What should I be and do?"

JESUS CALLS FOUR FISHERMEN, 1.16-20

Two brothers, Simon and Andrew, are busy in their daily task of casting a net into Lake Galilee, for they are fishermen. Passing along the shore, Jesus calls them to follow him. Immediately they leave what they are doing and follow him. This is an ironic way to start a kingdom. No one establishes a kingdom with four fishermen. But that is only one of the surprises that await us.

A little farther on, two other fishermen, James and John, are in their boat, mending their nets. Jesus calls them, too. They leave their father Zebedee in the boat with the hired servants and follow Jesus.

Mark's succinct account of Jesus calling the fishermen emphasizes his striking authority and the radical demands of his kingdom. Jesus appears; his word is authoritative. Those who hear, obey, without delay, without questioning. His word encounters them in the midst of their everyday lives. All prior activities and responsibilities fade in the light of the superior demands of the Kingdom. Their relationship with Jesus takes precedence over family ties (3.31-35; 10.28-31). Their lives change direction under the disruptive authority of Jesus; God's will becomes sovereign in their lives.

In terms of real-life situations, this is what it means to "repent and believe the good news" (1.15). The author does not leave us guessing. He gives us concrete examples of positive -- and negative -- responses of what it means to follow Jesus. The lack of details facilitates our own identification with those first disciples. In our daily contexts, so different from theirs, we, too, are called to radical discipleship.

Jesus' words to the fishermen contain an imperative ("follow me") and then a promise ("I will make you become fishers of men"). His authority, expressed in this command, does not override men and women but confronts them with a decision. To those who respond positively, he assumes the responsibility to remake them according his purpose. "I will make you" is conditional; it is a generous promise, but it is limited to those who follow him.

To follow Jesus is the inescapable responsibility of anyone who repents and believes the gospel. To follow begins with a first step and continues through life, a life of participation with Jesus in his journey "in the way" (**hodos**, 8.27). The follower does not understand all that is involved; it will become plain only as he follows. But he places his life in good hands. It is not basically involvement in a program; it is not joining a cause, movement or institution; it is not following a list of rules. Rather, it is personal devotion to the person of Jesus. "Follow me" is the first and last word from Jesus to his disciples (1.17; 16.7).

This pericope initiates one of the prominent themes of this Gospel: discipleship. In those days, an interested youth would request permission from a rabbi to become his disciple. As such, he could dispute with and possibly even replace his master. Not so with Jesus and his disciples. The initiative and choice are his; his word is authoritative. He establishes the way to be followed. He remains sovereign; the role of the disciple is ever to follow him. Discipleship is a blending of divine initiative and authority with human response.

Jesus becomes personally involved in the training of those who respond to his message. In leaving their nets and following him, the four give visible evidence of "repenting and believing the good news." Jesus responds to their first step by assuming responsibilities for making them into new persons with a new mission in life. It is a mission that grows out of a personal relationship: "I will make you fishers of men." The preaching of the Gospel demands the discipling of those who respond; the making of disciples is inseparable from evangelism.

Besides being a metaphor expressed in terms understood by the fishers, catching men may be an allusion to God's role as fisher, gathering men and women for judgment and restoration. This word-picture confronts each of us with the urgency of aligning our lives with God's rule through repentance and faith. Disciples are called upon to participate in this divine task.

Discipleship requires an individual response; it is not, however, individualistic. A disciple becomes a member of a new community; in this way, Jesus is creating the nucleus of the church, composed of his followers and centered in fellowship with him. Disciples are not related only to Jesus but also to each other, as Mark later paints in realistic brush strokes. Moreover, they have a ministry to those outside the community. Jesus specifies their role as continuing what he is doing. He is fishing for men; in the measure that they follow him, he will enable them to participate in creating the new people of God.

v. 16 - The "Sea of Galilee" is a fresh water lake fed by the Jordan River and many springs. Located almost 700 feet below sea level, it measures approximately 7 by 13 miles. It is called "Galilee" (Mk and Mt), "Gennesaret" (Lk 5.1) and "Tiberias" (Jn 21.1). Over the centuries, fishing has been a major commercial activity on Lake Galilee. The first century Jewish historian Josephus said that 330 fishing boats plied its waters. The circular nets used in New Testament times were around 12 feet in diameter.

• Mark does not relate any previous encounter with these men; cf Lk 5.1-11; Jn 1.29-42.

v. 17 - The invitation to follow Jesus and to be with him (3.14), implies the restoration of fellowship with God, a relationship broken by sin. Those who accept the rule of God are privileged to enjoy even now the presence of God and some of the blessings of the coming era. To follow Jesus is the greatest endeavor a person can undertake.

• Jesus created a radically different pattern of discipleship. The rabbis emphasized the Law with its multiple legalistic interpretations that controlled every area of life. With dialectical reasoning, they debated with their disciples: they never gave a personal opinion but cited the opinions of their predecessors. Jesus frequently affirmed his own position ("I say to you"), based on his authority as God's Anointed. As Ladd (Theology 107) said, "The rabbis offered something outside of themselves; Jesus offered himself alone. Jesus required his disciples to surrender without reservation to his authority....In him, men were confronted by God himself."

When Buddha was dying, he told his disciples not to bother to remember him, for his teaching, not his person, was what counted. With Jesus, on the other hand, it is the personal relationship with him that is central. He calls his disciples to follow him. Being with him, they come to know him, love him and commit themselves wholly to him. This is the heart of what it means to be a disciple of Jesus.

The Talmud states that "a master and his disciple...are regarded as one individual." To become a disciple is not a simple matter of acquiring information. "It is the cementing of a lifelong relationship to a person...that takes precedence over all other relationships" (Kenneth Bailey Eyes 30).

• Discipling was faithfully practiced (cf Ac 13.52; 14.20; 16.1) and taught by Paul (1Ti 4.6; 2Ti 2.2).

• Jesus' ministry recalls God's dealings with Abraham. Both are essentially personal. "Go to the land I will show you" (Ge 12.1) is rephrased in Jesus' "follow me." Both calls imply God's presence and personal leadership (Ge 17.7-8). They are followed by reaffirmations and expansions interspersed with testings. When Joshua, discipled by Moses, failed to prepare others to continue his work, confusion resulted: everyone did what was right in his own eyes (cf Jdg 17.6).

• God is pictured as a fisher of men in Jer 16.16 and Eze 29.4,5 and the concept is taught in some Dead Sea scrolls. The metaphor was a contextualization of "reaching people," a priority for all disciples, fishers and non-fishers alike.

• In 1.14-3.6 Jesus gathers and maintains disciple-companions who spend most of their time with him, imitate him, and are defended by him. Vernon K. Robbins (Jesus the Teacher 108-113) calls this "the initial phase of the teacher/disciple relationship."

FOLLOWING JESUS FOR 24 HOURS, 1.21-39

A good way to get to know a person is to accompany her in her day by day activities, seeing her in a variety of situations. Through a series of pericopes, Mark takes us with Jesus for a period of twenty-four hours. We see Jesus in action. The questions posed previously continue. "Who is Jesus?" is asked in one encounter. An initial answer is given to the question "Where is Jesus going?" He is going fishing for men and women. Those who follow him have the opportunity to learn something about that task as they observe him seeking people.

Of course, he is much more than a fisherman. Although he is the Anointed One empowered by the Holy Spirit, his identity is veiled from men and women. They see his authority expressed in different ways and ask, "Where does this power come from?" They are confronted with the necessity of making decisions with regard to him. In four short narratives about events occurring in one day in Capernaum, Mark gives us a bird's-eye view of initial responses to Jesus.

Jesus Demonstrates His Authority In A Synagogue, 1.21-28

In the first segment of this 24-hour period, Jesus begins to teach in the synagogue in Capernaum, a place where one would expect to find people deeply interested in living under God's rule. A man possessed by an evil spirit, however, interrupts his teaching.

1.21-22 - The four disciples follow Jesus, even as he called them. He begins their training in Capernaum, the hometown of Simon and Andrew (v. 29), taking them with him to the regular Sabbath meeting in the synagogue. Gathered to worship God through prayers and the reading of Scripture, the people should welcome the good news Jesus brings. It should be a good place to begin.

Mark doesn't mention the content of Jesus' teaching; we can presume that verse 15 presents the message in outline form. Mark does emphasize, however, the authority with which Jesus taught, in marked contrast with the scribes. Those teachers of the law (scribes) did not give straightforward answers but quoted varying rabbinical sources. They watered down the Scriptures by their traditions. Jesus, however, taught with the finality of divine authority.

The people's recognition of John as a prophet was aided by the fact that his clothing resembled Elijah's. The clues to Jesus' identify were not so readily evident. The authorities in Jerusalem did not sanction his ministry. The people did not know about his ordination by God (1.9-11). His words and his works are his credentials. They are part of his proclamation of the Kingdom. They are stepping stones, enabling those who observe him carefully to come to know him as the Promised One.

1.23-26 - On the positive side, Jesus' mission is to establish the Kingdom of God. On the negative side, he came to defeat Satan and the powers of evil in all their forms. To bring life and freedom, Jesus must destroy the Adversary whose purpose is to enslave and destroy.

So, as Jesus is teaching, demonic opposition surfaces. Satan understands that the consummation of God's rule guarantees the abolishment of death's empire. Jesus' baptism led to an encounter with Satan in the desert. Now the battle continues as Satan takes the offensive, confronting his opponent in the synagogue even though he knows that God's Son will ultimately destroy him.

The conflict is not limited to celestial powers; as they pursue their unholy purposes, evil spirits exert their power over humans and their institutions. The presumably peaceful environment in the synagogue suddenly becomes hostile as a man dominated by an unclean spirit screams at Jesus, declaring him to be the "Holy One of God." The Adversary seeks to destroy Jesus by revealing his true identity as the Son of God. If the people saw him as the Messiah, they might try to make him king prematurely, even by force. This would destroy Jesus' purpose just as surely as if he had succumbed to Satan's temptation (1.12-13; cf Lk 4.5-7) or if he were to drown in a storm (4.35-41). As will be seen later, his Sonship cannot be separated from his role as the Suffering Servant; he refuses to circumvent the cross. Therefore, Jesus orders the evil spirit, "Be silent and come out of him."

Although endowed by God himself (1.11), Jesus exercised his authority with great discretion. Whereas he *invited* the response of humans, Jesus *commanded* the obedience of the demon. In so doing, Jesus is acting within his cosmic purpose of destroying Satan. The evil spirit had no choice but to obey. Shaking the man violently, he came out of him screaming.

The scribes spoke and nothing happened. Jesus speaks and the demon flees. He speaks with authority coming from God, with the authority of the presence of God's kingly rule. The scribes belong to an era already passing; Jesus brings the good news of God's reign. His words and acts demonstrate that the Kingdom is present in his person. As Jesus said, "If I drive out demons by the Spirit of God, then the Kingdom of God has come upon you" (Mt 12.28). The power of God has invaded the enemy's domain, sealing its eventual fate.

1.27-28 - The people are amazed at his teaching (v. 22), at his new doctrine and at his expelling demons (v. 27), for all are done with an unaccustomed authority. His words and works are like no one else's. In their amazement, they ask, "What is this?" Mark poses the question in such a way that each reader is confronted with the necessity of reflecting seriously upon Jesus' person and deeds.

Jesus' first public teaching ministry led to his liberating a person from the power of evil. This news spread like wildfire over the whole region of Galilee (v.28). After relating Jesus' encounters with other persons in need, Mark will return to some of the effects of these reports (1.32-39,45).

By recounting this scene, Mark gives a vivid sketch of Jesus' authority at work, both in terms of human benefit and of demonic opposition. God's reign is God's power (authority) in action through Jesus. Clearly, this Kingdom is much more than an ethical concept. As Larry W. Hurtado (14) accurately observes, it is a "dynamic and material reality" involving "the deliverance from demonic forces of people like the man in this episode."

People perceive Jesus' unusual authority and are astonished by it. Many are unable to identify its source because of blindness caused by sin (2 Col 4.4, cf Eph 2.1). Jesus, however, knows its source. As uniquely anointed by God, he is fully aware that God is acting in word and deed directly through him, without intermediaries.

v. 21 - Located on the northern shore of Lake Galilee, Capernaum was a center of commerce, including salting fish for export. The large, partially destroyed synagogue known to modern tourists was built over an earlier structure that was probably the one in which Jesus taught.

• From ancient times, the Sabbath was designated as a day of rest and of remembering God's hand in national life. Its observance was essential to those who feared God (cf 2.23-28).

• The Temple in Jerusalem was the place of adoration and sacrifices. Synagogues had their beginning in the Babylonian captivity (597-539 B.C.) when the people were far from Jerusalem. By Jesus' time, synagogues existed in many places, formed wherever a minimum of ten adult males desired one. During the week, they were schools for the education of Jewish boys. On the Sabbath, the faithful gathered for the reading of the Scriptures and for prayer. There was no ordained ministry; local laymen led the meetings. A qualified person could be asked to interpret the Scripture in the Aramaic vernacular. In this capacity, Jesus taught in the synagogue (cf Lk 4.16-20). Mark emphasizes Jesus' teaching ministry more than any other New Testament book.

v. 22 - Jesus' authority (**exousia**) is emphasized in relation to his teaching (here), casting out evil spirits (1.27), forgiving sins (2.10), disrupting the Temple (11.28f, 33), and commissioning his disciples (3.15; 6.7; cf 13.34). Each time, the exercise of his authority confronts the observers (and readers) with the question, "What is my response to Jesus' authority?"

• In a sense, the scribes were descendants of Ezra of the Babylonian captivity. By Jesus' time, their role had expanded to that of "teachers of the law." As ordained theologians who had completed years of study, they constituted a respected body dedicated to studying and teaching the law of the Old Testament. They based their opinions on previous rabbinical decisions and thus created the oral traditions that governed every area of life. For many, these traditions became equal in authority to the Old Testament (cf 7.1-13). In the words of Ralph P. Martin (Action 14), the Jewish scribes "taught with the authorities; Jesus taught with authority." Jesus never deferred to human authority. He spoke as God's Son, drawing upon God's will as revealed in the Hebrew Bible.

This encounter is the beginning of conflict between the teachers of the law and Jesus.

v. 23 - The modern mind, schooled in the secular empiricism of Western philosophy, is often inclined to consider the subject of Satan, demons and demonic control as superstitious nonsense. The notion of his nonexistence is one of Satan's great triumphs.

We understand the existence of Satan and his subordinates to be a central theme of Scripture, and as such is to be taken seriously. Certainly Mark intends for his readers to understand that Jesus is engaged in a power struggle with Satan, the personification of evil, and with his emissaries who literally take control of individuals.

On the other hand, we seek to avoid practices contrary to Scripture, such as attributing all illnesses to demonic control. Nor does this concern justify such measures as the burning of witches; these "were due, not to taking the New Testament too seriously, but to failing to take it seriously enough" (Cranfield 75). Nor does this orientation lead to questioning the role of natural law. The Biblical accounts of the miraculous are largely confined to periods of crises in redemptive history.

The Gospels carefully distinguish between the ill and those who have demons (cf 1.34; 3.10-11). For example, in addressing Jesus, only evil spirits employ terms such as the Holy One of God (1.24), Son of God (3.11), and Son of the Most High God (5.7). These titles are never used by the physically ill. Moreover, while faith is ascribed to a sick person, no demon-possessed person is ever said to have faith. Their healing is related either to a parent's faith (7.24-30; 9.14-29) or to Jesus' authority over demons (1.21-28; 5.1-20).

• "Unclean spirit" (3.11; 5.2; 6.7) does not mean a "physically dirty" spirit. Rather, it signifies an invisible spirit associated with evil and under the influence of Satan, capable of taking control of a person. Such a person is said to "have a demon" (cf 1.34, 39; 3.22; 5.1-20; 9.14-27) and is thus ritually impure and excluded from the synagogue.

• Based on her studies of spiritism in Brazil, Neusa Itioka (109, 159) affirms that the characteristics presented in the demoniacs in the New Testament are also found in contemporary cases of demonized persons. Moreover, she declares that "many times the seductive spirits are present in the midst of God's people, counterfeiting the Holy Spirit."
• At this point in the narrative, the people recognize Jesus only in terms of his authority. The demonic forces, however, recognize him immediately. The question "What do you want with us?" implies the perception that Jesus' appearance will result in their destruction. Their fear indicates that Jesus won a decisive victory over Satan in the desert (1.12-13), even though Mark does not state this. While their ultimate ruin (not annihilation) is inevitable, they continue their struggle. Jesus did come to defeat completely the evil spirits and their ruler, but their final destiny awaits his second advent (cf Mt 25.41, Rev 20.10). The Gospels dedicate little space to this final defeat, since their emphasis is on Jesus' first advent.
• Nazareth is mentioned infrequently in this Gospel (1.9; here; 10.47; 14.6 and 16.6; cf 6.1). With the two terms (Jesus of Nazareth/the Holy One of God), the demon may be speaking of the human/divine nature of Jesus. See our comments on 5.7 for another possibility.
v. 25 - Mark's statements about Jesus' injunctions to silence (1.25,34,44; 3.12; 5.43; 7.36; 8.26,30; 9.9) were interpreted in 1901 by W. Wrede to mean that Jesus did not claim to be the Messiah nor was he recognized as such by his disciples during his lifetime. His messiahship, Wrede claimed, was imposed upon the Gospel after the resurrection, when the disciples came to regard Jesus as Messiah. This theory of the "Messianic Secret" became the center of much discussion. In response to Wrede, Cranfield (79) correctly argues that "the reasons for this secrecy are to be found in the very nature and purpose of Jesus' ministry and of the Incarnation itself."
• Jesus cast out demons with a single command, in contrast to the rituals of the Jewish exorcists. What is one to think of our contemporaries who wrestle physically with persons in order to expel demons?
• The similarities between healings and exorcisms in the Gospels and Hellenistic miracle stories are only superficial, as C. S. Mann (213) says. He adds: "The true parallel to Hellenistic wonder stories lies in advertisers' claims for the panaceas being offered on modern commercial television."
v. 26 - The phrase **phone megale** ("with a load voice") occurs twice in reference to the expulsion of evil spirits (here; 5.7) and twice in reference to the crucifixion (15.34, 37).
• In Mark's eschatological emphasis, Satan and his agents are under God's judgment *already*. But since God's judgment is *not yet* consummated, they continue to thrash about in panic. Cf 4.39; 5.7, 9.36.
v. 27 - "Astonished" (1.22; 6.2; 7.37; 10.26; 11.18) usually expresses the reaction of uncommitted onlookers to Jesus' words and actions. "Amazed" (1.27; 10.24,32) also expresses strong emotions.
• The Greek **kainos** ("new") refers to quality, to something unprecedented, unfamiliar or previously unknown, in contrast to **neos**, which has a temporal reference, meaning "recently."

Jesus Heals Simon's Mother-In-Law, 1.29-31

We may miss the significance of this short pericope because of the simplicity of the writer's style. It takes place on the same day, in the same city, with the same disciples present. But there the similarities end.

After the tumultuous scene in the synagogue, Simon and Andrew take Jesus along with James and John to their home in Capernaum. Upon hearing that Peter's mother-in-law is ill with a fever, Jesus seeks her out (as he had previously sought the fishermen). He raises her up by taking hold of her hand. Her cure is instantaneous, enabling her to serve them.

By his words and acts, Jesus demonstrates his compassion and his power. In the synagogue, the reaction to his power was amazement; here, it is service. Having been served, "she began to wait on them." Her continuing service (as indicated by the imperfect tense of the verb) shows her gratitude and also implies that she became Jesus' disciple, for service is an essential characteristic of a disciple (9.35; 10.43-45). Both here in the beginning and in the end of his Gospel (15.41), Mark tells of women serving Jesus.

Jesus' ministry is not only in the places of worship; he goes with disciples into their homes. He becomes involved in their family life. He is concerned about individuals, not just crowds, about women, not just men. His disciples feel free to talk to him about a family concern and Jesus meets that need. He ministers wherever and whenever he is, without public fanfare. He accepts their hospitality and is served along with the others. While he is making disciples, Jesus is forming a new family (3.31-35) given to serving one another (9.35) even as Jesus serves others (10.45).

v. 30 - Mark clearly indicates that Peter was married (as were most of the apostles, 1Co 9.5). The New Testament gives no support to insistence upon the celibacy of the clergy (cf 1 Tim 4.3, 1Co 7.38, Heb 13.4). Each Synoptic Gospel refers to Peter's mother-in-law. Her serving in the home does not demonstrate that Peter was a widower; 1 Co 9.5 implies that Peter (Cephas) had not renounced his marriage vows in order to become an apostle.
• In the beginning of Jesus' ministry, Mark presents two hurting people, a man and a woman. Through these and later examples, he makes it clear that Jesus came to liberate all who are bound, both male and female, Jew and Gentile, young and old (cf Gal 3.28). The author calls attention to Jesus commending women (e.g., 12.41-44; 14.3-9). Such commendation of women is uncommon in male-dominated societies. The Good News clearly gives women a new place in life. "Jesus knowingly overthrew custom when he allowed women to follow him" (Joachim Jeremias Jerusalem 376).

Jesus Cures Many After The Sabbath, 1.32-34

The people spread throughout Capernaum the news about Jesus' power to heal. Being pious Jews, they were fearful lest a Sabbath law be broken. So they waited until after sunset, when the Sabbath ends, before bringing to Jesus all the sick and demon-controlled. It looked like the whole city was crowding around Peter's door as Jesus healed many who were suffering from various diseases.

Jesus also cast out many demons, but he would not let them speak. Previously (v. 25), he commanded the demon to be silent. Shouting in the synagogue no doubt disrupted the whole gathering. Now Mark specifically states that Jesus' command to silence has to do with "who he is." The demons know and try to use that information to destroy him. So he demands their silence. He wants his true identity to remain unknown for the present, awaiting the appropriate time. Gradually, this important subject will become clear; but for the present, Mark gives no further explanation.

Jesus Prays In A Solitary Place, 1.35-39

That Saturday had been a very busy day for Jesus. On the first recorded Sunday in his ministry, Jesus arises very early and goes off to pray alone. While Luke frequently speaks of Jesus in prayer, Mark calls our attention to three occasions in which Jesus prayed alone and at night during special crises in his ministry (here, 6.46 and 14.32-39).

Seeing the crowds, the disciples probably consider Jesus to be an overwhelming success. But is this what God anointed him to do? Jesus faces the possibility that this good ministry may be an enemy of the best. Many people are destroyed by "success"; Jesus takes special precautions in the face of popular clamor. He does not bow to pressure; he does not allow people to determine his path. So he goes out early in the morning, seeking an uninterrupted time for prayer. He defines his priorities in his Father's presence, for he delights to do his will. He is a man entirely dependent on the Father. He rejects Satan's continuing efforts to tempt him.

Simon (later nick-named "Peter") and his companions track Jesus down. They cannot allow him to miss the golden opportunity of healing many. When they find Jesus, they rebuke him with the words, "Everyone is searching for you." These men have "in mind the things of men" (8.33), a point of view that will increasingly cause difficulties. Their understanding of Jesus is still very limited.

Jesus' reply must have been shocking to the disciples: "Let us go" to other villages. It is imperative that others have the opportunity to hear the good news. Meanwhile the people of Capernaum will have time to re-evaluate their motives in seeking Jesus. Jesus desires not "amazement" but repentance and faith (1.15) in response to his ministry. Since the Kingdom requires urgency, Jesus goes elsewhere, setting the example of spreading the gospel out to nearby villages, to all Israel and to all nations (13.10; 14.9).

Jesus reaffirms the nature of his mission: he came to proclaim (from **kerusso**, the public proclamation by an authorized herald who is God's messenger, as in 1.4 and 1.14). The response to his healing ministry in Capernaum was counter-productive; it was not leading to repentance and faith. Without these, the Kingdom does not grow; it is best served by giving priority to the proclamation of the good news.

Thus Mark brings to a close his bird's-eye view of twenty-four hours in the opening ministry of Jesus. The disciples have gained invaluable exposure to what is involved in fishing for men, as they observe Jesus in a variety of places (synagogue, home and street), in the midst of crowds and alone in a solitary place. His power is not impersonal; he does not ignore individual needs in the clamor of the crowds. He cares for both men and women.

Yet he is not a populist who leads the throng where they want to go. He knows his mission and will not be deterred from it. He touches home, double-checking with his Father as to priorities. With a sense of urgency, he establishes the pattern of extending God's reign to many places.

v. 36 - "Tracked him down" contains a sense of hostility, and "searching" (used nine times in Mark) connotes seeking out of wrong motives. This is the first suggestion of the blindness of the disciples. That's why they are called "companions" (v 36) here instead of disciples.

JESUS CLEANSES A LEPER, 1.40-45

Mark frequently closes a section by relating an incident that illustrates one of its major emphases. Sometimes it is a positive example (as in 10.46-52), sometimes a negative one (as in 6.1-6). After presenting the authority of Jesus in word and act, he rounds out this subject with a dramatic story showing a different facet of Jesus' authority. He identifies neither the time nor place in which this experience occurred; he draws it from his knowledge of Jesus' many encounters.

Leprosy has a distinct place in the Old Testament Scriptures. The term probably included various highly infectious skin diseases that were very difficult to cure. Infected persons were required by the Mosaic Law to live in seclusion and to shout "Unclean, unclean" (Lev 13.45-46) as a warning to anyone who approached them. In the light of these physical and social consequences, the victims were called the "living dead", and their cure considered as difficult as raising the dead.

Because of its parallels with the consequences of sin, leprosy is considered a "type" of sin. The illness was connected to punishment for sin (Nu 12.10; 2Ki 5.27, 15.5). A priest declared the infected person excluded from worship and, when cured, authorized his return upon making an offering for sin (Lev 13-14). The term **katharizo** is used both as purifying from leprosy (Mk 1.40ff) and as cleansing from sin (Ac 15.9; 2Co 7.1; 1Jn 1.7).

1.40-42 - Although this leper violates the rules of isolation and approaches Jesus, he is not reprimanded. Somehow he knows that Jesus is compassionate and able to cure him. Kneeling before him, he declares his faith in Jesus' authority: "If you are willing, you can make me clean." In other words, "You have such authority that you can do what you want." This is the highest acknowledgement that a person can make of Jesus' authority; it can be said about none other. Honoring such recognition, Jesus confirms his sovereignty: "I am willing. Be clean." Although Jesus did not come primarily for healing (1.38), Jesus does not desist from this ministry. In his battle against all evil, he frees people from all enslavement.

Lepers were not only isolated from society, they were *untouchable.* Anyone who touched a leper would become ceremonially unclean (similar to touching a corpse) as well as run the risk of becoming infected physically. While others shrunk from any such contact, Jesus touches the untouchable. Jesus does not become unclean; rather, he makes the unclean clean.

Jesus acts out of his characteristic compassion (cf 6.34). According to the best-attested manuscripts, however, the text does not state here that Jesus was moved by compassion (as most of our translations read). Rather, they read "he was moved by anger." Leprosy was a vivid example of the destruction wrought by evil. Jesus' anger is directed against Satan who was destroying the leper, just as surely as he enslaved the demoniac. This should not surprise us, for God's wrath is directed against all evil. We should not picture Jesus as a sentimentalist; he is engaged in the destruction of evil. His anger here is evidence of the presence of God's dominion that includes the judgment of sin as well as the offer of redemption. His future reign will bring the complete destruction of the forces of evil and the complete redemption of those who repent and believe (1.15).

Readers familiar with the levitical laws readily understand this story as expressing Jesus' power to redeem from sin, as well as his power to cure. He who is able to cure the leper and restore him to communion with God and the community can also cleanse the sinner and bring him into fellowship with God and people. This understanding is reinforced by the following pericope (2.1-12), in which Jesus' power to forgive sin is emphasized.

The Mosaic Law as to purification could not help the man; it was designed to protect the community from him. What the Law could not do, Jesus does (cf Ro 8.3). And he does it so simply, with just his words, "Be clean." The cure was immediate (v. 42). In accord with that Law, Jesus tells the man to get an official certification of his purification from the priest. This would guarantee the man's acceptance in the community.

1.43-45 - This instruction, however, was made with a strong warning: "Don't tell this to anyone." Publicity given to this cure would only add to people's amazement, making it more difficult for Jesus to fulfill his ministry (v. 45). Already, too many saw only his works, without hearing his words. Too many saw him as a miracle-worker, without seeking to know the man behind the acts. They needed time to weigh the evidences, to find out who Jesus is.

Previously, the leper impressed us with his faith and understanding as he knelt before Jesus. His clear perception of Jesus' authority should result in obedience to Jesus as an expression of true gratitude. Instead, his enthusiasm dictates his actions. Contrary to Jesus' strong warning, he tells widely what happened, as though emotions could substitute for obedience. He had eagerly sought Jesus' blessings, but he didn't accept Jesus ruling his life. It seems that he did not seek Jesus as a person; rather, he sought him for what Jesus could give him. His disobedience hindered the progress of the gospel. For a while, Jesus could no longer enter a town openly but had to stay in lonely places. Yet people from everywhere still came to him (v. 45).

This section (1.14-45) emphasizes Jesus' authority in establishing God's rule among men. He proclaims the good news with divine power. He commands some to come after him, and they immediately follow him. He teaches with authority. The evil spirits are subject to him. The sick are healed. However, Jesus' authority does not override a person's free will; the restored leper disobeys Jesus' strong warning. Jesus' power is self-limiting. His Kingdom is not yet an irresistible power, sweeping all before it. In the future, when he is exalted by God to the highest place, all will confess that Jesus Christ is Lord (Php 2.9-11). Meanwhile, he has limited the exercise of his power (Php 2.6-8). In the present age, men and women are confronted with the decision to follow Jesus. They can accept that invitation or reject it. Even those who richly benefit from his authority, like this leper, can insist on their own way. Apart from their personal loss, their disobedience limits God's reign among men and women.

v. 40 - The illness popularly known today as "leprosy" is not highly contagious and is not to be identified with the illness described in the Bible. Its correct medical term is "Hansen's disease."

v. 41 - "I am willing" removes healing from the subjective faith of the individual and places it within the realm of Jesus' sovereign will (cf 9.22).

v. 44 - The priesthood was an honored hereditary position, with no theological training required for consecration (the scribes were the trained theologians). In order to conduct public worship in Jerusalem, the approximately 7,200 priests were divided into 24 courses. These descendants of Aaron lived at their homes most of the year, journeying to Jerusalem for their functions confined to two one-week periods and the three annual pilgrim festivals. Their income from tithes and special taxes were supplemented by some professional activities (mostly manual work) in their home area.

• By presenting himself to the priest, the former leper would serve "as a testimony" that Jesus cleansed lepers. This would contribute to Jesus' eventual recognition as the Messiah (cf Mt 11.5; Lk 7.22). On the other hand, the demons' identification of Jesus as God's Son was designed, not for the establishment of God's reign among men, but for its destruction. Therefore, Jesus ordered them to be silent.

Through the man's testimony, Jesus would be known as one who recognized "the validity of the Mosaic Law in cases where moral issues are not at stake" (Vincent Taylor 190). Jesus was not a "law breaker"; he was faithful to the Law and fulfilled its promises. In chapter 2, it appears that Jesus rejects the Mosaic Law. Upon closer study, his rejection occurs only when the practice of laws that are dictated by oral tradition and not Scripture itself contradicts the will of God (cf 7.1-13).

B. JESUS DISCLOSES HIS AUTHORITY IN THE MIDST OF CONFLICT, 2.1-3.6

The disciples are most likely gratified by Galilee's initial response to Jesus' ministry, in spite of some difficulties encountered. Progress seems inevitable, considering the authority Jesus has demonstrated in word and deed. They are confident that before long God will establish his reign.

This subdivision, however, makes it clear that some have doubts about Jesus as one sent from God. The Jewish religious authorities spearhead the opposition. On the basis of their traditions, they conclude that Jesus is an impostor. Step by step, they reject his claims and make accusations against him. Because of his growing popularity, they conclude that he is a danger to the religious life of the nation and must be eliminated. Still they are powerless to indict Jesus.

Meanwhile, Jesus reaffirms his authority as he intensifies his efforts to establish God's rule among men. He brings blessings that belong to the messianic era, such as the forgiveness of sins. These are further indications of his identity. However, he does not call himself the Messiah (nor does the word appear even once between 1.1 and 8.29), for popular connotations of the term "messiah" are unacceptable to him. He uses the phrase "the Son of Man" to identify himself and proceeds to fill it with rich significance as a part of his self-revelation.

This first appearance of the religious leaders (2.6) signals a growing controversy with Jesus. Mark narrates a series of five questions presented in five paragraphs. These balance another series of five controversial questions with leaders near the end of the Gospel (11.27 - 12.37). A third, shorter unit of controversy is related near the middle of Mark (7.1-23).

A careful reading of these five paragraphs reveals a lineal progression in the leaders' offensive against Jesus. They begin by accusing him in silence (2.6f). Then they question him directly (2.18), rebuke him (2.24) and finally plot to kill him (3.6). The number of people involved grows, and the hostility multiplies with each alleged offense. While all this is going on, Jesus gives clues as to his identify and his coming death.

These controversies arise from questions about Jesus' person, authority and untraditional behavior. Even the two healings are narrated in ways that emphasize the christological rather than the miraculous element. With pastoral concern for his readers, Mark includes these stories to strengthen their faith in the person and authority of Jesus. His first readers should know about the origins of Jesus' rejection by the Jewish establishment. Knowledge that Christian freedom from ritualism began with Jesus' himself will help heal relationships torn by differences between Jewish and Gentile believers.

1. Jesus Heals A Paralytic And Forgives His Sins, 2.1-12

Upon Jesus' return to Capernaum, many gather to hear his teaching, crowding inside and outside the house. Again, his teaching is interrupted, this time by the friends of a paralytic. This cure, however, takes on new dimensions, for Jesus says to the paralyzed one, "Your sins are forgiven."

Mark moves from Jesus' curing a leper (1.40ff, an illness related to sin in Old Testament symbolism) to the forgiving of sins. Simultaneously, he introduces us to a new element in Jesus' life: his rejection by the religious leaders. The shadow of Jesus' death will soon appear.

• 2.1-3.6 is a literary unit called "chiasmus" (i.e., in the form of an "x"). The first paragraph corresponds with the fifth, the second with the fourth, while the third (2.18-22) presents the climax of 2.1-3.6.

2.1-5 - After a few days teaching in less populated areas, Jesus is able to return to Capernaum. There, in a home, he resumes his primary ministry of teaching the word. While Mark does not explain what he taught, we can safely presume that he explains more about the Good News (cf 1.14-15; 1.21).

Crowds fill the house and yard, hindering four men from carrying their paralytic friend to Jesus. Undeterred, the four make an opening in the roof and lower the man to Jesus.

Seeing their faith, Jesus says to the paralytic, "Son, your sins are forgiven." He continues teaching, adapting his method to this interruption in his "teaching plan." The sufferer came for healing: that was his greatest felt need. He might have been startled or even disappointed by Jesus' words. But Jesus is not superficial. He goes to the heart of the problem. Since all suffering is rooted in humankind's separation from God, Jesus calls the paralytic's attention to his deepest necessity: he needs to be restored to communion with God. Jesus' healings are evidence of his much more profound authority, namely, to restore alienated men and women to communion with God.

2.6-7 - The narrator leaves no doubt as to the response of the teachers of the law (cf 1.22) seated there. They ponder such an affirmation from one gaining widespread fame as a religious teacher. Who does this man think he is?

Since they consider him to be a contemptible fellow, possibly carried away emotionally by such popularity, they do not charge him directly with blasphemy. They conceal their thoughts about "Why does this fellow talk like that? It is blasphemy. Who can forgive sins but God alone?" Since they know the Old Testament law (Lev 24.15f; 1Ki 21.13; cf Acts 7.58), the idea of punishing Jesus with death for the crime of blasphemy rises unsolicited. Yet they say nothing; their time will come (cf 14.64). Meanwhile, they are gathering evidence. By 3.6, they are already plotting his death.

2.8-10 - Jesus, however, deliberately brings their thoughts out into the open. "Which is easier: to say to the paralytic, 'Your sins are forgiven,' or to say, 'Rise up, take your mat and walk?'"

Anyone can *say* "Your sins are forgiven," but how does one prove it? On the other hand, to *say* "Get up and walk" invites immediate confirmation. Failure would identify the speaker as a charlatan. A paralytic walking, however, would prove that his word is to be trusted. So Jesus cures the paralytic, thereby giving tangible proof of his power to heal. Having deliberately connected the healing with forgiveness, Jesus affirms his authority to forgive sins. The man is restored to God just as surely as he is restored to walking.

God alone has the prerogative to forgive sins; no human being has this authority. But *this particular person* does, because he receives this authority from God. Daniel wrote of "one like a son of man" (Da 7.13-14) who, with authority given him by the Ancient of Days, represents and vindicates God's suffering people (Da 7.18,21,27). By referring to himself as "the Son of Man," Jesus accepts that mission. He is God's obedient servant who identifies himself with suffering humanity in order that he might bring redemption (Mk 10.45). He *already* exercises this God-given authority to forgive sins "on earth" (that is, here and now); he does *not yet* exercise his everlasting dominion over all peoples (Da 7.14; Mk 8.38; 13.26; 14.62).

By the term "the Son of Man," Jesus both conceals and reveals his identify as the Son of God. For example, in both 2.10 and 2.28, the Son of Man (a term that associates him with humanity) claims two prerogatives that belong to God alone: the authority to forgive sins and the Lord of the Sabbath. The Son of Man is, in fact, the Son of God *incognito*. Although his self-revelation continues, his full identity remains hidden from his contemporaries until he fulfills his role as the Son of Man. At that time, Jesus is vindicated by God and acknowledged to be the Son of God (cf 15.39).

2.11-12 - This cure (as well as the one in the parallel paragraph 3.1-6) is a restoration to normality. In the sight of all, the paralytic does as Jesus instructed. He is restored to health, to communion with God and to the fellowship of his home. Jesus responds to the needs of the whole person; his work is complete.

All the people are amazed. They ascribe to God the splendor (**doxa**, cf 8.38; 13.26) due to his name. But one gets the impression that the people are more interested in what Jesus does than in who he is. As Mark continues his narrative, we are left with no doubts as to the response of the religious leaders.

v. 1 - Mark does not indicate whose home this is. The word (**oikos**) may indicate Jesus' "in house" teaching ministry (3.20; 7.17; 9.28) especially applicable to the house-churches of Mark's first readers.
v. 2 - By the time Mark wrote his Gospel, "the word" meant the message of the gospel.
• Suffering is not necessarily the direct result of an afflicted person's own sin (Lk 13.1-5; Jn 9.2-3).
• Significantly, the first mention of the substantive "faith" (**pistis**, 2.5; 4.40; 5.34; 10.52; 11.22) is followed by Jesus forgiving sins. Faith is a prerequisite for reconciliation with God (cf Romans 3.22; 5.2; 9.30; Ephesians 2.8. These men (2.5) expressed their faith correctly: they sought Jesus.
v. 4 - Frequently, an outside stairway led to the flat roof of Palestinian one-room homes. These determined friends would have little difficulty in removing the sun-baked earthen covering over a matting of twigs and branches laid on crossbeams.
v. 5 - As William Barclay says (Words 118-122), "in the New Testament, **hamartia** ("sin") does not describe a definite act of sin; it describes the state of sin, from which acts of sin come." Every person is involved in and guilty of sin; it is the universal state of humanity. "Sin is not merely an external power that exercises sway over a man"; it dwells within him, rules over him, hardens his heart and results in death.

Jesus' authority includes forgiving sins (2.5-10) and defining forgivable and unforgivable sins (3.29-30). Mark's use of the present tense means, "your sins are at this moment forgiven" (Mann 224). Repentance in response to John's and Jesus' messages (1.4, 1.15) now finds fulfillment: Jesus offers forgiveness.

• The essence of **aphiesthai** (the most common word used to express forgiveness of sins) is that through Jesus Christ God releases us from the punishment and penalty that he had every right to inflict upon us. It emphasizes God's love in dealing with us, not according to what we deserve, but according to his mercy and his grace in Jesus Christ. While Jesus does not define forgiveness in abstract terms, he vividly portrays its meaning in actions such as including sinners in table-fellowship (2.15).

Authentic religion emphasizes the need of God's forgiveness because it recognizes both the holiness of God and the sinfulness of humanity.

• The rabbis had a saying, "There is no sick man healed of his sickness until all his sins have been forgiven him." (Barclay Mark 47).
v. 7ff - The Greek words used to pose the question "why?" increase in intensity throughout this section.
• Blasphemy constituted a transgression against God when a person claimed prerogatives that belong only to God. The accusations made against Jesus both here and in 14.64 are of this type. A direct charge is not made against Jesus here (they don't say what they are thinking). This, however, prepares us for the direct, spoken charge of blasphemy made forcefully by the Sanhedrin during Jesus' trial, followed by the demand for the death penalty (14.64).

The story takes an ironic twist when Jesus charges his accusers of blasphemy (3.28-29). Their blasphemy was that of persons knowingly or unknowingly attacking God or his representative.

• In the absolute sense, only God can forgive sins (Ex 34.6ff; Isa 43.25; 44.22). In the relative sense, people can forgive those who have wronged them (cf Ge 50.17; 1Sa 25.28, 35; Mt 6.12; Mk 11.25).
v. 10 - "Son of Man" is used fourteen times in Mark. It is Jesus' most frequently used self-designation; no one else in the New Testament refers to him as the Son of Man.

2. Jesus Associates With Outcasts, 2.13-17

Having demonstrated that the Son of Man has authority on earth to forgive sins (2.10), Mark now shows that this authority extends even to Levi, the tax collector, considered to be among the worst of sinners. Jesus' ministry, however, is not limited to wiping out past offenses. He transforms persons, even remaking this "sinner" Levi into one of his disciples. The remarkable story of Levi is thus tied to the preceding theme of Jesus' authority to forgive.

The confrontations with the religious leaders continue in these next three paragraphs of inverted parallelism. In contrast to the first and fifth pericope, no cures are involved in these encounters. Jesus does not take the initiative; rather, the leaders question him or his disciples as to their actions. Each time Jesus answers with a parable that reveals something more about who he is. Thus all five paragraphs are essentially christological against the background of contentions about religious rituals.

2.13-14 - Since Jesus came to proclaim God's rule among men and women, he continues to teach in homes, on the street and by the lakeshore. He buys up the time and does not stop because of the opposition encountered. Mark continues his report on the controversy over Jesus' authority (2.6-10) without neglecting, however, the positive results of Jesus' teaching.

As a fishing center beside Lake Galilee, Capernaum's commerce was subject to taxation by the Roman authorities. Among the tax collectors was Levi, the son of Alphaeus. Upon hearing Jesus' imperative, Levi follows him.

The call by Jesus and Levi's prompt obedience bring to mind the similar experience of the four (1.16-20). "Follow me" is the essence of his call to discipleship. By openly summoning anyone into the group of disciples, Jesus is expressing forgiveness and proclaiming to everyone that Levi is acceptable in God's Kingdom.

But Jesus' call to Levi is very different because Levi is a tax collector. In Jesus' day, "publicans" bid for their jobs and then exploited the people for all they could get beyond what was due the government. As a result, the people despised tax collectors.

Tax collectors' greed was bad enough. Worse than that, they were Jews who collaborated with the hated Roman imperialists. Detested by all who longed for the restoration of the Jewish nation, these traitors were outcasts from society, disqualified as witnesses and excommunicated from the synagogue. Ritually "impure" themselves, all they touched and any house they entered became impure as well.

Some rabbis taught that one should avoid association with sinners, even to introduce them to the Torah. Jesus, however, seeks out Levi rather than shunning this "sinner" who is rejected by "decent people." In the eyes of many, Jesus disqualifies himself as a religious teacher because he includes Levi among his followers.

2.15-16 - However, the worst is yet to come. Levi prepares a feast, inviting his friends and co-workers, "sinners" and outcasts like himself. That way they can meet Jesus. And Jesus accepts the invitation and eats with such disreputable people.

To receive someone at their table was especially significant for persons in the Near East. Since sharing a table meant sharing life, people were extremely selective in whom they invited. The guest's presence was a sign of peace, confidence and even amnesty (Ge 26.30, 31.54; 2Sa 9.7; 2Ki 25.27-29).

A religious person would shrink from eating with a non-religious person lest he, too, be defiled. In avoiding all such contact, the Pharisees (this name means "separation") expressed their concept of God as the holy One separated from sinners. They awaited a great messianic feast in which only those separated in this life from sin and sinners would participate. As preached by the prophets, that eschatological banquet symbolized Israel's salvation.

Jesus, however, is crossing barriers to bring the good news to those alienated from God. For him, table fellowship gives expression to his mission and message of the forgiveness of sins. He is demonstrating God's redemptive love by including "sinners" in the community of salvation in anticipation of the messianic feast.

This has adverse effects on Jesus, however. His association with outcasts leads to his being known as a "friend of tax collectors and sinners." He is accused of being "a glutton and a drunkard" (Mt 11.19). The religious leaders are convinced that if he were a truly religious man, he would be like the Pharisees and disdain table fellowship with sinners. They no longer have doubts about who Jesus is, for a man is known by the company he keeps. He not only condones sin; his participation in Levi's feast proves that Jesus is a sinner. He must be denounced openly. His table-fellowship with "sinners" is a scandal only to be surpassed by the scandal of the cross (1Co 1.23).

A direct attack by the teachers of the law must wait awhile. Now, rather than ask Jesus directly about his conduct, they ask his disciples: "Why does he eat with tax collectors and 'sinners'?" By raising doubts in the disciples' minds, they can possibly create a wedge between disciples and teacher. The disciples themselves may wonder about how God's rule can include such outcasts. How can the restoration of the Kingdom of Israel embrace anyone who collaborates with pagan Rome?

2.17 - Although the question is directed to his disciples (cf 2.18), Jesus answers for them with a parable. "It is not the healthy who need a doctor, but the sick. I have not come to call the righteous, but sinners."

Levi needs a physician as much as the leper and the paralytic. The Pharisees need help, too. In fact, they are worse off, for their self-righteousness keeps them from admitting how much they need the help that only Jesus can give. Little do these self-appointed "saints" imagine that they, too, are sinners. In reality, their religious self-image isolates them from God.

In saying, "I came to call sinners," Jesus affirms his purpose and mission (cf 1.38, 10.45). Other people try to avoid contact with the sick, but the doctor seeks them out in order to heal them. Jesus desires the undesirables. He loves the common person, so despised by others. He calls men and women to repentance and faith (1.15), offering them forgiveness (2.10), table fellowship (2.15) and more that the gospel story will yet unfold.

The benefits he brings are unavailable to the unrepentant, however, for such presume that they have no need. At the same time, it would be a mistake to think of these benefits as only future blessings. Jesus brings life from the future Kingdom into the present age, offering communion with God and humans, to be enjoyed now in the midst of this present evil world. Jesus' example of breaking down barriers carried a clear message to the early church, as it sought guidelines as to relationships between Gentile and Jewish believers, between Christians and unbelievers. This new life is to be expressed today, as well, wherever his followers seek to live as his church in the midst of communities torn apart by strife.

Levi shows us something of what it means to follow Jesus. The center of his life changes from self to Jesus. He shares with his own people the joy of knowing Jesus (cf 5.19). As one who follows Jesus, he is a "fisher of men" (1.17).

v. 14 - Levi is often identified with Matthew (Mt 9.9, cf Lk 5.27), since there is no reference to Levi son of Alphaeus in the list of the twelve disciples in Mk 3.16-19 (cf Mt 10.2-4, Lk 6.14-16, Acts 1.13).

• "Tax collector" or "customs officer" is the proper translation. "Publican" comes to us through the Latin and does not occur in the Gospels.

v. 15 - The possibility that Jesus himself was hosting these "sinners" enhances the significance of this event as a dramatized messianic parable. It becomes a preview of that eschatological banquet, where men and women, gathered from all social positions and coming "from the east and the west" (Mt 8.11), will be guests of the God who forgives sinners and welcomes them into his home. Communion, severed by sin, will be restored; social barriers will be destroyed.

As head of a new family (3.31-35), Jesus hosted (14.12-25) the celebration of the annual Passover, giving it new meaning, in anticipation of the messianic banquet.

• In the biblical sense, Levi and his friends were sinners, "missing the mark" and "falling short of the glory of God" (Ro 3.23). Tax collectors were despised for their low morals. In this context, however, "sinners" is used ironically. It signifies "irreligious people," i.e., people who were not zealous in observing the Law as interpreted and kept by the Pharisees. Their "sins" become especially apparent in the dietary and Sabbath regulations defined in detail by rabbinic traditions. As used by the Pharisees, "sinners" included workers in despised trades as well as those with disreputable lifestyles. They were outcasts, spurned by the ruling segments of society.

• This is the first use of the word "disciples" in Mark. Already there are many persons following Jesus. The "many" in this verse probably refers, however, to the tax collectors and "sinners" who followed Jesus.

• Jesus' joy in receiving sinners is not to be confused with approval of their conduct nor with a generous, egalitarian spirit. He neither denies that they are sinners nor makes light of their guilt. Rather, he points to their need and ministers to it. He rejoices when sinners respond to his message and, through repentance and faith (1.15), are forgiven and enter into fellowship with God.

• The teachers of the law (scribes) belonged to the party of the Pharisees, the largest religious group in the time of Jesus. As the spiritual descendants of the **hasidim** (the "devoted ones"), the Pharisees sought to separate themselves from the Hellenistic influences which dominated the Mediterranean world and threatened Judaism. They were highly regarded for their religious zeal and their patriotism. They considered themselves to be "the righteous ones."

• Table fellowship was a matter of concern in the early church, as seen in Ac 10.28; 11.3; Gal 2.12.

v. 17 - In Mark's Gospel, Jesus' use of parables begins simultaneously with the controversies. Parables veil their message from his adversaries while revealing it to "those who have ears to hear" (4.10ff).

• Once again we see Jesus identifying himself with sinners (cf 1.9ff). At the same time, just as a doctor is distinct from both the sick and the well, Jesus is distinct from both the sinful and the "righteous."

3. Jesus Answers Accusations Related To Fasting, 2.18-22

"To eat, or not to eat?" (with apologies to William Shakespeare). Ironically, both questions are posed to Jesus. After accusing him by asking, "Why eat with sinners?", religious leaders now denounce him with "Why eat?" (i.e., "Why not fast?"). His interrogators are concerned about keeping rituals, for these are the essence of their religion. Jesus, however, keeps insisting on their facing another question, namely: "Who is Jesus?" Therein lies the answer to their many questions. Jesus' presence changes everything, including all those rules that dominate their lives.

This pericope consists of three parts, beginning with the controversy over fasting and Jesus' answer in the form of a parable (2.18-19). In the center of the pericope and of the whole controversy narrative, Jesus identifies himself through a christological parable containing a strong allusion to his crucifixion (2.20). In closing (2.21-22), two parables answer the question of why Jesus' disciples do not fast.

With this pericope, we reach the climax of the chiastic structure of 2.1-3.6. Mark gives no indication of place, time, or the source of the question ("some people asked Jesus"). This implies that here is vitally important teaching, not limited to a specific occasion. Emphasis is given to Jesus' words. His verbal answer (not his actions, as in the neighboring pericopes) is central. The truths contained herein are the key to understanding what is going on, for they focus on the Person who is now present.

2.18-19 - Left to themselves when their leader was taken from them by force (1.14, cf 2.20), the disciples of John continued the practice of fasting as a sign of repentance in preparation for the coming of God's Kingdom.

Although the Law required fasting only on the Day of Atonement (Lev 16.29), the Pharisees fasted every Monday and Thursday (cf Lk 18.12). For them, this sign of mourning for their sins gained them God's approval in preparation for the Day of Judgment. Not only did they themselves practice and teach fasting, but in their role as defenders of the traditions, they protested when others did not.

Jesus does not break the Mosaic Law by not asking his disciples to fast. Others think he does, since they equate their traditions to the Law. So they ask Jesus why his disciples do not fast. Jesus is accused indirectly through his disciples, for their behavior implicates their teacher. Later he himself will come under direct attack. In his answer (v. 19-22), Jesus comes to his disciples' defense, justifying their different conduct in the light of something new--more accurately: someone new. Jesus brings a new reality. It would have been inappropriate for his disciples to fast, for "the time has come, the Kingdom of God has arrived" (1.15).

Jesus frequently answers a question with one of his own, to arouse his hearers (and Mark's readers) to thought. A short parable (v. 19a) answers their question and his own by relating a fact obvious to people familiar with Near Eastern marriage customs. "How can the guests of the bridegroom fast while he is with them?" A marriage is a time for celebration; to fast at such a time is unthinkable (v. 19b). A rabbi would even interrupt the giving of biblical instruction in order to join the festivities. So Jesus' disciples (the wedding guests) are not fasting because Jesus' presence is similar to a wedding feast: it brings joy, not mourning.

The Old Testament frequently uses marriage as a metaphor of the true relationship between God (the bridegroom) and Israel (the bride). God's final act of redemption is also described as a marriage to take place at the coming of the Messiah. In this light Jesus is declaring that the messianic era has already begun. Jesus is the bridegroom. His presence brings joy. His gift of forgiveness is a cause for rejoicing. God is fulfilling promises made to his bride, Israel.

2.20 - This joy, however, is not unrestricted. Normally, the guests leave the bridegroom. But Jesus says there will come a time when--not if--the bridegroom will be taken away, implying a violent removal (cf Isa 53.8). The Bridegroom will win his bride through suffering and death. So this joy cannot be divorced from mourning, for Jesus came to die as the Suffering Servant. During his absence, they will fast.

Jesus presents himself as the one who, through his own death, brings the joy of the Kingdom to forgiven sinners. His whole ministry is conducted under the shadow of the cross. This is the climax of this controversy section.

2.21-22 - Jesus continues to answer the question posed in v. 18 by telling two parables related to the daily life of his listeners. No one would patch a piece of new cloth on an old garment, for the new cloth would shrink upon being washed. The result would be a tear worse than in the beginning.

The second anecdote reinforces the first. No one would fill an old leather wineskin with new wine. As the wine fermented, it would expand, bursting the old, stiff wineskin. As a result, both the wineskin and the wine would be a total loss.

Yet the scribes (guardians of the traditions) and others are trying to do something equally ridiculous with Jesus. His good news can not be used to repair their worn traditionalism. God's reign is dynamic; it will not be restricted by old molds. Jesus brings a new message that requires new patterns of expression that cannot be bound by the old (cf 2 Co 5.17).

This does not mean, however, that Jesus rejects all that is old and accepts every new thing. His ministry is anchored in the Old Testament revelation. He rejects its misuse, twisted by traditions. He also gives new meaning to the old covenant without subtracting from it (e.g., 2.25; 7.6ff; 10.5ff; 11.17; 12.29ff, 35ff; 14.12ff.)

v. 18 - As members of a lay movement formed about two centuries earlier to combat the Hellenization of Judaism, the Pharisees belonged to various social classes, although most were merchants and craftsmen. Numbering about six thousand, they were spread all over Palestine. Only their leaders were scribes. They hoped to gain God's favor in response to their zeal for the Mosaic law.

Jesus' various charges against them contradict their claim to represent the true Israel through their strict fulfillment of the commandments. Wanting to be the holy ones, their dedication to obtaining strict external purity ignored humanity's greatest need, that of inward cleanliness (cf 7.1-24). Their piety was "at the service of their need to assert themselves" (Jeremias Theology 143-145).

• "How is it?" is more intense than the previous "why's?" and delves into the reasons behind the act. Their question opens the door for Jesus to deal with their motives for fasting. In the New Testament the practice itself is neither explicitly commanded nor prohibited. Religion is too often reduced to *what* one does, with little or no regard for *why* it is done. Like other spiritual exercises, the practice of fasting should avoid tendencies toward legalism and manipulation. Jesus declared that his presence among his disciples was cause for rejoicing, not mourning. Since the risen Christ is ever present with Christians today, this is also a time for rejoicing.

This passage met a special need of first-century believers, often divided over the place of Jewish customs in the churches. As to fasting in the early church, see Acts 13.3; 14.23; Ro 14.1-15.7.

v. 19 - Cf. Isa 54.5,6; 62.4,5; Jer 2.2, 32f; Eze 16.8ff. Hos 2.14-23 is especially pertinent here, for it speaks of both the bridegroom (v. 16ff) and the new wine (v. 22}. The messianic significance of the bridegroom is evident in Mt 25.1-13; Jn 3.29; 2Co 11.2; Eph 5.32 and Rev 19.7-9; 21.2.

v. 22 - "New" religions (which are basically modern adaptations of ancient ones) sometimes appeal to portions of the Bible as confirmation of their practices. However, they reject Biblical revelation as a whole. By distorting the meaning of their selected passages, they claim support for their religion. Their conclusions may appear to be "new wine," but they are based on false premises.

4. Jesus Is Tested Concerning The Sabbath, 2.23-28

A religious teacher must meet certain qualifications in order to be authentic. Jesus had failed the three tests already applied. Now the religious authorities will apply the acid test: does he keep the Sabbath?

Mark does not identify the synagogue where the incident took place; that is unimportant. The discussion revolves around what happened on a Sabbath day.

2.23-24 - Since in his creative acts God separated the seventh day from the others, humankind had a special obligation to observe the Sabbath. God's will was expressed in the fourth of the Ten

Commandments: "Remember the Sabbath day by keeping it holy," for the Lord himself had "blessed the Sabbath day and made it holy" (Ex 20.8-11).

That Law went on to say that no one should work on the Sabbath. But what constitutes work? In their desire to obey God in every detail of their lives, rabbis sought to define what activities were prohibited by that commandment. Their discussions led to the formation of thirty-nine main categories of work forbidden on the Sabbath. Later, these categories were defined in even greater detail.

The Decalogue, along with the Mosaic injunction to rest "even during the plowing season and harvest" (Ex 34.21), was interpreted in the third category as forbidding "reaping" on the Sabbath. This included picking a few heads of grain. Obedience to these details of the Law was of primary importance as expressions of one's submission to God. It distinguished the Jews from the Gentiles. Unlawful activity on the Sabbath could even be punished by death if the violator had been previously warned (Ex 31.12-17, 35.1-3; cf Jn 5.10).

The Pharisees' accusation is specifically concerned about what is allowed on the Sabbath. It is not a question of stealing, for the Law stipulated that some of the grain and grapes be left for the needy to eat (Lev 19.9f; Dt 23.25). It is a matter of Sabbath observance.

Once again (cf 2.18) Jesus is questioned concerning the conduct of his disciples. This is the first time the Pharisees themselves confront Jesus. Their "look, why?" is not a request for information. Their rhetorical question is in reality an accusation, based on the conviction that a good teacher would correct his followers' misbehavior.

2.25-26 - In the rabbinic mode of a counter-question that introduces an argument from Scripture, Jesus asks them, "Have you never read...?" His interrogators, reputedly authorities in the Scriptures, were bound by their traditions. Jesus calls them to take a fresh look at the Scriptures themselves. On the basis of Scripture, he defends the so-called unlawful action of his disciples with two arguments. The first is an appeal to the precedent of King David, one of the most honored figures in Jewish history. The second is an appeal to the principle of creation (v. 27; cf 10.6).

Fleeing from King Saul's wrath, David and his men were hungry and in need (1Sa 21.1-6). The urgency of their situation justified their breaking the rules. Likewise, Jesus and his disciples are travelling; their mission is urgent, for the gospel must be proclaimed. Their mission justifies breaking religious restrictions.

Moreover, David was special: Samuel had already anointed him as King, although he had not yet assumed the throne. Jesus, too, is a king awaiting the proper time to assume the throne. God himself has anointed him (1.11). By comparing himself to David, Jesus implies that what the great King David could do, he, too, can do. Some might ask, "Just who does he think he is, claiming authority equal to that of King David?" That is a very appropriate question, for it takes us back to one even more basic: who is Jesus? A partial answer is implied: Jesus is a King greater than David (cf 12.35-37).

A more complete answer is needed, however. Without delay, the reader is given additional information about Jesus' identity.

2.27-28 - Jesus now establishes a basic premise about the very purpose of the Sabbath, a principle already illustrated in David's experience: "The Sabbath was made for the good of man; man was not made for the Sabbath." The Sabbath was designed to meet humanity's need in relationship to God: it is a day for renewal in holiness (Ex 31.12-17). The Sabbath also emphasized human relationships and social justice (cf Dt 5.12-15). The Sabbath was God's gift to men and women, for he knew what his creatures needed. He ordained one day in seven so that, in breaking the burdensome day-to-day routine, they could maintain physical, psychological, social and spiritual equilibrium. It was a day of rest for all, slave as well as free, female as well as male, animal as well as human.

The Sabbath was functional; it was made to benefit people. In legislating the rabbinical code, however, the religious authorities lost sight of God's purposes in creating the Sabbath. God's guidelines for freedom were twisted into chains that enslaved the people. Rules dominated Sabbath observance.

Jesus rejects any reordering of God's creation. By virtue of his God-given authority, he clarifies the correct order. His two statements, "the Sabbath was made for man" and "the Son of Man is Lord even of the Sabbath," signify that:

1) The Sabbath was made for the benefit of persons. This is what God intended in creating it.

2) Men and women are therefore to be served and blessed by the Sabbath rather than be enslaved by it.

3) Jesus' claim to be Lord of the Sabbath is a claim to deity, for, as all Israel knew, God had created the Sabbath.

4) Jesus, the Son of Man, is Lord over humanity and over the Sabbath. The Sabbath is to serve persons, who are to serve the Lord.

The gospel liberates those who have been manipulated by religious legalism, as well as releasing people depersonalized by political or economic forces. Reconciliation with God (cf 1.15) restores individuals to their exalted position as the climax of God's creative acts. As men and women give personal priority to God's rule in the person of Jesus, they have the potential of becoming whole persons.

v. 23 - The disciples were not opening a path but were going along on a regular path through the fields of grain, travelling as a part of their mission. "Heads of grain" refers to grains like wheat or barley. Corn (maize) was unknown for it is a crop native to the New World.

v. 24 - The Pharisees seek Jesus' motives with their interrogative "Why? The rabbinical categories of work prohibited on the Sabbath, however, generally omit concern about motives. This lack is characteristic of legalism, where *what* is done takes priority over *why* it is done.

• The Sabbath prohibitions are presented in the Mishnah, a collection of rabbinic comments on the Law, compiled about 200 A.D. The Talmud, the authoritative body of Jewish tradition, is composed of the Mishnah and a commentary on it, the Gemara.

v. 25 - This reference to David prepares the reader for Mark 10.46-48; 11.10 and 12.35-37 where the relationship between Jesus and David is brought to a climactic conclusion.

• Here and in 2.17 Jesus emphasizes those who have needs. They are given priority over customs.

v. 26 - According to 1 Samuel 21.1-6, Ahimelech, and not his son Abiathar (1Ch 24.6), was the high priest when David entered the house of God. Various explanations are given to account for this discrepancy:

1) A gloss arose when a marginal note was moved into the text.

2) A scribe corrected what he thought was a case of dittography. Thus the original text identified the father by the name of his famous son, Ab (ba)-Abiathar (the father of Abiathar), similar to some Near East customs (Mann 240).

3) Abiathar was more closely associated with David than was Ahimelech.

4) Mark's statement means, "Have you not read *in the section of the biblical text concerning the high priest Abiathar*, that David ate the show-bread...?" This analysis results from a comparison with Mk 12.26, where the same grammatical construction is translated "Have you not read in the book of Moses, *in the passage concerning the Bush*, how God spoke unto him...?" (Lane 115f, following J.W. Wenham).

• The phrase "the consecrated bread" or the "bread of the Presence (of God)" refers to the twelve newly baked loaves which were placed every Sabbath on a table before God in the Tabernacle and later eaten by the priests (cf Lev 24.5-9; Nu 4.7).

v. 27 - In its struggle over the relationships between Judaism and the gospel, the early church also grappled with the question of Sabbath observance (cf Ro 14.5-6; Gal 4.10; Co 2.16). This pericope contributed to their discussion, for it shows Jesus in conflict with the strict Sabbath laws. Whereas the Sabbath symbolized the conclusion of God's original creation (Ge 2.2), soon disfigured by sin, the first day of the week recalled the new creation. Jesus inaugurated a new covenant (14.24); the Sabbath, symbol of the former covenant, gave way to the day of the resurrection, symbol of the new. Within the apostolic age, Sunday became the weekly celebration of God's new creation. Since Christians belong to the new covenant and have been freed by Christ from the legalistic obligations of the old one, they resist any bondage to a set of rules "with regard to a religious festival, a New Moon celebration or a Sabbath day" (Col 2.16). We do not worship the day but the One who is the Lord of all days.

v. 28 - The distinctive events of Acts 2 occurred on Sunday, for God had ordained that Pentecost be observed on the first day of the week (Lev 23.16). Also, on the first day of the week, the believers in Troas gathered to break bread and to hear Paul (At 20.7) and collections were set aside in Corinth, following similar instructions given in Galatia (1Co 16.1-2). The resurrected Christ appeared to John on the Isle of Patmos (Rev 1.10) on the day already known as "the Lord's day."

• Jesus offers the true joy which "lies in the freedom to transcend the prescribed duties of the Law for the sake of direct obedience to God's will and of immediate response to human need" (Anderson 111).

5. Jesus Reaffirms His Authority Over The Sabbath, 3.1-6

The religious authorities harden their stand against Jesus, for he does not live by their rules. Since they do not have irrefutable evidence to accuse him formally, they set a trap for him. By healing a man in the synagogue, he springs the trap. Can Jesus be blind to their intentions?

In this brief narrative, readers are given a clear answer to God's purpose in creating the Sabbath. As the story takes on a new, ugly turn, they are alerted to the seriousness of the accusations against Jesus. With simplicity, Mark brings to a close his initial presentation of the affirmation and rejection of Jesus' authority.

• This pericope closes this chiastic section. Its participants are similar to those in the first pericope (2.1-12). In both cases, Jesus speaks first; then he responds to an unexpressed accusation with a rhetorical question. He escapes immediate condemnation by the ways in which he cures the sick.

3.1-3 - Again Jesus goes into the synagogue (1.21). Some people come not to learn but to gather evidence that can be used in a formal accusation against Jesus. They do not doubt his ability to heal. Their concern is the proper observance of the Sabbath. We do not know if the man with a shriveled (or paralyzed) hand is there by personal choice or if the opponents of Jesus brought him as bait.

Tension is high as the Pharisees watch Jesus. Will he heal on the Sabbath? The question seems strange to us. It is paramount to them, however, for healing was included as one of the categories of work prohibited on the Sabbath as defined in the rabbinical code (see on 2.24). The Law permitted them to keep an injury from getting worse but not to make it better. It did not prohibit saving life in an emergency on the Sabbath. But this is not a case of the man's life being in danger. No harm would come to him if he waited another day to be healed, and Jesus would avoid this confrontation.

Jesus presses ahead, however. There is nothing secret about his actions. They take place in a synagogue, in the presence of religious authorities, where all can see. Jesus deliberately steps into the trap set for him by saying to the man, "Rise up in front of everyone."

3.4 - Jesus forces his critics to make a decision by asking them, "Which is lawful on the Sabbath: to do good or to do evil, to save life or to kill?" This is not an abstract question. A man's well-being is at stake. Surely, they who know *what one ought not to do on the Sabbath*, can answer this question. As they remain silent, Jesus shows *what one should do*. One should do good; one should love his neighbor.

But much more is involved than just Sabbath observance and showing compassion for the disabled man. In announcing good news to Israel, Jesus frees men and women from bondage. He brings forgiveness, restores fellowship with God and man. His presence is motive for joy. As Lord even of the Sabbath, Jesus shows that the laws of the old era are no longer binding. Every day provides an opportunity to celebrate his new creation, to do good and to save life.

By word and deed, Jesus is demonstrating that he is God's Anointed who is ushering in the future Kingdom. His attempts to bring true understanding, however, are met with silence. His opponents see him as a threat to their traditions. They conclude that he cannot be acting with divine authority. Although they are leaders in Israel, they fail to recognize God's Anointed.

3.5-6 - Zealous in guarding their traditions, the Pharisees are indifferent to the needs of suffering people. They are not ardent in good works, nor do they praise Jesus for his. They even use their zeal for the Sabbath to denounce him. As Lane (124) says, "In the name of piety they had become insensitive both to the purposes of God and to the suffering of men."

Their stubborn hearts deeply distress Jesus and move him to anger. This anger is frequently understood to be an expression of his humanity. Cranfield (121), however, raises an appropriate question: "Is it perhaps better to think here of the oneness of his person and to regard his anger as that of the whole Christ, God and Man--and similarly with his grief?"

Jesus cures the man on the Sabbath. Like God in creation, Jesus speaks and it is done. What God did then "was very good" (Ge 1.31). Jesus also does what is good (cf Mk 7.37; Eph 2.10). To omit doing good is evil. He does not withhold doing good (cf Pr 3.27; Ps 84.11b). Jesus frees both the Sabbath and man, for he is Lord of the Sabbath.

Jesus exercises his authority in such a way that he can not be condemned for breaking their traditions (cf 2.9-12). Jesus only says, "Stretch out your hand." There is no law against speaking on the Sabbath or against stretching out one's hand. Jesus renews the man's health, enhances his possibilities for gainful employment, and restores him to a meaningful life in the community.

The Pharisees, however, do not rejoice. They leave the synagogue and begin to plot how they might kill Jesus. The Law itself which commands "You shall not murder" (Ex 20.13) has become less important than the preservation of their Sabbath traditions.

Normally, Pharisees have no relationships with Gentiles or with anyone associated with them, for they are "unclean." In their desire to kill Jesus, however, this is all laid aside. They will need political allies, for only the Roman authorities have power to exercise capital punishment. The Herodians are politically minded Jews who support Herod Antipas and have some influence over him. These friends of Herod could possibly serve as lobbyists with the political rulers of the land.

Although they have little in common, the Herodians will cooperate with the Pharisees, for they can see political advantage for themselves in denouncing one who proclaims a new kingdom within the confines of the Roman Empire. Both groups are corrupted by power and use it for personal advantage. Since both groups see Jesus as a threat to their authority, they can make their religious-political coalition work.

They are devising ways to kill Jesus who is occupied in saving a man's life. This alliance continues in the background, to be mentioned again in 12.13. By registering this opposition early in his narrative, Mark alerts the reader to the seriousness of Jesus' ministry and to the possibility that those who follow him may also encounter opposition and even death.

v. 2 - The rabbinical observance of the Sabbath was an expression of their desire to obey God in the smallest detail. Jesus does not break those traditions because he is contrary to that desire. Rather, he knows that obedience from the heart is much more than fulfilling the letter of the law.

Following a principle of freedom that shocked his contemporaries, Jesus rejects their belief that God would repay their obedience as meritorious. As Schweizer says (76f), "Man must receive everything from God as a gift without any consideration of merit, and must open his heart to...serve God for joy alone... God's law will help him in this--not as a fence restricting him, but as a guide pointing the direction."

God brought his people out of the land of slavery (Ex 20.1-2) and proceeded to give them the Torah as instruction for the nation. It was not given as a means of salvation.

As with the Pharisees, religion can be a barrier to knowing God and recognizing his beloved Son.

• Devout Jews preferred to die rather than break the Sabbath. In several wars, Jewish soldiers were massacred by the thousands when, in strict observance of the Sabbath, they refused to defend themselves.

Sabbath observance continues to be a crucial issue in modern Israel. For example, some proposed that the elevators in Jerusalem be programmed to run automatically during the Sabbath, stopping at every floor, in order to avoid unlawful work on the Sabbath (that is, pressing an elevator button). For them, to obey the strict interpretation of the Law was more important than to conserve their nation's limited sources of energy.

v. 4 - Here, as at the close of the series of conflicts in Jerusalem (12.35-37), Jesus takes the initiative in questioning, and his accusers remain silent (12.34).

• To save (**sozo**, cf 5.34; 6.56; 8.35-37; 10.26; 13.13,20; 15.30f) is used several times in the theological sense. Here the primary meaning is physical.

• "The law, as it is here applied by the Pharisees, forbids doing good and allows doing evil on the Sabbath" (Paul J. Achtemeier Invitation 56). Jesus makes it clear that their position is a contradiction of God's will rather than an expression of it. In the name of the Law, they are in effect doing evil. Jesus rejects outright observances that prevent fulfilling the commandment to love.

v. 5 - From this narrative we understand that believers in all ages are called to do good (cf Ro 13.9-10), even when surrounded by controversies and hostilities.

• Because of their "stubborn hearts" they had identified religion with rules and regulations so completely that they were blind to Jesus' authentic human sympathy. They had become completely insensitive to the appeal of God and to human need. Such persons are on the way to a condition in which their hearts and consciences become petrified. Cf 6.52.

v. 6 - Palestine was divided into several provinces governed by Jewish or semi-Jewish princes, including members of Herod's family. Each was in his own way a collaborator with Rome.

• Conspiracies between religious leaders and secular authorities with the intent to destroy God's work occurred in the past (e.g., Ahab's alliance with worshippers of Baal, 1Ki 16.31ff), in Jesus' ministry (10.33; 12.13; 15.1ff) and are prophesied for the future (Mk 13.9; Rev 13). From its earliest days, the church has suffered under political-religious alliances. Knowing that Jesus was killed by such a coalition, believers throughout the ages persist in preaching to all nations, regardless of the cost.

• Under Jewish law, capital punishment could be imposed only if the person had been warned before witnesses and had acted deliberately. This encounter, along with 2.24, constitutes the second warning. Since that legal requirement has been met, the authorities meet to plan the occasion of his death.

• Some think that the plot to kill Jesus came much later in Jesus' ministry. However, Cranfield's (122) opinion that "it is intrinsically likely that the intention of his opponents to bring about his death developed quite early in the course (of his ministry)" shows greater understanding of the biblical data.

• This is the last cure Jesus performs in a context of conflict with the religious leaders. His only other appearance in a synagogue takes place in his hometown (6.1), where few cures were performed because of the hostile environment.

* * * * *

Looking back over 1.14 through 3.6, we recall that Jesus' ministry gets off to a good start. He proclaims God's rule among men and women, and some follow him. Although demonic forces oppose him, many people are attracted by his teachings and his power to meet their needs.

Jesus does not teach according to tradition. He gives them a taste of "new wine" (2.22). The religious leaders reject him and plan to destroy him, for they know his revolutionary message can burst their traditionalism at the seams. Step by step within these dramatic events, Jesus continues to reveal his mission, even giving a clue that he is going to his death.

This unit begins with the announcement of God's rule on earth. It closes with an implication that establishing his reign is inseparable from the cross. As the story progresses, we will see that the literary structure of Mark points to the crucifixion, for the cross is the heart of its message. The life of Jesus and his followers is to be seen as the way of the cross.

- PART 3 -
THE SOURCE AND NATURE OF JESUS' AUTHORITY 3.7 - 6.6a

We have accompanied the beginnings of Jesus' ministry in Galilee. In response to his initial proclamation of the Kingdom, four fishermen answer his call to follow him (1.16-20). Early in this division, Jesus appoints the twelve (3.13-19) in preparation for the third step (6.6b - 8.26) in which he sends them out on a mission.

The author tells how Jesus moves forward in his proclamation of God's reign. Having answered challenges to his disregard for orthodox religious practices, Jesus responds to false accusations about the source of his authority. With parables and with demonstrations of his God-given power, Jesus continues to provide clues as to the nature of God's Kingdom and to his own identity. This division, like the previous one, ends with rejection by some who would be expected to receive him.

A. RESPONSES TO JESUS' MINISTRY, 3.7-35

After giving a brief summary of the popular response to Jesus, Mark relates how Jesus prepares his disciples for the task ahead. He personally moves into the offensive as he affirms the source of his authority. His hearers (and Mark's readers) are faced with the need to decide which side they are on.

1. Jesus' Growing Ministry, 3.7-12

After the confrontation in 3.1-6, Jesus withdraws from official Judaism, as symbolized by the synagogue. Only once more, in his hometown (6.1-6), does he enter a synagogue where he only begins to teach before he is cut off from any significant ministry. Jesus turns to the people. From now until he reaches the Temple in Jerusalem (11.11), he conducts his ministry in homes or out of doors. Verses 7-12 summarize the widespread response to Jesus' activities by the anonymous crowds, the sick and the demon possessed.

• Mark probably breaks the chronological sequence at 2.13, in order to present the increasing intensity of the controversies, returning in 3.7 to the events that followed 2.12.

• According to Robbins (125f), in 3.7 to 5.43 Jesus introduces basic details that underlie his words and actions as he presents the Kingdom of God. This begins the first of four stages (3.7; 6.6b; 8.27; 11.1) in the intermediate cycle of interaction between Jesus and his disciples. The disciples only begin their participation in miraculous events in the second stage (6.6b).

3.7-10 - The first time Jesus walked by Lake Galilee (1.16), he was alone, soon to be accompanied by four. The next time (2.13), a large crowd comes to him. Now, on the third mention of this setting, he is accompanied by a multitude, from all parts of Israel.

Word about Jesus' deeds is spreading rapidly, for the people "heard all he was doing" (v. 8). Many come from nearby Galilee and from distant parts of Palestine. Others come from Judea and Jerusalem, regions John the Baptist prepared for receiving "the More Powerful One" (1.5,7). Some come from the far south (Idumea). People come from regions to the east (across the Jordan) and from the predominantly Gentile northern cities of Tyre and Sidon. While the leaders reject him, people from all parts of Palestine seek him (cf 1.45).

The new Kingdom is not limited geographically. All in Israel are welcome. Already Gentiles may be among those who seek Jesus. Later (11.17) he makes it clear that people of all nations are invited to submit to God's reign. Multitudes seek Jesus for healing. As the crowds increase in number, their self-control decreases. Pushing and shoving become the order of the day as they reach out to touch the miracle worker.

Jesus continues to heal the sick although he has much more to offer them. He does not use his extraordinary powers to protect himself. He instructs the disciples to keep a small boat in readiness to avoid his being crushed by the crowds. This is something the disciples can do; it is their first responsibility beyond following Jesus. Their faithfulness in this can lead to greater responsibilities (Lk 16.10). From the boat, Jesus can preach (cf 1.38; 4.1) and lead the people into a meaningful understanding of what his presence really means. He seeks to be known in ways that lead to faith and obedience, refusing to perform marvels that lure spectators.

3.11-12 - Mark draws a clear distinction between the sick and those controlled by evil spirits. Like the crowd, the sick welcome Jesus, although they have no real understanding of who he is. The evil spirits, however, know what is going on. They throw themselves on the ground before him and scream, "You are the Son of God." Because they know who he is, they fear him (cf James 2.19) and proclaim his real identity in order to destroy him through popular acclaim before he fulfills God's mission (see comments on 1.24-25; cf 1.34; 5.7).

v. 8 - Idumea lies over 125 miles south of Capernaum. Jesus himself goes to the regions of Tyre and Sidon (7.24-8.17) and "beyond the Jordan," beginning with Decapolis (5.20). He ministered in the places reported in verse 8 with the exception of Idumea. There is no mention of Samaria in Mark.
vv. 10-12 - In curing the sick, Jesus varied his methods as a part of his teaching ministry (cf 1.41; 3.5; 5.41). He refused to stereotype his methods in curing illnesses. In casting out demons, however, he employed one pattern only: he commanded them to leave.

2. Jesus Appoints Twelve Apostles, 3.13-19

Mark presents three phases in Jesus' call to discipleship. In response to his first call (1.16-20), the disciples follow and observe him. Now he designates the leaders for his expanding ministry (3.13-19). Since Jesus will not always be with them (2.20), others must be prepared to minister in his absence and to protect the flock from false leaders (7.6-8; 8.15; 12.38-40; 13.5-6, 22). In the third step, he sends them out on missions (6.6b - 8.26). Upon their return, they report to him and receive additional instruction. Their relationship to Jesus personally is central in each phase.

3.13-15 - Withdrawing from the crowds, Jesus goes up into the hills with those he wants to accompany him. He appoints twelve of them to be with him in preparation for the time when he will send them out to spread the gospel. His sovereign authority is evident here: he initiates this setting, he chooses his companions, he appoints the twelve and he specifies the purpose of his call.

First of all, they are to be with him. This personal relationship is implicit in "follow me," the first and last words of Jesus to his disciples in Mark's Gospel (1.17 and 16.7). He does not call them to a place or to an institution; he calls them to himself. They have much to learn about him and about themselves. Their character must reveal Jesus' qualities. Since character determines the quality of service rendered, character building must precede service. Otherwise their work will fail and they themselves will eventually falter. So Jesus does not rush to send them out.

Second, he calls them that he might send them out (**apostello**; their ministry to others actually begins in 6.7-13). Called out from the multitude, the twelve will be sent back to the multitudes, in contrast to the Qumran community isolated in the desert and the Pharisees separated from the impurities of the common people.

Jesus will send them out "to preach and to have authority to drive out demons." They will proclaim (**kerusso**; cf 1.4,14) what Jesus proclaims, namely, the good news of God. As men and women submit to God's rule, they are released from the bondage of sin; those controlled by demons are freed from Satan's rule (cf 1.23).

God's authority manifested in Jesus is made available to those who have been with him. His authority never becomes theirs; it always remains delegated authority. To be chosen by God is never a motive for boasting or for claiming privileges; it is a call to service (9.35; cf Ro 12.3-8). When disciples (and church leaders through the ages) seek power and glory for themselves (8.32f; 9.33-40; 10.35-45), the progress of the gospel is impaired.

Jesus' resolve to select the Twelve is one of the most crucial decisions in history. He does not write a book, erect monuments or build institutions. He disciples persons as the most effective way to perpetuate his ministry. He depends upon them to continue his work. The existence of the church proves the soundness of his decision.

v. 13 - Mountains had historical significance in God's relationships with his people of ancient times. It was on a mountain that God gave the Law to Moses and made a covenant with Israel (Ex 19.1-20.20). Jesus also chose mountainous settings for special occasions (6.46; 9.2; 13.3ff). The number twelve recalls the twelve tribes of Israel. The mountainous setting together with the number twelve signify the forming of God's new people, similar to the forming of Israel into a nation. Its life flows out of being with Jesus.

• To "call to oneself" (3.13,23; 6.7; 7.14; 8.1,34; 10.42; 12.43) "seems to have been almost a technical term for unreserved discipleship - cf John 12.19 and Jude 7" (Nineham 115f). To join one's self to another requires cutting off previous ties (1.16-20; 10.29).

Scholars disagree as to whether only twelve accompanied Jesus on this occasion or whether twelve were chosen from the many men and women now following Jesus. The phrase "serve Jesus," used of women (1.31, 15.40-41, cf Lk 8.2-3), describes the role of the disciple. If the Twelve had included women, it might have lost its symbolic significance, for women could not have symbolized the tribes of Israel in ancient oriental cultures.

• The verb "wanted" is in the imperfect tense. Apparently Jesus made the choice earlier but only makes it known at this time. Luke 6.12 relates that Jesus spent the previous night alone in prayer.

vv. 14-19 - The reference to twelve apostles is constant throughout the New Testament. The names listed, however, vary. A comparison of the lists (Mt 10.2-4; Lk 6.14-16; Ac 1.13) suggests that Bartholomew is Nathanael (Jn 1.45-51) and Matthew is Levi.

Jesus' choice of twelve was a symbolic prophetic action which answered to Israel's eschatological hope which included the restoration of the twelve tribes (Eze 37; 39.23-29; 40-48). The number twelve was so significant that soon after Judas' death, the eleven elected Matthias to take his place (Ac 1.24-26).

Jesus forms his new community in the midst of diversity. In creating unity, he respects the individuality of his followers which is further enhanced by the diverse gifts of the Spirit (cf Gal 3.26-28; Ro 12.3-8; Eph 4.2-16; 1Co 12-14). Jesus himself is not included in the list of those who represent the true Israel. He creates it but stands outside and above it.

3.16-19 - Simon Peter, the first one called to follow Jesus, heads up all lists of the Twelve in the New Testament, calling attention to his place of leadership. Peter, James and John receive nicknames, just as the leaders of ancient Israel (Abraham, Ge 17.5, and Isaac, Ge 32.28) received new names. These three were witnesses chosen by Jesus to accompany him on three occasions (5.37; 9.2 and 14.33). They are the only ones who are quoted in Mark (Peter, frequently; James and John, in 10.35-37; and John in 9.38).

The group is very heterogeneous. Different personality traits are to be expected in twelve men coming from diverse backgrounds. Their individual ambitions provoke their colleagues' indignation (e.g., 10.35-41). While Mark does not mention it, it is easy to imagine sharp conflicts arising between Levi, whose profession ties him to the hated Romans, and Simon the Zealot, whose sympathies lie with a nationalist movement which favors subversive guerrilla activity against Rome. Apparently Jesus deliberately chose the Twelve from different geographical regions and different groups within the nation to demonstrate his call to all Israelites. Moreover, Marks' readers are hereby encouraged to accept in their churches persons coming from diverse backgrounds (cf 11.17).

The twelve are not chosen on the basis of unblemished character (for example, Simon is not surnamed Peter, a rock, because of his character. cf 8.32; 14.29). Their frequent mistakes demonstrate imperfections and slowness to learn. Jesus does not manipulate them but gradually forms them into his own likeness (cf Ro 8.29) while respecting their individual characteristics. By God's grace and not by personal merit, they will play a significant role in founding God's new people. The new family of God is composed of imperfect persons who often disagree about politics, etc., but they learn to live together in harmony as a part of their submission to the Lordship of Christ.

The last name on the list is that of Judas Iscariot. The meaning of Iscariot is contested. Many say it indicates that he came from Kerioth, a village in Judea. Some connect the word with the Latin **sicarius** (knife), thus implying "assassin," while others consider it a nickname meaning red-haired. The text adds that this Judas will be involved the plot to kill him.

As one of the twelve, Judas is included when Jesus calls those he wants (3.13). Why does Jesus choose a traitor, unless he is going to the cross, not as a martyr, but as a volunteer? Therein is the mysterious interplay of Jesus' sovereign choice of his traitor and of Judas' freedom of action (for which he was held accountable, cf 14.21).

This introduction to Judas is especially relevant for readers who suffer in the hands of traitors within the Christian community (cf 13.12; Ac 20.29-31; Rev 2.13, 20f).

v. 17 - In the ancient Near East, a name was intimately involved in the very essence of a person's being and inextricably intertwined with his personality. A change of name symbolized the transformation of character and destiny. The surname "sons of thunder" could refer to James' and John's character or to their future as linked with Jesus in his suffering (10.38-40).
v. 18 - The Zealots waged a whole series of revolts against Rome, motivated principally not by political motives but by their desire to hasten the coming of God's Kingdom.

3. Who Are Jesus' Allies? 3.20-35

This literary unit begins with a short narrative about Jesus' family relationships (3.20-21). Before returning to this subject (3.31-35), Mark inserts his account of the accusation made by the scribes from Jerusalem: Jesus has an unclean spirit (3.22-30). The family's accusation against Jesus is similar to that of the religious authorities in so far as mental disorders were considered by some to be a form of demonic possession. These pericopes bear a closer affinity, however, in that they present two opinions about why Jesus does what he does and his own affirmations about his identity.

JESUS' FAMILY (part A), 3.20-21

Having selected the Twelve, Jesus again takes up his ministry in a home (cf 2.1). He and his disciples are so busy attending the crowd that gathers that they aren't even able to eat. When Jesus' family hears about this, they become concerned about his well-being and want to rescue him. They even have doubts about his sanity.

Mark will return to the subject of Jesus' family in verses 31-35. For now, he points out that Jesus' teaching and works have made little impact on members of his family. According to them, anyone who serves others so intensely that he cannot eat is incompetent to run his own life; he is crazy. This is their explanation for his behavior.

• Ironically, Jesus (and/or his disciples) was denounced for eating with Levi's friends and for eating while others fast (2.16, 18). Now he is judged to be out of his mind because he does not take time to eat.

THE SOURCE OF JESUS' POWER, 3.22-30

A committee of theologians from Jerusalem, the center of Judaism, arrives to press charges against Jesus, for his divergence from the traditions endangers the religious life of the nation. Their charges cannot go unanswered. First Jesus shows the logical self-contradiction in their accusations (vv. 23-26). Then in a parable, Jesus declares who he is and what he is really doing (v. 27). He then gives a very strong warning to his accusers and affirms the source of his authority (vv. 28-29). Just in case some reader misses the point, Mark adds his word of explanation (v. 30).

3.22-27 - Everyone agrees that Jesus is powerful in word and deed. Even his opponents concede that he has supernatural power. How then can he be denounced? The scribes design a strong attack, built around the question, Where does this power come from? With the authority of Jerusalem behind them, these official theologians declare that the source of Jesus' power is not God but Satan. Jesus' proficiency in expelling demons is proof that he himself is controlled by the powerful demon, Beelzebub.

The teachers of the law charge that Jesus is working in league with Satan. If such a partnership existed, Jesus answers, it would be self-destructive. Satan cannot drive out Satan any more than a kingdom or a household divided against itself can stand. Their accusation is illogical. It is also contrary to the facts; not even his accusers would claim that Satan's realm is about to disintegrate.

Having denied the charge that he drives out demons in collaboration with Satan, Jesus now answers with a parable the accusation that he is demon-controlled.

Jesus says that, in reality, the true situation is similar to that of robbing a strong man's house (cf Isa 49.24-25). First, the strong man must be tied up. Only then can his possessions be carried off (cf Isa 53.12).

In this way, Jesus declares his superiority over Satan (1Jn 4.4) and disclaims any alliance with him. He is engaged in a frontal assault on Satan's realm, overpowering him to rescue captive humanity from his control (cf Gal 1.4).

This parable is understood as a part of the cosmic conflict between God and Satan who plundered God's creation, holding it an unwilling captive. Jesus, however, enters this domain uninvited and constrains Satan, dealing him a preliminary defeat as he inaugurates God's reign over all (cf Lk 11.20). Satan's final defeat awaits the culmination of God's redemptive acts.

v. 22 - Beelzebub ("the lord of the flies") recalls the god of the Philistines in Ekron (2Ki 1.2). Beelzebul is the Canaanite "prince of demons." The name could mean "lord of dung" or the "lord of the house" (which would tie in with v. 27). Regardless of these variations, they are judged to be alternate names for Satan.

v. 23 - These verses qualify as parables, for they shatter the scribes' reasoning (cf 4.2). Jesus began using parables in the context of controversy (2.17) although here is the first use of the word in Mark.

v. 24 - Jesus begins his answer with a series of three conditional sentences ("if, if, if") which are essentially conditions contrary to fact. The *true* situation is introduced in v. 27 with the adversative "but."

v. 27 - The word "bound" appears in Rev 20.2 and is interpreted by amillennialists as illustrative of what happened to Satan at Christ's first coming, as described in this parable. For them, the millennium is another symbol of the present church age. Pre-millennialists claim this verse refers to Jesus' first advent whereas in Revelation, John describes future events to take place at Jesus' Second Advent.

Excursus: The Binding of Satan

The "binding of the strong man" means that Jesus has accomplished a defeat of Satan so that his power is broken and no longer has the right to rule. The expression does not mean Satan is incapacitated: he is "a strong man." He continues his resistance, as seen in Jesus' subsequent ministry (5.1-14, 8.33; Lk 22.31, etc.) and in the churches (E.g., 2Co 2.10f; Eph 4.27; 6.11; 1Pe 5.8f; Jas 4.7; Rev 2.9, 13, 24; 3.9). Jesus is giving his disciples neither a commandment to bind Satan nor instructions on how to cast out demons (he teaches this in 9.28-29). By this parable he is illustrating how his coming initiated God's victory over the forces of evil.

This conquest over God's enemies involves three stages. The first has already occurred when the Kingdom of God in the person of Jesus invaded this present evil age, the realm of Satan. Jesus' presence and earthly ministry--all are a part of this binding. His death, resurrection (Col 2.15) and ascension (1Pe 3.22) seal Satan's final and absolute defeat. The driving out of Satan's representatives is evidence of the fact that the Adversary's power is broken and that Jesus has forced an entry and plundered Satan's goods. This is the first stage of the cosmic struggle in history. It is not the full story, however, for Jesus will be Satan's consummate conqueror only at the end of all things (1Co 15.24-28).

The second stage is underway now. "Satan is the god of this Age, yet the power of Satan has been broken that men may know the rule of God in their lives. The evil Age goes on, yet the powers of the Age to Come have been made available to men" (Ladd Gospel 50). This is an age of tension between the *already* ("the Kingdom has come," Mt 12.28) and the *but not yet* (thus we pray, "your Kingdom come", Mt 6.10). As Hebrews 2.8 clearly states, "God left nothing that is not subject to (Jesus). Yet at present we do not see everything subject to him." Therefore persons freed from demonic control need discipling, pastoral care and companionship within a Christian community.

During this present age, Satan is still strong. "Even after the Cross and the Resurrection and Ascension have completed the victory, the power of Satan, though broken, will still be strong... Not till the Parousia will it be resolved" (Cranfield 138). Just as God's reign is *already present but not yet fully manifested*, Satan's defeat has *already* been accomplished, but is *not yet* fully culminated.

The third stage is the Second Coming of Christ in power and glory (8.38; 13.24-27; 14.62) when he will consummate God's redemptive work, bringing this church age to a close. This eschatological defeat of Satan is presented in the Book of Revelation (20.1-10) in two stages (even as it presents the resurrection from the dead in two stages; cf 1Co 15.20-38). At the beginning of the Millennium, Satan is bound and thrown into the abyss, to be released for a short time at the end of a thousand years. Then will come the final struggle, and Satan will be "thrown into the lake of burning sulfur" (Rev 20.10). As Ladd (Presence 151) says, "The universal establishment of God's reign will mean nothing less than the destruction of the very principle of evil in the spiritual realm."

3.28-30 - In the previous verses, Jesus has been accused of acting under the power of Satan. He denies this by showing that their logic is fallacious. Now he indicates positively the source of his authority.

The Greek word **amen** ("I tell you the truth;" "Verily I say to you") is a very significant term in Jesus' vocabulary. It occurs over 59 times in the Gospels (13 in Mark), and only on Jesus' lips. **Amen** precedes a special emphasis or even a shocking truth. Just as "thus says the Lord" in the Old Testament declares the divine origin of what follows, this word guarantees the truth of Jesus' declarations (cf 2Co 1.20; Rev 3.14). More than that, it is a christological statement. He is making an explicit claim as to who he is: he speaks as God's Anointed.

Jesus calls people to repentance (1.15). This would be meaningless if there were no forgiveness. He already declared that "the Son of Man has authority on earth to forgive sins" (2.10). Now he defines the length and limits of God's forgiveness. The rabbis maintain that many grave sins are unforgivable, including blasphemy. This sin is punishable by death and is the keynote of their accusations against Jesus (2.1-12; 14.64). Jesus, however, declares that all sins and blasphemies will be forgiven except one: "Whoever blasphemes against the Holy Spirit will never be forgiven."

The scribes do not mention the Holy Spirit in their accusations; their attacks are directed against Jesus. Jesus is the one who brings the person of the Holy Spirit into the discussion, because anyone who denounces Jesus is actually denouncing the Holy Spirit who indwells him. By not talking about blasphemy against himself but against the Holy Spirit, Jesus declares the source of his authority. He is led by the Holy Spirit who is present and at work through him (1.10, 12). Jesus is not possessed by Satan; *he is indwelt by the Spirit of God.*

This teaching on the person of Jesus, with special reference to his relationship to the Holy Spirit, is so important that Mark adds his own "aside" as reinforcement (v. 30). Jesus' critics were saying, "he is possessed by an evil spirit", when they should have been saying "he is indwelt and led by the Holy Spirit."

What then constitutes the unforgivable sin? Jesus incarnates God's forgiveness of sin (cf 2.17; 10.45). Therefore, a person who persists in resisting and scorning God's offer of forgiveness in Jesus is excluded from forgiveness. "To accept Jesus is to be accepted (forgiven) by God. To reject him is to reject God (and his forgiveness) as well." The scribes are doing just this: they are rejecting Jesus and God who anointed him when they insist that Jesus' authority is from Satan rather than from God (cf Isa 5.20). This rejection is "the one limitation to God's limitless forgiveness of sin" (Achtemeier Invitation 64).

Jesus' words are addressed to persons whose repeated accusations against him are arrived at after much thought. With their eyes wide open, they are trying to destroy Jesus. Such fixed attitudes evoke Jesus' warning. One the other hand, forgiveness is available to a person who denounces God or his acts in moments of anguish. Doubts which arise from honest inquiries can also be forgiven (cf Isa 1.18). The overwhelming fear of having committed the unforgivable sin is in itself evidence that the person has not committed it. All fears, including the fear of having committed the unforgivable sin, should be humbly acknowledged before God. Jesus declares that "all the sins and blasphemies of men will be forgiven them" (v. 28; cf 1Jn 1.9).

Jesus invites men and women to repent and believe the good news (1.15). He does not, however, force anyone's response. Any person who persists in unbelief will not find forgiveness; for although freely offered, God's forgiveness is limited. For this reason, Jesus draws a contrast between "the lavishness of God's grace that freely forgives all, and the incredible hardness of those who by their willful spurning of that grace shut themselves off from its blessing" (Anderson 123).

Mark 3.20-30 provides further evidence as to who Jesus is by pointing out who he is not. Jesus is not an agent of Satan; rather, he is Satan's enemy. He is engaged in a frontal attack on Satan, to limit him now and eventually to destroy him. He drives out demons as a part of this strategy. He accomplishes this as one empowered by the Holy Spirit of God. Jesus knows who he is and what his mission is. The rest of the story is to be read in the light of the fact that Jesus is both Spirit-filled and Spirit-led in all that he says and does.

Already the Twelve learn about the seriousness of their mission. Satan and the religious power structure are aligned against them. Slander and false accusations are a part of their weapons. Family ties are not even a guarantee of support.

vv. 28-29 - The marvel of the extent of God's forgiveness is frequently forgotten as Christians debate "the unforgivable sin." Similar to Adam and Eve (Ge 3.2-3), we tend to concentrate on the negative, ignoring the wide scope of God's positive provisions. With the Psalmist (103.1-5), our emphasis should fall on praising the Lord who forgives all our sins.

v. 29 - Church leaders and theological teachers need to heed Jesus' warning directed to scribes, for they, like the scribes in ancient times, are today's teachers of God's people.

• Blasphemous words against the Trinity and the Bible and other violent reactions are all characteristic manifestations of control by evil spirits (Itioka 178).

v. 30 - "The scribes accuse Jesus of expelling demons in the name of the prince of demons. However, they do something far worse: they exorcise the Holy Spirit himself" (Alessandro Pronzato I 176).

Excursus: Contemporary Exorcisms

Mark's Gospel, in keeping with the rest of the Bible, gives repeated warnings against false teachers and prophets (8.15, 12.38-40 and 13.5-6, 21-23; cf Dt 13.1-4). The Scriptures recognize that even those opposed to God are able to work miracles (cf Ex 7.11; 8.7; 2Th 2.9; Rev 13.13). Some persons associated with the scribes drive out evil spirits (Mt 12.27, Lk 11.19). Paul encountered some unconverted Jews engaged in expelling demons (Ac 19.13f). Thus we conclude that the ability to perform signs and miracles does not authenticate the miracle worker as God's representative. In fact, such a person may be working against God, attempting to deceive God's people (13.22).

In our day, some people engaged in occult activities claim to cast out demons by the power of evil spirits. Are these cases of Satan opposing himself and bringing about his end (3.26), or was Jesus mistaken when he argued that demons don't cast out demons?

Their methods and the end results of exorcisms by occult religions may look like those of Jesus. A careful comparison of their methods, purposes and end results with those of Jesus will reveal, however, that the differences are very great.

As to his methods, Jesus commanded the evil spirits to leave. He spoke, and it was done. Not once in the expulsions described in the four Gospels is it recorded that he touched a demon-controlled person. He never demanded faith on the part of the possessed. He drove out demons by the power of his word. His *authority* in freeing persons from demonic control--not the fact that he did it--was the cause of much admiration (1.27). Jesus' method was very different from the strange rituals of words and actions employed by others, both in New Testament times and now.

As to his purposes, Jesus drove out demons in order to that the person might be free from bondage. Free so that he or she could choose to follow Jesus (cf Mk 5.18, Lk 8.1-3). Free to live under God's rule and enjoy fellowship with other persons. Free from control by an evil spirit, to be indwelt by the Holy Spirit who brings the fruit of love, joy, peace, etc. (Gal 5.22f). Free to become a whole person.

Spiritualists, however, have very different purposes in "driving out demons." When an army of occupation changes the guard, it doesn't free the nation. It maintains its control through another platoon or company of soldiers. For similar reasons, spiritualists, mediums, etc. call upon evil spirits to drive out other demons when this results in greater control over the possessed individual. They have no interest in benefiting the person controlled; their exorcisms strengthen their own position. The person is not freed but is manipulated to become increasingly dependent upon a more powerful evil spirit. Satan's kingdom is not destroyed; it is benefited. Satan and his agents extract high prices from those whom they have "freed."

In sharp contrast to the occultists, Jesus drives out evil spirits in order to free the person from demonic control. In answering the scribes' accusation, Jesus is making a play on words. He is saying that if demons were driving out demons *the way that he is driving them out*, then Satan's domain would be self-destructing. They, however, are not doing what Jesus is. They are not expelling demons to release people; they are just "changing the guard." Through an agreement with their evil allies, they perpetuate Satan's control. Jesus, on the other hand, literally drives out demons. He does this by the power of

God in opposition to Satan and he will ultimately destroy evil and the evil one. Jesus' expulsions are authentic; theirs are not. If they were authentic, Satan would be destroying himself.

Satan and his agents are capable of all types of deceit. They appear to do good; their "good," however, is only temporary and eventually leads to evil. They stage scenes in which they appear to be freeing a person by "driving out" evil spirits. As a part of the Deceiver's tactics, his agents seek to imitate God's liberation; but the Devil's purpose is to gain control over them forever. When those who have been "freed" discover they have been deceived, it may be too late, for their "liberated" souls have been taken over by more powerful evil forces. Their final condition is worse than before (Lk 11.24-26). This is a part of the Adversary's attempt to win his battle against God and his Anointed One.

Occultists may claim that Jesus cooperates with them in their religious practices. Jesus, however, categorically denies any kinship or collaboration with Satan and his agents. He is in mortal combat against Satan and all his works. This pericope (3.20-30) constitutes a warning to all individuals and religions that claim Jesus as their ally. Jesus does not belong to them or to any other. One must belong to Jesus, for he is God's anointed. He is the Sovereign Lord. To declare knowingly that Jesus is cooperating with other evil spirits is blasphemy against the Holy Spirit who fully indwells and leads Jesus. This sin is unforgivable (3.29).

Words of caution are necessary for those who are acknowledgedly Christian; for there are tragic consequences when major biblical truths are neglected, misconstrued or misdirected. While Jesus' cosmic warfare with Satan is biblical, we must maintain balance regarding it, neither denying its existence nor making it dominant. Jesus is preeminent; Satan is not. Not Satan, not demons, not even expulsion of demons can ever be given centrality in the Christian community. As Jesus himself cautioned, "do not rejoice that the spirits submit to you, but rejoice that your names are written in heaven" (Lk 10.20). Unfortunately, the demonology of some people is stronger than their Christology. The lordship of Jesus Christ (Php 2.9-11) must never be neglected. God's plan is that in everything Jesus Christ "might have the supremacy" (Col 1.18), leading us to enjoy God and rejoice in him in our daily lives and ministries.

At the same time, no Christian should presume that, because Jesus bound Satan, the forces that oppose the Gospel today are so weak that the cosmic war is only a figure of speech and not a life-and-death struggle. Satan was defeated but he was not destroyed; he still possesses power to cause great damage. This is clearly seen in Jesus' warning Peter that his faith would be tested to its limits (Lk 22.31-32).

In order to "resist the devil" (1Pe 5.9, Jas 4.7), Christians are commanded to "watch and pray" with fear and trembling (Eph 6.12; 1Pe 5.8). They realize that Satan can hinder God's servants from doing things they earnestly desire to do, even as he did in Paul's ministry (1Th 2.18). To avoid giving "the devil a foothold" (Eph 4.27), the believer puts "on the full armor of God so that he can take his stand against the devil's schemes" (Eph 6.11).

In seeking the release of a person controlled by an evil spirit, Christians proceed as representatives of Jesus Christ. They intercede for that person, asking for his or her release on the basis of the fact that Jesus has *already* bound Satan. By faith, through prayer (Mk 9.23,29), God's servant claims the results of Jesus' work. Believers can never claim that authority as their own nor twist it for their own purposes or glory.

Furthermore, Christians involved in casting out demons must not use methods that contradict the way Jesus drove out demons. They refuse to manipulate the person who is under demonic control. They use the name of Jesus reverently, recognizing his absolute sovereignty. The believers' purposes must be identical to those of Jesus: to free the person in order that he or she might live under God's rule that provides continuing freedom. To drive out an evil spirit without introducing the freed person to Jesus as Lord and Savior is inadequate and leaves the person open to greater evil (cf Lk 11.26).

JESUS' FAMILY (part B), 3.31-35

The division of opinion about Jesus has become acute. Beyond his self-identification in previous encounters, Jesus now makes further significant affirmations, both about himself and about those who follow him. Mark closes this unit (3.20-35) with a very positive assertion about those who accept Jesus, in contrast to those who don't understand (3.21) or reject him (3.22-30).

3.31-35 - In verse 21, the reader was introduced to the adverse attitude toward Jesus by his own family. Now Mark returns to that subject, after dealing with the scribes' denunciation. Jesus' mother and brothers are separated from him in two ways. Physically, they are outside, making no effort to get in. They send in word to Jesus, probably "to take charge of him" (as in 3.21). At this point in time, they are also "outsiders" for they fail to understanding who Jesus is.

Mary, the mother of Jesus, does not play a prominent role in Mark's Gospel; she is mentioned only here and in 6.3. During his years of ministry, Jesus' own brothers do not believe in him (Jn 7.1-5). Mary's presence at the crucifixion is mentioned in John 19.25-27, with no indication of her understanding at that time. When the change came is not indicated in the New Testament. After the resurrection, however,

Mary and the brothers of Jesus join others in prayer (Ac 1.14). His brother James becomes a leader in the early church (1Co 15.7, Gal 1.19, 2.9). Their conversion is an encouragement to all who have unbelieving relatives.

Even in the light of his family's rejection, "Who are my mother and my brothers?" seems like a harsh question. No doubt it jolted his hearers into thinking about relationships (cf 7.9-13; 10.2-12, 29-31). Family obligations, reinforced by God's laws (cf Ex 20.12), were top priority in Near Eastern culture. Jesus' purpose here is not to discredit his kinsfolk but to show by contrast the meaning of a new kinship. So his provocative question prepares his hearers (and Mark's readers) for his call to radical discipleship, with its high demand and its remarkable promise.

"Here are my mother and my brothers!" Jesus' disciples become his true family. This family is not limited to the twelve; it includes those in "the circle around him" (v. 34). Moreover, Jesus invites others into his family by adding, "*Whoever* ..." This kinship is not "according to the flesh", as determined by family, tribe or race. These fundamental relationships are replaced by a new social order, God's gift to all people through fellowship with Jesus (see comments on 14.24; cf 2Co 5.17).

Jesus (and by implication, his followers as well) has been accused of working for Satan (v. 22). He strongly denies that. He is doing just the opposite: he is doing God's will! That is the overwhelming purpose of his life (as he declares in 14.36). In following him, his disciples also are doing God's will. Anyone who wants what God wants will follow Jesus, for that is the will of God. Moreover, all who do God's will enter into a unique relationship with Jesus. United by their common obedience to God, they become Jesus' brothers and sisters and he becomes their brother. All those who do God's will belong to this new family.

God's Kingdom is not impersonal, ruled by an absentee potentate. It is a family, God's family. Its citizens are brothers and sisters one of another. They are also brothers and sisters of their sovereign Lord who is not ashamed to call them his brothers and sisters (Heb 2.11f; cf Mt 25.40). This new family relationship takes priority over one's biological family. Jesus claims authority over his disciples greater than that of their own parents (cf 1.16-20, 10.28-30).

This new kinship is not composed of those who *say* they do God's will but of those who *do* it (cf Mt 7.21-23). While its members are not perfect in their obedience, they seek to express their faith through obedience. They respond to the proclamation of God's Kingdom with repentance and faith (1.15). They are not evading God's will; they are doing it by following Jesus, even though their understanding is fragmentary (4.13, 8.32) and their faithfulness inconstant (14.27). As they continue to follow Jesus, they realize increasingly that their membership in the family of God is not a result of their obedience, but of God's grace. It does not depend on their faithfulness but on God's.

Down through the ages, those ostracized as a result of doing God's will (cf 13.12f) have been consoled by knowing that Jesus shares that experience. Others sever their blood ties in order to follow Jesus (10.28-30). They find their closest earthly ties in the church, "the household of God" (Eph 2.19) which transcends ethnic and cultural boundaries (11.17). Their fellowship and loving care for each other is an outgrowth of their fellowship with the Father and with his Son, Jesus Christ (1Jn 1.3).

v. 31 - Jesus' brothers and sisters are mentioned here and in 6.3. This in no way contradicts the doctrine of the Virgin Birth of Jesus (Mt 1.18), held by all Christian orthodoxy. This doctrine emphasizes the uniqueness of Jesus. It does not mean that Mary was not a sinner (in Lk 1.47, Mary "rejoices in God my Savior") nor that she would be exempt from the possibility of unbelief.

With the emphasis upon asceticism (including celibacy) in Jerome's time (c 380 A.D.), the idea that Mary remained a virgin perpetually gained favor, later becoming an Eastern Orthodox tradition and a Roman Catholic dogma. According to that view, the brothers and sisters of Jesus were either children of Joseph by a previous marriage or cousins of Jesus. There is no exegetical basis for either idea. Moreover, Jesus' description of his followers as his own "brothers and sisters" would be weakened if the comparison were reduced to "cousins."

"Father" is omitted as a relationship within this new family (3.33-35), for Jesus had but one Father--God himself (cf 14.36). He had no human father; his mother Mary conceived through the Holy Spirit (Mt 1.18, Lk 1.35). On the other hand, in this new family Jesus has many brothers and sisters and mothers. While the New Testament holds Mary in high esteem, it contradicts claims that she is the "Mother of God."

B. PARABLES ON THE NATURE AND GROWTH OF GOD'S RULE, 4.1-34

With high expectations that God would soon establish his Kingdom, the disciples follow Jesus. But they (and the reader as well) are troubled. Why does the number of those opposed to Jesus grow almost as fast as the size of the multitudes that seek him? Those most likely to follow Jesus--the religious leaders and his own family--are his strongest opponents. The Roman soldiers aren't going to be driven out of Palestine by a group of fishermen and some uncontrollable crowds. Jesus talks about giving the disciples authority but he still hasn't sent them out. Have they invested their lives in a lost cause?

The parables that follow offer some necessary answers to such questions. The disciples need to know more about how God works before they go out and proclaim the dawning of his Kingdom. Jesus gives the parables as "the great assurance" (to borrow Jeremias' phrase) to answer their reservations about what is happening. Nevertheless, they have difficulty in understanding them.

Mark's Gospel is known for its action. While much emphasis is given to Jesus' teaching, it is normally presented in bite-sized pieces. Three longer teaching units, however, are distributed in the overall structure of this Gospel: parables in the early chapters; Jesus' teachings on defilement near the middle (7.1-23); and his reply to questions about the end times (c 13) near the closing chapters.

An understanding of the disciples' thoughts and emotions is necessary for a proper understanding of the parables. The descriptions interspersed in and around these parables (vv. 1-2, 10-13 and 33-34, with 21-25 playing a double role) also point to their function of explaining the way God's Kingdom grows. The whole passage offers encouragement for those who are despondent over the apparently stagnant growth of God's reign in the midst of unbridled evil.

Jesus Teaches In Parables, 4.1-2

By sitting in a boat a little off shore, Jesus gains some freedom from the pressure of the sick who push forward to touch him for healing (3.9-10). This allows him to give priority again to his teaching (1.38). He is really no longer welcome in the synagogues, having been rejected by official Judaism. By the lake, there is space for all who desire to hear him.

"Hearing" is the key to understanding the passage. Since understanding is dependent upon hearing correctly, the two words are linked together. Many of those looking only for healing have not been listening to Jesus. They need to hear in order to see.

The word "parable" (meaning "thrown alongside" and thus "comparisons") is used in the New Testament (like **mashal** in the Old) for a variety of figures of speech such as proverbs, riddles, hyperboles, word puzzles and any out-of-the-ordinary or striking speech. Jesus used many of these forms to get his listeners to perceive something new and to involve them in reflection upon his teaching. Jesus skillfully employs them as dramatic confrontations in which he demands a response from his listeners.

Approximately one-third of Jesus' teaching in the Synoptic Gospels is in the form of parables. In Mark, they first appear in the context of controversy (2.17); they are a part of his instructing friends and of debating with foes (12.12). Although designed to gain attention, they are much more than captivating stories with a twist to them. While in a sense they are "earthly stories with a heavenly meaning", the parables confront us with our responsibilities and opportunities in this life, for that heavenly Kingdom is already present in our world.

Through his parables, Jesus presents characteristics of God's Kingdom while answering wrong ideas about it. His words have different effects upon his hearers, even though they understand the literal meaning of his words. His words bring light and life to some, while serving as instruments of judgment to others, depending upon the hearer's response. Since it takes two to communicate truth (one to speak, the other to hear), the same parable hides truth from some, while revealing it to others.

Parables are not allegories, although they have been frequently interpreted as such. An allegory is an artificial story. In creating it, the author can give each detail a special meaning, like a description in code where every item stands for something else. Those who interpret biblical parables allegorically often employ their creative imaginations with little regard for the biblical text and context. As a result, they may miss Jesus' intended meaning.

Most contemporary scholars reject the allegorical interpretation of parables. They seek the *one* single theme of the parable instead of *many* allegories. This means that the interpreter should concentrate on the punch line of the story as a whole, as perceived *in the context of Jesus and his ministry*. Only after discovering what the parable meant for the original audience can one proceed to find its message for today. Parables speak of experiences and objects familiar to the original listeners. The background details have no independent significance; they arise from real life and often contribute little to the truth intended.

Some writers argue, however, that in moving from the "irresponsible extravagances of the past, a number of scholars moved to the other extreme and rejected *all* allegory, insisting that there is only *one* teaching in each parable." Kenneth E. Bailey (Eyes xxi) made a major contribution to the interpretation of parables by claiming that "parables have in them more than a single theme and that these themes can be understood without either destroying the unity of the parables or falling back into the allegorizations of the past."

The interpreter must begin by observing with care how the original audience understood the symbols of the story ("a symbol *represents* something else; an allegory *is* something else and has no other existence"). The cultural background and the literary context and structure of the parable contribute to finding this initial response. Having done this, one can then discover what the parable means for us today by discerning *the theological cluster*. Bailey continues (Eyes xxii-xxiii): "Once we identify the original listener and perceive the single response expected of him, we can discover the cluster of themes that evoked that response. It is in that cluster of theological themes that we find the message for all people in any place at any time"

Jesus employs parables for a variety of purposes. Through them, he instructs about the nature of God's rule. He uses them to stimulate faith and to invite participation in God's Kingdom, to form attitudes and to change behavior. His parables train his followers and warn those who reject him.

At the same time, Jesus fully recognizes that each person hears according to his own frame of reference. Some are prepared by previous teachings and by a receptive attitude toward Jesus. Others (whom Jesus calls "outsiders," v. 11) are predisposed to contest his words. Frequently both groups compose his audiences. A variety of attitudes is present, even when he addresses the disciples alone. We conclude that Jesus not only uses parables for various purposes but that, on occasion, he uses a given parable like a missile with a multiple warhead, designed to strike the consciences of different people at different levels. The parable penetrates our defenses, entering our consciousness because it is a beautiful story. Passing through our thoughts for a while, it suddenly explodes in different places, hitting a prejudice here, a preconception there, a doubt in this place, an unwillingness in that place, and a fear someplace else.

We will seek to benefit from these insights into the interpretation of parables, while always giving priority to the way each parable functions in the text. Jesus' purpose is communication, not the preservation of literary forms.

v. 2 - A comparison with Matthew and Luke indicates that some of the teachings presented here may have been presented in other contexts; nevertheless, the composites represent the mind of Jesus.

• Many distort parables by seeking the allegorical meaning of every detail. For example, in the parable of the Good Samaritan, there is no hidden meaning in the man "going *down* from Jerusalem to Jericho." That's real-life background, for the road descends rapidly from the mountains to the deep valley. Nor does discovering the parable's message involve identifying the donkey. The common practice of reading parables with no consideration of their biblical and cultural setting also distorts their meanings.

On occasion Jesus used some allegorical details, as in the parable of the soils (4.3-8) and in the parable of the tenants (12.1-12). However, Jesus' parables are not true allegories, because the truths contained are only reinforced by the details; the messages are not dependent upon them. His infrequent use of semi-allegorical elements does not license allegorizing all parables.

• I am indebted to my colleague David Richard Jackson for the apt comparison of a parable with a missile. He adds, "The parables refuse to fit into any of our neat categories. The greatness of the Lord is seen by the fact that his stories judge us, rather than our judging them."

1. The Parable Of The Soils, 4.3-9

"Listen!", Jesus says as he begins this parable. He closes it with a similar admonition: "He who has ears to hear, let him hear." These two commandments call attention to the importance of this parable. Later (4.13) Jesus says that it holds the key to understanding all of the parables.

This unit of parables (4.3-32) is basic to discerning all that is going on in the Kingdom of God.

4.3,9 - "Hear, O Israel!" This phrase rang out in the Old Testament (cf Dt 6.4), marking occasions when God had a special message for Israel. God spoke frequently to his people in those times; however, there followed a long period of silence. Now he speaks again, through Jesus, who begins with the ancient command: "Listen!" and closes with "He who has ears to hear, let him hear." Now Jesus speaks with the authority of God himself; for he is not only anointed by God (1.11), he is God's Son (cf 9.7; 12.6; Heb 1.1-3). It is crucial that all listen carefully.

v. 3 - akouo (translated "hear," "listen," and "pay attention") occurs eleven times in chapter four. Related admonitions to hear and understand are repeated in 6.52; 7.14,18; 8.17, 21; 9.7; 12.29.

4.4-8 - The parable must be understood according to ancient Palestinian agricultural practices. The sower ("farmer") walked through the field, throwing seed by hand over the unplowed ground. In the process, seed scattered all over, some falling on the path, on rocky ground and among thistles, as well as on good soil. Only after the seed was broadcast was the ground plowed, burying the seed.

Like other parables, this one calls attention to something specific about a familiar experience or object. Here Jesus relates a common experience: a farmer sowing seed. He emphasizes a specific fact about it: depending upon the type of soil on which it falls, some seeds produce a crop, and others do not.

Those who hear Jesus would clearly understand this much, for sowing is a part of their cultural milieu. But what is the comparison between the story and what is happening in Mark's story? Specifically, what does it mean in terms of Jesus' ministry? Unable to make the connection, the disciples ask what the parables means (v. 10).

As Jesus proclaims the arrival of God's reign, two things stand out: the remarkable person and power of Jesus on one hand, and the different ways persons respond to him on the other hand. This part of the parable's historical context is very evident to the reader. Behind the scene, however, is the Jewish expectation of the nature of God's Kingdom. Contemporary apocalyptic pronouncements claimed that the Kingdom would come with an irresistible display of God's power, sweeping all before it. John the Baptist, Jesus' disciples and the multitudes share this belief. Since this is not happening, the disciples are puzzled and the scribes denounce Jesus as Satan's special agent. How, then, does the parable relate to their kingdom expectations?

Actually, the parable bears high relevance to what is happening. The Kingdom of God has already come; it is present and active in the proclamation of the good news. Contrary to popular expectations, it is not destroying the wicked. Rather, it is God's gracious offer to humanity, a gift that can be accepted or rejected. It is like a seed sown in a Palestinian field. Sometimes the seed is snatched away; sometimes it does not even germinate. But other times it produces an abundant harvest (cf 14-20).

v. 4 - This parable is reinforced by the details (the path, rocky ground, etc.), but it is not dependent upon them (as would be the case in a true allegory). The common experience (some types of soil produce, others do not) would not be altered if other impediments to growth had been cited. The details (discussed in 4.14-20) play a supportive role.

v. 5 - In much of Palestine, the typical field is small, with limestone boulders just beneath the soil. With great effort, farmers attempt to clear the land of rocks to form terraces and walls. Some large rocks remain, however.

2. The Secret Of God's Kingdom, 4.10-13

The teaching in verses 1-34 is not limited to the three well-known parables. Four short paragraphs (4.1-2, 10-12, 21-25 and 33-34) are intertwined with them, providing indispensable orientation as to the occasion, reactions and purposes of the parables.

Jesus' own followers acknowledge they don't understand him. Not just this parable, but the parables in general perplex them. They do the right thing, however: they ask Jesus himself. Maybe they think he can give them some secret essential to understanding. Anyway, he answers in terms of the **mysterion** ("secret") of the Kingdom of God.

While the religious cults, philosophy and gnosticism of the ancient world each gave their own nuances to the term, **mysterion** carried a common connotation for all. It signified something hidden; it involved secrets of something that could not or should not be revealed. These concepts of "mysteries" underlie today's occult and oriental religions, where mystic and esoteric practices continue. Just as the Old Testament denounced the strange gods of that day, the New Testament rejects the validity of the mystery religions. God is not hidden, nor is he "found" through secret processes. He has revealed himself in Jesus Christ (cf Heb 1.1-4). This knowledge is not esoteric, that is, available only to a few who are specially initiated; rather, all are openly invited.

In the New Testament, **mysterion** is almost always used with verbs that denote revelation or proclamation, in sharp contrast to the "mysteries" in the ancient world. In other words, **mysterion** means "that which is revealed." Specifically, the Kingdom of God has arrived in the person of Jesus. While the disciples submit to God's rule by following Jesus, they still do not understand fully what it is all about. It is still partially hidden from them. However, this lack of understanding is temporary, for, as Jesus says, "the secret of the Kingdom of God has been given to you."

By using a Semitic form of speech ("the secret is given"), Jesus is saying that God is the Giver of the **mysterion**. It does not come through evil spirits; they are forbidden to manifest who Jesus is (3.12). The hidden is disclosed (4.22) by the grace of God. Just as Israel was chosen by God's grace, the disciples are chosen (3.13,14) to share with others the knowledge of the God who has revealed himself. The gospel is the "secret now revealed," for God is actively implanting his promised Kingdom. As this message is proclaimed, even those presently on the outside are given the opportunity to hear and understand (cf Ac 28.26-28).

This **mysterion** is proclaimed to all. Understanding is given to those who respond (that is, believe and follow). Many, looking for God's Kingdom to come openly and in overwhelming power, reject the hidden way in which it appears in Jesus. It doesn't make sense to them--it is ironic. So are the parables. Through them, Jesus is explaining how God's rule is actually at work in the world. Those who hear the parables only as interesting stories are rejecting an opportunity to understand what God is doing. The fact that the Kingdom of God entered the world "quietly" in the person and works of Jesus remains hidden to them because they do not "listen" to Jesus (4.3,9). They are outsiders. They are soil in which the seed does not bear fruit.

Jesus then indicates that this division within humanity (belief and unbelief) is nothing new. The prophet Isaiah was sent to an unbelieving people (Isa 6.9-10), with the promise that his mission would have a two-fold result. God would be a sanctuary to those who regard him as holy; at the same time, he would be a stumbling stone to the unbelieving (Isa 8.14-15). Like Isaiah, Jeremiah (5.21) and Ezekiel (12.1), Jesus also faces people with calloused hearts. His ministry brings blessing to those who understand and divine retribution to those who reject his rule.

This division into insiders and outsiders comes through hearing Jesus; it is according to God's design. Similar teaching about the two-fold purpose of God's work is encountered in both the Old (cf Isa 28.13; Jer 23.29) and New Testaments (Lk 2.34; Jn 12.40; Ac 5.3ff, 28.26; Ro 9-11; 2Co 2.14-16; Heb 4.12; 1Pe 2.8). As Cranfield (157-158) explains, "No outward compelling evidence of divine glory illumines the ministry of Jesus. It is a necessary part of the gracious self-abasement of the Incarnation that the Son of God should submit to conditions under which his claim to authority cannot but appear altogether problematic and paradoxical. In the last hours of his life his incognito deepens until...he becomes the absolute antithesis of everything that the world understands by divinity and by kingship." The revealing and veiling are held in tension (cf Mt 11.25ff; Lk 10.21f). God's truth revealed demands a decision; his truth hidden gives people sufficient room to make one. By veiling the revelation, God gives humanity freedom to believe.

Verse 13 both closes Jesus' dialogue with his disciples about the importance of understanding the parable of the soils and introduces his interpretation of it.

v. 11 - Although those disciples do not understand at this time, "to you is given" promises that future understanding will be granted to them through further revelation of who Jesus is. God's selective choice is taught throughout Scripture. First, he chose Israel, then a remnant. Now through Jesus God chooses the disciples to begin the new Israel.

v. 12 - Both **hina** ("so that," "in order that") and **mepote** ("otherwise," "lest," "in order not") express purpose. Many commentators, stumbling at this, go to great lengths to seek other meanings. The division of humankind into two groups according to their response to Jesus is repeated throughout this whole section by various comparisons: fruitful/unfruitful, insiders/outsiders; revealed/veiled; have/have not). Mark intends for us to understand that humanity is not divided into Jews and Gentiles but according to its response to God's word.

• As Jeremias said (Theology 205), "Jesus lived in the Old Testament. His sayings are incomprehensible unless we recognize this... He was particularly fond of the prophet Isaiah."

3. The Explanation Of The Parable Of The Soils, 4.14-20

In answer to the disciples' inquiry (4.10), Jesus interprets the parable of the soils, thereby enhancing its importance as a key to understanding any parable (4.13). His explanation is relevant to those who heard him then and now.

Mark clearly intends that we understand this interpretation of the parable of the soils as originating with Jesus. However, some writers contend that the early church created it, citing linguistic characteristics (for example, the explanation lacks Semitic flavor and employs several words that occur only in the Epistles). More likely, however, Mark related Jesus' explanation, expressing it in his own words, in terms pertinent to his readers and in language well understood by the early church. To communicate in terms of the needs and language of their hearers is, of course, the desire of all who proclaim God's word.

• Some critics claim that this interpretation of the parable did not originate with Jesus but with the early church. More likely, Jesus himself made the change from seed = word (v. 14) to seed = hearer (vv. 16,18,20), for he was an excellent communicator who involved his hearers directly in the message of the parable. In 14-20, the demonstratives, prepositional phrases and participles are all masculine, for the parable concerns people, not seeds.

Parables are not found in the "church documents" (i.e., the Epistles). The cultural background of the parables confirms that they originated with Jesus. After living for years in a Middle Eastern, oral-tradition peasant community, Bailey (Eyes, page x) significantly observes, "we find no convincing reason to question the basic authenticity of the parables as parables of Jesus of Nazareth. The material is Palestinian. No doubt the material has been reused by the evangelists for their own theological purposes. But it is our view that this reuse does not significantly obscure the original intent of the material."

Jesus does not identify the sower in his parable. Anyone who sows the word is included. They, like the farmer, need to be aware of how the seed grows.

The seed, on the other hand, is identified as "the word" (**ho logos**). This term is already used in Mark (2.2) in reference to Jesus' teaching (cf 8.38; 13.31). The good news he brought forms the core of the Christian message which is called "the word" (or "message") in Mark (4.14, 33; 8.32) and in the church (Gal 6.6, 1Pe 2.8, 2Ti 4.2). Although diluted by some (Col 2.8) and distorted by others (Ac 20.30, 2Co 4.2), the proclamation of the word remains the distinct contribution of the church to a dying world, for it is the power of God (1Co 1.18).

The comparison made between "seed" with "word" is dynamic: in v. 14, the seed is the word; in vv. 16-20, it is identified with the hearers of the word. Both comparisons occur midway through the transition, in v. 15. Such a change may not be technically precise, but it is good communication as Jesus moves from the impersonal to the personal, exhorting his hearers to be "good soil." As hearers accept the word of God and give themselves to it, it becomes a part of them, molding them and transforming them so that they produce results (cf Jn 15.7,8; Ps 1.2-3; Jer 15.16). All who teach the word need to understand the dynamics involved. Each one who hears is challenged to ask, "What obstacles prevent my full obedience to God's will?"

As a part of his cosmic attack against God, Satan actively seeks to destroy the word before it can even begin to grow. His intermediate agents of destruction are not specifically identified but they are many. Neither Rome nor his various other instruments are the true enemy; Satan is the force behind them. He no doubt is also active in the rocky and thorny places (vv. 16-17). He continues to combat the message, for he knows that it is a part of the Spirit's weapons (cf Eph 6.17) against the Adversary. Satan closes the minds of many even before they hear the gospel.

The rocky places (vv 16-17) depict people who show initial promise that does not materialize. Both their superficial response and their falling away are "quick." Affliction ("trouble", "distress") and persecution (10.30) come into their lives because of the word. As a result, they "turn back" (**skandalizontai**; cf 6.3; 9.42). This "falling away" does not specify permanent abandonment. The disciples themselves show some of the characteristics of rocky and thorny ground at this point in time, but later they produce much fruit. One's heart can become more receptive as a person perseveres in hearing Jesus' word.

Many of Mark's first readers chose Jesus and as a result faced physical persecution and even death "because of the word." Not a few, today, decide to follow Jesus in spite of fierce opposition.

The word grows in lives afflicted by internal conflicts (vv 18-19), but it is unfruitful when the drive for status in the community, for possessions, for material security bring anxieties which choke out desires for God. This list of brier patches is not exhaustive but only representative of obstacles to fruitfulness, as the Epistles bear out by repeating similar warnings. In the life of any believer, thistles choke the word and make it unfruitful. Any obstacle to the growth of the word needs to be uprooted.

Despite all the impediments, some seed bears fruit--thirty and sixty and a hundredfold (v 20). Such results surpass all expectations. By closing the parable with such a surprise, Jesus focuses attention on the amazing growth of God's rule in spite of all barriers. Jesus' presence is proof that God has begun his rule among women and men. What God has begun, he will carry to completion. Aware of these realities (and possibly in tears, Ps 126.5-6), the wise farmer sows more extensively so as to obtain a more abundant harvest.

This parable and its explanation evoke several theological motifs. God's Kingdom comes to men and women as the seed of the gospel is sown everywhere. Its growth is hindered by Satan and by lives dominated by external pressures and internal ambitions. Nevertheless, an abundant harvest is assured as God is now speaking through Jesus, calling each person to listen and bear fruit, for fruit-bearing is an essential mark of the Kingdom.

Mark adds emphasis upon the gospel for all nations by using different demonstrative pronouns to denote the different soils. "These" (**houtoi**, near) fell by the way and among rocks; "others" (**alloi**, over there), among thorns; and "those" (**ekeinoi**, farther away) produced abundantly. This indicates that good soil will be found among the distant Gentiles, as Swartley (Mark: Way 217n5) points out.

The parable challenges those who lack understanding (like the disciples, 4.13) to overcome hindrances to bearing fruit. Obstacles abound, but those who are faithful in sowing the seed are encouraged to expect an abundant harvest. To outsiders, the parable is an invitation to hear and obey instead of succumbing to difficulties.

• These responses appear within the events narrated in Mark. For example, Satan tries to take away the word from Peter (8.33). King Herod likes to listen to John the Baptist (6.20; cf Pilate, 15.5), but the word sown in his heart, a rocky place, does not take root. The disciples experience life among thorns where desires for status (9.34; 10.37) choke the word. They themselves fall away quickly when persecution arises (14.50), although later they follow Jesus (16.7). The rich young ruler exemplifies the unfruitful seed: his heart, a thorny place, is deceived by wealth (10.22). Seed sown in most unpromising places, however, produce amazing results (e.g., 2.13-15; 5.1-20).

4. Sayings About Hiddenness, 4.21-25

No indication is given as to the occasion on which the statements in this pericope were originally made. The other Synoptic writers use some in other contexts. Mark places them here to augment the reader's understanding of the surrounding parables.

Instead of saying, "Jesus asked," the text begins "he said to them," for these two verses contain three *rhetorical* questions, which are in reality declarations. Rhetorical questions serve two purposes: they provoke the hearers to think, and they imply the answers to the questions raised. So actually we have two parallel statements ("he said," vv. 21-22, and "he continued," vv. 24-25) balanced on the pivotal declaration in the middle (v. 23) of a chiasmus. (The phrasing in the Greek text is not always evident in translations). The structure is designed to aid our understanding the pericope.

4.21-22 - The first two questions Jesus poses stir up an unspoken negative response from listeners: "of course not, no one hides a lamp under a bowl or a bed." The third question elicits a positive reaction: "you put a lamp on its stand." Everyone knows that. By "asking" something so obvious, Jesus gains the undivided attention of his hearers.

This positive answer is reinforced by v. 22, with two declarations that emphasize the same truth: if one does hide something, it is with the purpose of bringing it out later. While modern readers do not easily understand the construction of these verses, the Hebrew parallelism employed aided the original audience. The different forms of comparisons found in this pericope are all "parables" in the broader sense of the term.

What is hidden will be revealed. But what is hidden? The identity of Jesus, the presence of God's reign among men, even the meaning of Jesus' teachings--these are all hidden (and are inseparable here). They are hidden in order to become known. That **mysterion** of v. 11 is kept before us, for it is important. The strange expression, "does a lamp come?" (translated "do you bring a lamp?") alludes to the coming of Jesus and the Kingdom. Jesus came to be revealed. Not immediately, but after a period of concealment, he will be revealed as God's Son. This is God's purpose, as declared four times in two verses by **hina** ("in order that;" cf 4.12).

The hidden will be disclosed. By whom? The evil spirits were "ordered not to tell" (3.12); the manifestation of the Son belongs to the Father. God will bring it out into the open; he will reveal the secret to those who listen. Slowly, the disciples gain insight into "who Jesus is." They will know him clearly, however, only after his crucifixion and resurrection.

Like the parables (cf the abundant harvest of 4.8), these two verses offer encouragement. Going beyond the hidden/revealed in vv. 10-12, they add the time element, teaching that the obscurity is only temporary. They reaffirm that Jesus' identity is purposely veiled until the right time (cf "until" in 9.9). Doubts should give way to hope, for the concealment is a part of God's purposes.

v. 21 - A small, simple clay lamp with a wick lying in olive oil was normally placed on a vertical stand to illumine better. "Bowl" ("bushel") indicates a large vessel for containing over 2 gallons of grain.

4.23 - This little verse--the pivotal point in this chiasmus--presents the theme of the pericope and forms a bridge between the encouragement (vv. 21-22) and the exhortation (vv. 24-25).

Having indicated that God will unveil what is presently hidden, Jesus teaches that our responsibility is this: Listen to Jesus! People are given ears in order to hear. They are responsible to use them. In so doing, they become recipients of the promise that the hidden will be manifested. "Anyone with ears"--not just a privileged few, but anyone, including a person who understands a little and one who doesn't even understand enough to ask questions--is encouraged to give full attention to Jesus' teachings. This is the way to gain understanding.

4.24-25 - These pithy statements begin with an appeal to "see in order to hear" (or "consider carefully what you hear"). The three proverbs which follow overflow with Semitisms. In form, they reflect the Hebrew style of writing. In expression, God's name does not appear, lest it be used in vain. In context, they teach about God's work, not about economics. Jesus could have created these riddles, for his wisdom is greater than that of Solomon (Mt 12.42); or he could have cited popular sayings.

The beginning of v. 24 goes beyond the previous exhortations to hear (vv. 9,23). It is a warning: listen carefully now. Why? Because understanding will blossom when God unveils the mystery. The reasoning behind this is presented in figures of speech (24b and 25) that are different from the parable of the soils, but the message complements previous teaching.

In this context of repeated emphasis upon hearing, "measure" probably substitutes for "hear." A modern paraphrase to this riddle could be, "God will give you understanding according to how much you hear. It won't be given on an arithmetical one-for-one basis; he will give you understanding in geometrical proportion to how carefully you listen." On the other hand, the one who does not listen will fall into greater ignorance and judgment. These consequences are both temporal and eternal.

Far from being an incomprehensible mixture of unrelated sayings, this paragraph is closely knit around the promise ("the hidden will be unveiled") and the exhortation ("hear"). It fits very neatly into this section for it reinforces the themes presented in 4.3-32.

v. 25b - This negative statement balances the positive in 24b-25a. The same divine principle is also seen in Luke 8.18 and 19.26.

5. The Parable Of The Seed Growing Of Itself, 4.26-29

Two more comparisons complete this section of parables. They are a part of Jesus' teaching the crowd, related to us without commentary. Both continue the imagery of the seed and agriculture, offering encouragement for all who sow the seed, especially when results are invisible. Both are clearly identified as parables of the Kingdom of God. The omission of any exhortations to "hear" indicates that their purposes differ from that of 4.3-20. These two parables answer his hearers' doubts about why the Kingdom doesn't appear as they expected. They also convey instruction especially helpful to all who proclaim the word. What is one's responsibility after "sowing the seed"? What are the end results?

"A man scatters seed on the ground." From such a beginning, the listener might expect teachings on soil analysis. Quite to the contrary, this parable talks about the sower. To be more accurate, it focuses on what happens when the farmer is off duty. It is a surprising way to teach, but with it, Jesus catches the crowd's attention.

After sowing, the farmer's daily routine ("he sleeps and gets up") is unperturbed by anxiety over the seed planted. He is content in the knowledge that the soil produces grain "all by itself" (**automate**). In other words, he leaves it up to God, who works through mysterious ways unknown to the farmer. The sower knows that harvest will delay but it will certainly come. Men and women sow, but the seed and the harvest are God's work.

This parable is eschatological, for the Kingdom of which it speaks is eschatological. The Kingdom is present both in the seed and in the harvest. It is embryonic now, full kernel then; hidden now, fully manifested then. In symbolism of the end times, the harvest (with words drawn from Joel 3.13) stands for judgment that will be followed by abundant blessings in the consummation of God's Kingdom (cf Joel 3.18).

Humanity longs for a just society, with freedom from hunger and violence. God promises much more: his eternal Kingdom will be fully consummated after the harvest. Meanwhile, it is present in the person and ministry of Jesus. Among the disciples, for example, Simon the Zealot (3.18) would likely be frustrated by Jesus' way of working. The zealots advocated political (and even military) action as necessary for achieving freedom and justice. To some today also, preaching the word appears irrelevant to achieving a just society. Yet sowing is **sine qua non** to the harvest (cf 13.10,27; Ps 126.5-6).

Since this comparison is one of the few passages in Mark that does not appear in any other Gospel, we can presume that Mark's first readers especially needed this encouragement. They saw many problems and few results for their labors. The Christian worker needs a "farmer's patience." Anxiety will not help; in fact, it hinders. In other words, "Don't take yourself too seriously; sow and wait" (cf 4.38a; Ps 27.14; 126.6). A life built upon God's promises is free from anxiety (cf Php 4.6). "Be patient, then, brothers, until the Lord's coming" (Jas 5.7; cf 1Pe 5.7).

Jesus desires that his hearers (and Mark's readers) sow the seed and remain confident that the harvest will come. The Kingdom is God's creation. He is building it according to his own blueprint and time schedule. People are invited to receive it; men and women are commanded to sow; God retains sovereign control over its growth. In the face of frustrations and even scoffing ("where is his coming?" 2Pe 3.3ff), programs and institutions are created to "bring in the Kingdom." Such plans and maneuvering can easily obscure the true dynamic, namely, "the zeal of the Lord Almighty will accomplish this" (Isa 9.7).

• The stages of growth (stalk, head, full kernel) probably are not meant as a description of the gradual growth of the Kingdom (or the church). They are a part of the narrator's art of stressing the wonderful, although mysterious, God-given harvest that begins with simply scattering seed on the ground.

• George Muller of Bristol, England, once said, "any believing child of God may safely gauge the measure of his surrender to the will of God, in any matter, by the measure of impatience he feels at the obstacles in his way." He added that "when a man's chief business it to serve and please the Lord, all his circumstances become his servants."

v. 29 - Waiting for a harvest involves the passing of time. It is difficult to reconcile this with the assertion by some writers that Jesus thought God's reign would be consummated soon.

6. The Parable Of The Mustard Seed, 4.30-32

At this point of time in Jesus' ministry, the Kingdom of God proclaimed by Jesus is not very evident to his followers. Moreover, his critics denounce him as a fraud.

In the midst of such attitudes, Jesus arouses the interest of his hearers by asking rhetorically: "What shall we say the Kingdom of God is like, or what parable shall we use to describe it?" By including his hearers in these questions ("what shall *we* say?.. *we* use?"), he challenges them to think as he proceeds to tell this parable: the Kingdom of God is like a tiny mustard seed; when planted it grows into a plant so large that birds can nest in its shade.

The mustard seed is a proverbial symbol for that which is tiny and insignificant. From such a small start, a planted seed grows and becomes a very large garden plant. This is a story of contrasts between a small beginning and an amazing conclusion, between present hiddenness and future visibility. The Kingdom of God is like such a seed. Its present size and seeming insignificance are in no way indicative of its consummation which will encompass the whole universe (13.24-27, cf Rev 5.9-13; 7.9). The Kingdom is already present, hidden in the person and work of God's Son incognito. In the future, however, "men will see the Son of Man coming in clouds with great power and glory" when Jesus establishes his eternal Kingdom (13.26-27; cf Rev 1.7).

In this way, Jesus is saying, Do not be deceived by appearances. Let all be encouraged to participate in the Kingdom. Have faith in a great God. God's present "weakness" will pass away when God manifests his sovereign power.

This eschatological parable recalls what the Sovereign Lord said about the cedar in which birds "find shelter in the shade of its branches" (Eze 17.22-24; 31.6). In keeping with this and the symbolism in Daniel 4.11-12, the birds in Jesus' parable are probably an illusion to the Gentiles' finding refuge in God's Kingdom. This is consistent with Mark's emphasis upon the worldwide outreach of the Gospel (11.17; 13.27; 14.9).

v. 30 - Ladd (Theology 111) says some writers misinterpret this parable because they fail to perceive that "the church is the community of the Kingdom but never the Kingdom itself... The Kingdom is the rule of God; the church is a society of men." This parable describes the Kingdom, not the church. It teaches neither slow, gradual church growth nor that the church will grow into a great institution.

v. 31 - The black mustard plant, grown in Palestine for its mustard and oil, attains a height of over ten feet.

v. 32 - Nineham (144) points out that growth processes are a modern concern; Jesus' hearers typically concentrated on the contrast between the smallness of the seed and the size of the tree.

Jesus Speaks The Word In Many Parables, 4.33-34

Jesus does not state in abstract terms the precise nature of the Kingdom of God. First of all, he demonstrates God's rule in his own person and deeds. In addition, he speaks of it in word pictures, employing familiar objects. The parables challenge his hearers to listen with their whole being in order to experience God's rule in daily life. If Jesus had spoken to the multitudes openly, he would have forced a decision before they were ready. Mature understanding is necessary to avoid superficial discipleship. Along with the disciples, readers are urged to seek more understanding, for they are continually dependent upon Jesus' word.

The Gospels include only a sampling of Jesus' parables. He continues to use this form of teaching, even though many do not understand. The disciples need further explanation (cf 4.10,13; 7.17). After his resurrection, Jesus explains much that they were incapable of understanding before the crucifixion (cf Lk 24.27ff) and the Holy Spirit also made known to them the things of Jesus (Jn 16.12ff). As a result, the New Testament, breathed by God the Holy Spirit (2Ti 3.16; 2Pe 1.21) unveils Jesus Christ, the Son of God who will be gloriously manifested at his return (8.38; 13.26-27; 14.62).

Jesus' "comparisons" are full of contrasts: fruitful/unfruitful, insiders/outsiders, revealed/veiled, have/have not, sow/harvest and smallest/greatest. By grouping these parables together, Mark intends that we remember that God's Kingdom is already present in the person of Jesus. Obstacles to faith and perseverance exist, but God guarantees surprising results. The mystery awaits the proper time for unveiling its hidden identity. The Kingdom's small beginning is no indication of the outcome.

The preceding section of parables explains what is happening in God's Kingdom. It instructs all disciples on what to expect as they work in it and assures them as to the future. At the same time, it exhorts each one to self-examination. The section is a warning about judging God's role in the world by external appearances. Although each parable has its own emphasis, through them all Jesus continues to confront men and women with their need to respond to his person.

C. THE MIRACULOUS POWER OF GOD'S RULE, 4.35 - 6.6a

After the calm scenes portrayed in the parables, this new section of the Gospel jolts the reader into realizing that Jesus is far more than an excellent teacher. It is filled with action described in vivid details, suggesting eyewitness accounts. It may reflect sermonic material from the apostle Peter.

The grouping is clearly thematic. The miracles in this unit demonstrate God's power to resolve extreme problems that are beyond human solutions. Beautifully woven through this tapestry are two other threads: one portrays faith and doubt in unexpected places and another answers the question, "Does Jesus care?" The religious opponents are absent from 3.30; their somber presence, however, will return in 7.1.

Through the parables, the reader gains important insights into the nature of God's reign. However, these insights are incomplete, for the parables present the Kingdom of God as weak in its hiddenness. Now we see the Kingdom as the power of God overcoming all foes. The parables tell of the Kingdom already present; the miracles demonstrate God's care for people who, like Jesus (15.34), call out to him in the midst of undeserved suffering. They also give insight into the Kingdom when consummated. The dual aspects, "already" but "not yet," are skillfully compared by the juxtaposition of the two literary units, 4.1-34 and 4.35-6.6a. First came Jesus' word, its significance hidden; then comes his miraculous power, unveiled.

The present hidden nature of the Kingdom continues, however. While some are admonished to silence (5.43) and others are blind (6.1-6a), surprising exceptions arise. For example, Jesus tells one, "Go and tell how much the Lord has done for you" (5.19) and he calls upon another to tell what she wanted to keep hidden (5.30).

Woven through the whole tapestry, however, is that question which each person must answer, Who is Jesus? It dominates the first scene; through an unexpected turn of events, it also provokes serious reflection in the closing pericope (6.1-6b).

1. Jesus Calms The Storm, 4.35-41

The disciples face an extreme test as they follow Jesus' command. In their fear, they rebuke Jesus, who calms the storm and he in turn rebukes the disciples for their lack of faith. Will the experience open their eyes to understand who Jesus really is?

4.35-36 - Interrupting his ministry by the shore of Lake Galilee (1.16; 3.9; 4.1; 5.21), Jesus himself initiates his first journey to the eastern shore, saying to his disciples, "Let us go over to the other side." Jesus soon falls to sleep in the stern, tired from the constant demands placed upon him (3.20). Like the man who scattered seed on the ground and slept untroubled (4.26f), Jesus rests, certain that God will care for him and for the seed he has sown. On the eastern side of the lake, he will sow more seed, extending his ministry (1.38).

v. 35 - Specific references to the time of day, the presence of other boats as well as vivid details about the storm and the disciples' behavior indicate first-hand information, probably related to Mark by Peter. As C.F.D. Moule (42) says, "The evangelist meant the story to be taken quite literally."

• The possibility of miracles has been denied **a priori** or rationalized by those who presuppose a closed view of the universe. Since scientific "laws" are descriptions of normal occurrences experienced and measured in nature, it does not follow that something different cannot take place under any circumstances. The God who reveals himself in the Bible did not create a mechanistic, self-operating universe. He actively participates in the world he created, even occasionally exercising his prerogatives to employ his power in ways that are not his normal operative procedures. Jesus' presence and miracles are a part of God's special participation in the world he created.

v. 36 - Jesus had been teaching from a boat just off shore (cf 3.9, 4.1). Apparently he did not go ashore; the disciples "took him along, just as he was, in the boat" as they began crossing the lake. The "other boats" may have been brought along side Jesus' boat for their occupants to hear his teaching, unmolested by the crowds. They were sailed back to nearby fishing villages when the disciples shoved off for the eastern shore. Josephus reports that 350 fishing boats plied the lake at his time.

• In 1986, a boat (measuring approximately 7.5 feet wide, 26 feet long and 4.6 feet high) was found buried in mud near the western shore of Lake Galilee. All evidence indicates it was constructed in Jesus' time. The boat's layout fits the details in Mark. It could be propelled by sail or by four oarsmen (with the helmsman completing the five-man crew; cf Mk 1.20) and accommodate fifteen people (cf Jesus and his twelve disciples). The ballast was stored in the stern beneath the platform called the pillow, on which it was possible for a person to sleep, undisturbed by the activities of the others.

4.37-40 - Situated in a basin, the lake is subject to sudden storms when winds whip over the surrounding mountains, quickly changing the atmospheric pressure over the lake. On this particular evening, an unusually violent storm arises. With gale force, it threatens the safety of the boat and its occupants as the waves nearly swamp the boat. Although several of them are fishermen who practically live on the lake, the disciples fear for their lives. Jesus, however, continues to sleep in peace (cf Lev 26.6; Pr 3.24).

Stricken with fear, the disciples resent the fact that Jesus is asleep, oblivious of their plight. They awaken him with a reprimand, "Teacher, don't you care if we drown?" In this hour of despair, the disciples address him only as "Teacher."

Their harsh accusation, "Don't you care?" would hurt any caring person. Because he does care, Jesus humbly submits himself to this and to other rebukes by his disciples (cf 5.31; 6.37; 8.4,32). Later, because he cares, he gives "his life as a ransom for many" (10.45).

Also, Jesus cares enough to rebuke his disciples for their lack of faith. They crossed over the lake in obedience to Jesus' direct command. There will be other times when their lives are endangered as a result of obeying Jesus' word. In order for their faith to grow, they must face up to the reasons behind their fears. When Jesus is nowhere near, will they quickly fall away "when trouble comes because of the word" (4.17)?

Answering their cry, Jesus rebukes the wind and the waves. Nature submits to his word, the wind dies down and the waves become calm (cf Ps 107.26-29). As God "stills the roaring of the seas" (Ps 65.7), an atmosphere of complete peace comes over the lake.

The vocabulary of Jesus' words and the responses to his authority are similar to those used when he addressed an evil spirit (1.23-27):

"He sternly commanded the wind and said to the lake, `Be silent! Be quiet!'" (4.39).	"Jesus sternly commanded him, saying, `Be quiet!'" (1.25)
"The disciples asked each other, `Who is this? Even the wind and the lake obey him'" (4.41).	"The people were all so amazed that they asked each other, `What is this? A new teaching--and with authority! He gives orders to evil spirits and they obey him'" (1.27)

Jesus speaks to the wind and waters with the same words he uses when he addresses the evil spirit because he recognizes that Satan is behind both attempts to nullify the dawning of God's reign. Having failed in his opposition to Jesus in the synagogue in Capernaum, Satan now seeks to destroy Jesus in the storm before he initiates his ministry in Gentile territory (5.1ff). Jesus, however, demonstrates his superior authority over the Adversary in both the spiritual and natural realms.

"Do you still have no faith?" Jesus asks. In his efforts to strengthen their faith, Jesus had assured them in the parables of the eventual triumph of God's Kingdom. He had forewarned them of besetting dangers. The disciples' faith is still limited, however; they need to listen more attentively (cf 4.3,9,23; Ro 10.17). At the same time, faith does not come instantaneously; it is strengthened through testing (cf 5.36).

4.41 - Awe-stricken, the disciples ask each other, "Who is this? Even the wind and the waves obey him!" Their fear and their lack of faith all come down to one thing: they do not know who Jesus is. As their fear of the storm and of dying fade, they are overcome with a different type of fear, a sense of awe that God is right there. God has intervened in their lives; he has saved them. And in a peculiar way, it is all related to Jesus. Jesus has done what only God can do.

Mark intended that this and the other nature miracles be understood primarily as substantiating Jesus' divine authority. Yet from ancient times, this narrative has been allegorized as a description of the church tossed on angry seas. "Storms" certainly have tossed the church through the ages (cf Paul's own experiences related in 2Co 11.23-28). Believers do not face trials alone, however, for Christ helps in times of troubles and delivers us from the fear of death (Heb 2.14-18). While the allegorical interpretation seems apropos, we should not allow it to detract from the event's christological emphasis.

After the lessons of the parables, the disciples fail to pass a "surprise test". Jesus does not give up on them, however. After rebuking them, he proceeds to reteach them. Through his ensuing ministry to others (5.1-43), perhaps the disciples will see how much he really cares. Perhaps their faith will become strong as they see the faith of others under trial.

v. 41 - Literally, "they feared a great fear." The Greek word **phobos** can mean fear in the sense of the panic that the disciples' felt when they met behind locked doors after the crucifixion (Jn 20.21). It is used more frequently in the New Testament for "awe," humankind's essential reverence in the presence of God (cf Lk 1.12; Ac 9.31). After "it was completely calm," the disciples probably experienced both "fear" and "awe" (cf 6.50; 16.8). They gained a sense of reverence in the presence of Jesus' awesome power over the lake they knew so well. Yet "they were terrified," for their insight into his identity was incomplete.

• This short narrative dramatically presents side by side the human and divine natures of Jesus. Tired from the heavy demands of his ministry, he falls asleep. Upon being awakened, he speaks and the forces of nature obey their sovereign Lord, the Creator and Sustainer of the universe.

• As seen in this miracle, the Bible does not equate God with nature, a doctrine of ancient and modern pantheistic religions. Although Satan presently exercises power in the realm of nature, the triune God is still sovereign Lord over nature. Western thought has isolated nature from its Creator.

2. A New Life For A Demon-Controlled Man, 5.1-20

This and the following pericope continue the theme of Jesus' mighty works in extreme circumstances that are beyond human solution. These events provide additional clues in answer to the disciples' question, "Who is this?" (4.41). They also answer the disciples' accusation ("Don't you care?" 4.38) by showing Jesus' caring for three people, each in a hopeless circumstance, all of them ceremonially unclean. Probably Peter supplied the many details in the story, for they bear the marks of an eyewitness.

Jesus extends his ministry to a new territory where he does what no knowledgeable farmer would do: he sows among the tombs, with startling results (cf 4.8,20).

• This event does not take place in the town itself (v. 14) but in the "region of the Gerasenes." Archaeologists have located the ruins of a village called Gergesa (modern name: Kursi) on the eastern coast of the lake. Tombs exist in the caverns in the steep slope near the shore south of the locale. The name has been confused with Gerasa (about 45 miles southeast of the lake, Jerash in modern Jordan), and with Gadara (about 7 miles away). Changes in administrative territories and scribal guesses at other names may have resulted in the various names found in the manuscripts.

5.1-5 - Upon arriving on the eastern shore of Lake Galilee, Jesus is met by a man with an evil spirit. Lest the reader assume that this is "just another case" of demonic control, Mark reviews the Gerasene's tragic history before describing his encounter with Jesus (v. 6ff).

This man disrupted his community so much that people had often tried unsuccessfully to control him with chains. He tore apart all restraints; nothing worked. Rejected by society, his anguish continued night and day. From the cave-like tombs on the steep hillside, the echo of his cries filled the air with terror. He turned his despair against himself, lacerating his own body. He was his own enemy.

This living-dead man is a vivid, realistic picture of the disorder, confusion and fear in Satan's kingdom. A murderer from the beginning (Jn 8.44), Satan seeks to destroy the image of God in man. Failing to accomplish this immediately, he cripples a person, degrading and dehumanizing him as he drives him to ruin and self-destruction.

Although all reject this man, Jesus cares about him, frees him from very dire circumstances and restores him to true life.

• For the orthodox Jew, this scene overflows with ceremonial impurity. It is Gentile territory. Demonic control and contact with the dead transmit the highest degree of ritual impurity.

• This man resembles those who reject the truth and are given over to progressive degradation (Ro 1.18-32). They are spiritually dead and in bondage to evil (Eph 2.1-3).

5.6-10 - The author now describes this man's encounter with Jesus. Upon discovering that Jesus has landed nearby, the man runs and falls on his knees before him (3.11; cf Php 2.11; Jas 2.19). Fearfully, he acknowledges Jesus' superior authority, for the news of Jesus' invasion of Satan's domain (3.27) has been spread to his evil agents. In response to what Jesus is already commanding ("Come out of the man, you evil spirit!"), the man shouts "at the top of his voice, 'What do you want with me, Jesus, Son of the Most High God?'" In desperation, he is crying out for God to protect him from the Son of God: "Swear to God that you won't torture me!" Realizing who Jesus is, the evil spirit fears sharing in Satan's final judgment.

Jesus asks the Gerasene, "What is your name?" He replies, "My name is Legion, for we are many." A Roman Legion, composed of approximately 6,000 soldiers, was the finest professional fighting machine of ancient times. Satan had sought to destroy Jesus in the lake before he reached this territory under his control. Unsuccessful in that attempt, he meets Jesus' beachhead landing with an enormous force designed to repel any invasion of non-Jewish areas. Like the Roman legions which occupied land not their own, Satan has long reigned uncontested in the Gentile world; he is determined to stop Jesus at all costs.

The scene presents a power encounter with cosmic consequences. Each recognizes the power behind the other. Satan sees his kingdom invaded by Jesus (3.27). Nevertheless, he plans a counter-attack by an army of evil spirits, hoping against hope to regain dominion. The mention of a Legion of unclean spirits would frighten anyone into retreat. Jesus, however, by the power of his word, strikes terror in the demonic army.

v. 7 - "The Most High God" was a title used by non-Jews in reference to the God of Israel (Ge 14.18f; Isa 14.14; Da 3.26; 4.2; cf Ac 16.17). The use of this title, the geographical references and the presence of a herd of pigs all confirm that this takes place among Gentiles.

v. 8 - Jesus does not touch the demoniac; much less does he use rituals or inflict pain as others did in their exorcisms. He casts out the evil spirits with a word (cf Mt 8.16).

v. 9 - In the pagan world, "it was commonly believed that knowledge of a person's identity and the use of his name conferred magical power to harm and defeat him" (Nineham 43). Some commentators allege that evil spirits identified Jesus (1.24; 3.11) as "their only hope of avoiding destruction by him" (ibid. 113). They presume that Jesus is following popular magical beliefs and asks the Gerasene demoniac's name in order to control him. This interpretation ignores: 1) this is the only case in which Jesus asks for a demoniac's name, and 2) the numerous cases in which Jesus expelled demons without identifying them. More likely, Jesus asks, "What is your name?" because he wants the Gerasene to reflect upon his own identity and he wants the disciples to realize the massive force aligned against him.

• Sometimes the man speaks in his own name, sometimes as mouthpiece for the powers that possess him. This switching from singular to plural underlines the man's chaotic condition.

v. 10 - The concept of the territorial domain of spirits (cf Da 10.12-14,20; Ac 19.35) is reflected in the "high places" (Nu 33.52, etc.) and the "gods of the plains" (1Ki 20.23). Animistic people believe that certain spirits are lords over a territory or a house and make it their abode.

In the Babylonian captivity, Israel struggled to learn that God's presence was not limited to the Promised Land. Jesus taught that true worship is not geographically determined (Jn 4.19-24).

5.11-13 - Defeated in their attempt, the once boastful legion of evil spirits is reduced to begging, again and again, not to be sent out of the area. After inhabiting a man, they now plead to enter a large herd of pigs feeding on the nearby hillside. Although they realize that Jesus is in control, they continue to maneuver. Jesus complies with this request, for he knows the havoc they could wreck if they were to return to the Gerasene (Lk 11.24-26). Far better that they destroy pigs than humans. Characteristically, the evil spirits create more confusion: the pigs rush down the steep bank and drown in the lake over which Jesus has already shown his lordship (4.39).

When Jesus begins teaching in Jewish territory (Capernaum), he is opposed by an unclean spirit (1.24). Later, Satan seeks to destroy Jesus as he crosses the lake to begin his first mission among the Gentiles (4.37-41). Upon arriving in a non-Jewish region, Jesus is opposed by Satan in massive show of strength as portrayed by the name "Legion." These pieces fit together as part of the larger picture of Satan's opposition to God's reign.

There are close parallels between the driving out of evil spirits in Capernaum and in the Decapolis. In both episodes: 1) Jesus initiates his ministry in a new place; 2) the question posed ("What do you want?") has the same construction; 3) the demoniac identifies Jesus in relationship to God; 4) he is fearful of destruction/torture; and 5) he cries out in a loud voice (cf 1.26). The latter case, however, involves a multitude of evil spirits. In other words, what happened in Jewish territory is repeated here in Gentile territory, but under greatly intensified demonic opposition.

Furthermore, in Capernaum the demon identifies Jesus as being from Nazareth, implying that his jurisdiction is limited to that town. In Decapolis, the spirits request repeatedly not to be sent out of the area of their domain (5.10). This implies that Satan claims Gentile country as a part of his realm and that these areas are assigned to these evil spirits as a part of the administrative program of the principalities and powers. In both cases, however, they soon realize that Jesus is not outside his territory; God's Kingdom is not confined geographically (cf 13.10,27; 14.9).

Jesus, "the Holy One of God" (1.24), "the Son of the Most High God" (5.7), is claiming the whole world as God's jurisdiction. Nevertheless, Satan mounts strong opposition against those who penetrate new areas to proclaim the gospel.

vv. 11-13 - Mark avoids the risk of losing his narrative in minutia. Moreover, the Bible does not reveal many details about the inner workings of the spirit world. Where the Scriptures are silent, our explanations must be tentative.

v. 12 - The demons' plea to go into the pigs is a subterfuge to stay in the area in order to reestablish a base of operation. Jesus gives them permission to go into the pigs, not because they ask, but because it is in line with his purpose. The pigs' drowning in the lake probably means that the demons go into the abyss (cf Lk 8.31), their destination until the day of judgment (Rev 9.11; 17.8; 20.1,3; cf 2Pe 2.4; Jude 6).

v. 13 - Any of the following motives could possibly justify the destruction of the pigs:

1) As the ex-demoniac witnesses the great herd of pigs rushing down the steep bank into the lake, he understands that he is now permanently free from further torment. The memory of that sight would be a constant antidote to temptations to doubt his complete break with the past.

2) Israelites were commanded to destroy the instruments of paganism (Ex 23.23-24; Nu 33.52; cf At 19.19). Itioka (202f, 213ff) points out that complete liberation from demonic manifestations is not fully achieved apart from the destruction of everything utilized by the demons for their activities. Otherwise, the spirits can return with greater evil consequences (cf Mt 12.43-45). Thus the destruction of the pigs is a blow against the return of these evil spirits.

3) Their destruction demonstrates Jesus' power in Gentile territory and provides outward signs to convince all observers of the intensity of demonic activity and of its overthrow by Jesus. This prepares the people of the area to hear the gospel.

4) Kelber (Story 31) claims that "By the drowning of the swine Gentile land is exorcised, that is, cleansed of Gentile pollution."

• In the dominion of darkness (Col 1.13) governed by the god of this world (Jn 12.31; 2Co 4.4; 1Jn 5.19), Satan uses every means possible to turn people aside from worshipping the true God. Economic systems, for example, are turned from benefiting humankind into idolatry, enslaving nations through greed and materialism. These pigs may have been raised to be sacrificed to pagan gods in a temple in Gerasa. The loss of about two thousand pigs strikes against Satan's economic and religious control of Gerasenes. The text does not say the pigs were a complete loss; we cannot rule out the possibility of the owners mounting a salvage operation to cut their losses by salting the meat and utilizing the skins.

5.14-17 - Upon hearing from the herdsmen the bad news about the pigs, many from the town and countryside rush out to see for themselves what happened. They are overcome with fear, for they see with Jesus the man none could restrain, seated there, clothed and in a sound mind. Witnesses told them what happened to the man and to the pigs. Since Jesus was the cause of all their upsets, the people plead with him to leave.

No doubt the people reject Jesus for several reasons. Fear of the unknown and the destruction of the area's economic life play a part. They had no interest in the man himself. Their system of values is all distorted. They don't even ask what Jesus can do for them. They just want to get rid of him. So

Jesus embarks for the other side of the lake--after leaving a witness in Decapolis. Although he triumphs over a legion of demons, he does not force himself upon the people.

v. 15 - We assume that Jesus is teaching this man seated at his feet (Lk 8.35) about how God is mercifully establishing his rule among all peoples. As in all other New Testament cases of expelling demons, Jesus does not require that the man have faith as a prerequisite for liberation. Faith comes afterwards, strengthened by Jesus' teaching, tested by his command and demonstrated by obedience. Miracles do not necessarily lead to faith (cf 6.1-6; 8.11-12)

5.18-20 - When they first met, this man wanted Jesus to leave, for they had nothing in common. Now he begs Jesus to allow him to stay with him, for they have everything in common. The man who was set free from demons is now committed to God (cf Ro 6.18). He is bound no longer by chains but by gratitude to Jesus. He begs to be with the one who cares about him.

His new life brings a new desire (2Co 5.17; cf Eph 2.1-10): he wants to go with Jesus (cf 1.16-20, 3.14). His first prayer, however, receives a negative answer. Jesus tests his submission to God's rule by asking him to do something he does not wish. Denied the privilege of following Jesus physically, he follows Jesus' word.

Jesus asks some persons to leave family as a part of following him (1.16-20; 10.29-30). However, he sends this man home alone (cf 6.7) to his people who had abandoned him to a living death. He is given no promises of wealth, comfort or success. Rather than free him from a stressful world, Jesus sends him back into it to initiate reconciliation in his family and community. Those who heard his story from others must hear from the person himself the truth of how God saved him, extending his mercy to such a forsaken Gentile.

Obeying his Lord, the man tells his personal testimony in Gentile territory where Jesus established a foothold. All are "amazed," but this is an inadequate response. Mark does not report other results to the man's witness; he does imply, however, that among the Gentiles there is much "good soil" (cf 4.8,20) where the seed, once it is planted, will take root and produce in others as it did in the Gerasene (cf 7.24ff).

Although the disciples observe what Jesus is doing, it will take them a long time to accept persons of other ethnic groups as potential brothers and sisters in Christ (3.35; cf Peter's attitude toward the Gentile Cornelius, Acts 10). No doubt they will remember this experience and be encouraged when they finally penetrate other Gentile territories to tell about God's mercy.

Jesus' historic victory over a legion of demonic powers alerts those who penetrate new frontiers with the gospel to expect satanic opposition to the advance of God's rule. It also points to Jesus' final victory over the forces of evil.

v. 19 - Among the Jews, Jesus commands the evil spirits to be silent about his identity (1.43; 5.43; 7.36); in Gentile territory, he tells the ex-demoniac to relate what the Lord has done.
v. 20 - Decapolis was a league originally consisting of 10 cities modeled on the Greek pattern of life. Almost all were located east of Lake Galilee. This is Jesus' first entrance into this predominantly Gentile territory, although some from the area had previously come to him (3.8). He ministers to Gentiles again in 7.24-8.9.
• Those Mark describes as "amazed" lack genuine faith and insight into who Jesus is (cf 1.22-27; 2.12; 5.42; 7.37; 9.15; 12.17; cf disciples in 6.51). Some who reject Jesus are amazed (6.2-4; 15.5,44).

3. Jesus Is Victor Over Illness And Death, 5.21-43

The theme of God's mighty power continues in this pericope, giving further insights into Jesus' care for people facing problems that are beyond human solution. Both cases bring ritual uncleanness. Throughout, Jesus affirms the participants' faith and, through instruction and testing, encourages its growth.

Both the sick woman and Jairus' family could well have asked the question, "Why me, Lord?" Like the disciples in the storm and the Gerasene demoniac, these also might reasonably ask, "Why has this happened to us?" In the following narrative, Jesus not only cares for these people in their pain and isolation, he also resolves these "inexplicable problems" as a part of his tender mercies. As Michael Wilcock (28) points out, "Although as sinners we deserve nothing better, it is encouraging to know that Jesus can deal not only with sin and its consequences, but also with the evils we commonly call undeserved."

• Jesus also suffered undeservedly and blamelessly (Heb 2.14-18; 4.14-16). Having shared in our humanity, he cares for us so that we can share with others the comfort received from God (2 Co 1.3-7).

5.21-24a - After his brief entry into Gentile territory, Jesus returns to the other side of the lake (possibly to Capernaum). The Gerasenes had pled with Jesus to leave, but here a large crowd welcomes him. No doubt he resumes his teaching ministry. He is interrupted again, this time by a man named Jairus, who prostrates himself at Jesus' feet, pleading with him on behalf of his dying daughter. "Please come and put your hands on her so that she will be healed and live."

Now Jairus was chief of the synagogue, responsible for the town center with its religious services on the Sabbath and for the school and law court during the rest of the week. Most of the religious leaders would never seek help from Jesus, for as a group they reject him as an impostor (3.6). But Jairus publicly begs Jesus' intervention. A father intercedes for his daughter who is beyond earthly help. By his humble request, he evidently believes that Jesus has supernatural power from God.

Jesus goes with Jairus, without discriminating against him because of the attitudes of other religious leaders. Jesus even does it Jairus' way ("come and touch"). He frequently varies his "methods" (e.g., he cures without touching, 7.24-30), for healing does not depend upon *what Jesus does* but upon *who he is.*

v. 23 - Other parents interceding for their children are presented in 7.26-30 and 9.17-27.
• Jesus transformed interruptions into opportunities to minister. He was sensitive even to importunate people, taking time from the crowds to serve their individual needs. He is the Lord of Time as well as the Lord of Eternity.
v. 24a - Jesus granted Jairus' request, even though religious leaders as a class rejected him.

5.24b-34 - A large crowd follows them, pushing and shoving in their eagerness to see what Jesus will do. Along the way, Jesus suddenly turns around and asks, "Who touched my clothes?" The question brings a disgruntled answer from the disciples. After all, there's always a lot of elbowing in a large crowd.

Jesus, however, keeps looking around to see who had touched his garments. Then a woman comes and falls at his feet. Trembling with fear, she relates her whole story. During twelve years of suffering from a chronic female disorder, she keeps getting worse. Human resources were of no avail, and now her money is all gone. On top of all her physical problems, her hemorrhage makes her and all she touches ceremonially unclean (Lev 15.25-27). She is cut off from the synagogue and the community. "If I just touch Jesus' clothes, I will be healed" (cf 3.10) was the thought that drove her through the crowd to Jesus.

When the woman touched him, Jesus immediately perceived in himself that the power (**dynamis**) which dwells in him had gone forth from him" (v. 30). This power proceeds from Jesus, not from the sick woman. His God-given power is personal in source and personal in application.

Upon hearing her story, the disciples probably wonder about all this delay for just a woman, a poor one at that. Helping her is not like helping Jairus. She's alone, a social outcast. Jairus is a man of status. Maybe he will influence the religious leaders to reverse their attitudes toward Jesus. After twelve years, the nameless woman could have waited a few moments longer. Now that she is healed, why doesn't Jesus attend to Jairus' daughter and talk to the woman later?

Jesus, however, does not rush on. This is an opportune time to teach the woman and the entire crowd, so he says to her, "Daughter, your faith has healed you. Go in peace and be freed from your suffering." She is no longer alone, for she belongs to God's family (cf 3.35). Hopefully Jairus learns that Jesus cares for other "daughters" as well as for his little daughter.

Then Jesus declares, "Your faith has healed you." In Lane's words (193), "it was the grasp of her faith rather than her hand that had secured the healing she sought." Jesus' words counter the popular belief that healing power is transmitted through touching. God honored her faith, even though it was imperfect (cf 9.24), because it was faith in Jesus. Her cure (from the Greek verb **sozein**) is neither automatic nor impersonal; it is the result of God's own gracious decision in response to her faith. Moreover, she has received spiritual salvation as well, for the New Testament characteristically uses **sozein** in a distinctive way to signify "that which saves from all that would ruin one's soul in this life and in the life to come" (Barclay Words 270; cf 3.4).

Jesus gives this woman much more than she sought. By publicly confirming her physical healing, he releases her from hidden fears and lays the ground for her acceptance in the community. She had come to think of herself as a nobody; Jesus gives her dignity. He values her as a person. By enduring the pain of openly telling her story, she gains freedom from her public fears.

In dealing with her basic insecurities, Jesus does not promise her freedom from difficulties (contrary to some popular preaching today). As the Hebrew **shalom** indicates, "Go in peace," means security and wholeness even in the midst of conflicts. Such peace flows from a person's relationship with God (cf Isa 26.3). Through faith in Jesus, she begins a new life.

By combining three important terms (faith, saved and peace), this story presents a dramatic portrayal of God's gift of salvation through faith in Jesus. The example of this woman calls upon each reader to reexamine her/his faith in Jesus Christ.

v. 24b - While Mark sometimes frames one scene in the middle of another, it does not follow that all narratives with one story inserted within another are purely literary constructions. We understand that the woman's interruption was historical and that Jesus used it to teach Jairus as well.

v. 27 - The Hellenistic concept of power transmitted through "touching" finds similar expression today in the precepts of mystic religions such as Hinduism, Buddhism and the New Age. Miracles supposedly come through tapping impersonal "cosmic energy" by "touching." All three Evangelists, however, quote Jesus' affirmation that her faith healed her, a denial that it was a result of magic or fate. In addition, Mark's account refutes any notion of an automatic flow of impersonal power.

v. 30 - Cf **dynamis** in Mark 9.1; 12.24; 13.25, 26; 14.62 (cf Lk 5.17).

v. 34 - Faith (**pistis**, see 1.15) is not mere mental assent to biblical teaching but reliance upon God as actively fulfilling his purposes through Jesus. Faith is a personal response to God's faithfulness.

• Jesus overthrew custom in his attitude to women and children. While a son brought joy, the birth of a daughter was often greeted with indifference; Jesus, however, was deeply concerned for the girl. This woman followed custom, remaining unobserved in public. It was not customary for a man to converse with a strange woman and it was a disgrace for a scholar to speak with a woman on the street (cf Jn 4.27). Furthermore, the "unclean" woman may have sought to avoid making Jesus "unclean" by touching him clandestinely. Jesus, however, does not become "unclean" but the woman becomes "clean" (cf the leper, 1.40-45). He values this woman, speaking with her and publicly commending her for her faith.

5.35-43 - Hopefully, the disciples are learning from Jesus' conversation with the woman. Jairus, too, could benefit, for Jesus' instructions could help him face a more severe testing. While Jesus is still speaking, some men arrive from Jairus' house, saying, "Your daughter is dead. Why bother the teacher any more?"

What Jairus dreaded most has happened. His beloved daughter is dead. He knew she was dying when he went to Jesus, hoping that he could possibly arrive in time to heal his daughter. Now all is lost, for death is so final. If Jesus had not delayed (cf Jn 11.21) to talk to that unimportant woman... As resentment begins to surface, Jesus breaks into his thoughts, telling him to ignore what the men had said. But how can he ignore the heart-breaking reality of his daughter's death?

"Stop being afraid; keep on believing." Jesus claims that the delay does not render him incapable of helping. Not even death should hinder Jairus' confidence in Jesus' ability to confront crises with the power of God invested in him. Jairus' faith is being tested; it will grow as he continues to look to Jesus (Heb 12.1-2) whose word dispels fear.

Peter, James and John are chosen to continue with Jesus. Apparently, they are more responsive to what they have already received and so they are given the opportunity to receive more (cf 4.25). This will afford them an excellent opportunity to know who Jesus is and to convey that to the other disciples.

Jesus prohibits the crowd from accompanying him. There is enough confusion around Jairus' home already. Following Palestinian custom, the sound of wailing and chanting, accompanied by flutes and clapping, fill the air in a public display of mourning. Having asked them the reason for all the commotion (for they were wailing like people who have no hope; cf 1Th 4.13), Jesus affirms, "The child is not dead but asleep." In response, the mourners scoff at Jesus. So he puts all these people out as well.

The mourners, the men who had informed Jairus and the parents themselves know that the girl is dead. Jesus says she is only asleep, for he makes a *theological prognosis*, not a physical diagnosis. Many say death is the end. They see it as a period, whereas it is only a comma. Death, however, is not permanent; it has lost its awful power (1Co 15.54-57). From God's standpoint, it is sleep from which there is an awakening. But Jesus promises more than that. Even though she is dead, it is no more permanent than sleep, for he is going to raise her up. Just as the Old Testament prophets interpreted national and international events theologically rather than politically, Jesus interprets her physical state from God's standpoint.

Fulfilling this implied promise, Jesus takes the girl by the hand and says, *"Talitha koum!"* These words in no way constitute a magical formula or incantation. Mark feels that the richness of Jesus' words could not be conveyed in translation, so he quotes the original phrase before attempting to give its meaning. As Martin (Action 39) beautifully expresses it, Jesus speaks to the little girl in her mother tongue (Aramaic), choosing tender words exactly suited to the occasion and tones as natural as a mother's morning call to a drowsy infant, saying, "Little girl, it's time to get up" (5.41).

The girl stands up and walks around, for she is healed immediately. Her appetite is restored. Her astonished parents can now feed her and care for her. Jesus commands them "not to let anyone know about this," for he is also concerned that the girl be allowed to grow up in a normal way, without being an object of curiosity. Those who scoffed would eventually imagine that she had just been asleep after all. In making provisions for her physical and psychological needs, Jesus shows his concern for the quality of life.

Who is Jesus, this man who restored a dead person to life? This remarkable event gives further insight into that question which underlies the whole gospel, unveiling Jesus as the Lord of life. Yet full knowledge of Jesus as the Victor over death would await that day when death "conquers" him, for it is only through his death that he can be fully known.

The secret of God's rule as present and active in the person of Jesus is revealed to those who "listen" while at the same time it is withheld from "those on the outside" (cf 4.11-12; 4.21-25). In keeping with this emphasis, Jesus "gave strict orders" that they should not tell others what had happened. Those outside had laughed at Jesus (v. 40), unwilling to listen to him. His identity is *hidden* from them. If "those outside" had known who he is, they would have demanded as their right (not as God's merciful act) that he raise their dead before God's appointed time. Jesus' present mission would be thwarted, so he avoids the trap of being known only as a miracle worker.

Jesus' command to secrecy was not universal. He told the Gerasene to tell (5.19). The sick woman tried to keep things secret, but Jesus brought her story out into the open and publicly proclaimed her cured. Along with the girl's parents, three disciples are chosen to witness the miracle (see 5.37). In each of these cases, faith is present, opening their understanding as well as saving them. But it does no good to reveal who Jesus is to people who already have their own answers, as the following narrative portrays (6.1-6).

So in the context, Jesus does not command absolute silence. That would be an impossibility. Rather, he wants it kept as private as possible. By avoiding unnecessary publicity, he can continue his ministry, actively bringing salvation and peace in this world.

v. 36 - Jesus' words, "Fear not," remind us of the same phrase in the theophanies (Ge 15.1; 21.17; 26.24; 46.3; Jdg 6.23; Da 10.12,19), when God appeared to his servants to save in times of crisis.
v. 37 - These three will also witness the transfiguration (9.2-8), with its proleptic view beyond death.
• While "sleep" is a New Testament term used in reference to death (Jn 11.11-13; Ac 7.60; 1Ti 4.14-15), it does not deny the reality or heartache of death. Rather, since Jesus conquered death (Jn 14.19; 1Ti 1.10; 1Co 15.26), no believer should behave in the face of death as those who have no hope.
v. 39 - The parents are convinced that the girl is dead. This is borne out by their "complete amazement" (v. 42) when she is immediately and completely alive. Her resurrection contradicts the advocates of reincarnation who claim that, after death, rebirth occurs in a new body or a new form of life.

In these three narratives (4.35-5.43), the mighty power of the Kingdom of God is demonstrated in the present age, under the compassionate authority of Jesus. They are proleptic, giving the believer insight into that day "when death shall die." All who are in Christ *already* experience the results of Jesus' resurrection, although *not yet* in their fullest measure.

4. Jesus Is Rejected In His Home Town, 6.1-6a

This pericope is noticeably different. In the preceding narratives, faith was growing; here, in Jesus' hometown, it is lacking. As a result, Jesus limits his teaching to a short proverb and his healing to a few sick people. In spite of these differences, this paragraph forcefully confronts the reader with the same question, Who is Jesus?

Both the previous division (1.14-3.6) and this one (3.6-6.6a) close with rejection of Jesus resulting from failure to discern who he is. Jesus responds to both groups with a proverb. Following each of these units, Mark reports how Jesus intensifies his ministry and prepares his disciples for service.

6.1-3 - As a rabbi accompanied by his disciples, Jesus goes to his hometown and begins to teach in the synagogue (1.21, 38-39; 3.1). His wisdom amazes his audience and the reality of his mighty works is acknowledged by all. Yet they question the source of his capabilities (cf 3.22; 11.28).

The whole community knows that Jesus' brothers and sisters are just ordinary people. They know Jesus, too, for he grew up and learned a trade in Nazareth. His very humanity is an obstacle to thinking of him in any other way. The town buzzes with exclamations like: "Where did this man get these things?" If God were the source of his teaching and miracles, why wasn't that evident when he was a child among them?

To top it all off, they know about Jesus' birth. Normally, a man is known as the son of his father. To call Jesus "Mary's son" is a calculated slur on the legitimacy of his birth, for in the East no man, whether his father were living or not, was known by reference to his mother.

Refusing to believe that God is at work through Jesus, they express their resentment by referring to him contemptuously as "this man" (cf "this fellow" in 2.7). Initially many were amazed at Jesus; now they reject him.

v. 1 - Although the text mentions only "his home town," this scene took place in Nazareth (cf 1.9, 24; 10.47; 14.67; 16.6), possibly later than the experience recorded in Luke 4.16-30. This narrative prepares the reader for Jesus' rejection on a much wider scale.
v. 3 - Following custom, Jesus probably learned Joseph's trade of a craftsman before beginning his ministry. Many skilled Nazarene craftsmen worked in Sepphoris, an hour's walk away.
• This slur on Jesus' birth supports the historicity of the Virgin Birth. It is inconceivable that Mary's conception before marriage could be kept secret in a small town like Nazareth. The people know about it but they reject Mary and Joseph's explanation (Mt 1.18-25; Lk 1.26-45).

With its parallel in Mt 13.55-56, this verse presents the most detailed information on the family of Joseph and Mary. Mt 1.25 is understood to mean that children were born to Mary subsequent to the birth of Jesus. Mark nowhere mentions Joseph, who may have died earlier. Although Jesus' own family did not believe on him at this time (Jn 7.5), certain members play prominent roles in the early church after the resurrection (e.g., Acts 1.14; 15.13; 21.18; 1Co 9.5).

This is Mark's last reference to the mother of Jesus. In Acts 1.14, the last reference in the New Testament to Jesus' mother, Mary prays along with the others. Prayers are not directed to her nor through her as though she were a mediatrix (cf 1Ti 2.5). To consult her subsequent to her death would be in violation of Dt 18.11. The greatest respect that can be shown to Mary, "blessed among women" (Lk 1.42), is to follow her only recorded order, "Do whatever Jesus tells you" (Jn 2.5).

• The Greek word **skandalizo** connotes more than "take offence." It means that they reject Jesus and turn away from God. As rejection here led to proclaiming the gospel in the surrounding country (6.6b; 7.24ff), so rejection by Israel in general led to the mission to the Gentiles (Ac 13.46; Ro 9.33; 1Co 1.23).

6.4-6a - Orthodox Jews were convinced that the Spirit of God had been quenched due to Israel's sin, and thus the prophetic line had been cut off since the death of Malachi. By referring to himself as a prophet, Jesus reiterates his message that God's reign is dawning. The Spirit is present, God is speaking, and Jesus is his eschatological messenger. While some in Israel consider Jesus to be a prophet (6.14-16; cf 14.65), in 8.27-29 he makes it clear that he is much more than a prophet.

Jesus is a particular kind of prophet: he is "a prophet without honor." He is not the first of God's servants to be rejected by his own people, however. Comparing his experience to theirs (12,4-5; cf Heb 11), Jesus applies a popular saying to this occasion: "Only in his hometown, among his relatives and in his own house is a prophet without honor." Even though the people of Nazareth deny it, Jesus is a prophet. He teaches and interprets the will of God, and like other prophets, he is scorned by his own people.

Earlier, we noted that Jesus' authority was limited by human will (1.40-45). Now (v. 5) we see that his power is also limited by the lack of faith. "He could not" does not mean that Jesus is powerless apart from people's faith. As Cranfield (197) explains, "in the absence of faith he could not work mighty works *in accordance with the purpose of his ministry*; for to have worked miracles where faith was absent would, in most cases anyway, have been merely to have aggravated men's guilt and hardened them against God."

His mighty works (**dynameis**) are a part of his self-revelation. They are not an end in themselves; they are a part of the proclamation of the gospel. They are, however, subject to misinterpretation. Where there is no perception of who Jesus is, where there is no sensitivity to his person, the result is astonishment (v. 2), leading to open unbelief (v. 3). Jesus does not force belief. The Nazarenes know that Jesus has power but they lack faith that God is at work in him. Nor do they respond to his teaching, an essential key to understanding his work. As a result, he withholds his miraculous works from them (cf 4.24-25).

The pericope closes on a sad note: Jesus is amazed at their lack of faith. In spite of all their advantages, the people of his hometown have no idea who Jesus really is. By rejecting him, they reject God's rule and the opportunity to reach their potential as individuals.

6.5 - This passage does not mean that Jesus works his cures by suggestion and is powerless when the sick person has no confidence in him. The power resides in Jesus, not in the person cured (5.30).

Neither does it mean that each sick person can be healed only if he or she has enough faith (or that a person is not healed because of lack of faith; cf 9.24). Healing is not dependent upon the subjective faith of the person but upon Jesus' will (cf 1.40-41). Many ask the wrong question: Do I have enough faith for Jesus to heal me? The correct question is: Am I willing to commit myself to Jesus' rule, following him along the way, trusting his will to be best for me? (Adapted from Swartley Mark: Way 83-85).

The sick who go from one religious group to another, seeking to be healed, may find temporary relief. Many are manipulated to become dependent upon the "healers." Full satisfaction escapes them. On the other hand, those who seek God himself, for what he wants to give, are never disappointed. They find fulfillment in the whole of their being.

• Many people seek miracles above all else. Miracles of themselves, however, do not bring persons to true faith. Best (Disciples 194f) warns the church to "beware of presenting Jesus as a miracle worker to the world, for the world may see the miracles and not be convinced."

v. 6a - Jesus' humanity is seen here in his being astounded by the intensity of the rejection by those whom he has known since boyhood. The fully human character of God's Son is one of the glorious aspects of the gospel. Unfortunately, his humanity has frequently been neglected or forgotten, with emphasis given almost exclusively to his divinity. Docetism, a heresy that began in the early church, denied Jesus' complete humanity, affirming that he only seemed to be human.

- PART 4 -
THE EXPANSION OF JESUS' MINISTRY 6.6b - 8.26

We have accompanied Jesus as he creates the new people of God. Mark pictures three steps in the expansion of this eschatological community. First, Jesus calls four *disciples* and leads them in basic experiences; then, he creates the *twelve*, teaching them about the kingdom through parables and mighty works and giving them insights into the nature of the opposition. These two steps constitute two divisions of Mark's Gospel (1.14-3.6; 3.7-6.6a); the next division begins with 6.6b.

In this third step, Jesus sends them out as *apostles*, an extension of his own mission. As the disciples' responsibilities increase, however, their understanding does not grow at the same pace. As a result, their failures become more evident. Sometimes they resemble the opposition, in marked contrast to the response of Gentiles whom Jesus graciously serves.

This division includes two cycles of events, the second repeating the pattern of the first:

6.35-44	Miraculous provision of food	8.1-9
6.45-53	Crossing the lake	8.10
7.1-23	Dispute with the Pharisees	8.11-13
7.24-30	Conversation about bread	8.14-21
7.31-36	Healing miracle	8.22-26
7.37	Confession of faith	8.27-30

The first events in Galilee, followed by the negative reaction of Jewish authorities (7.1-23), are set in contrast to the examples of positive responses as Jesus does among the Gentiles (7.24-8.9) what he did among the Jews.

These experiences are not mere repetitions. Jesus is deliberately providing opportunities for his disciples to understand his person and mission. Through their experiences, Mark invites the reader to take a second look and see their significance for all disciples. The author skillfully employs the words "bread" (sometimes translated "food"), "understanding" and "desert" (or "wilderness") to bind the whole unit together. As the narrative progresses, the reader begins to realize that these terms have a deeper meaning than meets the casual eye.

Throughout this division, the pressure on the disciples to know and understand Jesus increases. As it closes, the reader senses the tension, wondering when the disciples will see clearly. This question leads into the second half of Mark.

• Rhoads and Michie (47f) affirm that "the two-step progression is the most pervasive stylistic feature in the gospel," occurring in phrases, episodes, etc. These progressions enable the reader to see crucial emphases or clarifications that often lie in the second step.

• Swartley (Structure 198ff) calls this the "wilderness-section." Just as God sustained Israel in the wilderness (cf Ps 78), so here Jesus feeds, tests and teaches the new people of God.

A. JESUS GIVES THE TWELVE MISSIONARY RESPONSIBILITY, 6.6b-56

In the very beginning of this new phase, Jesus sends the twelve out to continue and extend what he has been doing. Upon their return, however, their ability to assume additional responsibilities is hindered by lack of understanding.

1. Jesus Sends Out The Twelve, 6.6b-13

In parallel with the beginning of the two previous divisions (1.14; 3.7), this one also begins with Jesus' public ministry and leads immediately to the disciples. They are central in Jesus' plans to continue and extend his ministry. Here, for the first time, the disciples are separated from Jesus for a period of time as he sends them out, on their own.

The "sent ones" are not novices. They have already spent time with Jesus. They have learned some of the basic principles of discipleship. Jesus will continue to instruct them as they gain experience in serving people.

6.6b-7 - Rejected in Nazareth, Jesus takes the initiative of presenting God's rule to the surrounding villages as a part of his itinerant ministry. Having called the disciples to be with him (1.16-20), he had chosen the twelve (3.14) and was teaching them by word and deed (3.20-6.6a). Now he sends them forth (**apostellein**) on their first mission, even though their knowledge is incomplete (cf 8.21) and their faith weak (4.40). Upon their return, he will continue their training, for the workers must be prepared to minister in his absence.

On this tour among the villages, the twelve are to do as they saw Jesus do on previous missions. Although they are empowered by him, the authority is not theirs; it belongs to him. It is an unmerited gift. To be "given authority" means they serve under Jesus, are dependent upon him and are responsible to deliver his message according to his instructions. They should never forget that their mission is an extension of his.

He sends them out "two by two" (the pairs are named in Mt 10.2-4). As two witnesses (Dt 17.6; 19.15; Nu 35.30), they will confirm the message preached and report on the response to their ministry. Working in teams is the norm for the churches in the New Testament (Acts 8.14; 15.36ff; 1Co 9.6), expressing the community of faith formed around the person of Jesus. It emphasizes partnership in ministry, in contrast to the personality cult so frequently created around a charismatic leader in modern religious movements.

v. 6b - The Jewish historian Josephus reported that Galilee had 204 towns and villages, none with less than 15,000 people. While he is frequently accused of exaggeration, Galilee was an impressive field for ministry.

v. 7 - The verb "send out" (**apostello**) appeared first in 1.2, and returns repeatedly throughout Mark. The "sent ones" (6.30) are given authority and responsibility to transmit God's word. "Apostle" is used in the New Testament in reference to the Twelve, to Paul (Gal 1.1) and to others as well (Ac 14.4, 14; Ro 16.7; 1Co 15.5-7, etc.). The twelve were sent out as an expeditionary force to be followed by others.

While some are separated in a special way for missionary endeavor, all believers are called to participate in the spread of the gospel. This is God's plan for the church.

• Just as "the twelve" signified the forming of God's new people (3.14), the concept of God's people as his flock (Jer 23; Eze 34) is implicit in Mark, especially in 6.6b-8.9. The True Shepherd sends out his twelve undershepherds to continue and extend his work, forming the new Israel.

6.8-11 - Beyond giving them a ministry to perform (cf 1.17), Jesus proceeds to brief them on how to perform it. Their acts and attitudes must reinforce the message they proclaim.

He instructs them to take a staff and sandals for travelling from village to village. These are essential items for their urgent mission, just as they were when the Israelites undertook their journey (Ex 12.11).

Jesus sends them out to give (they have so much to give, for their message is related to God's "indescribable gift", 2Co 9.15). They will receive in return. They need take no provisions; God will provide for Jesus' ambassadors. They need no beggar's bag, since they are God's servants and not like the beggar-priests of that day. They will not "peddle the word of God for profit" (2Co 2.17) but freely give the message. By not taking bread, they learn to trust in God's ability to supply (Mt 6.11), rather than in their own means. Without money or extra equipment, they can not bargain as a back-up measure. By learning to trust God for these daily needs, they will be prepared for much greater demands upon their faith.

Jesus instructs them as to life in the villages, too. A second tunic, normally used for covering at night, is not needed because God will provide them with shelter at night. They are to accept the hospitality offered, without seeking better accommodations. Moving from house to house might create a competitive spirit among the people, as well as involve the twelve in a round of time-consuming social activities. A simple life style sets apart Jesus' emissaries from those religious authorities known for their love of feasts and pride in dress (cf 12.38-40). To spread the word is top priority; all else is secondary.

God will provide for their needs through the people they serve. As people repent in response to the message, they form a community of faith in which interdependence is acknowledged and mutual care is practiced. The twelve share the word; those who receive it share food and shelter. Their mutual dependence and reciprocal care are God's provision for each.

In this way, Jesus is laying the foundations for his church. Interdependence and mutual care are a part of life in the body of Christ as exemplified by the believers in Jerusalem (Acts 2.42-47; 4.32-35). Those who receive the word "share all good things" with those who teach them (Gal 6.6). By sticking to the task, those who concentrate on teaching "earn their keep" (Mt 10.10, Lk 10.7; 1Ti 5.18; cf Acts 16.15). They humbly accept without complaint what is offered them, even though that is a very difficult task for fishermen and other self-sufficient folks. These characteristics, however, are essential for the community of faith. "The Christian principle is not proud independence, but a willingness to accept the risk and obligations of mutual dependence" (Moule 48).

Jesus was not received in every place (5.17; 6.1-6), and his servants can expect to be rejected in some places, for they are not greater than their Master. Pious Jews returning from Gentile regions shook the dust off their feet as a sign of separation from defilement. In like manner, Jesus instructs his emissaries to make it clear that those who persist in rejecting them and their message, whether Jews or Gentiles, are heathen and must answer for themselves before God (cf Acts 13.51; 18.6). Any person who receives/rejects the messenger, receives/rejects Jesus who sent him or her (cf Mt 10.40).

These instructions do not constitute literal commandments for all time and all cultures; their temporary nature can be seen in 8.14 and Lk 22.35f. They are set in the Palestinian social customs of that time. The principles behind them, however, were valid for missionaries sent out by the churches in Rome--and continue to be valid today. They call upon messengers to trust in God's provision for a simple life-style while they live out the gospel they preach and clarify to all the ultimate issues of accepting/rejecting God's rule.

v. 8 - In relating Jesus' instructions to the twelve, Matthew and Luke both share Mark's emphasis: God will sustain them, for they go as Jesus' ambassadors. The differences in some details are possibly due to the Evangelists' emphases upon the cultural situations of their original readers.

• "Bread" (or "loaves") is a key word in this division, used 17 times between 6.6b and 8.19. It is linked to "hearing" (4.12) and to "understanding" (6.52; 7.14; 8.17, 21) and to failing to understand (7.18; 8.17). Here "bread" is meant literally; later, it acquires symbolic significance (cf 6.38; 14.22).

• A staff as a walking stick is readily understood. Some writers believe it had symbolic meaning. "The staff permitted in Mark is the walking stick or shepherd's crook which became the symbol of office, while the rod prohibited by Matthew and Luke was the shepherd's club designed for protection" (Lane 207). Minear (80) suggests that since the same word was used for the shepherd's rod and for the king's scepter, "staff" symbolized that the twelve are sent by the Shepherd-King.

• As a caring community, the church is instructed to share with God's people (Ro 12.13). "Created in Christ Jesus to do good works" (Eph 2.10; 2Co 9.8), its loving concern extends "to all people" (Gal 6.9-10), even to one's enemies (Lk 6.12; Ro 12.9-21).

• Prior to following Jesus, the fishermen supported themselves through their own efforts. To depend upon others now would be a difficult adjustment for the twelve, requiring humility on the part of those who receive as well as the generosity of those who give.

v. 10 - To offer hospitality is emphasized for all believers (1Pe 4.9) and is a qualification for overseers (1Ti 3.2; Tit 1.8). Because some itinerant workers abused the hospitality offered, the *Didache* (a second century church document) limited their stay to 1 or 2 days. A three-day stay indicated false intentions. The modern saying is less gracious: guests, like fish, smell after three days.

6.12-13, 30 - The twelve are not responsible for others' response, but they are responsible for their own obedience. As commanded, they go out and "preach." When they return (v. 30), they report all they had "taught." They have not disobeyed Jesus' instructions to "preach"; good preaching always includes teaching.

The twelve pattern their mission after Jesus' own ministry. They teach what Jesus proclaimed, that men and women should repent for God's Kingdom is near (1.15; cf 1.4). They present evidences of the power of God's rule by freeing the demoniacs and healing the sick (v. 13).

After inserting the story of another preacher of repentance (6.14-29), Mark states that the apostles reported back to Jesus (v. 30). Beyond stating that their ministry provoked Herod's guilty conscience (vv. 14-16), the author does not elaborate on the mission's success, although "many people coming and going" (v. 31) implies a popular response.

v. 12 - The terms "preach," "teach" and "speak the word" are often synonymous in Mark.

v. 13 - The reason why the twelve (unlike Jesus) anointed sick people with oil remains uncertain. Oil was widely used as medicine in the ancient world (cf Isa 1.6; Lk 10.34). Possibly it symbolizes God's grace, although it may have been used as an aid to faith.

The use of oil in prayers for the sick is prescribed only in James 5.14. Although Mark 6.13 and James 5.14 are claimed as precedence for the Roman Catholic sacrament of supreme unction (which includes "forgiveness of sins"), neither passage supports this practice. Henry Swete (119) says "Traces of a ritual use of the unction of the sick appear first among Gnostic practices of the second century."

2. The Death of John the Baptist, 6.14-29

The beginning (verses 14-16) of this narrative about Herod ties this event to the mission of the twelve (6.12,30). After introducing Herod's opinion about who Jesus is, the narrative about John the Baptist's death provides insights into the question of where Jesus is going.

In contrast to those who live to please God, the sketch of Herod portrays the character of one who lives according to his own desires.

6.14-16 - Word about Jesus reaches all classes of people. They all concur about his miraculous powers; they disagree, however, about the source of Jesus' authority. While the religious authorities denounce him as an agent of Satan (3.22), others recognize him as a man of God like the ancient prophets. Some claim that he is the prophet Elijah, whom God promised to send "before that great and dreadful day of the Lord comes" (Mal 4.5; 3.1; cf Dt 18.15).

Reports of the mission of Jesus' ambassadors reaches Herod Antipas, tetrarch of the territory where the disciples are working. As he wonders about Jesus, Herod naturally remembers John the Baptist, whom he knew to be "a righteous and holy man" (v. 20). Herod has special reasons to be interested in John the Baptist, for he had ordered John's death. He concludes that Jesus is none other than John, raised from the dead (cf 8.27-29; 15.35).

Thus the question, "Who is Jesus?" gives Mark the opportunity to return to the story of John the Baptist, last mentioned when he was imprisoned (1.14). John's death took place earlier. Nevertheless it is appropriately mentioned here, for the Twelve, like John, preach repentance. Will they also be imprisoned and killed?

v. 14 - By local custom, Herod Antipas, the youngest son of Herod the Great (Mt 2.1), was called king, whereas his official title was tetrarch (Lk 3.19). He ruled over Galilee and Perea ("beyond" the Jordan) from 4 B.C. to 39 A.D. Only Luke (23.7-12) records Jesus' appearance before him.

• Christian work done out in the villages does not escape the attention of the authorities. When "local councils" or "governors and kings" bring them to trial, Jesus' ambassadors have the opportunity to witness to them as well (13.9). Political leaders also need the opportunity to hear, repent and believe.

v. 15 - Elijah was one of the great personalities of the Old Testament (1Ki 17-19; 21; 2Ki 1-2). On the basis of Malachi 3.1 and 4.5, Elijah or one like him was expected to prepare the way for God's judgment and salvation in the last days (cf 1.6). He appears in the Transfiguration (9.2-8); his relationship to John the Baptist is discussed in Mark (9.10-13). Some say he is one of the two witnesses in Revelation 11.

6.17-20 - Mark fills in background on John's death. Herod knew John was a good man and "liked to listen to him" (cf the seed in rocky places, 4.16-17). Full of contradictions and conflicts, Herod also feared John and was greatly puzzled by him (v. 20). He did not repent, although John kept telling him, "It isn't lawful for you to have your brother's wife" (Lev 18.16; 20.21).

Herodias, however, was determined to kill John. Since she was aware of Herod's ambiguous feelings about his prisoner, she awaited the opportune time to manipulate him into ordering John to be beheaded. That opportunity came at Herod's birthday banquet.

v. 17 - Josephus attributes political motives to Herod for John's arrest. Mark, however, gives the moral reason. Each writer reported the same fact in keeping with his basic interpretation of life.
• According to Josephus, John was imprisoned at Machaerus, a fortress east of the Dead Sea. The Synoptics do not name the location of his death.

6.21-29 - This tragic story is well known for its dramatic elements. Nevertheless, the reader may wonder about why Mark, known for the brevity of his descriptions, dedicates so much space to this account. Since Mark began the pericope with opinions about who Jesus is, he most likely intends to confront the reader with this same question in terms of a king and of a preacher of repentance.

Jesus came as the herald of God's Kingdom (1.14-15). The subject of his kingship really comes to the fore in chapter 15. Here, near the middle of his narrative, the author provides a sketch of an earthly ruler, to encourage the reader "to contemplate in what ways and to what extent it is appropriate to speak of Jesus [as king]" (Robert M. Fowler 121).

The contrast between God's Kingdom and Herod's stands out in this pericope. Herod binds a free man and delivers him to death; Jesus frees the enslaved, giving them life in God's Kingdom. In Herod's kingdom, authority is exercised for personal benefit; Jesus came to serve others with compassion and to give his life as a ransom (10.45). Herod and Herodias, controlled by frailties, adultery and intrigue, are a sad but true picture of much of humanity. Refusing to live by God's decrees, they assert their independence; their self-rule delivers them over as slaves to their own passions. Vengeance becomes more important than honor; grudges lead to violence and death.

John is pictured as the forerunner of Jesus in ministry. Similar to that preacher of repentance, Jesus preaches "Repent and believe" (1.15). After stating that John was "delivered up" to prison (1.14), Mark repeatedly calls attention to Jesus being "delivered up" (9.31; 10.33; 14.10,41; 15.15; cf Isa 53.6). John's condemnation by Herod invites comparison with Jesus' trial by Pilate (15.1-15). Their judges also show similar character traits. Herod and Pilate are impressed by God's servants and are reluctant to condemn them. However, both are people-pleasers, manipulated by others, authorities without authority.

In death, John is also a forerunner of Jesus. John's call for repentance (1.4; 6.18) brought him imprisonment and death. Jesus also preaches repentance (1.15) and he will be killed by evil men. Paradoxically, the Kingdom Jesus proclaims is made possible by his undeserved suffering and death. John's death prepares the reader for Jesus' death. What happened in John's life finds fulfillment only in Jesus, and what happened in Jesus' ministry has the cross in view.

In a sense, Jesus becomes the "forerunner" of the disciples, for they are called to follow him. They may also face death as a result of preaching repentance. So Mark seeks to prepare his readers to pay the price of following Jesus, lest they "quickly fall away" (4.17). God's present rule does not mean freedom from suffering (8.34).

In this hedonistic world, where suffering is to be avoided at all costs, today's readers need to understand that the gospel does not promise freedom from difficulties. Rather, in following Jesus, one must be prepared to leave behind family and possessions (6.8-10; 10.28-30), to leave behind life itself (6.27; 8.34-36). Along the way, however, one does not walk alone. The disciple is in good company, for he or she is following Jesus in the way of the cross.

John's disciples pay him the final tribute of taking his body and laying it in a tomb (v. 29). Jesus did not receive this care from his disciples; his body was taken and laid in a tomb by an outsider (15.43). He was abandoned by those closest to him.

Mark's account also constitutes a final tribute to John as one who did not hesitate to incur the wrath of the great and powerful. His illustrious example of moral courage ought to characterize all believers. Anyone who is a respecter of persons does not serve God well.

v. 21 - Herod's banquet for the elite stands in contrast to the simple fare of Jesus' emissaries (in the preceding pericope) and to the plain meal Jesus offers the multitude (in the next narrative).

v. 22 - Normally, custom would not permit a member of a ruling family to dance before strangers. However, Herodias' daughter's sensual dancing (as implied) is consistent with the immoral lives of the Herodian family and this vitiated occasion. Consumed by a desire for vengeance, Herodias willingly sacrifices her daughter's honor in order to get back at John. The whole scene demonstrates the progressive degeneration of godlessness. Those who refuse God's revelation are delivered over to their own sinful desires, lusts and depraved minds (Romans 1.24-32).

v. 23 - Herod did not have the power to give away any of his territory; he ruled at Rome's good pleasure. When he lost favor in A.D. 39, he was deposed and sent into exile.

3. Jesus Feeds Five Thousand, 6.30-44

The feeding of the five thousand is one of the few stories narrated in all four Gospels. Mark refers back to this miracle (6.52) and later relates a similar event (8.1-10). Jesus himself calls attention to both miracles (8.14-21). Evidently it is significant to the development of the gospel and to the perception of who Jesus is.

Although the crowds supply the occasion for this miracle, Mark does not focus on them. He directs the readers' attention to Jesus' compassion and actions on behalf of the multitude in contrast to the attitudes of the disciples towards these people.

Presenting all the evidences of an eyewitness account, this vivid narrative brings to a close one mission of the twelve (6.7-13; 6.30) while introducing other missions (6.33-56) prior to the culmination of Jesus' Galilean ministry.

6.30-34 - In this transitional passage, verses 30 and 31 look backward, closing the narrative about the mission of the Twelve (6.7-13). The apostles (6.7) report back to Jesus on all they had done and taught. Although their ministry benefited those served (6.12), Mark emphasizes the needs of the disciples themselves.

Jesus' invitation to rest is an expression of his pastoral care for the disciples. Beyond his concern for their physical welfare, his call also envisions their need for quality time alone with him. After facing the pressures of the crowd in his first mission, Jesus withdrew to pray. This led to a clear definition of his mission (1.35-39). While healing others, disciples are not exempt from the stress of working with people. Mindful of their needs, Jesus calls them apart.

Verses 33 and 34 look forward, describing the desert setting of Jesus' ministry to the multitude. In Israel's experience, the wilderness (i.e., uninhabited area) meant a place of rest (cf Jer 31.2) and of testing (Ex 16). Mark's triple mention of the solitary place (6.31, 32. 35) informs the reader that this will be a proving ground for the disciples, as it had been for Jesus (1.12).

The crowds cut short the disciples' time alone with Jesus. Nevertheless, they have many opportunities to learn as Jesus teaches the multitude. At the end of the day, Jesus focuses on the disciples' particular needs as he tests their motives and gives them unparalleled opportunities to gain insights into their mission.

Upon arriving in this remote place, the disciples find a large crowd waiting for them. Will this crowd increase the disciples' workload and give them no opportunity to eat or rest (3.20; 6.31)? Will these undershepherds be false shepherds who "only take care of themselves" (Eze 34.2)?

Jesus saw the crowd as "sheep without a shepherd." Centuries earlier, a leader named Moses taught Israel (Ex 24.12; Dt 4.1; 6.1) and knew its needs. As he neared the end of his life, he asked God to appoint a leader "so the Lord's people will not be like sheep without a shepherd" (Nu 27.17). Later, God promised to send a king like David to be their shepherd (Eze 34.23f). Now Jesus appears as the Shepherd-King, tending the flock (Isa 40.11; Mic 5.4-5). In this beautiful scene of loving care, Jesus fulfills God's promise that "I myself will tend my sheep" (Eze 34.15).

This Shepherd is no mercenary, motivated by self-interest (cf Jn 10.1-18). Although tired and hungry like his disciples, he has compassion on the people and begins to teach them many things, "guiding them in the paths of righteousness" (Ps 23.3).

v. 31 - The "you" is emphatic here ("you yourselves come") and in verse 37 ("you yourselves give them something to eat").
• The phrase "come rest" reminds José C. Pallares (35) of the phrase "beside restful waters" in Psalm (23.2), just as Jesus' "teaching" (6.34) guides in the righteous life God desires (23.3).
v. 32 - Mark's geographical information here is scanty, but we can approximate the itinerary. After the twelve reported to Jesus, they traveled toward Bethsaida (Lk 9.10-12), less than 3 miles east of Capernaum. Probably the boat kept close to shore, visible to the crowd as it ran ahead. Jesus taught and fed the multitude "in a remote place" where food and lodging were not obtainable. That evening, Jesus sends the boat on ahead to Bethsaida (6.45). After hours of rowing against the wind (6.48), the disciples land at Gennesaret (6.53), approximately 5 miles west of Bethsaida. After another boat trip (8.13,22), they finally reach Bethsaida. Then they go north to villages near Caesarea Philippi (8.27).
v. 33 - Many "saw *them* and recognized *them*," i.e., the missionaries who had served in their villages. In 6.54, "people recognized *Jesus*."
v. 34 - Expressing the highest type of sympathy, the word "compassion" is used in the New Testament only of Jesus (8.2; Mt 9.36; 14.14; 15.32) and denotes a deep concern which expresses itself in active assistance. In Mt 18.27; Lk 10.33; 15.20, Jesus uses the word in figures that have a close connection with himself.
• Jesus is the true Shepherd-King, in contrast to Herod, who cares only for himself. As Lane (226) observes, Mark's comments "provide the indispensable background for understanding the feeding narrative that follows." The author returns to the imagery of "sheep without a shepherd" in 14.27.

Both Nu 27 and Eze 34 speak of caring for the flock "in the wilderness." God's people are frequently called sheep (e.g., Psalms 23, 77, 78, 80; Zec 7-14). The concept of the Shepherd-King is implicit in Jer 23.4-6. John 10 emphasizes Jesus as the true Shepherd. The Book of Revelation enhances this imagery with its portrayal of the Lamb who is the Shepherd (7.17).

6.35-38 - Jesus continues his teaching through the day. It has been a long day for the disciples. By late afternoon, they are ready to quit. They express their resentment of the crowd which had interfered with their need for rest and food by asking Jesus to send the people away to take care of themselves. They neither understand what Jesus is doing nor share his compassion for the people being served. True shepherds don't send sheep out on their own; they care for them (cf 4.38). Mark's analysis of Jesus' motivation serves to remind his readers then--and now--that compassion is indispensable in Christian service.

In response, Jesus commands them, "*You* give them something to eat" (v. 37). No doubt this word comes as a shock. Does Jesus really expect them to feed the multitude? He is testing them, hoping to awaken more understanding (cf 6.52); he "already had in mind what he was going to do" (Jn 6.6).

Startled by his command, their first reaction could have been, "Who do you think we are?" Their second response might be, "Who are you, commanding us to do the impossible?" When terrified earlier, they asked, "Who is this?" (4.41). Yet they have not faced that question seriously enough to come up with the answer. The correct answer is the missing piece essential for the whole picture to begin making sense. Even their own identity is dependent upon knowing who Jesus is.

If they had known who he is, they could have said, "We can't do that; but you can, for you are God's Anointed. You can perform greater deeds than Moses did in the wilderness. We'll be glad to obey you in any way we can."

Rather than accept Jesus' challenge, with a tone of reproof they argue the impossibility of buying enough bread for such a crowd (cf Nu 11.13). By becoming defensive, they avoid further risks.

The compassionate Jesus then guides them in accord with their level of understanding. He proceeds to feed the multitude just as he would have done had they responded correctly. He involves the disciples in the process, giving them rudimentary commands which do not require understanding, only obedience. Hopefully, understanding will increase with their participation. In the future, when Jesus is no longer with them, they may recall that Jesus is the Shepherd of leaderless people.

Faced with Jesus' command to feed the people, the disciples see only the impossibility of complying. Their resources are few (6.8-9); their mission experience has made them aware of the cost of bread in terms of the income of the villagers. A day laborer would work for almost a year to make enough money to buy bread for such a crowd. The disciples emphasize what they do not have.

Jesus is not distressed about what they do not have. He tells them to take an inventory of what they have. When that is turned over to Jesus, with his blessing it is more than sufficient.

v. 35 - Judaism's eschatological expectation included the belief that the last and decisive age of salvation would begin with the appearance of the Messiah in the wilderness.

v. 37 - The disciples' question finds parallels with Moses (Ex 17.4) and with Elisha's servant (2Ki 4.43)], with lack of understanding (Nu 11.22) and with the abundance provided (Ex 16.8, 2Ki 4.44).

• A farm worker was paid a denarius for a day's work. Considering Sabbaths, seasonal unemployment, etc., 200 denarii represent approximately a year's income.

v. 38 - The second--and main--meal of the day was normally eaten in the late afternoon and consisted of bread, fruit, a hot dish and water. Meat and wine only appeared on special occasions. Similar to pita bread, the flat circular bread used by the common people was made of the less expensive barley. The fishing industry on the shores of the lake offered dried and salted fish for local consumption and for export.

• Many writers find symbolic meaning in the numbers (e.g., the five loaves represent the five books of Moses). The allegorical interpretation of miracles is questionable (as with parables).

While some scholars deny the miraculous element and seek only symbolic significance, I understand that the narrative reports a miracle parallel with the manna in the desert. The details are dictated by the event itself, not by its theological significance. The numbers show that only God could perform the impossible task of providing for so many with so little. "The miracle is a sign of the presence among men of the final Redeemer in whom God's promises are being fulfilled" (Cranfield 222).

At the same time, "bread" appears to have symbolic overtones in Mark. It is a metaphor for the teaching of Jesus, which is as inexhaustible for the community as the bread was for the multitude. The disciples pass on to the church the words they have received from Jesus. "Bread" will gain more significance as the narrative develops (cf 7.27; 8.14ff; 14.22).

6.39-44 - Jesus directs the disciples to have the people sit in groups of hundreds and fifties. Just as Moses organized the Israelites in the desert (Ex 18.21-25; Nu 31.14; Dt 1.15; cf 1Sa 8.12), Jesus continues to form the new Israel. The scattered sheep are united under their Shepherd. From the beginning, God's people are to be an orderly people (1Co 14.40), not an unruly mob.

As host, Jesus follows the normal procedure of a religious home of that time. Taking the bread and fish and, looking up to heaven (cf 7.34), he blesses God before the meal, possibly using the family formula, "Blessed are you, O Lord our God, King of the universe, who brings forth bread from the earth." He then breaks the bread and gives it to the disciples for distribution to the people. In the same way, the fish are given to all. All eat and are satisfied. Since God's gifts should not be wasted, the disciples gather up the scraps.

This event recalls cases of physical hunger in the Old Testament, vividly remembered in Israel. Through Moses (called a prophet in Dt 18.18), God provided food for another multitude in another desert (Ex 16.32; cf Nu 11.13-22). Experiences of the prophets Elijah and Elisha also come to mind (1Ki 17.8-16; 2Ki 4.42-44). Is this Jesus whose actions satisfy the physical hunger of so many, "a prophet, like the prophets of long ago" as many were saying (6.15)? Such an answer is unsatisfactory. His actions excel by far those of all the prophets. He is God's answer Moses' plea for a shepherd for the flock (Nu 27.17). He is "the eschatological Savior, the second Moses who transforms a leaderless flock into the people of God" (Lane 230). Jesus proves that God can "spread a table in the desert" (Ps 78.19). David's promised successor, the Anointed One, satisfies his people with food (Ps 132.15-17).

In addition to looking back to God's saving acts in the past, the picture of Jesus providing food points forward to the great messianic feast. The prophets saw those events in the Exodus as foreshadowing God's future acts of salvation (cf Is 25.6). The feeding stories, like all the other miracles, "are seen by Mark as indications that the time of salvation announced in the prologue has arrived. The feeding of the people, like their healing, is a sign of the wholeness of life which is found in the Kingdom" (Hooker 47-48).

Through the provision of manna, God affirmed that "you will know that I am the Lord your God" (Ex 16.12b). What God did then, Jesus does now. His disciples, however, fail to understand the significance of what is happening. They will come to know who Jesus is, not through miracles, but through his crucifixion (15.39).

Without doubt, this event emphasizes the need for Christians to express true compassion in concrete, sacrificial acts that benefit those in need. Also, through the ages the church has correctly understood Jesus' words "you give them something to eat" as a commandment to offer to all the "Bread of Life" (Jn 6.35), rejecting the idea of leaving each to fend for him- or herself. Those who respond to the invitation to submit to God's rule discover that their new King is the Shepherd who tends the flock and satisfies the deepest hunger of men and women. Even in New Testament times, the teaching of the Word was often expressed in terms of feeding the flock. This continues to be central in the ministry of undershepherds (cf Jn 21.15-17; 1Co 3.2; 1Pe 2.2, 5.2; Heb 5.12) in recognition of the fact that "man does not live by bread alone." Caring is not limited to the Shepherd and undershepherds, however. As the Shepherd's example molds the whole flock, the whole church becomes a caring community.

v. 39 - The vivid descriptions suggest the reminiscence of an eyewitness. The green grass probably indicates springtime (cf 8.6; Jn 6.4,10). From June through September, the skies of Palestine are normally cloudless and the grass dry.

v. 41 - Although some interpret this meal as a type of eucharist (14.22), the language is that of the meal described in Acts 27.35. As Achtemeier (Invitation 102) correctly observes, the Lord's Supper "is based not on Jesus' miraculous deeds but rather on his sacrifice on the cross."

• Mark gives no indication that the people had any notion of the miracle that was being performed. As Lane (232) explains, "The messianic meal remained hidden from the thousands. The event is intended to be revelatory to the disciples alone.... Jesus actively involved them in the total proceeding.... The disciples do not understand him although they were given an abundant opportunity to see his glory. That is why they alone are reproved for their hardness of heart (6.52; 8.17-21)."

v. 43 - These were small wicker baskets (**kophinos**) which Jews carried as a part of their attire. Village people could make some on the spot.

v. 44 - The presence of 5000 men (according to oriental custom, only the men were counted) is indicative of the widespread interest in Jesus and of the enormity of the miracle.

4. Jesus Walks on the Water, 6.45-52

This story is a continuation of the feeding of the five thousand, bound together by the people involved and by chronological and geographical references. The two miracles are complementary revelations, for, as Mark declares (v. 52), an understanding of the two is interdependent. The prominence given to the disciples' activities in both pericopes calls attention to the theme of the disciples' mission begun in 6.7. This narrative gives evidence of an eyewitness' memory of an actual incident.

6.45-46 - These two verses compose the transition from the first phase of this continuing story. They tell of Jesus' actions in relation to the disciples, to the crowd, and to God. They also fill in the background of that night's activities and hint at their purposes.

After feeding the five thousand, Jesus *makes* his unwilling disciples embark for Bethsaida, while he dismisses the crowd. Why this resistance on the part of the disciples? Since Mark does not specifically state the reasons, the reader must seek answers in accord with the context of this Gospel.

Earlier (6.7), Jesus sent out the twelve on their first mission. Going two by two (without Jesus), they went to the villages of Galilee, apparently with good results. Upon their return, Jesus directs them in performing additional services (6.37-43). Now he sends them on ahead on a new mission, to Bethsaida.

Apparently they are reluctant to initiate the evangelization of a new area, especially since many Gentiles live in the region. Moreover, they haven't forgotten the extreme hostility encountered on a similar mission (5.1-20). The disciples may also be fearful of what might happen on the lake on a previous night when they nearly drowned in a storm (4.35-41). Even with Jesus present, those had been two terrifying experiences, involving confrontations by evil spirits. They may have forgotten, however, that Jesus had freed them from both dangers and that he had given them authority over evil spirits (6.7).

In spite of their reluctance, Jesus insists on sending them to people who have yet to hear the good news. This is why he came (1.38); it is a priority for his followers. As seen throughout this division (6.6b-8.26), Jesus is preparing them for missionary service in his absence.

The hour is late and the people have a ways to travel to their homes. After sending the disciples ahead, Jesus dismisses the people for he does not want the crowds to endure the disciples' ill will (6.36).

Then Jesus goes up into the hills to pray. This is the second of three occasions recorded by Mark when Jesus prays alone at night at a critical point in his ministry (1.35; 14.32-42). Again the reader is left to infer within the context of Mark why Jesus communes alone with his Father (1.11; 9.7). Certainly Jesus is concerned about the disciples' failure to understand who he really is and their need to have compassion for the many sheep without a shepherd. So on a Galilean hillside, Jesus prays alone.

v. 45 - The word is **anagkazo** ("made" or "compelled," implying unwillingness) instead of **apostellein** ("send off") as in 6.7. Why did Jesus compel the disciples to embark (contrast 8.10)? Robert Alter (183) says Biblical writers often lead their readers to inferences through oblique hints rather than through explicit statement.

Many commentators draw from John 6.15, explaining that Jesus sent the disciples away without delay in order to avoid their joining the crowd to make him king. However, Mark gives no indication of any such intention. We have sought to understand Jesus' action within the context of Mark's narrative.

Some writers imagine that an intense confrontation had arisen between them. On the contrary, Jesus is seeking to cure their hardness of heart. He does this by teaching, testing and re-teaching them through word and example, adjusting his methods to the disciples' comprehension (cf Jn 16.12).

After their many opportunities as observers, Jesus increases their role as participants (beginning in 6.7). They are "on their own" in their first mission. In 6.37, Jesus enlarges their assignment yet more. In the light of their failure (6.52), he temporarily diminishes their participation (see 8.1-9) and increasingly teaches them apart from the crowds, even at night on Lake Galilee.

6.47-51 - Although geographically separated, Jesus is mindful of his disciples who unwillingly began crossing over to Bethsaida as ordered and are now rowing against a strong headwind. He not only continues to watch out for them from his vantage point on land, but he is also praying for them in their struggle. As the true Shepherd, he leads his sheep out (cf Jn 10.3-4) by praying for them.

As in the previous storm (4.35), the disciples find themselves in this plight as a result of their obedience to Jesus' command. This time he is not even with them in the boat. Jesus sees them straining at the oars, however, and goes out to them, walking on the lake. The phrase "to pass them by" recalls a similar expression used in reference to Moses and Elijah, prominent persons both in Mark and in the Old Testament. When they (like the disciples) were afraid to go ahead (Ex 33.15ff; 1Ki 19.10ff), the Lord appeared to them, "passing in front of" his troubled servants. Similar to those previous epiphanies, Jesus' intention is to reveal his glory as the Son of God by "passing in front" of the disciples.

The disciples, however, can not believe that they see a man walking on the water! They are terrified, for they think they see a ghost. Immediately Jesus says to them, "Take courage! It is I. Don't be afraid." Although their cry is one of fear, Jesus responds immediately, for "the Lord's power to answer is not limited by the inadequacy of our asking" (R. A. Cole 116).

While the words "It is I" (**ego eimi**, literally, "I am;" cf 14.62) could be simply self-identification, they have a much greater meaning here. Based on God's statement to Moses ("I am that I am," Ex 3.14), "It is I" appears in the Old Testament as "almost a title or formula of divine self-disclosure" (Hurtado 91; cf Isa 43.25; 48.12; 51.12). Moreover, in the Old Testament, God declared, "Be not afraid, it is I," when his manifestation was not recognized at first and responded to in awesome fear. In the same way, Jesus seeks to calm the disciples' fears, "Take courage! Don't be afraid" as he identifies himself to them with the most revered name, "I am."

The convergence of so many factors cannot be accidental: Jesus is demonstrating who he is. The One who walks on the water and makes the wind die down, who talks the way God talks and does what only God can do--he is the transcendent Lord. Furthermore, Jesus climbs into the boat with the disciples, for he is also human. He is a man among men. He understands humans, though they do not understand him. The Sovereign Lord over nature is present among and caring for his people.

A few moments earlier, the disciples had screamed aloud in terror. Now, upon hearing Jesus' words, they are completely amazed.

v. 47 - It was late in the day when the disciples came to Jesus as he was teaching (6.35). Jesus sees them in the boat "when evening came," an expression which means "late in the evening" (Cranfield 225).

"In the middle of the lake" does not specify the boat's distance from the shore. Rather, the boat was "out on the sea" or simply "on the water," an expression parallel to Jesus' presence "on land."

v. 48 - Since this occurs near the time of the Passover Feast (Jn 6.4), the full moon gives enough light to reveal the boat. By the time Jesus arrives near the boat, the moon had probably set.

• Jesus and the disciples finally reach Bethsaida in 8.22.

• Mark notes the time according to the Greco-Roman system, in which the period from 6 p.m. to 6 a.m. was divided into four watches of three hours each. Thus the fourth watch extended from 3 a.m. to 6 a.m. The Jews divided the night into three watches.

• Jesus was walking on the water: the preposition is **epi**, meaning "on top of the water." Martin (Action, 54) says "walking on the sea" is in the Old Testament "a manifestation of the divine presence. See Ps 77.19; Job 38.16; Isa 43.16." See also Isa 51.9-16, especially the phrases "I, even I, am he who comforts you.... I am the Lord your God who churns up the sea so that its waves roar."

v. 50 - "Do not be afraid, it is I," see Ge 15.1; 26.24; 46.3; Isa 41.13.

• See also "I am" in the New Testament, especially in John's Gospel (e.g., 8.24, 28, 58; 13.19; 18.4-6).

6.52 - For some time now, the disciples have been with Jesus, with unparalleled opportunities to know him. They have seen his mighty works and have been privileged to receive instruction beyond his teaching to the multitudes. The seed has been planted and carefully cultivated. Jesus expects the disciples to understand who he is and what he is doing. In times of testing, however, their lack of understanding becomes evident in their meager faith.

This is not an occasional problem; it is persistent and growing. The disciples need understanding more desperately than they need rest, food or a calm sea. In words (v. 52) that possibly "reflect Peter's humble confession as he looks back" (Cranfield 224), Mark gives readers of his Gospel insight into the hearts of the disciples as a warning and a challenge to avoid similar pitfalls in their own lives.

The disciples "had not understood about the loaves" means there was more than meets the eye in the feeding of the multitude. Like the parables, the miracles convey a meaning that is hidden but meant to be revealed. If the meaning of the loaves had been grasped, the miracle on the lake would have been clear. Understanding comes by building one insight upon another (8.19-21). The lack of understanding is not static; if not overcome, it becomes misunderstanding and results eventually in failure. The disciples' spiritual blindness has progressed to the point where Mark describes them with a phrase similar to his description of the Pharisees (3.5): "hardness of heart."

What do they not understand about the loaves? First of all, they still do not really understand who Jesus is or the relationship between his giving bread and God's reign among men and women. Secondly, Jesus' disciples (including readers of Mark's Gospel) need to comprehend and fulfill "the immense privilege and responsibility of offering to the multitude...the living Word that alone can satisfy their hunger" (Anderson (179). Without understanding these, they are fearful and go about their mission unwillingly (v. 45).

Hopefully, his disciples will learn that there is no need for fear when dangers arise as a result of obedience to Jesus' command. Whether present or absent physically, his concern for his disciples is always operative; his power is able to dispel all fear. Jesus has not forsaken them but is interceding for and is present with his church as it persists against all obstacles in order to give others the Bread of Life. Although the night is long and the contrary wind is severe, those who persist, even to the fourth watch, "will see the Son of Man coming with great power and glory" (13.26; cf 1Ti 6.14; Tit 2.13).

v. 52 - Introduced in 4.12, the word "understanding" (**suneimi**) returns in 7.14 and reaches its maximum emphasis in 8.17,21, where it appears again in connection with "bread." The ability to imitate without possessing clear understanding is characteristic of the second stage of the teaching/learning cycle, as described by Robbins (156ff).
• "Hardness of heart" does not mean "hardhearted," in the sense of "unfeeling" or "pitiless." Rather, it is a lack of understanding, perception, insensibility or blindness.
• See "hiddenness" in 4.11-13, 21-22. Cf Isa 6.9-10; Jer 5.21; Dt 29.4; 32.28.
• Regrettably, some stumble at these nature miracles, rationalizing them of any supernatural elements. Is it correct to presume that their explanations arise from hardened hearts, resulting in the failure to understand that Jesus is God Incarnate?
• The disciples experienced difficulty in identifying Jesus as the Son of God because, as Jewish scholar Robert Alter (157) says, "the whole spectrum of biblical thought presupposes an absolute cleavage between man and God; man cannot become God, and God...does not become man."

5. Jesus Heals All Who Touch Him, 6.53-56

The cycle of ministry to the villages of Galilee, begun by the disciples in 6.7, draws to a close, and with it, the first part of the literary unit extending from 6.6b-8.26. This brief paragraph also closes the smaller literary unit (6.30-56) identified earlier. Following this pericope, Mark will reintroduce the subject of opposition by the Pharisees (7.1-23) before narrating a cycle of ministry outside Galilee (7.24ff).

Here Mark relates Jesus' healing ministry in the area of Gennesaret. After having presented the teaching ministry of Jesus (6.34, with no mention of healings), he now relates his healing many people (6.55-56, with no mention of teaching).

6.53-56 - After a long night on the lake, the disciples land at the town of Gennesaret, their boat having been blown off course by the strong wind. Upon recognizing Jesus, the people lose no time in taking advantage of his presence to heal their sick. Throughout that fertile valley and beyond, they run to wherever Jesus is, carrying the sick to him.

In the midst of these demands, Jesus continues his usual itinerant ministry (cf 1.39,45; 6.6b). Word about his location spreads quickly; many people flock to him, sparing no effort in their desire to be healed. That same Person who a few hours earlier appeared in a theophany as the transcendent Lord is very approachable and touchable.

In their first missionary activity, the disciples had engaged in teaching (6.12,30) and healing (6.13). Now there is no mention of their participation. Apparently they still lack the compassion which creates a willingness to serve others (6.36,45).

Many sought Jesus unaided by their friends. Mark, however, mentions twice (vv. 55-56) that the people of the area serve others, bringing them to Jesus who graciously heals all who reach out to him in their afflictions (6.56). They are doing what the disciples fail to do. The act of touching Jesus does not cure them, however. As he explained earlier to the woman who touched him (5.28, 34), "Your faith has healed you."

v. 53 - Gennesaret was located on the northwestern shore of Lake Galilee, gateway to a small but fertile valley. The lake itself was also known as Gennesaret (Lk 5.1).
• The people recognize Jesus and rush to bring others to him. In contrast, the disciples had not recognized him the night before. They were terrified by his presence (6.49), and were not eager to serve others (6.36, 45). In the following pericope (7.1-23), the Pharisees seek Jesus for yet other reasons. They come to criticize. They have eyes to see only the disciples' failure to observe ceremonial rituals.
v. 56 - In accord with Nu 15.37ff and Dt 22.12 (cf Mt 23.5), Jesus wore tassels on his clothes, one of many evidences of his Jewishness. In the following chapter, he discusses ritualism with the Pharisees.

• Jesus' healings cannot be stereotyped. Sometimes he touched the person (1.41); sometimes the person touched him (3.10; 5.28; 6.56); on other occasions, no touching was involved (3.5; 7.29).

B. TRUE AUTHORITY AND SURE DEFILEMENT, 7.1-23

Somewhat abruptly, Mark switches from relating popular support of Jesus' ministry to the religious officials' denunciation of his insurgent religious movement. This section is divided into the question of "unwashed hands" (7.1-13) and Jesus' subsequent teaching on the true nature of defilement (7.14-23).

The dialogue that follows is carefully sandwiched between the two sections relating the expansion of Jesus' ministry while training the disciples (6.6b-56; 7.24-8.26). The debate about Jewish traditions prepares the reader for a new incursion into Gentile territory (7.24ff). His Galilean ministry has faced controversy with the religious leaders almost from the start (2.1ff); it closes now with this sharp demarcation of fundamental differences.

Jesus espouses the authority of the word of God; the religious authorities hold to their traditions. Jesus knows that God gave the Scriptures to guide and judge human life, whereas the Pharisees use the Bible to approve their actions and elevate their status with God. Jesus shows that he has the authority to interpret the word of God and to lay aside erroneous interpretations and traditions. Throughout, Jesus provides additional evidence as to who he is.

By relating this dispute, Mark calls upon his readers to stand with Jesus against legalism that would destroy their freedom purchased by Christ (cf Gal 5.1). He also warns them against substituting human traditions in the place that belongs exclusively to God's inscripturated self-revelation. Of special value for guiding the early church through its controversies, these basic principles continue to distinguish Christianity from all other religious systems. The church must know the truth in order to avoid that which is false.

• Swete (142) suggests that this discussion takes place on the western shore of Lake Galilee. [The committee from Jerusalem would have easier access to this area, for the ancient international highway called Via Maris, or "the Way of the Sea" (Is 9.1) passes nearby.] He also suggests that the discussion arose because the disciples were eating some of the broken pieces of "day-old" bread (6.42). Contact with many sick people in the crowded marketplaces (6.53-56) could also raise the subject of ritual cleanliness.
• Controversies with members of the religious establishment form an undercurrent in the whole Gospel narrative. Questioning Jesus begins early in Mark's account (2.1-3.6; 3.22-30); it reappears near the middle of Mark's narrative (here; 10.2). In Jerusalem, the controversy heightens (11.27-12.40) and culminates in Jesus' trial and condemnation (14.53-65).

1. The Source of Religious Authority, 7.1-13

Although Jesus has been ministering in the small towns of a northern province, word about him reaches authorities, both religious (3.22) and secular (6.14). Once more, teachers of the law (scribes) are sent out from Jerusalem, the religious capital, to combat this non-conformist who is gaining much popular support in the provinces. Joining the local Pharisees, they observe Jesus, waiting for a deviation from their teaching or practice that could be used against him. They strike at him by criticizing his disciples (as in 2.18, 24).

Scrutinizing the disciples' failure to observe certain rituals, the religious authorities ask, "Why?" Jesus' answer is two-fold. First, such rituals are based on human traditions, not on God's commands. Secondly, in reality those practices nullify the word of God. Jesus illustrates his argument by showing how a gift to God (**Corban**) was used to justify disobedience to God's commandment.

7.1-5 - These verses provide the background for this phase of the controversy with the religious authorities. Mark includes a brief explanation of the custom in question for his Gentile readers who are not acquainted with such rituals (vv. 3-4). (We have included additional background for our readers.)

Within his purposes of creating "a holy nation" (Ex 19.6), God commanded "Be holy, because I am holy" (Lev 11.44). But how can one "be holy"? Over a long period of time, oral traditions were created in an effort to clarify the way to holiness as taught in the written law (the first five books of the Old Testament, the **Torah**). These traditions were developed as a "fence" around the written law, to protect it by instructing the faithful on how to fulfill it. For example, as seen in Mark 2.23ff, the command to "keep the Sabbath day holy" was spelled out in detail, defining all types of work and thus "protecting the law" from being broken even inadvertently. In the third century after Jesus, the **Mishnah** was compiled as a written summary of these oral laws.

The charge that the disciples were "eating with unwashed hands" had nothing to do with hygiene. It was strictly a matter of the ceremonial laws of purification. In order to remain pure (see 7.14-23), a zealous Jew sought ways to avoid contact with all that was ceremonially unclean. According to rabbinical tradition, "impure" included far more than things declared unclean in the Levitical code (e.g., Lev. 11). These traditions grew as the scrupulous attempted to define and avoid all impurity. For example, the shadow of a Gentile falling upon a pious Jew's food would make it "impure," since Gentiles were the personification of impurity.

Thus the rabbinical tradition on "washing hands" determined the "when" and the "how" of obtaining ritual purity. Each step was detailed, even specifying the minimal amount of ceremonially clean water to be used. With fingers pointing upward, the water was poured over the fingers and hands, running down to the wrists. Then each hand was scrubbed with the fist of the other. Finally, with fingers pointing downward, additional water was poured over the wrists, running off at the fingertips.

The Old Testament did not command this elaborate procedure. It was an oral law which grew out of the written law (the Old Testament) requiring priests to wash their hands and feet with water from a bronze basin prior to entering the Tent of Meeting (Ex 30.19; 40.12). Zealous laymen also sought to keep themselves pure from contamination through such practices "and many other traditions, such as the washing of cups, pitchers and kettles" (v. 4b). Their separation from the masses and from all else that contaminated proved their dedication to God. These rituals reflected the conviction that the sources of evil were external; impurities came from contact with unclean persons or things. After denouncing such practices (7.1-13), Jesus defines the true source of evil (7.14-23).

In serving others, Jesus and his disciples expose themselves daily to many "sources of defilement." They were already known for their violation of the Sabbath and for eating with sinners. Now they come under additional scrutiny by the authorized leaders. If they were authentic religious leaders (according to the reasoning of the committee of scribes and Pharisees), they would zealously observe the rituals established for all who aspired to holiness. Likely perceiving strain in the relationship between Jesus and his disciples (cf 5.31), the committee denounces the disciples to Jesus, possibly hoping to create a gap between them. Their question about the disciples' motives ("why?") is a veiled accusation aimed at Jesus himself. His decisive answer (vv. 6-13) comes to grips with the main issue.

v. 3 - Mark's phrase "the Pharisees and all the Jews" is used in the sense of the strict, orthodox minority who regarded these traditions as of equal or greater importance with the written Law. The Sadducean party (cf 12.18ff), however, rejected the oral traditions.

v. 5 - The "tradition" means the teaching that was handed down from antecedent teachers of the Law (**presbuteros**) and was transmitted (generally in oral form) from generation to generation. It instructed how to "be holy" as commanded in Lev 19.2. Elsewhere in Mark, **presbuteros** means "elders" and refers to the contemporary older men who, with the chief priests and scribes, composed the Sanhedrin.

7.6-8 - There can be no doubt about the sincerity of the teachers of the law and the Pharisees. Like Saul of Tarsus (Ac 26.5), they lived according to the strictest sect of their religion. Sincerity in religion is not enough, however. It must be based on a true understanding of what God has revealed about himself. God's revelation was given in order that we might know our sins (Ro 3.20b) and cast ourselves upon his grace. But their forefathers ("elders," v. 5) manipulated that revelation, changing it into rules for self-justification. They had accommodated God's laws to human nature, instead of seeking God's forgiveness in order that they might, by his mercy, live according to his will. Since their zeal was not according to the truth (Ro 10.2-3), their dedication to their traditions led away from God and to reject Jesus as well. They were sincere in their convictions; but they were sincerely wrong.

Jesus responds to their question, basing his reply on the Old Testament. He not only knows the Scriptures intimately, he declares they were given by God ("the commandments of God," vv. 8,9; "the word of God," v. 13) and are thus authoritative. Jesus does not attack the law (cf 10.2-10); he affirms it and denounces those "defenders of the law" for sabotaging it.

Jesus meets the challenge of the committee by identifying the origin and the authority behind the custom itself. The disciples had not violated the teachings of the Old Testament. The ritual they failed to observe was a part of the oral law. "Rules taught by men" (6b) which faithfully expressed the spirit and truth of God's laws could conceivably have authority. But that was not the case with this oral law. Their authors may have had good intentions, but their interpretation of God's teaching was progressively disastrous. According to Jesus, those who lived according to the traditions of the elders:

"let go of the commands of God" (v. 8),
"set aside the commands of God" (v. 9) and
"nullify the word of God" (v. 13).

They did this while claiming that their traditions were according to God's laws. As teachers of the law, the scribes should have been alerted to the danger, for Isaiah had prophesied (29.13):

"These people honor me with their lips,
but their hearts are far from me.
They worship me in vain;
their teachings are but rules taught by men" (7.6-7).

Jesus makes it very clear that externals can be harmful when one's heart is not in the right place.

Since they substituted their customs in the place of the true intention of the law, Jesus rightfully calls them "hypocrites" (v. 6; cf Mt 23). "Although they made an outward fuss about worshipping God they did not give him true heart worship; scrupulosity in the things that he had not commanded was accompanied by subtle evasions of what he did command. Such worship could only be in vain" (I. Howard Marshall Mark 26).

v. 6 - Used only here in Mark, the word "hypocrite" originally referred to stage actors, as their role involved pretending to be another. It has come to mean a person concerned only with appearances; one who pays more attention to reputation than to character; one who emphasizes his or her own virtues and others' sins. Here Jesus uses the term in reference to those who, while pretending to follow God's will, are in reality invalidating it.

v. 8 - "The oral law was professedly a 'fence' [around] the written law; in practice it took its place and even reversed its decisions. When the two were in competition, the tradition was preferred" (Swete 148).

7.9-13 - By his answer, Jesus continues to challenge the authority of the oral law: "You have a fine way of setting aside the commands of God in order to observe your own traditions." He accuses them directly, citing an example of substituting what Moses said (v. 10) by what *"you* (emphatic) say" (v. 11). Their traditions are not based on the divine command spoken by Moses (as the teachers of the law defend); they actually contradict God's purposes. As a result, God's word is in effect made void. As an example of how obedience to the written commandments is being avoided with the sanction of the oral law, Jesus chooses one of the Ten Commandments which defines one's responsibilities to others: "Honor your father and your mother" (Ex 20.12; Dt 5.16). Then (v. 10b) he quotes the law concerning the legal consequences of cursing one's parents (Ex 21.17; Lev 20.9). With official sanction, a way had been devised to set aside this commandment which emphasizes family responsibility. By declaring his property **Corban** (that is, "an offering to God"), a son "neither promised it to the Temple nor prohibited its use to himself, but he legally excluded his parents from the right of benefit" (Lane 251). The scribes would not allow the son to renege on his vow, even if his parents were in desperate need; for the law commanded that "he must not break his word but must do everything he said" (Nu 30.1-16; Dt 23.21-23). In this way, personal vows (even bad ones) were sacred, more sacred than God's rules.

Jesus insists that children--even adult children--are responsible to honor and care for their parents. This is a primary, life-long responsibility (cf 1Ti 5.8). Jesus puts "God's will for human life in its fullness at the top of his list" (Martin Action 65). He is uncompromising in his denunciation of the source of such unethical acts. When human traditions are placed above divine command, they sap the strength out of God's laws. They even lead people to violate the commandments of God.

The "old wineskins" (2.22) of Judaism were rigid, reducing life to a set of external rules. To the scribes and Pharisees, these rules and regulations were the essence of religion. A person who subscribed to these rules was bound by a closed system. He became independent from God and self-sufficient, for within the system he had the formulas for leading a religious life. It allowed no room for the law of love (which, in God's Kingdom, replaces legalism; cf 12.28-34). A wide chasm separated Jesus from such human commands and teachings (cf Col 2.22).

Attempts to reduce the Christian life to a set of rules were a major problem in the early church and continue until this day. Jesus' declarations here should also alert Christians today to the fact that exaggerated emphasis upon certain truths leads to their distortion and runs the danger of eventually losing their original meaning and value. As Cranfield (244) warns, "All human handling of the Word of God is continually beset by the temptation to try to turn the Word of God into a business of conventional piety and morals."

v. 10 - Taylor (340) emphasizes that, "while oral tradition is assailed by Jesus, the Law in the Decalogue is accepted by Him as binding; what God said through Moses stands (cf 10.3)."

• Since "all Scripture is God-breathed" (2Ti 3.16), the interpretation of the Bible must reflect the unity of all Scripture. One passage cannot be interpreted in ways that contradict another. When two passages seemingly contradict each other, the meaning of either one can only be properly ascertained in the light of the other. Here, this principle means that any oath that negates "honor your parents" cannot be valid.

• "Jesus' words are really an indictment of the whole idea of purely legal religion" (Nineham 195-196).

• Satan's efforts to distort values is seen in C. S. Lewis' portrayal of Screwtape instructing his apprentice demon, Wormwood, to keep a youth preoccupied about his mother's soul but unconcerned about her rheumatism.

v. 11 - The inscription on an ossuary lid recently discovered in a tomb near Jerusalem states that the deceased gave everything inside as an offering (**Corban**) to God. A.E.J. Rawlinson (95) suggests that Jesus may have cited a contemporary *cause célèbre*.

v. 13 - In classical Greek, **akuroo** ("nullify") was frequently used in canceling wills.

Excursus: Scripture and Oral Tradition

Several aspects of the controversy between Jesus and the Jewish leaders merit further clarification. First of all, Jesus is not questioning the validity of Scripture but rather the validity of the Pharisees' interpretation of Scripture. As Cranfield (243f) points out, the oral law was an attempt to manipulate God's Law. The Pharisees could live with the demands of oral traditions for they were compatible with their self-righteousness and complacency. They were determined to establish their own righteousness rather than face their need for God's forgiveness. In their hands, God's law eventually lost its original meaning and value.

Second, the teachers of the law and the Pharisees were rightfully concerned about defilement and God's commandment to be holy. However, (as Jesus emphasized in 7.1-8) they erred completely by seeking purification through external means. Their wrong premise (namely, that the source of contamination is external) brought a wrong conclusion. Regardless of how elaborate the process employed, washing one's hands only cleans one's skin; it does not remove inward contamination. In 7.14-23, Jesus identifies what really makes a person "unclean."

Third, Jesus is in no way attacking moral cleanliness per se. The New Testament also emphasizes that God "called us to a holy life" (2Ti 1.9). It distinguishes between what is pure and what is impure (as Jesus does in 7.20-22) and closes with the declaration that "nothing impure will ever enter" the New Jerusalem (Rev 21.27, cf Eph 5.5). Christians are called upon to purify themselves from that which contaminates (2Co 7.1; Eph 5.3-5; 2Ti 2.20-22). Unfortunately, some are unconcerned about avoiding defilement. Anyone who disregards God's command to be holy is evidently insensitive to the holiness of God himself.

Fourth, many (such as the Pharisee in Lk 18.9-14) tried to become holy through obeying aspects of the law. This twisted the purpose of the Law. God gave the Law as a mirror, to show his people their sinfulness and their need of cleansing. In no way can a mirror cleanse. The Law was given to lead us to Christ Jesus (Gal 3.24), who did not come to abolish the Law or the prophets, "but to fulfill them" (Mt 5.17). He does what the Law could not do: he makes the impure clean (1.40-45; 2.1-12; cf Ro 8.1-4). Jesus, the Holy One of God, is seeking "unwashed sinners," for he forgives and cleanses according to his grace, not according to the observance of rituals. As someone has said, "The Law gave me neither hands nor feet to do what it commanded. God's grace, on the other hand, invites me to fly and gives me wings as well."

2. The Source of Defilement, 7.14-23

Jesus is not superficial. He insists upon penetrating into the heart of thoughts and practices. He made it clear that God's word, not human traditions, is the source of religious authority (7.1-13). Now he focuses on the source of defilement. Calling for all to listen carefully, Jesus tells a parable which gets at the heart of the debate over cleanliness. After declaring a general principle on defilement (v. 15), he gives further explanations to the disciples in private (vv. 17-23).

These teachings prepare for the encounters which follow (7.24ff), where Jesus demonstrates what he has taught by ministering to Gentiles whom some advocates of the ritual laws of purity regard as the personification of impurity.

7.14-16 - Since the false concepts of the religious leaders sway the minds of the people as well, Jesus calls the crowd to him and exhorts all: "Listen to me, everyone, and understand this," for his pronouncement is applicable to all. Jesus has not forgotten the basic question behind the leaders' accusation (7.1-5), namely, How can one be holy? (or, in other terms, How to can a person be "clean" before God?) He returns to that question now, fulfilling the priestly role of teaching the people "how to distinguish between the unclean and the clean" (Eze 44.23).

When Micah (1.1-2) called out, "Hear, O peoples, all of you," he spoke as a prophet proclaiming the word of the Lord. Jesus speaks, not as one prophet among many, but as God's Son, his uniquely Anointed Messenger (cf 1.11; 4.3). He alone can command everyone, "Listen to me," for his words have an authority equal to that of the word of God itself. (Later, in 9.7, God confirms this by saying, "Listen to my Son, whom I love!") Having rebuked the religious leaders for letting go of the commandments of God (v. 8), he offers all a word from God, speaking an uncommon truth that would set Christianity free from the bondage of legalism.

Human traditions claim that external influences are the cause of "uncleanness." Jesus affirms just the opposite: a person is "unclean" because of what is inside in his or her heart. These words mark a fundamental difference between the Kingdom of God and Pharisaic Judaism. As Swete (150) points out, Jesus had stressed "the principle that the merely external cannot purify;" now he presents the converse: "the merely external cannot defile man's spiritual nature." Human moral nature is the source of moral defilement. What defiles people is not what goes into them, but what goes out of them. Quoting Lane (258), "Jesus does not alleviate the demand for purity but sharpens it.... The capacity for fellowship with God is not destroyed by material uncleanness of food or hands; it is destroyed by personal sin."

vv. 14-23 - In Barclay's judgment, "This passage, when it was first spoken, was well-nigh the most revolutionary passage in the New Testament " (<u>Mark</u> 172).

v. 15 - This is called a parable because it is designed to provoke thought: it undercuts a central facet of rabbinical teaching. Jesus' accusers could not use this against him, however; to them, the parable is enigmatic.

v. 16 - Some versions include the saying "if anyone has ears to hear, let him hear." While this exhortation is parallel to verse 14b (cf 4.9), it is omitted in most versions for lack of more solid manuscript evidence.

7.17-19 - Having heard this principle in the form of a parable, the disciples ask Jesus what it means. His strong rebuke, "Are you so dull?" (v. 18a; cf 6.52; 8.17-18, 33), is not unmerited, for the disciples are responsible for their lack of understanding. Given the amount of time they have been with Jesus, they should have perceived more (Cf 4.40b; 9.19; Heb 5.12). Hopefully this rebuke might startle them into thinking deeply about Jesus' unprecedented teaching as to the source of uncleanness.

The disciples observe Jesus and participate actively in his ministry. That is not enough, however. Jesus is teaching and training his followers with the desire that they understand the basic principles behind what he does and teaches. Nevertheless, their question reveals that there are still gaps in their comprehension of Jesus' message.

Jesus' teaching here is so contrary to popular concepts that he repeats to the disciples (vv. 18b-20) the truths he just taught the crowd (v. 15b). To make sure that no reader misses this important teaching, Mark also emphasizes its meaning: "In saying this, Jesus declared all foods clean." In spite of this repetition, the church is slow to realize the implications of these teachings. As Minear (86) says, it is "quite doubtful if the Church has ever understood. And, to come closer home, which of us has fully understood, if we define understanding by obedience?"

v. 17 - "He entered the house" means Jesus went indoors after teaching the crowd outdoors. Mark frequently designates a place of instruction as "the house" (9.28,33; 10.10) where God's family gathers

• Robbins (140) calls Jesus' efforts to explain systematically the principles that underlie his theology the "intermediate phase in the teacher/disciple cycle."

v. 19 - "Heart" (cf 2.6,8; 3.5; 6.52; 7.6; 12.30) does not mean the physical organ but a person's whole inner personality. It is the seat of one's moral nature. As Nineham (191) aptly says, a person's relationship to God is determined by the "state of his heart rather than upon what he ate."

• When the publican beat upon his chest (Lk 18.13), he was confessing the fact that "out of the heart come evil thoughts." He then pled, "God have mercy on me, a sinner" (Bailey Eyes 153).

v. 19b - Very likely, Peter related Jesus' explanation to Mark. Then Peter may have added, "In saying this, Jesus declared all foods 'clean'" (v. 19b). He possibly concluded with a personal confession: "I was so dull then. Years later, I finally understood what Jesus meant after God repeated three times that vision in Joppa (Ac 10.9-23). Mark, don't fail to emphasize that Jesus was declaring all foods 'clean'."

• The early church's lack of understanding these teachings is evident in its discussions over eating with the uncircumcised, attitudes towards foods, etc. Some deep animosities in the Christian communities in Rome arose over these matters (Ro 14-15).

7.20-23 - Jesus goes on to indicate some of the things that come from the human heart and make the person unclean. He mentions twelve sins. The first six nouns are plural, and, according to Swete, (153) refer to "successive acts of sin, as they emerge from the inner source of human corruption; the more subtle tendencies to evil which follow are in the singular (v. 22)." The list is not meant to be exhaustive. Jesus enumerates these sins in order that his followers might avoid committing them, for they would create barriers between disciples and disrupt life in God's family (3.35).

Significantly, evil thoughts ("evil devisings") are indicated first, for beyond being sinful in themselves, they do not remain alone. They conceive and give birth to other sins (cf Jas 1.14-15), some of which are mentioned in the following list of degrading acts and vices.

Two of the six nouns in the plural, indicating evil acts, explicitly name sexual sins. Sexual immorality (**porneiai**, often translated "fornication") is a broad term that includes every kind of sexual immorality. Adultery (**moicheiai**) is a narrower term, denoting sexual relationships that involve marital infidelity. (In 10.2-12, Jesus emphasizes life-long faithfulness to one's spouse as God's purpose from creation.) Pornography is not innocent entertainment; through the "lust of the eyes" (1Jn 2.16), it stimulates evil thoughts which give birth to evil acts.

Sexual immorality takes away a person's moral purity; adultery steals what belongs to marriage. Two other types of theft follow: stealing another's possessions (**klopai**), and murder (**phonai**), which is taking another's life.

Greed is the desire to have, a sieve that can never be filled. Among its many facets, greed hungers for that which belongs to others; it craves power; it lusts after the flesh. It is found in the heart of those who seek happiness in things instead of in God.

Malice (**pleonexiai**) describes a person who actively pursues evil with a desire to harm. Like the Evil One, such a person seeks to make others corrupt as well.

The next six nouns refer to the vices themselves, beginning with deceit (**dolos**, "guile"). This cunning treachery will be seen later in the chief priests and teachers of the law (14.1).

Lewdness (**aselgeia**, "indecency," "debauchery") signifies resentment of all social and moral restraints. Lewd persons shamelessly dare to do with open and flagrant excess anything their wanton insolence desires.

Envy is a vice that begins with jealous thoughts as one looks with malice upon another's possessions. It, too, is a bitter root which grows, often producing stinginess in oneself and causing trouble for others as well (cf Heb 12.15). While **ophtalmos poneros** literally means "an evil eye", even in Old Testament times this Semitic phrase meant "regarding another with envy." The meaning here is far removed from its use in pagan magic whereby one "casts an evil spell" upon another person, often to gain vengeance.

Slander (**blasphemia**) here may be defamatory or abusive speech against other persons, although in the Old Testament it always describes an affront to the majesty of God, thus, "blasphemy."

Arrogance (**huperephania**) may not be shown ostensibly, but one's contempt for everyone else inflates a person's heart with pride to the point where the individual even sets oneself up against God. As with the other vices, "God opposes the proud" (Jas 4.6).

The last term, "folly" (**aphrosune**), refers to one "who is morally and spiritually insensitive; he does not know God and he does not wish to know him" (Lane 257).

We must acknowledge that this list accurately portrays the evil that lies within the human heart. We see the results of these vices in the pages of our newspapers. We admit they hide in the depths of our own beings, threatening to charge out when we are sufficiently upset. These evils cannot be corrected by ritual or by diet; laws (religious or civil) cannot control them, for they are a part of our fallen nature. They come "from within, out of men's hearts."

The only remedy is *a new heart*. It is harder to have a clean heart than to have clean hands. In fact, it is impossible to have a life acceptable to God apart from God's gracious cleansing of our contaminated hearts. Jesus calls upon each of us to face up to the reality of our sinfulness by repenting and believing (1.15) in God's mercy demonstrated in the death of his Son (10.45).

Only God can free a person from bondage to evil thoughts (Ro 3.21-26), for the moral quality of the mind is determined by the power to which it is subject (Ro 6.16). To present one's body as a living sacrifice to God is the highest expression of worship (Ro 12.1). To think God's thoughts after him is the highest mental activity a person can achieve (cf Ro 12.2). These nurture the righteous life that God desires.

Repentance not only marks the beginning of the Christian life, it is a continuing practice as the Christian sees with increased clarity that sin exerts itself in his or her thoughts, words and deeds (Ro 7.21-23; 1Jn 1.8-10). To live under God's rule includes cultivating a Christian character through fellowship with God and with his people (Eph 4.13-16).

This parable with Jesus' explanation to the disciples is like new wine that bursts old wineskins (2.22). Its theological cluster includes teachings that are as relevant today as when they were given.

By attributing defilement to causes exterior to human beings, the teachers of the law infer that people are, by nature, pure. Failing to recognize the holiness of God and their own sinfulness, people seek to justify themselves before God through rules and regulations. Through good deeds, rituals and social actions, they make demands upon God and save themselves. Jews and Gentiles alike mistakenly concentrate on the external instead of the internal.

In the plainest of terms, Jesus says that sin springs from within the human heart. The source of defilement is internal. Since humankind is not pure but prone to sin, salvation must come from without. Sensitive to the human predicament, God mercifully offers men and women a "new heart" through Jesus. Only by his grace can his requirement of inner cleanliness be realized. With sovereign authority, Jesus cancels these rules and regulations, offering men and women freedom through faith in him. In this way, each one is able to live for God. Mark publicizes in these verses the charter of Christian liberty (cf Ro 5-8) and alerts believers to their tendency to create extra-biblical rules for themselves and for others.

God's command to "be holy" includes his concern about thoughts (even those that don't take shape in acts) and moral behavior. Both thoughts and conduct are important to God. All the religious rituals in the world cannot change a person's heart (Ps 51; Isa 58; Am 5.21-24). The gospel works from the inside out, providing the inner motivation necessary for acquiring righteous character and for getting "rid of all moral filth and the evil that is so prevalent" (Jas 1.21). God enables those who follow his leading to live on a different plane, for "the good man brings good things out of the good stored up in his heart" (Lk 6.45).

v. 22 - Greed is frequently associated with terms describing sexual sins, as in Eph 5.3; Col 3.5.
• Ladd (Theology 124f) says the Old Testament legislation, which distinguished between clean/unclean foods, vessels and people, was brought to its full intent and finished by Jesus and thereby canceled.
• Since no similar list is recorded from Jesus' teaching, some writers presume that the list originated with the early church. More likely, Mark faithfully adapted Jesus' teachings to his original readers. As Achtemeier (Invitation 111) observed, this passage is "an accurate reflection of the mind of Jesus." As a good teacher, Jesus varied his vocabulary according to the content of his teaching and the capacity of his hearers (cf Jn 16.12).
• Advocates of situation ethics attempt to justify each decision in the light of the circumstances in which it is made. This leads to the sanctioning of immoral acts and the loss of a sense of guilt. Any society that fails to discern between good and evil is in serious trouble.
• No religion can fulfill its role without facing seriously the plight of sinful humans before the holy God.

Excursus: Liberation Theology

In general, Liberation Theology emphasizes the corporate sins of society and turns a blind eye to evil thoughts and to the sinful acts of individuals. When only society's sins are condemned, it follows that only those responsible for social evils would need to repent. The Bible, however, states that *all are sinners*--both the oppressed as well as the oppressors, the poor as well as the rich (cf Ro 3.10-23)--and alienated from God. Corporate sins are the institutionalization of individual sins. While Jesus denounces the injustices of the religious establishment (11.12-18; 12.38-40), he identifies the human heart as the source of the problem. By calling upon all to repent (1.15), he deals with the root of sinfulness and not just its manifestations. Hearts transformed by God become the source of positive changes in society.

C. JESUS MINISTERS OUTSIDE GALILEE, 7.24 - 8.26

This new section constitutes a definite geographical break in the narrative, for Jesus' Galilean ministry ends in 7.23. At the same time, these events are a commentary on the preceding verses, for Jesus transforms the logic of his teaching in 7.1-23 into concrete experiences and demonstrates its meaning by including "unclean" *goyim* in God's Kingdom. He does among the Gentiles what he has been doing among the Jews, for he is their Shepherd, too. Their response contrasts sharply with the antagonism of the Jewish authorities.

After experiencing a cycle of events similar to those in 6.6b-56, the disciples finally arrive on the threshold of making their first open declaration of who he is.

1. A Syrophoenician Woman Accepts Crumbs, 7.24-30

Through his encounter with a Syrophoenician woman, Jesus illustrates what he has been saying about "clean and unclean" (7.1-23). Pious descendants of Abraham daily thanked God that they were not born Gentiles (i.e., "unclean"). By going to Tyre, a predominantly Gentile region, Jesus rejects that distinction and makes it crystal clear that the gospel is intended for all. The basis of being accepted by God is not ethnic background; it is based on relationship to the person of Jesus.

The emphasis of this narrative is not upon driving out an evil spirit. Jesus' pithy parable and the ensuing dialogue revolve around "children" and "food" (i.e., bread and crumbs).

• The ancient city of Tyre is located some 50 miles northwest of Lake Galilee, on the Mediterranean coast of modern Lebanon where Elijah ministered to the widow at Zarephath (1Ki 17.8ff). Phoenicia was part of a Syrian political unit. Although many Jews lived in this region, in general the people of Tyre were unfriendly to Jews. Like the inhabitants of the Decapolis, they followed pagan religions.

• Scholars debate as to whether Jesus ever taught in Greek. They agree, however, that he certainly spoke it. Jesus no doubt communicated with this woman in her mother tongue.

7.24-26 - Jesus now leaves Galilee, closing his ministry there. Those who considered themselves to be "righteous" did not recognize their need of this doctor (2.17). People who recognized their need had come to Jesus from Tyre and Sidon (3.8); now he goes to those in the vicinity of Tyre, taking his disciples outside Israel.

As soon as she hears about Jesus, a local woman drops everything she is doing and hurries to him. Since Greek is her cultural background and Syrian Phoenicia her birthplace, she has no claim to the promises that God made to Israel. She does not observe the rules of Jewish piety. In the eyes of the Pharisees (7.1-13), this Gentile is "unclean." According to the rabbis, she had the misfortune of being a woman. She has nothing going for her. What can she, a doubly unqualified person, possibly hope for in making a request on behalf of her daughter who is "unclean" due to demonic control? Nevertheless, with profound respect she comes and falls at Jesus' feet, interceding with him on behalf of her daughter.

v. 24 - Earlier (3.6), Jesus left the synagogue in Capernaum, closing his ministry there.
• There are two possible explanations why Jesus did not want his presence in Tyre known. His ministry was first to the Jews. Also, separated from the religious opposition and the pressures of the crowds, he was teaching his disciples (as in 9.30-31a), giving them an opportunity to reflect upon what has been happening and overcome their dullness (6.52; 7.18).
v. 26 - Mark presents other case studies of intercession: Jairus' intercession for his daughter, 5.23; a father's for his son, 9.17; friends' for the sick, 2.3; 6.55, and for little children, 10.13.
• The various cases of demonic control related in Mark show that Satan works his evil in Gentiles as well as Jews, in children as well as adults (cf 9.21).

7.27-30 - In answer to the mother's insistent appeal, Jesus tells a parable: "First let the children eat all they want, for it is not right to take the children's bread and toss it to their dogs."

God's call to Abraham (Ge 12.3) marked the priority of the children of Israel, a concept taught throughout Scripture. Jesus concentrated his ministry in serving the Jews and now he affirms this priority, declaring "first the children." Of course, a family does not deprive its own children in order to give food to household pets.

The Greek woman readily understands Jesus' parable and responds with one of her own. She accepts the fact that she is not a member of the household of Israel, with the rights and privileges of its children. She is aware that as a Gentile, she is an outsider. Unlike the Pharisees, she claims no status or merit; she has nothing with which to bargain. She knows that the granting of her request will not deprive the children of eating all they want. God's grace is more than sufficient to meet their needs and the needs of others as well. She will be content with crumbs.

As Jeremias (Theology 107n1, 164) says, "The faith of the Gentile woman does not consist in the fact that she gives Jesus a quick answer, but in the fact that with her 'Yes, sir, but' she acknowledges him as the giver of the bread of life (v. 28)." She "declares herself content with a crumb of what is really meant for Israel."

Having tested her understanding, motives and faith, Jesus again tests her faith, saying, "You may go; the demon has left your daughter." By informing the mother that the child has been freed although she is some distance away, Jesus invites her to believe that he possesses power and knowledge that belong to God alone. Without any external evidence, based only on Jesus' word, she goes home and finds her child lying on the bed. (Perhaps the departing evil spirit had convulsed the girl, leaving her exhausted; cf 9.26.) The girl is on the way to full recovery (cf 5.43). Just a crumb from Jesus brings untold satisfaction!

By accepting the scrap not as a child of the household but as a dog, she becomes a child, entitled to table fellowship in the house of God along with all the children. All who come to Jesus in faith find acceptance (salvation), based not on merits or privileges or race, but on expecting God to act in mercy through Jesus. The Greek mother recognizes that she is last, and thereby she becomes the first woman convert among the Gentiles (cf 9.35; 10.31).

The Syrophoenician woman exemplifies a mother's intercession for her daughter. She persists in spite of obstacles and she expectantly believes in God's merciful answer to her prayer. Jesus' response shows the abundance of God's grace.

Jesus faithfully follows God's design that his Servant first "restore the tribes of Jacob" and then to be "a light for the Gentiles" (Isa 49.6). The church's privilege and responsibility of inviting Gentiles everywhere to submit to God's rule (cf 11.17; 13.10; 14.9) is already envisioned in this ministry of Jesus. The Gentiles' potential for a positive response to Jesus (e.g., this woman and the Gerasene, 5.15-20) is comparable to the best responses among the Jews. The Syrophoenician "is a spokeswoman for the non-Jewish world which will become beneficiaries of Messiah's bounty after Israel has been offered the divine mercy" (Martin Mark 222).

In the early days of the church, many Jewish believers had serious doubts about accepting Gentiles into God's Kingdom, resulting in sharp clashes over the church's mission to Gentiles. Since Mark had experienced that struggle when he participated in the events which led up to Paul and Barnabas' decision to "turn to the Gentiles" (Ac 13.46), he writes with sensitivity to his original readers involved in this contention. He makes it clear that Jesus (and not Paul) initiated ministry among the Gentiles. Mark is concerned that the church follow Jesus' initiative and be faithful in expanding his ministry to "the ends of the earth" (13.10; 14.9; Ac 1.8).

v. 27 - A "first" (**proton**, 13.10; cf Ro 1.16; Ac 1.8) implies a "second," when others will have their opportunity. God revealed himself first to Israel so that Israel might proclaim his glory among the nations (cf Ge 12.18; Isa 66.19f; Mic 4.1ff; Zec 8.20ff). Confusing "first" with "exclusive," Israel failed in its missionary responsibility. Paul understood God's purposes, turning to the Gentiles after offering salvation to the Jews (Ac 13.46; 18.6). As Peter said, "God does not show favoritism but accepts men from every nation who fear him and do what is right" (Ac 10.34). The wall of separation is broken down. In Christ Jesus, "there is neither Jew nor Greek" (Gal 3.28).

• The expression translated "eat all they want" literally means "eat until satisfied." It is found only here and in the two feeding narratives (6.42; 8.4,8). Hurtado (103) notes that increasingly, "bread" becomes a symbol for the blessings of the Kingdom of God.

• To the Jews, Gentiles were "dogs" by comparison with God's Chosen People. Jesus is not being rude to the woman; he uses the diminutive which means "puppies," household pets free to roam about the house (not the fierce dogs that roam the streets). He may have added an understanding smile, removing further any possible misunderstanding. The mention of "puppies" may have brought pleasant memories to the woman. Other animals would be unsuitable for the metaphor. She recognizes this as a parable and not a direct form of address. Her reply shows that Jesus' words are not at all offensive.

v. 28 - The crumbs are from the bread that the children are eating, not pieces of bread people used to wipe their fingers while eating, then throw under the table. There is no thought of the eucharist here.

• Nothing, not even a crumb from the floor, can make a person "unclean" (7.17). The Syrophoenician woman gratefully accepts a crumb; the Pharisees rejected the bread.

• Persistence is a virtue frequently missing in a society that demands instant results. However, its rewards are significant (cf Dt 4.29; Am 5.4; Mt 7.7-8).

v. 29 - By not going to the girl, Jesus avoided being identified by the evil spirit (1.24f; 3.11f; 5.7).

2. A Deaf Man Hears and Speaks Clearly, 7.31-37

Jesus continues among the "unclean" the work he had performed among the Jews. By extending his ministry to the Gentiles, he makes it clear that women (7.26) and men (7.32) of all nations are invited to live under God's rule.

Based on Isaiah 35.5, people were saying that "When the Messiah comes, he will unstop the ears of the deaf." Since Jesus does just that, this narrative adds new evidence about his identity.

7.31-35 - In the Decapolis, friends bring a man to Jesus, begging him to help this deaf man who can speak only with great difficulty or a stammer. Jesus takes him aside, away from the "background noises" of the crowd. He needs to communicate with the man in his own way, free from the intervention of those who would insist on "helping" Jesus converse with a deaf man. Due to his limitations, the man probably knew little about Jesus. By taking him aside, Jesus is saying "I value you as an individual." This personal relationship helps Jesus emphasize that the healing power proceeds from his own person (cf 5.30).

Jesus adapts his communication to the man's ability to understand. Knowing that the man does not speak correctly because he does not hear adequately, Jesus puts his fingers into the man's ears; then he spits and touches the man's tongue. Step by step, he gains the man's confidence as he communicates by an informal sign language the message that "I am here to help you; trust me."

By looking up to heaven, Jesus conveys to the needy man that, as God's agent, he is praying with him and on his behalf. He enters into the man's suffering and shares his anguish. With a deep sigh, he visibly expresses his strong emotion against the evil in the world that ravaged another life (cf 1.41). Jesus commands, "Be opened!" and the man is cured from his dual affliction. His ears are opened, his tongue loosened. As a result, he begins to speak plainly.

Ancient magicians used incantations of foreign words or nonsense syllables like "abracadabra" to perform their acts. **Ephphatha** is not one of these; this authentic Aramaic word (meaning "be opened") was normal speech for Jesus. Mark translated the word, thereby showing that Jesus used a simple command and not a magical formula to achieve the desired cure.

v. 31 - From the limited information Mark gives, it appears that Jesus goes north from Tyre, through the region of Sidon, then takes a circuitous route east and south to the region east of Lake Galilee, the area of 5.20. Lane (265) suggests that Jesus takes this route in order to avoid entering Galilee.

• The Decapolis was considered "unclean" because of the predominance of Gentiles.

• Based on the geography and the context, we conclude that this scene portrays the healing of a Gentile. Jesus' use of Aramaic to speak to him does not prove the man was a Jew, for Aramaic was widely used in the region.

v. 32 - Lane (266) points out that "Mark's use of an extremely rare word to describe the man's speech defect is almost certainly an allusion to Isa 35.5f which celebrates God as the one who comes in order to unstop the ears of the deaf and to provide song for the man of inarticulate speech. The fulfillment of the prophecy was expected in the Days of the Messiah (and) took place in the ministry of Jesus."

• Compare with its "matched pair" in 8.22-26. These two healings point to who Jesus is.

v. 33 - The phrase "he took him aside" is frequently used by Mark to indicate private clarification.

• Jesus "spit and touched the man's tongue." Saliva is not mentioned. Did Jesus spit on the ground, symbolically getting rid of an impediment on the tongue? Did he transfer spittle to the man's mouth (directly or on his finger), indicating therapeutic value in the spittle? The Greek does not say.

Modern concepts of hygiene find this procedure distasteful. In New Testament times, however, it was neither strange nor unbecoming (cf 8.23, Jesus spat "on the man's eyes;" Jn 9.6). In many parts of the world, saliva is regarded as therapeutic. Who has never put a bruised finger in his mouth?

v. 34 - The phrase "with a deep sigh" describes Jesus' strong emotions (cf 1.41; 8.12; Jn 9.33, 38). The deep sigh was not audible to the deaf man; but it was clearly visible, conveying to him Jesus' emotional involvement.

v. 35 - Literally, "the bond of his tongue was loosened." Some regard the man as having been controlled by an evil spirit (cf Lk 13.16). However, we see nothing in the text to indicate demonic activity.

7.36-37 - Overwhelmed with amazement, the people begin to tell everyone that Jesus "has done everything well." By recalling Genesis 1.31, the reader sees this as public recognition that Jesus' acts were such as only God can do. As Hooker (43) says, some in that mixed crowd would possibly surmise that "the time of salvation has arrived in the person of Jesus" (1.15) for God is at work, restoring the wholeness of life he intended at the creation (cf Isa 29.18-19; 32.3-4).

Why, then, does Jesus command them not to tell? Their idea of Messiahship is tied to the healing. They are more interested in what Jesus can do for them than in who he is. Jesus wants in-depth understanding, not limited comprehension. He is not a "stunt-performer, using his extraordinary powers merely to attract people. The miracles are indeed performed, but to meet human needs." Hopefully, those benefited can by faith see "the health and wholeness that Jesus provides" and the reader can see "the defeat of the demonic powers and the healing of mankind in preparation for the coming of God's Kingdom" (Kee 171-172).

Also, Jesus wants to avoid what happened earlier, when the crowd's talking hindered his ministry (cf 1.44-45). Healings also aroused antagonism against him (3.22). In the light of these facts, it is not so strange that Jesus commanded the crowd not to tell.

He could loosen the tongue of the stutterer. His authority was limited, however; he could not oblige the crowd to obey. The more he told them not to tell anyone, the more they kept talking.

v. 37 - Mark implies that "Jesus is God's pledge that the new era has arrived and in him God's age-old promises of deliverance are made good" (Martin Mark 170).

3. Jesus Feeds Four Thousand, 8.1-10

As we read this narrative while working our way through Mark's Gospel, we recall the previous story of the feeding of 5,000 (6.34-44). The two stories are similar in the following ways: Jesus and his disciples gather with a multitude of people in a desert setting. After conversing with the disciples about the situation, Jesus asks, "how many loaves do you have?" After their reply, the crowd is instructed to sit down. Jesus prays, then breaks the bread. The disciples distribute it to the people. The same is done with the fish. After all eat and are satisfied, the disciples gather the fragments into a recorded number of containers. The number of people is noted. The crowd is dismissed; a boat trip follows.

We also detect differences between the two narratives. We readily notice variations in the numbers. As Lane (272) comments, "even among the so-called parallel expressions, there are striking differences" in situation, motivation and detail.

Although many writers understand that Mark relates two different occasions on which Jesus feed multitudes, Schweizer (156) and others argue that "this story is a duplicate of the account in 6.32-44." The reader should study the following text of 8.1-10, for in it the major differences found in 6.32-44 are indicated in smaller type within brackets. Additional comments are made on the items marked with an asterisk (*).

Mark 8.1-10 [1]During those days another [**palin,** another account, not a variant of the previous] large crowd gathered. Since they had nothing to eat, Jesus called his disciples to him [earlier, they had interrupted Jesus to present the problem, 6.35] and said, [2]"I have compassion for these people" [here, Jesus speaks of his compassion which leads him to feed the multitude. In the earlier narrative, 6.34, the author ascribed compassion to Jesus, adding, "...because they were like sheep without a shepherd. So he began teaching them many things."]; "they have already been with me three days [only one day in 6.35] and have nothing to eat [his compassion results in feeding them]. [3]If I send them home hungry ["Send them away," the disciples had said, 6.36], they will collapse on the way, because some of them have come a long distance" [no mention of distance in the previous case].

[4]His disciples answered, "But where in this remote place can anyone get enough bread to feed them?" [Jesus does not repeat his command, "You give them something to eat," 6.37*].

[5]"How many loaves do you have?" Jesus asked.

"Seven," they replied [five on the first occasion].

[6]He told the crowd to sit down [previously, Jesus directed the disciples "to have all the people sit down in groups" of hundreds and fifties, 6.39f; Jesus by-passed his reluctant disciples this time] on the ground ["green grass," 6.39]. When he had taken the seven loaves and given thanks, he broke them and gave them to the disciples to set before the people, and they did so. [7]They had a few small fish [two previously] as well; he gave thanks for them also and told the disciples to distribute them. [8]The people ate and were satisfied. Afterward the disciples picked up seven basketfuls [12 units of a different sized container*] of broken pieces that were left over. [9]About four thousand men [people*] were present. And having sent them away, [10]he got into the boat with his disciples and went to the region of Dalmanutha [strikingly different*].

From such marked differences between the two narratives and in the light of 8.19-20 where both events are expressly mentioned, we conclude that Mark reports two different events. As Hurtado (109) says, "The fact that Mark devoted space to two accounts of the same sort of miracle suggests that each one had for him a special significance and that neither could be omitted without losing something important." One occasion alone is enough to prove that Jesus could perform this miracle. Two accounts indicate that there is something more to learn. We will discover what that "something" is by examining the similarities and differences.

As noted previously, 8.1-29 follows the pattern of 6.35-7.37. Jesus employed repetition as a part of his teaching method in an effort to drive truths home. As every teacher knows, repetition is especially essential when social and psychological barriers hamper student learning, as with the "dull" disciples. Jesus is giving his disciples a second chance.

• The feedings of the five (6.35ff) and the four thousand (8.1ff) have intrigued scholars for a long time. Some regard the two stories as variants of only one event. One even rejects Mark 8 as a "stupid repetition," claiming that the disciples' reaction would be "psychologically impossible." We maintain that the author composed the stories as a matched pair. The differences force us to recognize the integrity of each story as a distinct event, while the similarities demand that we relate the two. In this way, we reach an understanding of the distinct--though similar--purpose of each of the two events.

• The Decapolis and the context of Mark 7.24-8.10 indicate this a predominantly Gentile setting, although Jews of the dispersion live there. The phrase in 8.3 ("a long distance") is used in the OT to describe foreign areas and a future ingathering of the people of God from such distant lands (cf Isa 60.4,9; Jer 46.27). The same word is used in Ephesians 2.13: "in Christ Jesus you who were once far away have been brought near." These three narratives (7.24-8.10) demonstrate that the Kingdom includes Gentiles.

8.1-5 - In this new setting, why don't the disciples ask Jesus to feed this multitude as he did on the earlier occasion? There are fewer people (4,000 people/5,000 men), with greater necessity (3 days/1 day), and still the disciples don't talk to Jesus about the people's need of food as they did in 8.35-36.

Have the disciples forgotten the miracle of feeding 5,000? By no means. The problem is not a faulty memory (when Jesus asks them later, they remember details of both occasions, 8.17-20). The problem is they remember *too much*. They remember that Jesus had commanded them, "You (emphatic) give them something to eat" (6.37). They are so afraid that Jesus will repeat that command that even on the third day they avoid mentioning the subject of food. They see no way in which they can feed the multitude and they want to avoid the embarrassment of another failure.

This time Jesus takes the initiative by declaring his compassion and the pressing need of the people (8.2). Then, even before the disciples can suggest their previous "solution" (6.36), he declares its impossibility (8.3). In this way, Jesus gently offers them a second chance to feed a multitude. But they attempt to escape all responsibility by saying, "But where in this remote place can anyone get enough bread to feed them?" If Jesus wants to do something, fine. The disciples, however, remove themselves from any involvement. Without contesting their "Don't count on us," Jesus proceeds. However, he involves the twelve noticeably less than on the previous occasion.

Their "dullness" (7.18) is not a question of forgetfulness or mental debility; they suffer from a lack of understanding due to the hardness of their hearts (6.52). They still do not know who Jesus is. If they had known, they still might have doubted that he would do for these Gentiles what he had done for the Jews previously. For the disciples, the occasion is full of danger. For them, the less they have to do with this crowd, the better.

v. 2 - Jesus reveals the Christian God who is "the Father of compassion" (2Co 1.3; cf. Isa 40.11; Mic 5.4). The "force" and other "energies" in the occult religions are incapable of compassion.

• "Three days" does not necessarily mean 72 hours, but one whole day and parts of the previous and following day (as in the period between the crucifixion and resurrection). The phrase is used in the three predictions (8.31; 9.31; 10.34) and also in 14.58.

•Bratcher and Nida (245) say that "have nothing to eat does not mean that they had eaten nothing for three days, but that they now had nothing left to eat."

v. 4 - This last reference to "remote place" draws the "wilderness-section" (6.6b-8.26) to a close and prepares for the "way-section," 8.27-10.52. (Swartley Structure 202)

vv. 4-5 - Lane (273f) finds an indirectness in the disciples' response here that is different in tone from their "disrespectful irony" in 6.37. They "refer the question of procuring bread back to Jesus (which) is tantamount to asking, What do you intend to do? Jesus' counter-question concerning the number of loaves available to them, on the other hand, is equivalent to the affirmation, I know what I am going to do."

v. 6 - Donald Senior (58) understands "bread" as a symbol of Jesus' universal mission "to gather and nourish the scattered people of Israel and to break beyond these boundaries to feed the Gentiles as well."

8.6-9 - Determined to feed this multitude, the compassionate Jesus personally tells the crowd to sit down. Only after giving thanks and breaking the loaves of bread does Jesus involve the disciples as in the earlier miracle. Apart from the numbers of food items, fragments and folks, the rest of this account is similar to the previous one.

Centuries earlier, God provided manna for his people in the desert. It could not be left over; it had to be consumed at once. On both of these occasions, however, Mark reports the large quantities of food left over, demonstrating that Jesus brings blessings surpassing God's provisions for Israel in the wilderness. The children of Israel ate first (cf 7.28); now Gentiles and Jews scattered abroad are being fed as well, and still there is more bread for the hungry. God's grace is for all people (13.10; 14.9); it does not divide; it heals breaches (Eph 2.14-22). The new people of God is a "mixed community." This is good news for all churches, like those in Rome, that struggle because of ethnic diversities.

v. 8 - More fragments were left over on the second occasion, for the 7 hampers (**spuris**; each one could hold a man, Ac 9.25) had a greater capacity than the 12 small wicker baskets (**kophinos**, 6.43).

v. 9 - In 6.44, there were "five thousand men," as befitting an oriental banquet. Here the text reads "four thousand persons," presumably including men, women and children. This is another subtle indication of a new community open to all (Gal 3.28). Could this large crowd be (at least in part) a result of the Gerasene's telling "in the Decapolis how much Jesus had done for him" (5.19-20)?

• Many writers see symbolism in the numbers. For example, the number twelve represents Israel; seven (indicating perfection and universality) signals the inclusion of Gentiles, etc. With Lane (274), it appears that "all such symbolic interpretation finds little support in the Markan text. The numbers are carefully noted because they were important" in 8.17-21.

8.10 - The events that follow the two feedings are also very different. In the first, Jesus made his disciples go ahead of him by boat to Bethsaida near the north shore before he dismissed the crowd (6.45-46). Then he went to pray and later walked on the water to join the disciples. Here, after he sends the crowd away, Jesus joins his disciples in the boat and heads west to the region of Dalmanutha.

This event provides further evidence as to Jesus' identity. He does what only God can do. In the light of Old Testament references amplified by contemporaneous Jewish expectation, "the miracle is a sign of the presence among men of the final Redeemer in whom God's promises are being fulfilled" (Cranfield 222).

Jesus is gracious towards those who are slow to learn. Like his Father, he is compassionate. He responds to the needs of the whole person, including physical hunger, and provides that which fills and satisfies. This is a proleptic picture of Jesus as host of the messianic banquet in the consummation of the Kingdom (Isa 25.6ff; Lk 13.29, etc.). From God's inexhaustible supply, all the needs of countless thousands will be met (cf Rev 21).

The miracle points to the Kingdom of God that includes men, women and children of every tongue and nation. The exclusive privileges of the Jews terminated; God shows his concern for all peoples by opening the Kingdom to Gentiles as well as Jews. This message is especially significant for churches torn between ethnic groups such as Jewish and Gentile believers.

4. Yeast and Bread, 8.11-21

After their absence from several events that demonstrate Jesus' mighty power, the Pharisees reappear, seeking Jesus. Their motives differ dramatically from those of the Gentiles. Their opposition to Jesus has not softened; rather, it stiffens. They taunt him; they insist on a sign from heaven. He refuses to grant their demand, however, for he knows that they, like Israel in Moses' day, respond to miracles with stubborn rebellion.

• Jesus' discussion with the Pharisees on the shore sets the context for his dialogue with the disciples in the boat (14-21). First employed together in 6.52, "bread" and "understanding" (key words in 6.6b-8.26) are reunited in these two paragraphs. Here "bread" is contrasted with "yeast" and the disciples' lack of understanding is compared to the Pharisees'. Verses 11-21 pull together much of the preceding chapters in preparation for the climax hinted at in 8.22-26 and reached in 8.29.

8.11-13 - Upon Jesus' return to the western shore of the lake (v. 10), the Pharisees seek him out and begin to argue (cf 1.27; 9.14,16; 12.28) with him. Disagreements between the Pharisees and Jesus have continued from their first encounter (2.1-3.6; 7.1-23; cf 3.22-30). Now they demand that Jesus perform a miracle as proof of the source of his authority (cf 11.28ff). In reality, they have already made up their minds about him. As Mark says, their purpose is to trap (cf 1.13; 10.2; 12.15) him. If they succeed, he must die as a false prophet (cf Dt 18.20-22).

Jesus has already done many mighty works that provide demonstrable proof that his power (**dunamis**, cf 5.30) comes from God. But the Pharisees want outward compelling proof (**semeion**, "a sign") from heaven (a Semitism meaning "from God"). After all Jesus has done, their demand is absurd. The mighty works are already there and offer sufficient evidence for those who have eyes to see and ears to hear. The Pharisees, however, are blind.

In another expression of his human emotions (7.34; cf 1.41; 3.5; 6.6; 10.14; 14.34), Jesus sighs deeply and asks, "Why does this generation ask for a miraculous sign?" Through mighty acts, God had delivered his people from bondage in Egypt. Yet the people tested God, demanding further miraculous signs from Moses (Nu 14.11,22). Another perverse generation (**genea**, 8.38; 9.19; 13.30) has arisen, confronting the One who is greater than Moses.

Again Jesus claims divine authority for his words by using that expression which only he used: **amen lego** ("I tell you the truth," cf 3.28). His refusal is absolute: "No sign will be given to" such people. The Pharisees are unable to recognize the signs that God gives them; nevertheless, they demand signs of their own choosing. To grant their demand would, as Cranfield says (258), "make faith impossible (for it would preclude a personal decision) and would abandon the messianic path of veiledness ordained by the Father."

As a token of his rejecting their demand for a sign, Jesus leaves them, getting back into the boat with his disciples.

v. 11 - The Pharisees knew that false prophets could perform signs (Dt 13.2; cf Ex 7.10-12). Jesus later warned his disciples that false Christs and false prophets would appear and perform signs in an effort to deceive (13.22).

• Mark indicates Satan (1.12,13), the Pharisees (8.11; 10.2; 12.15), and, by inference, Peter (8.32-33), as those who tempt Jesus.

• Translated "sign" (here and 13.4,22), the Synoptic writers, as Cranfield (257f) explains, "use **semeion** to denote an outward compelling proof of divine authority--something which unbelief demands but Jesus resolutely refuses to give." Since Jesus' miracles are not signs in this sense, the Synoptists call them **dunameis** (power; cf 5.30). The Gospel of John, however, uses **semeion** as a sign (miracle) pointing to Jesus as the manifestation of God's glory.

Like Jesus' parabolic teaching, his mighty works are ambivalent (for example, they had different meanings for Jesus and for the scribes, 3.22; cf 6.2-3). They are part of "the indirect presentation of Jesus as the hidden Son of God on earth" (Martin Mark 170f), performed to cause faith which leads to obedience. Human nature wants proofs ("signs") before venturing out in simple trust. However, in the words of Anderson (199), "Faith ceases to be faith when it clamors for visible or tangible proof." Rebellious Israelites who demanded further signs of God's powers were called "an evil generation" (Dt 1.35; 32.5; Ps 95.10). The Apostles also warn against the "corrupt generation" in Ac 2.40; Php 2.15.

v. 12 - Some versions read "sighing in his spirit," meaning in the center of his personality.

• Alan Richardson says "Jesus refuses to show the signs of the Kingdom of God to those who will not understand them, since he does not work miracles for their own sake--either as exhibitions of power or as spontaneous deeds of compassion. The working of miracles is a part of the proclamation of the Kingdom of God, not an end in itself" (cited in Swartley Mark: Way 85). Those who seek signs will be disappointed: anyone who seeks the Lord himself will never be disappointed.
• "The claims of God can be known only by committing oneself in loyalty to him, not by standing outside and arrogantly saying, 'Produce your evidence!'" (Moule 60f) Cf Jn 7.17.
• Jesus' refusal does not mean he cannot nor would not perform any additional mighty works but that he must choose to do them. He refuses to place himself under the control of any person (later, however, he does just that; cf 10.33; 14.53ff). "The lonely cross on the hill is the only sign still to our world that *Jesus is God's message of love to all men.*" (Martin Action 64; italics his). And yet that "sign" is "a stumbling block to Jews and foolishness to Gentiles" (1Co 1.18-24).

8.14-21 - While crossing over to the other side of Lake Galilee, Jesus warns the disciples, "Be careful; watch out for the yeast of the Pharisees and that of Herod." Knowing that yeast is employed in making bread rise, the disciples conclude that Jesus must be rebuking them for forgetting to bring bread for the trip. They are so preoccupied with their own problems that they fail to consider what Jesus is saying to them about the Pharisees and Herod.

The disciples are to avoid that "yeast" which, although unseen, is working havoc in others. The Pharisees' legalism, shrouded in false and inconsistent piety, dulls their understanding, making them incapable of accepting the truth Jesus presents. Their very religiosity separates them from God. Herod, lawless and godless, refuses the truth spoken by John (Mk 6.19-20). In spite of their apparent differences, the Pharisees and Herod demonstrate a similar hardness of heart. They neither repent nor believe. As Hooker (49) concludes, their "yeast" affects their whole personality, giving them a rigid, self-righteous attitude, making them "uncomprehending and hard-hearted, so they are unable to see the evidence when it is presented to them."

Aware of the disciples' discussion among themselves (cf 9.32-34), Jesus explains this short parable by means of a series of questions designed to make them think. His questions are provocative, designed to jar them loose from their concern about having no bread on board. Jesus hopes to open their eyes to see the meaning beyond the facts, to see beyond his words and works to his person.

Earlier, Jesus had stated the difference between his followers ("the secret of the Kingdom has been given to you," 4.11-12) and outsiders who are characterized by hardened hearts, blind eyes and deaf ears. Neither the Pharisees nor Herod see. They are outsiders. Then Jesus asks, "Do you disciples still not understand?" In other words, Are you outsiders, no different from the Pharisees and Herod?

This is strong admonishment, but Jesus is not talking about an abstract possibility. The disciples don't understand the parables, in spite of his explanations given to them in private. They abandon some religious customs related to the Sabbath and ritual washings, without really knowing why. They tend to keep the yeast of the outsiders and reject the bread Jesus gives. They still don't know what is going on. The strength of Jesus' rebuke is directly proportional to the magnitude of the danger.

In the boat, separated from other voices, Jesus juxtaposes questions about the feedings of the two multitudes in order to help the disciples understand. Through these questions, Jesus is saying to them, You have the necessary pieces; put them together and you will see the whole picture. The disciples' answers testify to the excellence of their memory; their understanding, however, is poor. Failure to understand the feedings is failure to understand Jesus himself, for they point to him as the One in whom God's reign breaks into the Jewish and Gentile worlds.

Jesus repeats his opening question: "Do you still not see?" (cf Jn 20.9). The disciples are blind to the abundant grace of God in Jesus, but they are not hopelessly blind. Read on! Their eyes will be opened, as dramatized by the story that follows.

v. 14 - As we all know from personal experience, the fact that people can "forget to bring bread" in no way detracts from their ability to remember past experiences.

v. 15 - In both Testaments, yeast ("leaven") often symbolizes evil (cf Ex 12.14-20; 1Co 5.6-8; Gal 5.9), with emphasis upon a little bit affecting the whole. Jesus' ministry is characterized as "giving bread" whereas the Pharisees and Herod are disseminating "leaven."

vv. 17-18 - The reappearance of "understanding" and "bread" (cf 6.52) and "see" and "hear" (cf. 4.12) indicate that Jesus is doubling his efforts to open the eyes of the disciples, warning them about a danger already present. Had they listened attentively, they would have understood and avoided several pitfalls. Symbolically, they would have bread and no yeast; as it is, they have yeast and no bread. The exalted Lord, who walks in the midst of the churches, continues to warn and rebuke his disciples (Rev 1.12-3.22).

vv. 19-21 - This dialogue would be meaningless if the feeding of four thousand were just another version of the feeding of five thousand. See comments on 8.1-10.

• Just as God frequently called upon Israel to remember his mighty works, Jesus asks the disciples to recall their experiences of God's faithfulness as a step towards overcoming their crisis in faith.

• By reflecting on "how many basketfuls of pieces" they picked up, the disciples should remember that Jesus provides enough and to spare, relieving their anxiety about having only one loaf in the boat.

vv. 22-23 present several verbal similarities to 7.32-33; the differences arise from the peculiar needs of each disability. In addition, neither account mentions the disciples or faith. A word-for-word comparison in parallel columns makes the similarities and differences evident.

v. 20 - The next reference to "bread" (14.22) is the last in Mark, where "bread" points to Jesus himself. Thus "you give them bread" in 6.37 means "you give them Jesus" (Cf John 6.34-35).

v. 21 - Lest we be too critical of the disciples' slowness to understand, we need to remember that they had to overcome two serious barriers to identifying Jesus. Their hope centered in a victorious military-political Messiah; in addition, the thought of the holy God living as a man among sinners contradicted all they had been taught. Soon, a third barrier would arise for Jews and Gentiles: the offense of the cross.

• Robbins (158, 162) analyzes this as the second stage of learning, in which "people learn how to do things before they understand the implications of what they do." In the third stage (8.27-10.45), they learn the meaning of what they have already been doing.

5. A Blind Man Sees Clearly, 8.22-26

The unique characteristics of this miracle beautifully interpret and conclude the preceding emphases upon seeing in order to understand. The giving of sight to the blind man climaxes the first half of the book while preparing the reader for the second half which begins with a breakthrough in the disciples' understanding (8.27-29).

• Fowler (107) concludes that 7.31ff and 8.22ff "were composed by the author as a matched pair: the similarities invite us to compare the stories while the dissimilarities force us to recognize the integrity of each story as a distinct episode within the Markan narrative." Bultmann, however, regarded them as duplicate accounts of the same incident. Apparently, blindness was not limited to the first century.

8.22-23a - After feeding the five thousand earlier, Jesus sent his disciples off to Bethsaida by boat (6.45). They arrived instead in Gennesaret (6.53). Now they arrive in Bethsaida, a village on the east bank of the Jordan River slightly north of Lake Galilee.

Once again, some people bring a needy person to Jesus (cf 2.3; 6.55; 7.32). They beg him to touch the blind man (this would have special significance for a person who learns much through his sense of touch). Jesus takes him by the hand away from the crowd (cf 7.33) in order to establish "communication with an individual who had learned to be passive in society" (Lane 285). Each is now attentive to the other, facilitating a personal relationship. No doubt having heard of Jesus' ability to cure, the man's hopes rise when Jesus spits on his eyes and touches him.

8.23b-26 - This miracle is unique in three details:

1. Jesus asks the man, "Do you see anything?" Nowhere else does Jesus ask anything like this of someone he is healing; he normally gives assurance of a completed cure (as in 5.34 and 7.29).

2. After looking up to double-check, the man indicates that his vision is fuzzy. The healing was only partial! By asking the question, Jesus seems to expect something different from his normally complete and instantaneous cure.

3. Jesus touches the man's eyes a second time, resulting in clear vision. From that hour, the man's faculty is restored; he sees perfectly.

The author closes this story quickly. Jesus sends the man home, telling him, "Don't go into the village." Mark neither explains these instructions nor mentions the reactions of the man or the people. Such details would have distracted from the central purpose of these miracles.

This miracle and the healing of the deaf man with a speech impediment (7.31-37) are unique to Mark. The similarities in the two narratives challenge us to seek the significance of these events in Mark's gospel. Both narratives allude to Isaiah 35, thereby announcing that Jesus is the Messiah. With him, the promise of redemption has become a reality, the new era has dawned (Isa 29.18; 35.5).

Together they imply that "hearing" and "seeing" are metaphors of spiritual comprehension. They dramatize the disciples' persistent lack of perception while Jesus perseveres in leading them into full understanding. Just as the healing of the deaf man led to singing a hymn honoring the one who does everything well (7.37), so the cure of a blind man contributes to the twelve recognizing Jesus as the Messiah (8.29). This is Mark's beautiful way of portraying how Jesus gives hearing and sight to those who lack understanding in order that they might follow him.

The man's clear vision came as a result of Jesus' second touch. Truth is almost always perceived in steps. Will a "second touch" be necessary for the disciples to clearly perceive who Jesus is?

What remains hidden in the first half of Mark's Gospel is unveiled in the next.

v. 23b - The use of spittle to cure, a common practice in ancient times, indicates Jesus' intent to cure.

• For emphasis, Mark employs five verbs to describe the man's newly acquired sight. In similar fashion, he made nine references to "hearing" in chapter 4 and used a profusion of terms to describe the disciples' blindness in 8.13-21.

v. 26 - The use of the verb **apostello** (see 6.7) here may indicate that Jesus gave him a mission to fulfil, similar to the Gerasene's (5.19). Local conditions may have been a factor in avoiding the village. Most modern editions of the Greek text omit the phrase "don't tell anyone."

• This division and the next one close with curing blind men. Each narrative is a metaphor of its division while preparing for the one that follows.

INTRODUCTION TO MARK 8.27 - 16.8

Upon concluding his report on Jesus' mission to Jews and Gentiles in Northern Palestine, Mark depicts Jesus' journey from Caesarea Philippi to Jerusalem (8.27-10.52). He then dedicates chapters 11 through 16 exclusively to Jesus' ministry in Jerusalem and its environs.

This new phase in Jesus' life and ministry is a startling reversal to what one would expect. The One replete with God-given power and authority appears as the servant of all. He submits himself to humans and makes himself subject to their evil designs; he suffers and dies in obedience to God. It is an incredible way to establish a kingdom. Nevertheless, Jesus invites others to follow him on the way of the cross.

The opening dialogue (8.27-30) brings to a climax the first half of Mark. Simultaneously, it serves as a transition and introduction to the teaching on the requisites for Messiahship and for discipleship (8.31-9.1) which follows without a break. Just as 1.1-13 introduces the whole Gospel and 1.14-15 served as the backdrop for the first half, these verses underlie the second half of the book.

Several new themes and vocabulary are introduced (e.g., the first explicit prediction of the passion, the first mention of the cross, the first reference to Jesus' coming in glory). The scenario moves from the northern regions to Jerusalem. New individuals appear, but the main characters (Jesus, the disciples, the people and the opposition) are dominant, their roles intensifying as the narrative progresses. In the title to his Gospel (1.1), Mark states that Jesus is the Christ, the Son of God. Only now, as the second half opens, does the title "Christ" reappear (in Peter's confession). The first human identification of Jesus as Son of God awaits Jesus' crucifixion, near the end of Mark's Gospel.

• The overall framework of this Gospel is a "two-step progression" which helps the reader identify and clarify themes and emphases by taking a second look (Rhoads and Michie 48-49).

ON THE WAY TO THE CROSS

MARK 8.27 - 10.52

Disciples confess: "You are the Messiah" 8.27	Jesus responds by declaring: THE WAY OF THE CROSS The Son of Man must Suffer, Die and Rise Again Jesus calls upon all Disciples to follow Him in the Way 1st Pronouncement 8.31	2nd Pronouncement 9.30	3rd Pronouncement 10.32
Requisites for Messiah	The Son of Man must: suffer and be rejected, be killed, after 3 days, rise again.	The Son of Man will: be betrayed to men, be killed by them, rise again.	The Son of Man will: be condemned by priests, be mocked and killed by Gentiles, rise again.
Requisites for Disciples (Individual and Community) *reader, continue this study:*	Anyone who follows Him must: have God's things in mind, deny himself, take up his cross, lose his life for Jesus,	Disciples will: serve others above self, accept others, not cause others to sin, avoid sinning at all costs,	Disciples will:

- PART 5 -
ON THE WAY TO THE CROSS
8.27 - 10.52

The beautiful organization of this Gospel is nowhere more evident than in 8.27-10.52. The author carefully weaves together three threads (a short word, a long journey and a dominant theme) to form a tapestry which, located at the hub of the narrative, emphasizes his central message to his readers.

The word "way" (**hodos**) suggests a journey, and this division presents a geographical progression, beginning near Caesarea Philippi (8.27) in the extreme north of Palestine and terminating in Jerusalem (11.1), the place of the crucifixion. Jesus proceeds on this journey, unhesitatingly and without detours. The disciples, on the other hand, vacillate a great deal, for they lack the heart of a servant who gives one's life for others.

The theme of Jesus' forthcoming death and resurrection dominates Mark's tapestry. Along the way, Jesus makes three pronouncements (8.31; 9.31; 10.33-34) that constitute part of his self-revelation. The division begins and ends with christological declarations ("the Christ," in 8.29; "the Son of David," in 10.47) beyond its seven-fold repetition of the title "the Son of Man." Although the cross is central, it is not the end. It is the way to the Kingdom that will be consummated in his coming in glory and power (8.38-9.1).

Each of the three distinct predictions is followed by a negative response from the disciples that lead to new teachings on Christology and discipleship. Jesus answers each of their objections. To their expectation that the Messiah rule by *power* (8.32,33), he defines the way of the cross. To their desire for *prestige* (9.32-34), he presents the model of a child. To their attempts to attain *positions* of privilege in the Kingdom (10.35-37), he takes the role of a servant (10.38-45). Jesus never asks the disciples to do what he himself is not doing. He himself models true discipleship.

Mark insists that only by a life of self-denial can a person substantiate his/her claim to know who Jesus really is. A true disciple gradually acquires Jesus' qualities of character by following him "in the way." As Swartley (New Way 83) says, "any view of Christianity that fails to emphasize discipleship as the heart of salvation renders itself inadequate and abortive."

This teaching unit includes the highest concentration of the words of Jesus and of his ethical teachings. "Way" (**hodos**, first used in 1.2,3) occurs in the first and last verses of this division, appearing five times more frequently than in the rest of the book. Few miracles are recounted; the crowds are mentioned infrequently. Jesus engages his disciples in intensive interaction through reciprocal questions and answers as they learn the meaning of his activities. They are taught concrete lessons about self-denial in interpersonal relations and material values.

A. DYING IN ORDER TO LIVE, 8.27 - 9.29

After many months of accompanying Jesus, the disciples make a break-through in their understanding and confess that Jesus is the Christ. Jesus does not praise their new insight, however. He begins the second phase of his self-revelation with clear teaching about his coming suffering, death and resurrection. In answer to Peter's protest, Jesus explains that self-denial is also the way of the disciple. This is a hard lesson to learn, as the disciples demonstrate repeatedly. After declaring that this is the way to glory, Jesus gives a select group of disciples a preview of God's Kingdom coming in power.

1. Requisites for the Messiah and Disciples, 8.27 - 9.1

In this well-crafted unit, Mark provides additional information as to who Jesus is and where he is going. The Son of Man must go the way of the cross, for it is inseparably tied to the coming of the Kingdom of God. Furthermore, anyone who follows him in the way gains his or her true self and a share in the Kingdom. The rest of the Gospel should be read in the light of this background.

THE DISCIPLES' CONFESSION, 8.27-30

Jesus takes his disciples to a new area, the villages around Caesarea Philippi. "On the way" (presumably separated from the religious authorities and the crowds), he asks them point blank about knowledge of his identity.

Contrary to the practice of the rabbis, who were questioned by their pupils, Jesus initiates this dialogue by questioning his disciples. Rather than introduce more rhetorical questions that he himself answers, Jesus poses questions requiring direct answers. By asking first what others are thinking, he gives his disciples an opportunity to reflect upon the answers of uncommitted outsiders.

Many acknowledged Jesus to be a servant of God, like John the Baptist and Elijah (6.14-16). The disciples, however, become increasingly dissatisfied with those opinions. They know that Jesus is unique among God's servants. Therefore when Jesus elicits a declaration from the group, their previous uncertainty disappears. Aided by Jesus' two-step questioning (cf 8.19-20), they finally put the pieces together and declare, "You are the Christ."

The disciples finally confess part of what we readers learned in the Title (1.1) of this Gospel: Jesus is the Christ. Although Jesus does not reject the title of Messiah, he warns the disciples against speaking to anyone about this, for they themselves do not yet know the Messiah's mission. In first-century Palestine, the title Messiah was ambiguous, subject to non-biblical nuances. Jesus combats efforts to change his universal mission into a nationalistic military movement intent upon overthrowing Rome. Consequently, instead of congratulating the disciples for their increased understanding, Jesus begins a whole new emphasis in his teaching ministry.

While Jesus is revealing who he is, he continues to follow the path of messianic hiddenness (cf 4.11-12). He will openly proclaim his Messiahship only when he is a helpless prisoner and his claim seems ridiculous. This command to silence is only temporary (cf 9.9); after the disciples see clearly who Jesus is, they will proclaim openly that he is the Christ.

• About 25 miles north of Bethsaida, Caesarea Philippi was long a center of pagan religions. Jesus possibly chose this frontier between paganism and Israel to indicate the universal outreach of the gospel.

v. 28 - Some contemporary religions say that Jesus is a prophet; others say the greatest of prophets. Such answers are inadequate if they do not also confess Jesus Christ as the Son of God. Those who deny the deity of Jesus Christ or claim that Christ only seemed to be human (a docetic teaching) fall into errors that have been denounced as heresies since the beginning of the Christian era.

v. 29 - The plural pronoun is emphatic: "you," the Twelve, in contrast to others. Peter answered for all.

• The title "Messiah" ("Christ") appears only seven times in Mark's Gospel: 1.1; 8.29; 9.41; 12.35; 13.21; 14.61; 15.32. By this time in Jewish history, many (including Jesus' disciples) thought of the Messiah as the one whom God would send to deliver Israel and establish God's righteous rule upon the earth. The Qumran community expected the Messiah as an eschatological prophet combining the offices of David's royal and Aaron's priestly functions. Cranfield (270f) affirms that the real significance of Old Testament references to the Messiah is only understood in the light of their fulfillment in Jesus. From this perspective, the title "Messiah" designates One who is the King, Priest, Prophet and "the One in whom the life of the whole nation of Israel finds its fulfillment and meaning."

THE SON OF MAN IN THE HANDS OF GOD, 8.31-32a

Jesus now begins to add new content to his teaching, designed to correct the disciples' inadequate understanding of the messianic role. "Who Jesus is" will be better understood in the light of "where he is going." Jesus lays aside the enigma of parables as he speaks plainly about the role of the Messiah. He will repeat and add to this pronouncement, for he seeks to prepare his disciples for his passion and resurrection.

The disciples' confession is followed by Jesus' confession of his identity. Avoiding the title of Messiah, Jesus again uses his favorite self-description: the "Son of Man." Based on Daniel 7.13, this title is not a claim to the status, privileges and honor ascribed to the Messiah by his contemporaries; rather, it is Jesus' acknowledgment and willing acceptance that God's will involves suffering: "the Son of Man *must* (**dei**; cf 13.7,13) suffer." Although he is God's Son, his passion is a necessity bewildering to men and woman but grounded in the will of God as expressed in Scripture (cf Ps 22; 69; 118; Isa 50.4ff; 52.13-53.12; Zec 13.7). Jesus follows the path of the suffering servant of God; it is essential to his Messiahship. The healer becomes the sufferer.

Among the "many things" he must suffer is rejection by those who should receive the Messiah, namely, the elders, chief priests and teachers of the law. The shadow of Jesus' death has already been seen in the narrative (2.20; 3.6; and implied in the prior death of John the Baptist, 1.14 and 6.14-29). Now for the first time, Jesus explicitly foretells that "he must be killed" and that, after three days, God will raise him from the dead.

v. 31 - By referring to himself as "the Son of Man," Jesus could give new connotations to his mission as the One who brings the good news that bursts old forms (2.21-22). In 14.62, Jesus substitutes the title "Son of Man" when asked, "Are you the Christ?" He avoids the title "Messiah" because of its political undertones.

• Mark mentions each of the three groups which comprised the Sanhedrin, the "Supreme Court" of Israel in religious and civil matters (cf 9.27; 14.43,53,55; 15.1). They were: 1) the elders, the lay members of the body; 2) the "chief priests," including the past and present chief priests and their family members; 3) and the teachers of the law or scribes. They appear increasingly until Jesus' prediction is fulfilled.

• Jesus did not die as a martyr who refused to renounce his convictions; he died as a part of God's redemptive plan (10.45; Ro 3.21-26). This is indicated by "must" (**dei**), a necessity based on God's sovereign will (8.31; 9.11; 13.7,10,14; 14.31) in his offer to redeem sinners.

• "He will rise again" is a Semitic way of saying "God will raise him from the dead." The phrase "after three days" is equal to "on the third day" (as in Mt, Lk and 1Co 15.4).

MUTUAL CONFRONTATION, 8.32b-33

Having just acclaimed that the hopes of Israel would be fulfilled in Jesus, the disciples fail to grasp what Jesus is saying about a suffering Messiah (cf 9.32). However, Peter understands enough to object. He has no desire to follow a person headed for failure. Possibly in order to spare Jesus the pain of a remonstrance in the presence of the other disciples, Peter takes Jesus aside and begins to rebuke him. After struggling so long to know who Jesus is, Peter rejects Jesus' new, clear teachings about who he is and where he is going.

In reply, Jesus rebukes Peter for setting his mind on human things. To follow Christ involves "having in mind the things of God" (cf Ro 8.5; Php 2.5-8; 3.3-10; Col 3.2), earnestly desiring to "take captive every thought to make it obedient to Christ" (2Co 10.5). Jesus does not disqualify Peter for rebuking him; he proceeds to explain to him the essence of discipleship.

Even while the disciples are growing in understanding, Satan is at work. He entangles Peter into thinking his way and seeks to use him in "an attempt to draw Jesus away from the path of obedience to his Father's will" (Cranfield 280). He succeeds in turning the confession into confrontation. To suggest that Jesus--or anyone--disobey God is the work of Satan. Jesus forcefully rejects all attempts to prevent him from going to the cross.

With a look at the other disciples, Jesus includes in his rebuke all who reject God's way. Jesus insists upon fulfilling God's will, which means going the way of the cross. The Son of Man does not rule by force but by weakness.

v.32b - As Anderson (206, emphasis his) aptly says, "Knowing him formerly, the disciples really did not know him. Knowing him now with greater clarity, they really *do not want* to know." Martin (Action 72) notes that "for Peter, the indication that the Son of Man will die is unthinkable. For Jesus, it is inevitable." Some people dishonor Jesus because of the cross; God honors him because of the crucifixion.

• The same strong verb (rebuked, warned) is used in verse 33; also in 1.25; 3.12; 4.39; 9.25; 10.13,48.

v. 33 - Wilcock (43) presents as a possibility that "when Jesus tells Peter to get behind him, he means him to return to the humble, teachable position of a disciple, which is what the same Greek phrase means in the very next verse ('come *after* me'; similarly in 1.17,20)."

• Satan, "the prince of this world" (Jn 12.31), infiltrates all areas of life in his determination to overthrow God. He manipulates people and even uses religions to immunize people against the claims of Christ. Without understanding what he was saying, Peter became Satan's advocate, casting doubt upon God's plan (cf Ge 3.1-5). His confession did not free Peter from prior ways of thinking that Satan exploited for his own benefit. Perhaps Peter remembered this experience when he wrote 1Pe 5.8. Satan continues to devour and to deceive (1Pe 4.15-19; 1Ti 4.1). By the time Mark wrote, a humbled Peter probably asked him neither to cover over his failures nor to exalt him.

REQUISITES FOR DISCIPLESHIP, 8.34-9.1

8.34-37 - Having stated God's requirements for the Messiah (v 31), Jesus now declares God's requirements for the disciple. Anyone who has played "follow the leader" knows that those who follow go where the leader goes. The nature and path of the disciple are patterned after who Jesus is and where he is going.

Discipleship is "following Jesus" in a living personal relationship with him. Rabbis bound the loyalty of their students to the Law and philosophers attached their pupils to the truth. The prophets stood aside so that their message, not their person, was everything. In marked contrast, Jesus calls for a personal alliance between himself and those who follow him. Personal fulfillment is only possible in relation to other persons; complete fulfillment is only possible in relationship to that complete Person, the Son of God. As men and women maintain a growing relationship with him, they identify themselves with him, just as the Son of Man identifies himself with men and women. Through discovering who Jesus is, I discover who I am. By following him, I am freed to live at my God-given potential.

Jesus calls the crowd to himself, for this word is not limited to the Twelve. Rather, it concerns all who long for the righteous life that God desires.

To "follow Jesus" requires self-denial. This involves: 1) shifting the center of gravity from a concern for self to reckless abandon to the will of God, 2) a sustained willingness to say "No" to oneself in order to say "Yes" to God, and 3) a radical denunciation of all self-idolatry, as Lane (307) points out. In opposition to self-affirmation, self-denial even includes disclaiming prerogatives to "human rights" (cf 1Co 9.12,15).

In this materialistically minded world, many think that "to deny oneself" means to give up the enjoyment of "things." In a sense, the disciples had already forsaken "things" such as the security of their homes and employment. The source of self-assertion, however, is internal, arising from the heart (cf 7.14-21). To deny oneself is, in Cranfield's words (281), "to disown, not just one's sins, but one's self, to turn away from the idolatry of self-centeredness" and allow Jesus to rule supreme where the ego had previously exercised full control.

The phrase "take up one's cross" has been twisted to mean simply to endure a petty burden or an unavoidable inconvenience or to deny oneself certain pleasures or objects. These "burdens" we grudgingly bear are not crosses we take up voluntarily, for we rebel against them. Crosses are taken up voluntarily as a part of following Jesus.

To men and women of the first century, to "take up one's cross" meant to be crucified as Jesus was. For many, the cross was literally the instrument of their death; for others, it symbolizes death by other means. Jesus calls all Christians to be willing to sacrifice life itself for him. This disposition to die for him is manifested in one's determination to live for him.

The rigors of true discipleship are spelled out in the four sayings that comprise verses 35 through 37. When given the choice to "renounce Jesus and live," some deny him and thereby lose their true self, the very thing they seek. On the other hand, one who loses his life will find a quality of life superior to what he lost, providing his motivation is doing all for Jesus and the gospel. In 1956, shortly before being killed in an effort to evangelize the Auca Indians of Ecuador, missionary Jim Elliot expressed this truth when he wrote: "He is no fool who gives what he cannot keep to gain what he cannot lose."

Carrying the paradox further, Jesus declares that to obtain this true life is the greatest gain. No price tag can be put on it. One who forfeits his share in eternal life cannot buy it back, even if he owns everything. His loss is irreparable. Life is not a commercial venture evaluated by profit over loss. The distinctive of a disciple is not to gain but to give; he gives the maximum, his own self.

Jesus does not ask us to abandon our desire for life, security and satisfaction; rather, he insists that we change our ways of seeking it. Authentic life is gained only as we deny our self-centeredness and become centered in Jesus.

What person can demand such absolute loyalty? Who can say that eternal life depends upon following him? It is through these demands that Jesus again implies who he is. He is not a megalomaniac, but God manifested in the flesh. As such, he can make these demands.

v. 34 - In words addressed to everyone ("the crowd," 34a), Jesus lays down (34b) and elaborates on (35-38) the basic principle of discipleship, concluding with the promise of 9.1. Each saying in verses 35-38 is introduced by **gar** ("for"), a conjunction used frequently in Mark to introduce a startling teaching. Radical discipleship begins with the disciple sharing in Christ's self-denial and concludes with sharing in his Kingdom of power (9.1).

• The aorist verbs in 8.34b (come after, deny, and take up) "denote processes which begin with the decision to follow Jesus and continue right through discipleship" (Best Following 33). The verb translated "deny" or "disown" is used in 14.31,32,72, always in reference to Peter's denial of Jesus.

• The cross was an infamous instrument of death. A Galilean named Judas led a rebellion against Rome and raided the royal armory at Sepphoris, situated an hour's walk from Nazareth where Jesus was living as a boy. In reprisal, Rome burned Sepphoris, sold its inhabitants into slavery and, on crosses lining the roadside for all to see, crucified two thousand rebels. Undoubtedly, Jesus knew about this horrible event.

• The "imitation" of Christ falls short of what Jesus meant by "follow me." The example of Jesus in suffering, rejection and death out of absolute loyalty to the will of God is a pattern for the believer. Yet the disciple cannot really imitate him, for Jesus was unique in his relationship to God: he was the very revelation in history of God himself. Jesus also occupies a unique position in relation to the disciples: he is to be obeyed (9.7). Jesus is much more than an example to be imitated.

• Contrary to the accusation that religion is an escape from the realities of life, Jesus identified himself with those who suffer and called upon his followers to do the same.

• Jesus' description of the nature of discipleship contradicts the health and wealth theology which promises joy, prosperity and miraculous healings as primary benefits to all who "follow Jesus." The message of "gain" and "profit" contradicts Jesus' demands to "give" and "lose." The disciple is more than a recipient of blessing, and happiness is not the supreme good. As James I. Packer says, "Sooner or later, God's guidance, which brings us out of darkness into light, will also bring us out of light into darkness. It is part of the way of the cross" (Knowing God, p 229). Jesus was not about to fulfill the popular expectations of the Messiah then, nor is he a personal Genie at one's beck and call now.

v. 35 - Suffering does not atone for one's sins; we are healed by Jesus' wounds (Isa 53.5), not by ours.

v. 36 - The word **psuche** should not be confused with the Greek idea of "soul" as the spiritual part of man, distinct and separate from a person's fleshly body. It is used here in "a double sense, first of a man's ordinary human life and then of his true self or personality" (Taylor 382).

8.38-9.1 - The Kingdom of God is *already present* as a mystery hidden in the humble Son of Man and his followers (8.31-37), but it has *not yet* come in its final consummation. Earlier (8.31), Jesus declared that, after his death, he "will rise again." Now he unveils more of God's plan and focuses on the Kingdom in its fullness. Jesus will return in the Father's glory, in the awesome role of the eschatological Judge of this adulterous and sinful age (**genea**). Then the Son of Man who came offering forgiveness (2.10) will reject those who are ashamed to follow the One who died a criminal's death. God will vindicate Jesus and those who now share his sufferings will share in his exaltation.

In a world intoxicated with its own glory, Jesus manifests God's glory "only because his own glory means nothing to him and the Father's glory means everything" (Lane 311). In this way, Jesus' entire life and ministry are set in the perspective of the Father's glory.

The chapter break after verse 38 is misleading. The first verse of chapter 9 does not drop the subject of the Second Coming. Rather, in 9.1 this theme is viewed from a different angle, as the following comparison demonstrates:

verses	8.38	9.1
comparisons	the Son of Man comes	the Kingdom of God comes
	in glory	in power
	a strong warning: he will come as judge	a sure promise: some standing here will see it
interpretation: verses refer to	the parousia	a preview of the parousia

In 9.1, Jesus makes a "sure promise" that the power of the Kingdom (presently hidden in weakness) will be manifested shortly. The transfiguration narrative follows, in verses 2-8. During their lifetime (i.e., before they "taste death"), some (three of the Twelve) of those "standing here" with Jesus "see" what transpires on the mountain. They have a foretaste of the coming Kingdom. We understand that Jesus' pronouncement in 9.1 introduces the transfiguration (9.2-8) as a preview of the Kingdom of God coming with power.

v. 38 - "Generation" (**genea**; cf 8.12; 9.19; 13.30) here signifies the age or period of time before Jesus' return. The expression "adulterous and sinful generation" is a rebuke based on the character of men and women who forsake God and live according to this age. It recalls the denunciations made by the prophets against idolatry (Isa 1.4,21; Eze 16.32; Hos 2.4).
• In Mark's Gospel, the Father acknowledged his Son only in private at his baptism (1.11) and before a select few at the transfiguration (9.7). That will change when God openly acknowledges this "mere man" as his Son and manifests his glory (**doxa**) in him, in recognition of his self-denial and cross-bearing.
• Jesus' reference to God as his Father corresponds to the Father's references to the Son (1.11; 9.7) and to Mark's in 1.1. It is used again in 11.25-26; 13.32; 14.36 (cf 3.35; 12.6-8).
• The statement "ashamed of me...the Son of Man will be ashamed" makes it clear that Jesus and the Son of Man are the same person. Also, "when he (i.e., the Son of Man) comes in his Father's glory" identifies the Son of Man as the Son of God. The saying "of me and of my words" indicates that Jesus' person is inseparable from his words. He himself is the message he proclaims.
• A person's reaction to Jesus and his words determine one's eschatological destiny.
• The eyes of the disciples are not to be on the rewards, on the end, or even on the way itself, but on the risen Lord who continues to lead his disciples (cf 16.7). Unfortunately, the institutionalization of the church results in a detachment from the person of Jesus whenever "serving the cause" becomes the primary goal. Cf Heb 12.1-3.
• Discipleship requires confessing Jesus before antagonistic representatives of a perverse generation, not just making a declaration of faith before a closed circle of sympathetic friends. "In all the records about Jesus, we hear him warning against reliance on verbal confessions alone" (Minear 94).
• The word **doxa** ("glory") reappears in 13.26 and 14.62; each of these three passages draw upon Daniel 7.13-14. Here, glory is an attribute of God the Father; in 13.26, it is attributed to the Son of Man himself.
• This verse is the first explicit reference in Mark to the Second Coming of Christ.
• Angels served Jesus in the desert (1.13) and will serve him and the elect at the **parousia** (13.27; cf Mt 13.41, 24.31; 1Th 4.16; 2Th 1.7). See angels in relation to Christ in Jn 1.51; Heb 1.6; Rev 1.1, 22.16.
v. 1 - The first verse of chapter 9 (along with 13.30 and Mt 10.23) is often cited as evidence that Jesus expected to return within a short time. By the time he wrote, however, it was evident to Mark that the preaching to all nations (13.10) would require a considerable period of time. This is one reason why he emphasized Jesus' teachings on discipleship.
• In each of the Synoptics, Jesus' prediction (9.1) is followed by the account of the transfiguration, an indication that those writers understood it referred to that event. Jesus is not speaking here of the Parousia itself, for that would contradict his statement in 13.32. Opinions vary as to whether the transfiguration previews Jesus' resurrection, his glory between the two advents (cf Rev 1.13-20) or his return in glory.

2. The Transfiguration, 9.2-13

The disciples are disturbed by Jesus' clear description of the way that lies ahead for him. Suffering and death don't fit into their scheme of things. The idea of their taking up a cross is shocking.

Such thoughts obscure anything Jesus says about resurrection and glory. They need a glimpse of the victory that lies beyond the suffering. Jesus gives three of them such a preview in an incomparable experience. Their discussion as they descend from the mountain gives further insight into the meaning of Jesus' words in response to their confession.

This scene is central in Mark's Gospel, located almost exactly in the middle between God's previous identification of Jesus (1.11) and the centurion's confession (15.39). Here God himself declares of Jesus, "This is my Son, whom I love." The reader may desire details not included in the account; on the other hand, Mark's succinctness underlines the central thrust of the transfiguration. While interpreters disagree as to what future event is depicted by the transfiguration, they agree that a new revelation is given.

A PREVIEW OF THE FUTURE KINGDOM, 9.2-8

9.2-6 - After six days, Jesus takes Peter, James and John with him up a high mountain. The description of this event is full of allusions to the revelation given to Moses. As Hurtado (130) says, this alerts "the reader that what is about to take place is a manifestation of God (a theophany) like that related in Exodus 24.15-18 and that a new revelation is here given that therefore surpasses the former one to Moses."

Jesus is transfigured before them. Using the terminology of a theophany, Mark indicates that "the veil of Jesus' humanity was lifted" as his "human appearance was perceptibly altered in accordance with the splendor of the transfigured world" (Lane 318). The transcendent Lord appears in heavenly glory; yet his humanity is also apparent as he converses with two men in the presence of three others (cf Da 7.9; Rev 1.13-16; 2Pe 1.16-18).

Since the text does not give an explicit answer as to why Elijah and Moses are present, the reason must be found in the context. Contrary to custom, Elijah is mentioned first, emphasizing his role as identified with John the Baptist. We now know (from 8.31) that the "way" (**hodos**) John prepared for Jesus is one of suffering and death. John had already walked that path (6.21-29); Jesus follows "in the way."

According to Jewish tradition (reflected in Mk 9.11-13), Elijah was known as a sufferer and martyr and Moses (Ac 7.35-44) was a rejected envoy of God. Their appearance confirms that the way of suffering--the way that Jesus and his disciples will tread (8.31,34)--had been a path followed by God's servants in the past.

Their presence has eschatological significance as well. Following Malachi's announcement (4.1-6), the faithful expected Elijah to reappear before the end. Some awaited the coming of the prophet who is like Moses (Dt 18.15) as a sign of the end-time. Their appearance thereby signifies that the fulfillment of Israel's hope for the glorious end-time has already begun with the coming of Jesus.

Elijah and Moses were prophets (6.15; 8.28) whose days on earth ended in unusual ways (Dt 34.6; 2Ki 2.11). Jesus, however, would come to glory through his death and resurrection. They appeared for a while, but Jesus remains (v 8). God himself denounces any thought of their equality with Jesus. Jesus is the Christ, the beloved Son of God who is to be obeyed (v 7). His uniqueness is indisputable.

The three disciples are overcome by fright mixed with supernatural awe, a normal reaction for anyone experiencing a theophany (cf 4.41; 6.50; 16.8; Rev 1.17; Isa 6.5; Eze 1.28). Impulsively, Peter asks Jesus if they should put up three shelters, one for each of them.

These shelters ("tabernacles") would be temporary constructions like those built during the celebration of the Feast (Lev 23.40-43). According to Jewish thought in Jesus' day, the Feast of Tabernacles had an eschatological significance, looking forward to when God would again "tabernacle" in Jerusalem with his people who together with the redeemed from all nations would worship the King (cf Zec 14.16-19).

In this context, Peter probably wants to erect shelters to celebrate the arrival of the Kingdom. According to his way of thinking, nothing is lacking, for the Messiah is present. He still does not have in mind the things of God (8.33). If he had listened attentively to Jesus (8.31), he would have known that Jesus must suffer and die first. This was a prerequisite to his coming. The transfiguration was not the Parousia but a private preview of it. There is no shortcut to the consummation of the Kingdom.

v. 2 - Because of the references to time and space and to both auditory and visual experiences, we understand that Jesus appeared in a historical, objective manifestation of glory, linked temporally and theologically with the preceding dialogue.
• Only here and in 14.1 does Mark make such a precise chronological reference. He intends for the reader to understand the transfiguration as at least a partial fulfillment of the promise in 9.1.
• Mark does not explain why Peter, James and John were chosen to accompany Jesus. They were among the first to be called (1.16-20), the first named in the list of disciples (3.16) and present when others were omitted (5.37, 14.33; cf 13.3, where Andrew was included as well). Were they "given more" (4.25) because they understood more?
• The reference to a high mountain recalls God's appearances to Moses and Elijah in theophanies (Ex 24; 1Ki 19). Possibly the Transformation occurred on Mount Hermon, a high mountain (9,232 feet) 12 miles north of Caesarea Philippi. Mount Tabor is the traditional sight, but this 1,200 foot-cone in the populated Galilean Jezreel Valley is harder to coordinate with the geographical references in 8.27 and 9.30.
• Mark employs the verb **metamorphoo** to express Jesus' transfiguration. In all NT references to metamorphosis, personal identities are preserved (cf 2Co 3.18; Ro 12.1-2). In oriental religions, metamorphosis means the transformation of a person from one order of existence to another until complete union with the universe is achieved.
v.4 - The word "appeared" (cf 1Co 15.3-8) cancels out the idea of a subjective visionary experience.
• The appearance of Elijah and Moses verifies future existence, negating teachings about annihilation.
• The transfiguration invites comparison with the revelation given to Moses. Both Jesus and Moses took with them three people who are mentioned by name, leaving others behind (9.2; Ex 24.1,9,12,15). Both took place on a mountain. Both accounts mention "after six days" (9.2; Ex 34.29-35), "tabernacles" (9.5; Ex 25.9) and that God spoke from the cloud (9.7; Ex 24.16). Jesus' transfiguration recalls Moses' radiant face (Ex 34.29-35). Upon descending from the mountain, both Jesus and Moses encountered unbelief (9.19; Ex 32.15ff). (Swartley Mark: Way 156f).
• Although this experience is sometimes interpreted as designed to encourage Jesus, the action is described in reference to the needs of the disciples--see the repetition of "them" in these phrases: transfigured before *them*; appeared to *them*; overshadowed *them*; no one with *them*.
• Elijah and Moses as symbols of suffering in the end times influences some interpreters to identify them as the two witnesses in Rev 11.3, although neither is mentioned there by name.
• Moses and Elijah are frequently seen as representatives of the Law and the Prophets. Best (Disciples 219) argues that Mark's inversion of the normal order of their names indicates that he does not take them as typical of the Law and the Prophets.

Moses is mentioned specifically in Mark in discussions related to the Law (1.44; 7.10; 10.3) and the resurrection (12.19,26) as well as implicated in other references or allusions to the Old Testament (see 9.7). Elijah is referred to in Mark 6.15; 8.28; 9.4,11-13 and 15.35-36 and alluded to in 1.4,6. Elijah (1Ki 17.8-16) and Moses (Dt 32.21; Ro 10.19) are also connected with God's offer of salvation to the Gentiles.
v. 5 - The text does not say explicitly what Peter intended. Some say Peter wanted to prolong the occasion by providing shelters; others claim he was equating Jesus, Moses and Elijah. Here he addressed Jesus as "Rabbi," although he had acknowledged him to be the Messiah (8.29).

9.7-8 - Peter confessed that Jesus is the Messiah. Following that correct but incomplete recognition, Jesus identifies his role as the Son of Man (8.31). Now God makes it plain that Jesus is more than a Messiah chosen from among men. In the capstone of all confessions, the focal point of the transfiguration, *God himself declares that Jesus is his Son whom he loves.*

Earlier, God spoke to Jesus personally, endorsing his identification with sinners by being baptized (1.11). Now, after Jesus openly declared his identification with humanity in death (the ultimate consequences of sin), God speaks again, to a selected group. The voice from the cloud testifies that the One who is about to die is the Son of God. Just as God ordered Abraham, "Take your son, your only son whom you love, and sacrifice him as an offering" (Ge 22.2), he now confirms that this Jesus, his Son whom he loves, is to suffer and die according to the will of God. Just as Abraham did not withhold his son, his only son (Ge 22.12), God does not withhold his Son, his only Son (cf 12.6; 10.45; Ro 5.8).

His Son's glory was not lost in the incarnation; it was hidden from sight. In this extraordinary experience, God takes away the veil temporarily so that the three disciples can see, for a few moments, the future glory of the One they are following on the way of the cross.

God tells the disciples to listen to his Son, for "the sayings of the earthly Jesus are also the sayings of the exalted Lord having behind them all the authority of revelations" (Best Following 58). They need to believe Jesus' words about his own death (8.31) and to listen and obey his words about discipleship (8.34ff). These are truths for all humankind to hear and accept, for revelation is more than information about God and his nature. It is an invitation to trust him.

Jesus had rebuked Peter, for he did not accept his pronouncements (8.31-33). Now there is an implied rebuke in God's words, for the disciples persistently fail to listen to Jesus. No disciple can afford to allow Jesus' words to be choked out (4.19) or be infiltrated by the yeast of the Pharisees and of Herod (8.15). The babel of religious authorities with their discordant voices confuses many in today's world. We must listen to Jesus (as God himself said, 9.7); all others, no matter how charismatic they may be, must be evaluated in the light of his words.

This proleptic view of the coming Kingdom manifested God's mighty power (cf Eph 1.19-21). With God's awe-inspiring disclosure resounding in their ears, suddenly the disciples see no one with them except Jesus. He is not raptured to heaven; Jesus remains on earth to lead the three down the mountain on the road to Jerusalem and his crucifixion.

v. 7 - As Swete (191) said, "It is the voice of the Father rather than the visible splendor of the Transfiguration to which attention is called" (cf 2Pe 1.18). God does not speak again in Mark's Gospel; even this revelation was not to be shared until after the resurrection (9.9).

• Clouds are mentioned in connection with revelations of Jesus' identity (13.36; 14.62; Ac 1.9-11; 1Th 4.17; cf Mk 1.10). In the Old Testament usage, clouds are "the vehicle of God's presence (cf Ex 16.10; 19.9; 24.15f; 33.9; Lev 16.2; Nu 11.25), the abode of his glory, from which he speaks" (Taylor 391).

• In his promise to establish forever the throne of David's descendant, God spoke of a father-son relationship with the future king. His words "I will be his father and he shall be my son" (2Sa 7.13-14; cf Ps 2.7) carry overtones of a messianic king. Thus Jesus' kingship is indicated both by the phrase "the Son of God" as well as by "the Anointed One" (cf 1.1,11).

• Jesus' repeated emphasis upon hearing his words (4.3-8.17) is now reinforced by his Father. Repeatedly, God commanded Israel to hear his words. He also promised (Dt 18.15) to "raise up a prophet like Moses; you must listen to him." Now God commands, "Listen to Jesus," for Jesus is God's Son as well as that promised Prophet. The ancient prophecy closed with a warning (Dt 18.19) similar to Mk 8.38.

As Achtemeier (Mark 75,78) noted, Jesus' power is "as fully available in his words as it is in his miracle-working presence." As a result, for us today, "his words are laden with the same power to change lives as was his miraculous presence in Galilee."

"Listen to Jesus" was a needed command for Mark's first readers contemplating a return to the Mosaic Law. As Hebrews 3.1-6 says, Jesus is worthy of greater honor, for he is God's Son.

• Schweizer (358) stresses that God, in making this revelation, did not refer to Jesus' miracles but to his words (9.7). "The faith which ascribes deity to Jesus on the basis of his miracles alone is merely the faith of demons (3.11; 5.7), and consequently should not be proclaimed under any circumstances." Jesus can be worshipped meaningfully only when he is known as the Son of God who gave his life as a ransom, not as a miracle worker.

v. 8 - "Jesus only" points to the centrality of Jesus while pointing away from venerating any of God's other servants. The glory of the Old Covenant fades; the surpassing glory of the New is eternal (2Co 3.7-18).

THE DISCIPLES' DISCUSSION, 9.9-13

On the way down the mountain, Jesus orders them not to tell what they have seen (cf 8.30). As the ensuing conversation reveals, the three still lack understanding. How then can they convey what they have experienced to the other disciples or to outsiders?

But this command to silence is distinct from the previous ones. Jesus sets a time limit: tell no one of his transfiguration "until the Son of Man has risen from the dead." This means that full understanding of Jesus is possible only in the light of his crucifixion and resurrection. As Hurtado (132) points out, Jesus "is not just a wonderful visitor from heaven or an especially favored man given mystic glory but the one called to 'give his life to redeem many people' (10.45). He can be worshiped intelligently only when he is seen as the divinely sent redeemer." The essential element of the gospel ministry is not eloquent preaching, healing campaigns, harmonious musical programs, well-structured institutions or beautiful cathedrals. Any of these that is not centered on Jesus crucified and risen again is shallow and confused.

Continuing down the mountain, the disciples discuss among themselves what Jesus' statement about "rising from the dead" means. Since it would make no sense if everyone were included in that resurrection, they may have concluded that he is talking about a special resurrection of the Son of Man before the general resurrection at the end of the age.

Then they ask Jesus, "Why do the teachers of the law say that Elijah must come first" (i.e., before the day of the Lord, Mal 4.5)? They are convinced that Jesus is the Messiah (otherwise the question is meaningless). But there must have been a slip-up somewhere, because Elijah has not already appeared, setting things right in preparation for the Messiah (Mal 4.6). What happened to Elijah?

The disciples (v 11) ask about Elijah's appearance which was generally believed to precede the open establishment of the Kingdom of God and the general resurrection. After briefly assuring them that Elijah must come first (v 12a), Jesus quickly returns to the central issue, namely, the suffering of the Son of Man. He asks them, "Why then is it written that the Son of Man must suffer much and be rejected?" (12.b). This question should help them face up to the teaching of Scripture about his suffering and death. Only when they realize that his death must precede his glory will they understanding what is happening.

With an authoritative "I tell you," Jesus declares, "Elijah has come." He thereby confirms that John the Baptist has faithfully fulfilled the mission prescribed in Scripture for Elijah. John was an Elijah-like figure who set things right by preaching repentance. He was also the forerunner of Jesus in his own rejection and death (6.21-29). Although "they have done to him everything they wished" (v 13b)--John (who fulfilled Elijah's role) suffered and died at the hands of violent people--his ministry and death were in accord with the will of God. Reflection upon John's death should help the disciples understand that, as it is written, the Son of Man will suffer and be rejected. In this way, Jesus declares that prophecies concerning Elijah have been fulfilled in John and they will certainly be fulfilled in the Son of Man.

v. 12 - Believing that Elijah must come before the Messiah returns, pious Jews leave a chair unoccupied at their Passover table. During the feast they open the door so that Elijah can enter with news of the arrival of the Messiah.

• Here "Jesus not only expressed his certainty that he would share the fate of the Baptist, but also hinted that his death would be fundamentally different from John's by alluding to Isa. 53.3" (Jeremias Theology 295). "It is written"--the early church understood Psalm 22 and Isaiah 53 as applying to Jesus' death.

• The transfiguration, which presents "the clearest story in Mark of the divine glory of Jesus," is bracketed by references to suffering (8.34-9.1; 9.9-13), making the point that "the path to glory begins as the way of the cross.... To be blinded by the glory of the risen Christ was poor preparation for the persecutions that soon began to overtake his followers." (Achtemeier Mark 114).

Excursus: Reincarnation

The idea of reincarnation is basic to several religions. In general, adherents describe reincarnation as the consecutive progress of a pre-existent personality from one human body to another. Through different reincarnations, people pay for their own errors or reap benefits according to their comportment. Through innumerable reincarnations they experience "metamorphosis" into a higher order of life. Each person is his or her own savior.

Leaders of spiritism claim that Mark 9.12-13 and parallel passages teach that John the Baptist was the reincarnation of Elijah. In reality, these passages contradict reincarnation doctrine that holds that a new reincarnation proceeds from the most recent previous reincarnation. By the time of the transfiguration, John the Baptist had already been killed by Herod, so he should have appeared in the mountain, and not Elijah, since John was the most recent reincarnation of Elijah. Furthermore, since Elijah never died but was translated to heaven (2 Kings 2.11), he was not even qualified (i.e., dead) for reincarnation.

Let John answer for himself. When asked "Are you Elijah?" he answered "I am not" (John 1.21). Jesus' identification of John with Elijah was functional and symbolic, not corporal. They were similar in their service to God. The idea of reincarnation is imposed upon the text rather than arising from within it.

Moreover, the whole thrust of biblical teaching is resurrection and never reincarnation. Throughout, the Bible teaches that "man is destined to die once [and not many times] and after that to face judgment [and not reincarnation]," as Hebrews 9.27 states. To be "born again" (John 3.3) refers to the new life one receives now, in this present body, upon accepting Jesus as Lord and Savior. This bears no resemblance to being reincarnated (or "born another time") into another order of existence after death. This new life is a gift of God, not the result of a person's merits. It will continue in a resurrected body (12.24), forever in communion with God.

3. A Hurting Father Struggles with Doubt and Belief, 9.14-29

Returning from the transfiguration, Jesus continues to serve the needs of people. Although he experienced a preview of his future glory, his conflict with Satan is not over. In a narrative full of vivid details suggesting recollections from an eyewitness, Mark describes the tense scene resulting from the disciples' unsuccessful encounter with an evil spirit.

The emphasis, however, is not on Jesus' success in casting out the demon but on the cause and cure of the disciples' powerlessness. Jesus specifies faith and prayer as necessary qualifications for discipleship and for continuing Jesus' ministry during his absence.

9.14-19 - A large crowd surrounds the nine disciples who stayed behind as some teachers of the law seize this opportunity to belittle the disciples and discredit Jesus before the people. An argument ensues. Upon seeing Jesus, however, the people are overwhelmed with wonder and rush to greet him.

Jesus asks, "What are you arguing about?" A distraught man answers, "Teacher, I brought you my son." Then he pours out the story of his son' desperate need. The boy is controlled by a demon; his symptoms resemble epileptic seizures (cf Mt 17.15). In Jesus' absence, the father expected that his disciples would be able to drive out the evil spirit. They failed, however.

Jesus cries out, "O unbelieving generation, how long shall I stay with you? How long shall I put up with you?" His words echo God's reproof of Israel in ancient times (Nu 14.27; cf Isa 65.2). While his indignation conveys the reality of his humanity, Jesus stands over and against the faithless generation (as verified in the contrast between "I" and "you"; cf Isa 63.8-10). He experiences loneliness, for he is "the one authentic believer in a world which expresses only unbelief" (Lane 332; cf 11.22-25). He also knows anguish, for he sees humanity from God's viewpoint. He who will judge (8.38) demands an accounting from men and women for their unbelief.

In his rebuke, Jesus suggest that the disciples "are indistinguishable from the unregenerate men who demand signs but are fundamentally untrue to God (8.12,38), as Lane (332) points out. He also alludes to his future absence. He is already on the way to Jerusalem, "to be taken away" (2.20). What will the disciples do during a prolonged absence? With infinite patience, Jesus continues to instruct the Twelve and prepare them for continuing his work (3.14f; 9.28f; 14.28; 16.7).

Jesus' indignation is tempered by sympathy for the afflicted. He commands "Bring the boy to me," drawing attention away from the disciples to his own person, just as God underscored Jesus' authority earlier (9.7). For disciples who will listen, Jesus proceeds to instruct as to the cause and cure of their powerlessness.

v.14 - Following each time God speaks in approval of his Son (1.11; 9.7), Jesus enters into conflict with Satan.

• Swartley (Structure 186f) sees Jesus as the new Moses who, upon descending from the mountain, encounters unbelief and brings deliverance.

v. 15 - The people detect Jesus' authority (which is entirely different from that of the teachers of the law) and respond with astonishment and fear (cf 1.22,27; 5.20; 10.24,32).

v. 16 - The text does not indicate to whom Jesus is speaking. It could be the scribes; the context favors the disciples; most commentators assume it was the crowd. All were probably involved.

v. 17 - All four cases of expelling demons related by Mark include emphasis upon who Jesus is. The parallels between the first two (1.21ff; 5.1ff) are strong. The last two (7.24ff and here) also form a pair, with a parent seeking help for a child. Neither narrative emphasizes the expulsion in itself; both center on who Jesus is by pointing to the attitude of those who seek help as being essentially faith in Jesus. In each, faith grows through teaching and testing. Hurting parents still bring children to Jesus and find he meets their needs.

v. 18 - Demonic control can vary in symptoms. "The psychological and psychiatric terms are more descriptive of the symptoms than of the causes." (Itioka 198).

v. 19 - This verse "is probably the most forthright declaration of Jesus' emotional response to human need in all the gospels and provides a window of access into the inner life of Jesus which is without parallel." (Martin Mark 109).

9.20-27 - They bring the boy, and of course the evil spirit comes along. Even before Jesus speaks or acts, the evil spirit, detecting Jesus' authority, demonstrates his control over the boy by throwing him into a convulsion.

Jesus asks, "How long has he been like this?" The boy's father indicates that these attacks have come and gone since he was a child. By his question, Jesus shows his genuine interest in the boy as a person and initiates a relationship with the father as well. He seeks to meet the needs of the father--and the disciples--while he attends to the boy's deep distress.

The father senses Jesus' concern. He made a veiled accusation earlier ("I brought you my son"); now he gives a desperate cry, "If you can do anything, take pity on us and help us." Jesus will soon prove he lacks neither pity (translated "compassion" in 6.34; 8.2) nor ability. The father suffers in empathy with his son; however, he lacks insight into the extent of his own need.

In reply to the father's "if you can," Jesus affirms that "everything is possible for him who believes." Jesus does not set any limits on what God can do. He lives as a man fully confident in God and completely surrendered to him. The father's unbelief, however, is a barrier to God's acting in mercy and power. Consequently Jesus summons this member--and every member--of the "unbelieving generation" to believe.

Hope springs up as a result of listening to Jesus (9.7b). Laying aside all pretense, the father confesses to Jesus the struggle of his soul, exclaiming, "I do believe; help me overcome my unbelief." In Swete's words (200), with "a cry as piercing as that of the demoniac son, he recognizes that the help he needs is in the first instance help for himself and not for his boy." Just as the disciples were preoccupied with what they did not have (6.38), the father is focusing on the faith he does not have. Now, in response to Jesus' words, he exclaims, "I do believe." At the same time, he does not hide his unbelief. Although his faith is still frail and imperfect, he trusts in Jesus.

Having helped the father, Jesus now helps the son by saying to the evil spirit, "I command you, come out of him and never enter him again." The "I" is emphatic; Jesus leaves the spirit no room to maneuver. Previously, it had entered and left as he pleased; now the spirit will "never enter him again" (cf 5.34), for Jesus has spoken. Jesus gives the boy a basis for facing the future with confidence. He has driven out the cause; the symptoms will also disappear.

As he leaves the boy, the evil spirit attempts to wreck further havoc (cf 1.26). With the father looking on, he convulses the boy violently. Upon seeing the motionless body, many cry out, "He's dead." Does the father wonder if Jesus has killed his son? His faith, so new and fragile, is being tested (cf 5.21-43; 7.24-30). It grows yet more as Jesus takes the boy's hand and lifts him to his feet.

v. 23 - Twice Jesus assures others with the identical words, "all things are possible" (here and in 10.27). The third time, he himself uses them in his Gethsemane prayer (14.36). As Senior (75) concludes, "Jesus prays as he had lived and preached...(he) knew 'the power of God' and trusted his life and future to it." Jesus' success (in contrast to the disciples' failures) results from his confidence in God. He is the pattern for the believer in dependence upon and obedience to God. While Jesus' power is available to believers ministering in his name, he does not promise that by believing a person can receive everything one wants, or that prayer will magically produce anything a person might desire, or that positive thinking resolves all one's problems.

v. 24 - The father's unbelief is not that mentioned in 6.6, but an embryonic faith mixed with doubts and fears, struggling to grow.

• From the father's anguish "is born the answer which is probably the finest ever given to this question" (Schweizer 188).

• "The Lord answers, not according to the poverty of the asking, but according to the riches of His grace" (Cole 147). Like the Syrophoenician (7.24ff), this man "pleads for divine mercy, not for his deserts."

• Lamar Williamson Jr. (165-6) observes that "the faith of the boy is not mentioned. In no case of exorcism in Mark is healing contingent on the faith of the demon-controlled person.... Healing in the present case becomes possible through the imperfect faith of someone else who cares deeply for the afflicted boy."

• As Anderson (231) correctly concludes, this narrative contradicts "the modern tendency to attribute Jesus' healings to the power of auto-suggestion in the patient."

v. 25 - Possibly Jesus had withdrawn from the crowd mentioned in v 14; now some of those people, joined by others, run to the scene not to miss anything. To avoid undesired publicity (cf 7.33; 8.23), Jesus commands the evil spirit to leave before they arrive.

v. 26 - The descriptions (the boy "is dead"; "raised up") remind the reader of the frequent references to Jesus' death and resurrection, beginning with 8.31. The vocabulary is similar to the raising of Jairus' daughter (5.39-42) and God's action in raising Jesus from the dead (14.28; cf Ac 3.15; 4.10; 5.30). In this way, Mark alludes to Jesus' victory over death and to the believers' resurrection. Lane (335) also sees the healing of the boy as pointing beyond itself "to the necessity of Jesus' own death and resurrection before Satan's power can be definitively broken."

9.28-29 - After Jesus has gone indoors (possibly to the home where the nine disciples have been staying), the disciples ask, "Why couldn't we drive it out?" This question is vital to all disciples who face their own inadequacy. They may not be ready to confess that they, too, are a mixture of belief and unbelief, but they know Jesus had included them when he denounced the "unbelieving generation" (v 19). They know they had failed and they now seek to learn from their failure by asking the right person the right question.

Jesus has already indicated that unbelief is the cause of failure (v 19); however, "everything is possible for him who believes" (v 23). Furthermore, through his dialogue with the boy's father, Jesus has demonstrated how faith is born and how it grows through testing. Now he states explicitly that prayer is essential for successful ministry. Prayer is a verbal expression of faith in God and of one's dependence upon him (11.22-25). Through prayer one appeals to God for faith to overcome unbelief.

Instead of recognizing their dependence upon God, the disciples had presumed the ability to handle this problem themselves. Success was guaranteed, for they had received authority to drive out demons (6.7) and demonstrated it in past accomplishments (6.13,30). There is, however, no automatic victory for those who follow Jesus. God maintains active control over his power. To imagine that it is ours, under our control and at our disposal "is tantamount to unbelief; for it is really trust in ourselves instead of in God" (Cranfield 305). Their self-confidence was a far cry from "disowning self" (8.34). Lane (335) emphasizes that "the power of God must be asked for on each occasion in radical reliance upon his ability alone."

Christology and discipleship continue as the primary and secondary emphases of this central division of Mark. Jesus, the Son of God (9.7), lives among women and men as the Man of faith and, at the same time, he is the object of their faith. With patience and compassion, he leads persons out of unbelief into *faith in him*. The disciples already knew *what* they were to do (1.16ff; 3.14f). Now they--and the reader--learn more about *how* to do it. Effective ministry is not the result of one's ability, past successes or program. Effective ministry begins with reliance upon Jesus expressed in believing prayer and leads suffering people to faith in Jesus and to freedom from Satan's domination.

Jesus is ready and able to help every helpless person--with imperfect faith or persistent unbelief--in response to his or her honest cry. The father's words "help me" are not a prayer for help until his unbelief diminishes enough to be worthy of a response from God; rather, as Cole (147) points out, it is a plea to "help me just as I am, a doubter."

Of course this does not mean one should be content with little or stagnant faith. "*Faith is God's free gift, but it's not cheap*," as Martin (Action 84, italics his) points out. "We have to exercise faith, cultivate it, live by it." We promote faith's growth by prayer but impede it by negligence, careless attitudes and dallying with sin.

Many have "faith in faith," which only reaches out to a void. True faith trusts in the Lord with all the strength at its command (cf Pr 3.5-6). Even if demonic power seems overwhelming, we, too, can cry, "Lord, I believe; help my unbelief."

Excursus: The Disciples' Frequent Failures

Why does Mark mention so frequently the failures of the disciples? Some writers imagine a deep antagonism between Jesus and the twelve; others claim it is Mark's polemic against unacceptable views held by the disciples. Best (Story 46) says some scholars may accuse Mark because they are "so used to writing polemically against one another that they assume it is the only reason why people write!"

To attribute such motives to Mark is neither necessary nor in accord with the internal evidences of Mark's purposes in writing his Gospel. He is reporting what happened when a group of individuals found themselves torn between the "things of men" and the "things of God" (8.33). They didn't always like the taste of the "new wine" (2.22) offered by Jesus in his words and deeds. They stumbled because, like most of us, they had a hard time changing their minds about their beliefs, practices and worldview.

Changing their wills was harder yet. They found it hard to deny themselves, with their very human desires for status, power and riches. They quarreled among themselves and attempted to put each other down. They found it harder to abandon their human ambitions than to leave their fishing boats. Not one of them was fit to be a disciple, but God's grace transformed them into his useful servants.

Jesus' rebukes were given not to shame or blame them but to awaken them and teach them how to take advantage of future opportunities without repeating their errors. Blessed are those who learn from their own mistakes. Mark offers his readers a greater blessing: how to avoid pitfalls by learning from the mistakes of the disciples. How fortunate we are to read the additional instructions Jesus gave his disciples because of their slowness to understand!

Peter, James and John are given nicknames (3.16f) and special opportunities (5.37; 9.2); they are the only disciples quoted in Mark. Mark shows the strong qualities of the inner circle; he also identifies them by name when guilty of reproachable action (Peter, 8.32f; James and John, 10.35ff). As spokesman for the Twelve, Peter's failures reflect the group's shortcomings. Mark is neither out to exalt them or denigrate them. They have their ups and downs, and Mark reports it like it is.

Mark's pastoral concern for his readers is very evident in relating the failures of the disciples. He wants his readers to see in them the kinds of problems any individual or congregation is likely to experience in following Jesus. The Christian life is not a bed of roses; the requirements of radical discipleship constantly put human nature to the test. The Twelve were not "sinners emeritus" any more than the church is a museum for perfect products. It is a hospital for the sick. The failures of the disciples demonstrate their need for the Great Physician (2.17). We also can count on God's strength to meet us in our weaknesses, just as it did in theirs (cf 2Co 4.7).

The early church struggled with the reality of believers who failed in the face of persecution, torture and death (cf 4.17-18). As Senior (153) says, "The church of Jesus is not a church of infallible humanoids but a flesh and blood church of frail disciples." Mark's account encourages the offer of forgiveness and reconciliation to those who, like the Twelve, fail in loyalty (14.50,72). To those who idolize human leaders (cf the Corinthian Church, 1Co 1.12; 3.21-23), Mark is saying, "your leaders are only human like you" (cf Ac 10.26; 14.15). His account leaves no room for canonizing any of the Twelve and serves as a warning against the personality cult so common in Christian circles. Anyone who would reject the gospel because of sinners and hypocrites in the church or because a leader stumbles should remember that Jesus' call is to follow *him*. He never fails to meet one's highest expectations. We are all dependent upon his merciful forgiveness.

The disciples were not super heroes but persons with whom we can identify. We take hope, because Jesus did not reject them, in spite of all their weaknesses and failures. *He entrusted the future of his mission to people like us.* As probable author of this Gospel, John Mark could personally confirm this, for his experience of "sharp disagreement" with other believers (Ac 15.39) was followed by reconciliation and useful ministry (2Ti 4.11). Jesus rescues his soldiers who fall on the field of battle (cf "tell Peter," in 16.7).

Mark presents the disciples as a mirror to enable us to look at ourselves. If we do not see elements of failure in ourselves, we will repeat their failures, with painful results. Their errors should warn us to make sure of our own understanding and obedience to Jesus; their persistence in spite of weaknesses should challenge us to finish well.

B. THE COST OF ENTERING THE KINGDOM, 9.30-10.31

Continuing on the way (**hodos**) to Jerusalem, Jesus repeats his prediction of what awaits him, adding that he will be "delivered into human hands" as a part of his doing the will of God personally.

Even though the disciples are following Jesus, their conduct is frequently in conflict with his. So Jesus explains to them what it means to live under God's direction in terms of daily activities. When they want to control others rather than to serve them, he shows the meaning of discipleship in human relationships and in material values. These instructions given "on the way" parallel the commandments--on the sanctity of life, marriage, property and desires--which God gave to his people of ancient times when they were on the way to the promised land (Ex 20.12-17).

1. In the Hands of Others, 9.30-50

Jesus will be delivered into the hands of other individuals, for this is God's will. His greatness lies in that he has become "the very last and the servant of all" (9.35). The disciples, on the other hand, are still convinced that, upon arriving in Jerusalem, Jesus will somehow reinstate God's rule over Israel. His chosen leaders argue about positions of prestige within a presumed hierarchy and seek to control outsiders. Jesus calls upon them to take a completely different posture towards others and toward self. Peace in God's new family flows out of true discipleship.

THE SON OF MAN IN HUMAN HANDS, 9.30-32

As he passes through Galilee heading south, Jesus avoids public ministry in order to gives maximum time to teaching the disciples (cf 8.24). He patiently repeats his emphasis upon his suffering.

While Jesus foretells his death and resurrection in all three "passion pronouncements," each has a special emphasis. In this prediction, Jesus reveals yet more about his suffering: "the Son of Man is going to be delivered (from the verb **paradidomai**) into the hands of men." This seems to be a denial of his God-given authority. The essence of the gospel, however, is that "the all-powerful one, chosen and commissioned by God and authorized to act in his name, *consents* by voluntary choice to be surrendered to the hands of his rejecters" (Martin Mark 191f).

The disciples' perplexity increases upon hearing that Jesus will be delivered into human hands, for they understand that rulers lord it over others rather than submit to them. Previously they had asked Jesus for explanations (4.10; 7.17; 9.11,28); this time they do not ask (cf 8.16-17). Is the subject too painful, or do they remember the rebuke incurred by Peter (8.33)?

v. 31 - Jesus understood the difficulty of overcoming preconceived ideas much better than writers who claim that the repetition of pronouncements about the Messiah's suffering came from Mark, and not Jesus. Teachers know the need for repetition in order to change ingrained concepts, especially those that deal with basic views of God and the world. Attempts to explain the pronouncements as created by the early church after the resurrection remain unsatisfactory.

• Because **paradidomai** (cf 1.14; 13.9-13) is used to describe God's action in handing someone over for judgment or punishment (e.g., Ro 1.24,26,28), Jesus implies that he will endure God's judgment against sinful humanity (cf 10.45; Isa 53.5,12; Ro 4.25). Nineham (249) suggests that "the Son of Man deliver up to men" is possibly a deliberate play on words, "for the whole passion of Jesus had its ultimate ground in God's initiative and his concern for the salvation of men."

• "Into the hands of men" also introduces the theme of human relationships which continues to 10.45. As before (e.g., 2.1-3.6; 4.1-34), once Mark introduces a theme, he may select additional material from Jesus' teachings on other occasions.

• Could Jesus have known the future, or was this history disguised as prophecy and created by the early church, as Bultmann argued? Marshall (35) replies, "We have seen sufficient already in this Gospel to realize that purely human categories are quite insufficient to explain this Person and that we cannot set arbitrary limits to what He may or may not have said."

RELATIONSHIPS AMONG DISCIPLES, 9.33-50

The Son of Man in the hands of other individuals sets the pattern for the disciple, who is called upon to serve others rather than trying to control or manipulate them. The following pericopes spell out the way to peace in the family of God by presenting case studies of inter-personal relationships.

• The importance of these instructions is stressed by various statements: they are given indoors (9.28,33) apart from the crowds (vv 30,31), by Jesus the Teacher (v 38) who sits down and calls the Twelve (v 35) but addresses the all-inclusive "anyone" (vv 41,42,49).

The Desire For Individual Superiority, 9.33-37

On the way south, Jesus overhears the disciples bickering among themselves. In the privacy of the house in Capernaum, he asks them. "What were you arguing about?" Although they do not answer, Jesus knows they have been arguing about who is the greatest. Jesus does not allow their silence to end the matter.

In spite of the deep personal hurt Jesus must feel because their desires are so different from his (cf 8.32-33), he gathers the Twelve together and patiently begins to reteach them. He goes right to the heart of their contention: the desire to be first. In the world, the one-on-top is served by all others. He manipulates others for his own advancement. Not so in God's Kingdom. The first places him- or herself in the hands of others, to serve them. He (or she) even disclaims the right to choose whom he will serve; he becomes "the servant of all." The Twelve, however, are not practicing Jesus' teachings. Self-denial succumbs to their desire for prestige and power. "If anyone wants" indicates that this is a facet of the essence of discipleship explained earlier in 8.34-37.

Following Jesus consists of thrusting oneself into the hands of God. It does not end there, however. God's rule embraces a disciple's whole life, including relationships to persons as well as to God. It includes placing oneself in the hands of others. We resist this, fearing that others may harm or betray us (whereas Jesus proceeded in full awareness that people ***would*** betray him). Like the Twelve, we want to control our own lives; we want to be a somebody; we seek to be served rather than to serve.

Jesus (a servant of all, even to death on a cross, cf Php 2.5-8) calls upon his followers to be servants also. He embraces a child to illustrate his point. As a part of their cultural background, the disciples think of a child as weak and do not expect a boy to keep the Mosaic Law until his initiatory ceremony (**bar mitzvah**) on his 13th birthday. The Greco-Roman world considered a child to be insignificant, gaining importance only through training and education. In both Aramaic and Greek, the term "child" could also mean "servant" and indicated someone without status or power, living at the mercy of others.

Jesus is not saying, "Imitate child-like qualities" (cf 10.13-16); he is urging his followers to treat well all persons least likely to receive attention. After the example of receiving a child (v 36), Jesus instructs about receiving fellow believers, affectionately called "little children" and "little ones" (vv 37,41). To receive into full Christian fellowship the least prominent believer is to welcome Jesus and God himself, for Jesus is present in those who are his. Jesus intends that his teachings on interpersonal relationships should characterize God's family.

In these few words, Jesus also reveals more of his own relationship to individuals and to God. He is the servant who cares for the least of his "little ones;" at the same time, his relationship to God is distinct and can be claimed by none other, for "to receive him is to receive God" (v 37). In this amazing paradox is hidden the secret of who Jesus really is. In caring for insignificant persons, we, too, identify who we are.

v. 33 - Although Mark does not give a detailed itinerary, he gives enough for the reader to see Jesus' unflinching determination to reach Jerusalem. Passing through Galilee and Capernaum (9.30,33), he proceeds south (he may have entered Samaria; cf Lk 9.51-53) and apparently turns east, crossing the Jordan River into Perea (the eastern part of Herod's kingdom of Judea). He recrosses the Jordan, heading west through Jericho (10.46) and goes up to Jerusalem (11.1). All this takes a considerable time.

• The fact that the disciples argued about who is greatest proves that Jesus had not designated Peter as head of the church.

v. 35 - Mark presents some of Jesus' teachings on discipleship as servanthood through word associations (e.g., little children, name, stumble, good/better, fire and salt), while retaining Jesus' own poetical forms. These catchwords aid memorization as a tool for teaching. After switching between "do this" and "don't do that," the pericope ends on a positive note. The unit begins with contention (v 33) and closes appropriately with a prescription for "peace with one another" (v 50).

v. 37 - As Jeremias (Theology 254) points out, Jesus used the phrase "welcomes the one who sent me" as a climactic declaration of his identity as God's unique representative.

• Politics, wealth, social class, religion--all are used for personal aggrandizement. In the Qumran community, each individual was ranked annually according to his worth to that sect. Similar questions of rank and precedence were not uncommon in regard to the synagogue, tribunals, meals (cf Jas 2.1-13). Ecclesiastical structures are also manipulated in an effort to be greatest. "Those who desire or grasp at spiritual position condemn themselves automatically to the lowest place in the Kingdom" (Cole 150). Those who desire to serve do not have to wait in line for opportunities.

The Struggle For Group Superiority, 9.38-41

Neither desires for individual superiority (v 33-37) nor claims of group superiority (v 38-41) are compatible with following Jesus.

The disciples had encountered a man driving out demons in Jesus' name. Although he performed a miracle through a direct appeal to Jesus' authority, the disciples do not consider that sufficient reason to encourage him. Rather, they told him to stop, because (as John reports their action to Jesus) "he was not one of us." Jesus counters their claim to an exclusive franchise in doing God's work: "Do not stop him." Rather, welcome him, for he did a miracle with the right motives and with Jesus' authorization. As Lane (343) explains, "The man had grasped that an essential dimension of Jesus' mission was the confrontation and defeat of Satan. The use of Jesus' name shows an awareness that it was Jesus who ordered the action." Best (Following 99) adds that the servant of Christ "accepts all who work in the name of Jesus, whether they appear to be outside the Christian community or are unimportant members within it."

Some of Mark's first readers looked askance at those who did not belong to their local congregation. They withheld fellowship from those who were different, arguing that those who were not 100% with them were against them. As a good pastor caring for his flock, Mark no doubt selected incidents in which Jesus combated similar misconceptions among his original disciples. These admonitions are pertinent to the church today.

Replying to such attitudes, Jesus says, "Whoever is not against us is for us." Rather than limit fellowship to members of your in-group, take a humble and hopeful stance, provisionally extending the hospitality that characterizes God's new family to *all* who bear the name of Jesus Christ. God does not disdain their most simple service, neither should you. Best (Following 84-85) points out that "The thought bites more deeply when we recall 9.14-29; the 'church' has been given the power to exorcise; it failed; a 'stranger' comes along and succeeds; the church wishes to exclude him; it ought instead to pray (9.28f)."

Jesus is rebuking a narrow, sectarian spirit, without approving neutrality, pluralism or syncretism. Belonging to an in-group is no fit test of discipleship; belonging to Jesus is essential. Individuals are either for or against Christ.

v. 38 - Hurtado (141) correctly perceives that "The point under discussion is not the practice of exorcism but whether a person who is not identified with the Twelve can still be a true follower of Jesus with the right to minister in his name. The thrust of Jesus' answer in verses 39-41 is to say that anyone who claims to be a follower of Jesus must be received unless he or she gives reason to think otherwise."

v. 39 - Jesus singles out Peter, James and John, the "inner circle" of disciples, for correction (cf 8.32-33; here; 10.35-40). Their greater privileges (5.37; 9.2; 14.33) impose greater accountability.

v. 41 - Cf Ro 14.13-15. As Minear (99) says, "In Rome there were house-churches which did not welcome certain Christians,.. strangers...either too careful or too carefree about observing the scriptural commands. It is with regard to such a situation that it became unusual for a congregation to grant table hospitality to a person on no other ground than that he bore the name of Christ (v 41)."

• On a different occasion (Mt 12.30), Jesus said, "He who is not with me is against me." The two statements are complementary; they must be taken together. False prophets appeared in New Testament times (Mk 13.22; Mt 7.22-1-23; Ac 19.13). They appear today in religious groups that use the name of Jesus in their rituals while denying that Jesus Christ is the unique Son of God.

• God rewards humble service (e.g., "receiving a little one," 9.37) and minimal acts of hospitality to a disciple ("a cup of water," 9.41). There are no trivial acts in God's Kingdom. These statements promise neither salvation nor awards for all good deeds. "Whoever wishes to raise a claim to reward, shows by that very act that he did not really do what he did for God, but for himself" (Schweizer 197).

Choosing the Better Way, 9.42-50

9.42 - Following Jesus' encouragement to positive action, this verse warns against causing any seemingly unimportant believer ("little ones who believe in me") to stumble. All individuals and churches are admonished to remove strife, rejection and everything else that causes others to lose faith in Jesus. Unbecoming examples and false teachings not only cause others to fall away from God; they also bring God's judgment upon any member of the community who harms an "unimportant" believer.

9.43-48 - The preceding admonition against causing others to stumble introduces warnings about causing oneself to sin (43-48).

How does one avoid causing others to stumble? The answer is clear: through rigorous self-discipline. The Twelve are harsh toward one another (v 38) but tolerant of their own weaknesses (i.e., 9.34; cf Mt 7.3-5). To his command to zealously avoid harming others, Jesus adds: be ruthless regarding temptations in your own life.

Jesus seeks to shock his hearers out of their complacency: cut off anything that endangers your fullest participation in the Kingdom of God. Any sacrifice is insignificant in comparison with the supreme value of belonging to Christ. While many people will do anything to avoid suffering, disciples should spare no effort to avoid doing wrong. Just as the surgeon will amputate a limb in order to save the life of the patient, the disciple will cut off anything that limits his fellowship with God. This self-discipline is indispensable for enjoying that life of quality that is gained by losing self (8.35).

To enter life means to live according to the will of God. It is costly, for it includes self-denial (8.34) and renunciation of possessions (10.21) and family (10.28f). Those who enter life value fellowship with God above all else. A person who chooses to assert his or her own will, refusing to live under God's rule, will be "thrown into hell." No special effort is required. As Marshall (36) says, "The fate of the sinner will be every bit as bad as Gehenna."

With this teaching, Jesus faces each of us with the inescapable responsibility of choosing between taking part in the Kingdom or being rejected by God. The absolute alternatives are either life in the fullest or Gehenna, a symbol of spiritual ruin in the most severe terms. Each person is responsible for his or her actions.

9.49-50 - The call to follow Jesus is a call to sacrificial living (8.34-9.48). In the Old Testament, sacrifices are associated with fire (v 48) and salt (Lev 2.13; Eze 43.24). These "catchwords" lead to a metaphor on discipleship: "Everyone will be salted with fire."

Just as salt is necessary for preserving life and preventing decay, the disciple's self-discipline gives life and preserves that which is good. Through the fire of trials and persecution (1Pe 1.7; 4.12; Isa 48.10) God purges away everything contrary to his will.

Salt is good. The impure salt from the Dead Sea, however, becomes worthless after the good is washed out. Disciples who reject being salted with fire lose their life-giving potentials. Those who are true to God, however, reap the benefits of discipline and trials.

"Have salt in yourselves." In other words, be a diligent disciple. Be a living sacrifice to God by disowning oneself (8.34; Ro 12.1-2) even if it means suffering in the hands of others or martyrdom (as awaited some believers in Rome). The way is rugged, but true discipleship leads to peace with each other.

v. 42 - This is the first use of expressions such as "it is better..." Both implicit and explicit comparisons continue into chapter 10 in this division's emphasis on Christian social ethics.

• The large upper millstone ground the grain poured onto the lower stone. To be thrown into the sea with such a weight tied around one's neck meant certain death. Some Zealots who rose up against Rome were drowned in this way.

v. 43 - "Enter the Kingdom" (9.47; 10.15,23,24,25) is a synonym for "enter life" (vv 43,45), an antonym for "go into/cast into hell" (vv 43,45,47).

• In no way is Jesus teaching self-mutilation. Amputation would not solve the problem, for "evil comes from inside" (7.23). Nor is Jesus calling for asceticism; the hand, foot and eye are evil only when they lead to evil activities.

• The Greek **gehenna** ("hell") is derived from the Hebrew **ge-hinnon**, the Ben Hinnon Valley south of ancient Jerusalem where children had been offered as sacrifices to Molech (Jer 32.35). Later it was the garbage dump where fires burned perpetually. It is the place of divine judgment (Jer 7.32; 19.6-7).

Taylor (411) warns against dismissing Jesus' words about **Gehenna** as simply "a picturesque metaphor." The New Testament indicates without ambiguity the certainty of divine judgment and that the essence of hell is exclusion from the presence of God.

Many notions about life after death contradict biblical teachings. Two examples are: the concept of a purgatory where sinners are purified and the penitent gain paradise; and universalism's doctrine of the ultimate well being of every person.

v. 48 - This free translation of Isa 66.24 is genuine here, but all modern editions of the Greek text omit its repetition in 9.44 and 9.46 as not original. Its repetition was included only in the *Textus Receptus.* This "generally received text" (from 1516 to about 1750) rested on manuscripts that are late in origin.

vv. 49-50 - These sayings are to be understood in the context of the disciples' responsibilities for one another. Any interpretation of these difficult verses must be presented humbly, for nuances obvious to the original readers may be obscure to modern readers.

v. 50 - Peace does not mean merely the absence of strife but also the positive "capacity for unruffled social intercourse and for sympathetic and thoughtful consideration of others" (Bratcher and Nida 306).

2. Marriage, Children And Possessions, 10.1-31

Following the preceding instruction on interpersonal relationships, discipleship is now presented in relation to the marriage partner, children and possessions. These teachings are to be understood in the context of Jesus' passion-resurrection predictions with his call to die in order to live as essential for entering the Kingdom. Each theme provides ample opportunity for self-denial.

MARRIAGE AS FAITHFULNESS TO GOD AND TO SPOUSE, 10.1-12

After teaching about life itself (8.34ff) and life in the broader social context (be kind to others and strict with yourself, 9.33-50), Jesus teaches about marriage and children. In these basic human relationships, his followers are not to "live according to the customs of the nations" (Lev 20.23) but to live under God's rule. To "be at peace with each other" (9.50) is especially needful in the home, often a scene of much strife.

Marriage and divorce were among the most acute social issues of that day, as they are today. The Pharisees' attempt to test Jesus on this question provides him with an opportunity to present more of his ethical demands on the life of discipleship. The subject of children appropriately follows discussion about marriage. Disciples should welcome the Kingdom as Jesus welcomes children, learn from them how to be blessed, and serve them. Again it becomes clear that to follow Jesus requires a total transformation of values.

10.1-2 - As he advances in his journey to Jerusalem, Jesus teaches the crowds of people who come to him, although (as v 10f indicates) he used each occasion to train his disciples. Some Pharisees appear with a question about the Law of Moses (cf 7.5f) and, like their Galilean colleagues, seek to "test" (**peirazo**, cf 1.13; 8.11; 12.15) Jesus in the hope of eliciting some evidence against him.

Their question, "Is it lawful for a man to divorce his wife?" was the center of much discussion in Israel. All Jews agreed that the Old Testament permitted a man to write a certificate of divorce and send his wife away if she displeased him (or did "something shameful," Dt 24.1). They disagreed, however, as to what constitutes "displease." Around 20 B.C., the rabbinic school of Shammai insisted something morally shameful (e.g., adultery) was meant, whereas Hillel affirmed that divorce was allowed for any moral fault or for anything which annoyed or embarrassed the husband (e.g., the wife burned the dinner). The broader interpretation of Hillel determined actual practice among the Jews of Jesus' day.

The Pharisees do not ask Jesus this question in order to understand and follow his teaching. This was unfortunate; for he, unlike the teachers of the law (1.22), taught with authority. He not only called everyone to live under God's direction; he revealed God's will, interpreted God's covenant with Israel (cf 7.6-23) and proclaimed the new covenant (14.24). He who defined sin and identified its source (cf 7.14-23) is the Son of Man who has authority to forgive all sins but one (2.10; 3.28-29). In this capacity, Jesus explains God's will regarding marriage, the most intimate of human social relationships. Surprisingly, he does not mention love; his emphasis is upon fidelity to God's purposes and to the marriage partner.

10.3-4 - With his counter-question, "What did Moses command you?" Jesus goes right to the heart of the subject. By twice referring to "commandment" (vv 3,5), Jesus shows his concern for God's will. His opponents, however, speak twice about what is "lawful" or "allowed" (vv 2,4). As Schweizer (203) says, "When a person begins to ask this kind of question, he is seeking the greatest possible advantage for himself within the limits of what is permissible. In so doing he will have destroyed the marriage before it has begun."

The Pharisees don't answer Jesus' question about a *commandment*. Instead, they reply that "Moses *permitted* a man to write a certificate of divorce and send her away." On the basis of Deuteronomy 24.1-4, the scribes and Pharisees established rules for making divorce morally acceptable in certain cases. While Jesus accepted the Law of Moses, he claimed the right to interpret it (e.g., 7.10). He explains *why* this provision was made for regulating divorce: "It was because your hearts were hard that Moses wrote you this law." God recognized through Moses that people were living in gross violation of his ordinance. Jesus implies that Moses' provision was an expression of God's judgment on human rebellion and obstinacy in regard to God's will.

In an effort to limit sinfulness, to control the consequences of sin already committed, and to prevent worse things from happening, Moses acquiesced to human frailties. On the positive side, the provision mercifully provided the woman a degree of protection through release from the marriage contract.

Like the Pharisees, we often fail to realize that "laws and other prescriptions are normally given to correct faults, not to spell out the ideal. Thus a law on divorce does not spell out the ideal for marriage, but what to do when something goes wrong" (Perry Yoder 40). Laws are usually remedial, with provisions that take into account fallen human nature and are designed to limit and control its consequences. It is an error to turn them into norms, for they do not present the highest standards. In general, laws focus on behavior, while ideals deal with the motives and inner life of the heart. By saying that Moses' decree (Dt 24) was given because of their hardness of heart, Jesus infers that it was a concession. Although commanded by God, it does not represent God's highest standards.

10.5-9 - Jesus zeroes in on the beginning of the creation story, for Genesis 1 and 2 present God's ideal in creating male and female in the first place. In so doing, he shifts the discussion from law to ideal, from divorce to marriage, from human legislation to the divine plan. Quoting Genesis 1.27, Jesus declares that "God made them male and female." God designed sexual union as a part of his "very good" creation (Ge 1.31). The male was created for the female and the female for the male. The sexes are complementary.

Proceeding in his biblical exposition, Jesus quotes Genesis 2.24 to emphasize God's intention in this creative act: "for this reason" a man will leave the strongest social ties he knows (his own parents) to "be joined to" (implying sexual intercourse) his wife. As a result of sexual union, the two become one flesh; they are no longer two, but one in a relationship that is not to be dissolved. These phrases presuppose monogamy and denote a relationship more intimate and binding than any other.

Jesus makes it clear that in the intention of the Creator, the sexual relationship is not only corporeal but also essentially a part of a total personal relationship in which the couple shares spiritual and intellectual values and accepts moral and social responsibilities. By challenging his hearers to make an unbroken, lifelong commitment in marriage, Jesus demonstrates his deep concern for a husband-wife relationship that is all encompassing and not just physical. Without a communion of minds, hearts and wills, the relationship is neither personal nor, in the truest sense, sexual.

"Forsaking" is the prerequisite for "being joined to." First the man "leaves," then he is "joined to his wife." Thus pre-marital and extra-marital sex are precluded in the divine plan. Sexual union is not an end in itself, isolated from the total relationship of man and woman in other spheres of life.

Nor is sexual intercourse given only for procreation. It is also God's gift for mutual enrichment and enjoyment (Pr 5.18,19; SS 2.3-4.7), as husband and wife under God's direction complement and complete each other. Their total commitment benefits all of society as a model of the highest ideal in personal relationships.

As Collin Brown (NIDNTT III 539) points out, the juxtaposition in verse 9 of the verbs "joined together" (used of the marital relationship) and "separate" (a technical term used in connection with divorce) is significant. The physical relationship does not exist merely on the human plane. God joins a male and female in "one flesh" via the physical union which makes the marriage; and the sexual act of one of the marriage partners with someone outside the marriage has the effect of putting asunder the relationship established by God.

With his words, "Let no one put asunder," Jesus' alerts both partners and third parties to avoid any action or attitude that contributes to the breakdown of the relationship that God intended. Where there is a lack of mutual love, respect and care, "the relationship already falls short of what God intended marriage to be (Eph 5.21-33; Col 3.18f). Where a partner refuses conjugal rights (cf 1Co 7.2-7), a step has already been taken to putting the marriage asunder. But the adulterous look is also such a step (Mt 5.27ff; cf Jn 8.7ff), and either partner who actually commits adultery is *de facto* putting the marriage asunder" (Brown NIDNTT III 539-540).

God's purpose of a life-long partnership is to be followed without dilution by all who "enter the Kingdom." Life under God's leading means that one's sex life is submitted to God's will. Anything less than faithfulness to one's life-long partner "misses the mark" (**hamartia**, the most common Pauline word for sin; cf Ro 5.12,21; 6.23) of the will of God, and, like all sins, stands under the judgment of God. Anything less distorts the meaning of sexuality, degrades both individuals and offends the God who created them and endowed them with sexuality. As Anderson (243) says, marriage as an indissoluble union is not "a remote ideal but a gift of God's creation, to be received gladly and celebrated naturally and spontaneously." Faithfulness to God's purposes includes faithfulness to one's spouse.

Jesus refuses to make a legal edict or get involved in an intellectual debate. Instead, he challenges each one to live in exclusive faithfulness to one's spouse as a personal response to God's purposes. We saw earlier (7.9-13) how the Pharisees reduced God's high standard of "honor your parents" to a set of rules that nullified God's commandment, just as they watered down Deuteronomy 24.1-4. Fallen human nature would do the same with any new rule. Laws are external and therefore ineffective in avoiding evils such as sexual immorality and adultery that arise from within (7.21-23). Once more Jesus refutes legalism and goes beyond the Law to marriage as God's gift of grace in creation. The church is responsible to follow Jesus' example, reaffirming God's purposes and calling upon men and women to live on the highest plain. God's ideals are obscured every time the church resorts to legalism.

v. 2 - This is the Pharisees' only appearance in Mark's journey narrative (8.27-10.52). They may hope to persuade Herod to collaborate further with them (3.6; cf 12.13) by imprisoning Jesus as he had John.
• The question "Is it lawful?" may betray a philosophy of life based on minimum standards instead of the higher demands of God. Individuals who do more than the minimum may think that God owes them something. In this way, they feel good about themselves and avoid the need for repentance.
v. 3 - Earlier, Jesus taught the disciples that traditions must be examined in the light of Scripture (7.1-23). Now he shows them "that even the ordinances of the Law are not to be followed blindly but are to be carefully considered in the light of the highest standards which Scripture exemplifies" (Lane 357).
v. 4 - If a husband wanted to send away his wife, he had to return the dowry he received from her father (unless she had engaged in sexual misbehavior) and give her a written certificate stating she was free to remarry. It was a simple business transaction between individuals; no court action was involved. The break-up of a marriage frequently resulted in adultery. Certain sexual offenses were punishable by death (Dt 27.20-23).

The husband could divorce his wife in an arbitrary way. The wife had no redress to her husband's act nor could she seek a divorce; her only recourse was to persuade her husband to divorce her. The prevalent interpretation of Dt 24 reflected the low esteem of women in society; they were often more property than persons.
• While some Jews claimed divine approval for divorce and abuse of women, the Gentiles needed no such excuse. They exercised an even greater contempt for women in their sexually permissive world.
v. 5 - "Hard-heartedness" signifies a stubborn, stiff-necked, unteachable attitude (e.g., Dt 10.16). A different Greek word is used to describe the spiritual dullness of the disciples (8.11).
• Biblical scholars disagree about the question of whether Jesus abrogated Dt 24.1-4. In this writer's opinion, he did invalidate the practice of twisting it to accommodate human desires. He did this on the basis of his prerogatives as interpreter of the Law (as in 7.10). However, Jesus did not revoke divorce as such but recognized it as a continuing concession because of humanity's proneness to sin. He is not setting God's commandment against Moses' word. Rather he is bringing out the real meaning of Dt 24.1, namely God made provision for divorce because he knows that the destructiveness of sin within some marriages is worse than the healing of a subsequent remarriage.
v. 6 - The text presupposes that these unions are to be heterosexual. Cf Ro 1.24-32.
• Contrary to gnosticism and its present advocates, both spirit and matter were created "very good." As Ge 2.16-3.7 clearly indicates, Adam and Eve's sin was disobedience to God and not sexual relations. Nor is sex sinful when engaged in as God intended (cf He 13.4). God can be glorified in one's body (cf 1Co 6.19). On the other hand, humanity's rebellion against God frequently leads to the perversion of sex, as seen in first-century Rome (Ro 1.21-32) and in the world today.

• Dwight H. Small affirms that "The biblical theology of sexuality is the theology of marriage" (Christian: Celebrate your sexuality. Revell, 1974, 125).

"God created man in his own image" (Ge 1.27) "to glorify him and enjoy him forever" (as the Westminster Catechism declares). We reflect God's image through a living relationship with him and with others. When pursued as God intended, sexual intimacy contributes to husband and wife finding their identity individually and collectively as created in God's image.

"The Creator's intent of a chaste and holy union must be a couple's moral intent in coming together sexually.... Sexuality is meant to reflect something more than our mere humanity in its physical and psychic interactions, however meaningful they must be. Sexuality must reflect our being in the image of God" (124). He adds, "The starting point of any theology of sexuality necessarily includes the mystery of the two sexes created in God's image." All "who are redeemed by Jesus Christ are renewed in the image of God"; therefore they are uniquely capacitated to "live out this image in their sexual being...within a full personal commitment in marriage" (106).

v. 7 - In the fellowship of those who follow Jesus, a man and a woman can grow in a love "that is free of any fraud or deceit, free of any lust for domination, a love so powerful and so pure that they come to be a single reality" (Pallares 55-56). People whose marriages are in shambles need a church that loves and accepts others as Christ has accepted them (Ro 15.7).

v. 8 - In God's eyes, "one flesh" exists as a result of sexual union, independent of legal or ecclesiological recognition. God has declared this reality and intends that the two who are now "one flesh" live in personal commitment and reciprocal dedication, in a life-long partnership.

The religious ceremony declares God's role in marriage. Legal procedures recognize that marriage has social implications and grant the couple public license to experience in private the physical union that unites them as husband and wife. Even in the absence of legal sanctions (as in common-law marriage, "live-in companionship," etc.), sexual union results in the couples becoming "one flesh."

v. 9 - Schweizer (204-5; italics his) argues that "Divorce *can* be a sign of repentance by which two people face up to their failure. It *can* be a confession that they have not succeeded in living according to God's will, i.e., on the basis of his gift. Divorce *can*, therefore, set one free to experience anew the mercy of God. On the other hand, the preservation of the outward appearance of a marriage which has actually been destroyed *can* blur that consciousness of guilt. But divorce is only the last resort after a person has made every effort to be reconciled to the other, and must finally, for the sake of the other person or for the sake of the children, face up to his own failure and suffer the practical consequences. What this means in practice is that the marriage of a divorced person cannot be forbidden in a rigid legalism; nor can divorce proceedings be started indiscriminately, or without considering the principles which have been declared here."

• Celibacy and not matrimony is God's gift to some individuals (1Co 7.7; cf Mt 19.11-12).

10.10-12 - The disciples ask Jesus about his answer when they are together (cf 9.28). As most of them are probably married (cf 1.30; 1Co 9.5), the subject of the marriage relationship is important for them as they contemplate the possibility of a disciple's wife returning to her parent's home because her husband is accompanying Jesus on his itinerant ministry (cf 10.29-30). Unlike the Pharisees who wanted to trap Jesus, the disciples ask because they want to know.

The disciples' question is apparently about the right to remarry. Jesus answers that anyone (man or woman) who divorces his or her spouse and marries another commits adultery. Jesus does not set forth a new law; his answer in verses 11-12 reinforces what he said in verses 6-9. In personal rather than legalistic terms, he simply and uncompromisingly describes remarriage as a failure to observe God's unchanging plan and a violation of the relationship created by the first marriage. Stated conversely, both husband and wife are under obligation to spare no effort in keeping their marriage intact.

At the same time, Jesus' answer recognizes that men and women frequently fall short of God's ideal in marriage. Jesus is a realist; he deals with people as they are. He knows hearts are hardened, just as they were in Moses' day. For that reason, Jesus does not abrogate the provisions of Deuteronomy 24.1-4. He recognizes human frailty and works within that framework, always sensitive to human needs. Just as Moses (under God) made provision for those who are neither pure nor sinless, Jesus' word on divorce is a part of God's benevolent provision for men and women who don't live up to God's purpose in creating male and female. It constitutes a part of Jesus' compassionate pastoral ministry.

In allowing divorce, Jesus does not approve of it nor does he disallow God's original purpose. As Cranfield (320) explains, "Human conduct which falls short of the absolute command of God is sin and stands under the divine judgment. The provisions which God's mercy has designed for the limitation of the consequences of sin must not be interpreted as divine approval for sinning. When our sinfulness traps us in a position in which all the choices still open to us are evil, we are to choose that which is least evil, asking for God's forgiveness and comforted by it, but not pretending that the evil is good."

In his exposition of Genesis 1.27 and 2.24 (vv 6-9), by emphasizing that both male and female are God's creation, Jesus implies that wife's dignity equals that of her husband. Now Jesus declares that a husband can be guilty of committing adultery against his wife. As Marshall (37) says, this is "a new and radical saying, for Jewish law did not regard the misdemeanors of men, but only those of women, as adultery. Jesus here puts woman on an equal level with man" and reasserts the man's obligation to marital fidelity. Based on the original creation pattern, Jesus rejected the double standard in marriage (vv 6-9). Now he rejects the double standard in divorce and adultery. "Like Old Testament prophets (e.g., Mal 2.10-16), Jesus defines marriage as a relationship in which both husband and wife are responsible both to each other and to God for maintaining its sanctity" (Hurtado 148).

v.11 - Swartley (Mark: Way 162) points out that "The term 'commit adultery' is one word, a verb, in Greek and is best translated 'to adulterate,' which means to weaken or dilute. What is adulterated? The first marriage bond! The sin and failure is in relationship to the former marriage failure. Remarriage, while not the sin itself, finalizes the sin of the former failure in covenant promise."

• Opinions vary about the relationship between Mark's accounts and Mt 5.27-32; 19.3-12; Lk 16.18 and 1Co 7.12-15. We understand that each writer sought to relate from the whole body of Jesus' teachings those which were most relevant for their original readers. Mark reports what was more germane for his readers in the Roman world where women had the right to initiate divorce. A correct understanding of Mark is compatible with the data in Matthew (5.32; 19.9) and Paul (1Co 7.10-16). In fact, Matthew's statement permitting divorce on the ground of adultery is implied in Mark, for divorce merely attests the fact that adultery has destroyed the unity.

• "Commit adultery against her" refers to the first wife. Jesus goes beyond Jewish Law, for under it, a man could commit adultery against another married man but not against his own wife. Jesus' declaration is without precedence in ancient Israel.

• In Mt 19.9 and Lk 16.18a as well as here, "the starting point is the marriage that already exists intact. What is condemned as adulterous is the action which causes the break-up of a marriage for the sake of contracting a new liaison" (Brown NIDNTT III 540).

• "Jesus was not content with bringing women up to a higher plane than was then the custom; but as Savior of all, he brings them before God on an equal footing with men" (Jeremias Jerusalem, 376).

• Some writers claim that this saying about a wife divorcing her husband did not originate with Jesus but was added by the early church in the Roman culture where that was practiced. To the contrary, Jesus himself was aware of Gentile practice and was preparing his disciples for taking the gospel into a world where divorce was rampant. Also, the disciples could have inquired about the role of women when they "asked Jesus about this." Mark included these words of Jesus as a part of his pastoral concern for his readers surrounded by such attitudes. Immorality (Ac 15.29) was a serious problem to the early church.

Excursus: Marriage, Divorce and Remarriage

In his call to discipleship, Jesus challenges all believers to deny self, to serve others, to avoid causing others to stumble, to cut off sin in their own lives and to be more strict with themselves than they are with others (8.34-9.50). These characteristics are also invaluable in building a healthy marriage. Jesus' teaching on sex and marriage goes further. He wants believers to abandon the sexual ethic of an egocentric world and he calls upon husbands and wives to live in faithful personal commitment and reciprocal dedication in a life-long partnership. As a part of living by God's high ethical standards, Jesus expects his followers to control their desires, even their gaze (cf Mt 5.8).

In a world of sexual permissiveness and marital infidelity, the church today must affirm God's plan for marriage, just as Jesus did. Its mission includes calling men and women to pay the price of commitment to God's standards and proclaiming the availability of his grace to live accordingly.

God's purposes presents the church with the difficult task of faithfully proclaiming his will and at the same time receiving even the most unworthy of sinners. Jesus did both. Our human tendency, however, is to lose this equilibrium, favoring either laxity or legalism. Permissiveness encourages the corrosion of God's purposes. Legalism is blind to God's compassion in the face of human frailty.

Since divorce is not basically a legal problem (as the Pharisees thought), it can neither be resolved nor avoided by legal means. (It is nevertheless proper for the state to make laws in the hope of regulating divorce.) Jesus saw it as spiritual, as symptomatic of our stubborn rebelliousness against God. In the light of this fact, "God's solution is not to legislate, but to deal with the hearts of men in transforming grace. By transformation God removes from our personalities...the lust that leads to adultery, and the unwillingness to forgive and be forgiven which leads to divorce" (Larry Richards Remarriage, a Gift from God Word 100). The church, too, must avoid legalism as it seeks to bring healing by the gospel of God's forgiveness.

Hard-heartedness (verse 5, an evil that comes from within, 7.21-23) is one of the destructive forces that contribute to adultery. Other symptoms of not living under God's dominion--addiction, physical and psychological abuse, cruelty, etc.--also lead to marriage breakdowns and prevent that total interpersonal relationship which God intends in marriage.

As Brown (NIDNTT III 542-543) points out, "The foundation of Jesus' teaching--'What God joined together let man not put asunder'--is a formula for avoiding the breakdown of marriage, and not an iron law putting into equal bondage the callous, the innocent and the penitent. In cases where a believing partner desires to remarry we should follow the example of Jesus and examine the situation in the light of God's purposes in creation and the two great commandments." Marriage (like the Sabbath, 2.27) was made for men and women (Ge 2.18). The need for physical relations and for the expression of one's personality does not terminate when a marriage collapses. These personal needs must be faced honestly and balanced out with the needs of children. Those who desire to remarry should ask themselves this question: "Do you believe in your hearts that in your new marriage you can love God, each other and those around you more fully than if you were to remain as you are?"

To deal with people as they are requires us to recognize their weaknesses and their needs just as God does (Ps 103.14). That is what Moses did when he provided a choice between two evils, taking into consideration the plight of women. Divorce is not the ideal, but it is (like Dt 24) better than most other alternatives and can prevent other disasters. It can be God's grace at work in his specialty of rebuilding lives distorted by sin. "Weakness in our natural selves" (Ro 6.19) should lead us to make provision for situations in which, because of human sinfulness, open divorce may be better than hidden adultery (Cf "better than" in 9.43-48).

While Jesus denounced every kind of sexual immorality (7.21), neither it nor divorce is an unforgivable sin (3.28-29). Forgiveness is available for adultery, including the sin of looking "at a woman lustfully" (which is adultery committed in the heart, Mt 5.27). We are redeemed sinners; nevertheless we are not sinners emeritus. The church is not a museum of perfect specimens, but a hospital for the sick, for repentant sinners who, although forgiven by God, still have difficulty forgiving others (cf 11.25).

God still allows divorce as a concession. But those who follow Jesus "in the way" are called upon to live according to God's highest standards, not his concessions. God's ideal is so high that our response should be to throw ourselves on his grace that is available to those who want to make a marriage work. In the larger context of this division (especially in 8.34-9.50), Jesus has already given several criteria for living "at peace with each other" (9.50) in interpersonal relationships. They are especially valid in marriage. Moreover, Jesus himself "offers to Christians the model of dying in order to live. Nowhere is that model more applicable or more necessary than in the intimate, long-term relationship in which two persons become one. Nor does any element in the gospel challenge more profoundly the usual understandings of self-actualization and self-fulfillment of an egocentric culture" (Williamson 181).

JESUS AND LITTLE CHILDREN, 10.13-16

Without any break in his narrative, Mark tells us that people are bringing children to Jesus, no doubt confident that his touch will convey blessings to them as it has to many others. The disciples, however, rebuke (cf 8.34-35) those people. Perhaps the disciples think that the **paida** (children from 8 days to 12 years of age) are too young to understand Jesus, for Jewish boys could only assume the yoke of the Law at age thirteen (**bar mitzvah**).

In those days, adults generally ignored children. Jesus, however, is indignant, for he values children. "Let them come to me," he says; "don't hinder them" (cf 9.39; 10.48). Then Jesus takes them in his arms and invokes God's blessings upon them. He who had time for children while on the road to Calvary still loves children and blesses them. This is the literal meaning of Jesus' actions.

By his words, however, Jesus introduces a deeper meaning into his acceptance of these children: "for the Kingdom of God belongs to such as these; anyone who will not receive the Kingdom of God like a little child will never enter it." Jesus is not saying, "Imitate child-like qualities" (such as innocence, purity and humility). Rather, he says, "Receive the Kingdom like a child receives something." In that culture, children were considered to be insignificant and undeserving; they could make no claims on anyone. They could only receive from adults what was offered. If a child was well treated, it was because of someone's love and generosity. In the same way, a person is to trust God and receive from him the Kingdom as a gift of grace.

Jesus is saying that the Kingdom does not belong to the "worthy" nor is it a fearful power before which people are compelled to bow. On the contrary, it is a gift; it "belongs to such as these" insignificant and helpless ones, not because they merit it but because God has willed to give it to them (cf Lk 12.32). Those who claim worthiness will never enter it, for God gives the Kingdom to those who have no claim upon it.

"Come to me", Jesus says, for he has made the Kingdom accessible, bringing it near in his person (1.14-15). With authority (**amen**, 3.28) he declares that coming to him signifies entering the Kingdom. Responsive "children" accept the gift of God's active rule over them here and now as the condition--and assurance--that they will inherit the future Kingdom in all its fullness. The Kingdom, present and future, belongs to them.

v. 13 - The verb translated "touch" is literally "to lay hands" on for the purpose of blessing (cf Ge 48.14,15). On the eve of the Day of Atonement, children were brought to the rabbis for their blessing.
• Men were involved in bringing the children to Jesus, for the pronoun in "the disciples rebuked them" is masculine. Dt 6.4-9 gives parents the primary responsibility for teaching their children God's word.
• Achtemeier (Invitation 146) cites a rabbinic saying which called paying attention to children "a pernicious waste of time,.. like drinking too much wine or associating with the ignorant." The not-uncommon dehumanization of children in the ancient world parallels child abuse and abandonment today.
v. 14 - As Cranfield (323) points out, the meaning here is that "the Kingdom belongs to such" and not that it "consists of such." Cf "the weak things of the world" in 1Co 1.26ff.
• Only here in the Gospels is indignation ascribed to Jesus. Godly sorrow brings indignation, 2Co 7.11. Cf his anger, 3.5; sighing, 8.12; and emotions in Gethsemane, 14.33ff.
• From the imperfect of the verb, Jesus probably invoked God's blessing upon the children one by one.
v. 15 - Jesus is teaching "justification by faith:" the Kingdom is received as a gift, not as a reward. Dietrich Bonhoeffer decried, however, that this great doctrine of God's free and boundless grace which cost the life of his Son has been received as though it were cheap grace which costs us nothing.
• As Schweizer (207) says, infant baptism is not what is being discussed nor can any direct evidence be derived for its practice. Nevertheless, this story has long been used to support the baptism of infants. This passage does show, however, that Jesus loves, receives and asks God to bless children and implies that children may become full members of the church upon coming to Jesus as "little children."
• "One way the gracious rule of God becomes a reality in human life is as wife and husband openly receive each other in their life together, and as both receive gladly the children God gives. Perhaps this kind of receiving is the greatest gift we can offer each other" (Williamson 182).

POSSESSIONS AND THE KINGDOM OF GOD, 10.17-31

As Jesus resumes his journey to Jerusalem, he makes another startling declaration on the demands of discipleship. Through his dialogue with a rich man, Jesus presents the Kingdom of God as a gift that cannot be earned; it belongs to the totally unpretentious. At the same time, to enter requires a commitment to do things God's way instead of one's own way (1.15). Then Jesus answers the disciples' lingering question about rewards for those who have left all to follow him.

10.17-22 - Healthy, influential adults also seek Jesus. According to local practice, a person of distinction would not run in public. A certain man breaks this custom, however, running to Jesus with an intense desire to find the answer to a profound question. Falling down on his knees before Jesus, he asks, "Good teacher, what must I do to inherit eternal life?" He has rejected the standard orthodox answer that salvation is for the circumcised Jews who keep the commandments. With reverence, he asks the right person for the answer, while implying that it is within his abilities to acquire eternal life.

With his question, "Why do you call me good?" Jesus challenges the fellow not to use the adjective "good" unthinkingly or flippantly. God is the only one who is absolutely good. Yet (Jesus seems to imply), "From your question, you apparently think of yourself as being good, although you admit that you are not good enough to deserve God's acceptance."

Jesus directs him to the Ten Commandments, considered by the Jews as establishing the norm for proper conduct. By focusing on the "second table" (Ex 20.13-17) of the Decalogue, Jesus is asking if he is "good" by these standards which deal with the highest social values: life, property, truth and family. This is a fair test, for human relationships are easily verified, whereas compliance to the "first table" (relationships to God, Ex 20.3-8) is not so evident.

"Teacher," he replied, "all these I have kept since I was a boy." His naive reply indicates that for him, as with many people, behavior is a matter of outward obedience to the letter of the Law, not of the inner character and the motives of the heart. He lacks understanding of the commandments and is blind to his failure to keep them. Used correctly, the Law is a mirror to show men and woman that they are sinners in need of the grace of God.

Jesus' question is not an academic one. The man's eternal life is at stake. Avoiding any stereotyped approach, Jesus focuses on the man's need to gain insight into his true condition. To help him renounce his self-righteousness and call upon God for his gift of life, Jesus declares, "You lack one thing." This should jar him out of his complacency. Then Jesus charges him with a series of five short imperatives which, in Williamson's words (184), "fall on the man's ears like hammer blows." A promise, "you will have treasure in heaven," separates the imperatives into two movements: "Go, sell everything, give the proceeds to the poor," and "Come, follow me." The five imperatives are essentially only one command demanding one response. The fellow must renounce the particular object of his affection before he can live under God's rule.

Jesus' word is designed to show the man the secrets of his heart (cf Ro 2.16). In reality, he has broken the tenth commandment (he covets wealth) and the first (wealth is his god; Col 3.5) and is giving false testimony about himself in violation of the ninth commandment. He has allowed "the deceitfulness of wealth and the desires for other things to come in and choke the word, making it unfruitful" (4.7, 19). He must lose his life in order to save it (8.35).

The fellow thinks that his riches are an unmixed blessing from God (cf Job 1.10; 42.10; Ps 128.1-2). While the possession of riches in itself is not wrong, riches frequently possess the individual. Wealth gives people a means to dominate and exploit others, the inverse of the servant role of the disciple (9.34ff; 10.42ff). To begin with, this man must reject (as the first Commandment requires, or in the words of Mk 9.43, "cut off") any and all things that would take the place that belongs to God. If he had followed Jesus, he would have fulfilled the first commandment (for in saying "Come, follow me," Jesus reaffirms his oneness with the God who alone is good). Our hearts have room for only one all-embracing devotion (as Bonhoeffer has said), and we can only cleave to one Lord.

Jesus looks upon this rich man with love, sensing his inner conflict. His love, however, does not lead him to reduce the requirements for discipleship in order to make an easy convert. Jesus tells the man to divest himself of his wealth and of its claim on him. When people are under the power of their wealth, they are not free to follow Jesus who alone can give what wealth cannot.

Jesus offers himself to those who seek life; he fully satisfies the needs of those who follow him (Ps 23). He does not reject the man; he loves him. He points out the man's lack and gives him the freedom to make a conscious choice. The fellow goes away sad, leaving the One in whom God delights (1.11) and whose presence brings joy to humankind. The rich man becomes the poorest of the poor.

v. 17 - By "good teacher," he probably meant "good" in the sense of "kind," not "a capable teacher" or "perfect goodness." Jesus gives "good" the connotation of moral attributes (Bratcher and Nida 317f).

• This man no doubt believed that this age will end in judgment and that the new era will be limited to those who have eternal life (cf Da 12.2). Jesus confirms the coming of a new era (v 30), but not as something to be awaited passively. The Kingdom has come in the person of Jesus; it is to be seized with commitment.

v. 18 - Jesus' words "Why do you call me good?" do not imply that Jesus was conscious of sin; he is directing the inquirer's attention to his Father, who is the only source of goodness.

v. 19 Since stealing, deceit and coveting frequently operate together, "do not defraud" may express the 8th, 9th and 10th commandments in a form especially pertinent to one possessed by riches.

• "Do not murder." The unequal distribution of national and individual wealth contributes to the death of millions by starvation.

v. 21 - In contrast to many advocates of Liberation Theology, Jesus loves the poor without hating the rich.

• The imperatives ("Go, sell, give") are aimed at this fellow's particular stumbling block. "Come, follow me" are universal imperatives, repeated throughout the gospel. The fellow's basic need is not limited to the rich. He is not "called to poverty for its own sake, but to discipleship to Jesus" (Hurtado 152).

• To claim "treasure in heaven" as a reward for giving alms is to misconstrue Jesus' teachings. The young man no doubt gave alms; but Jesus commands him to give up the very sources of his income ("sell everything" includes property and fields) as preliminary to complete devotion to Jesus. These hard demands placed upon him are comparable to the hard commands given to the disciples (8.34ff) and to husbands and wives (10.9).

• Jesus did not tell the fellow to "follow the way of God (even as I do)." Rather, he tells him, "Follow me," for Jesus is "God's unique agent through whom obedience to God is appropriately expressed." Bailey (Eyes 163) adds that "To follow Jesus is the climax of what is required of him."

v. 22 - Matthew 19.20 adds that he was young; Luke 18.18, that he was a ruler. Only at the end of the dialogue (v 22) does Mark identify the man as rich.

10.23-27 - With the rich man's inquiry as background, Jesus elaborates on the difficulty of entering the Kingdom of God. In a three-step progression, he challenges popular concepts of life:

v 23 - "how hard it is for the rich to enter;"
v 24 - "how hard it is (for anyone) to enter;"
v 27 - it is impossible for anyone to enter;
conclusion: only God can save.

The disciples are increasingly amazed as Jesus undercuts the widespread opinion that good people can earn eternal life. Such merit is as impossible to earn as it would be for a camel (the largest animal known in Palestine) to go through the eye of a needle (the smallest opening).

While he does not make a universal call to voluntary poverty, by his life and proclamations Jesus places a strong emphasis upon detachment from wealth and possessions. He teaches that one cannot have real life without being ready to lose life (8.34f) and that one cannot be really rich without being willing to lose one's riches.

As seen in 8.34-10.31, discipleship includes several things that are neither natural nor possible for us. They are presented, however, as things we must do, as though the Christian life were a matter of human achievement. This seems to contradict Jesus' emphasis upon receiving the Kingdom as a gift. In 10.23-27 he transforms the apparent contradiction into an astonishing but true paradox as he brings these two teachings together. Eternal life is a gift from God; our response is a life of obedience to him. God's gift of life (10.13-16) is not cheap grace. Jesus (in 10.21) "demands our best obedience and all we have. Yet all we can do is not enough to achieve the life we seek" (Williamson 185). God's grace makes both salvation and discipleship possible; his gift and his high demands go together (cf Php 2.12-13).

v. 23 - This in no way implies that the poor will enter the Kingdom easily. While the possession of riches may be no sin, poverty is not necessarily a virtue.

• This narrative continues the theme of "enter the Kingdom" (9.47; 10.15, 23-25) with its synonyms, "enter life" (9.43,45, that is, "eternal life") and "be saved" (10.26). This is the true life (cf 8.35) in which one experiences God's rule in daily life now. It is also "eternal life" since the believer shares in the life of God in the present and future Kingdom.

v. 24 - Some manuscripts (including NIV) insert "for those who trust in riches." But Jesus has already advanced beyond the difficulty for the rich (v 23) to the difficulty for anyone to enter the Kingdom. Then he tells the proverb about the camel in preparation for the "shocking" conclusion of his step-by-step reasoning: the human impossibility of saving oneself (v 27). Explanations such as the "needle's eye" referring to a small gate in the wall of Jerusalem are without foundation. Moreover, they contradict what Jesus is saying. "To enter the Kingdom of God" is more than difficult; it is impossible apart from God's miraculous work.

• The "gospel of prosperity" attempts to identify economic betterment with spirituality. This is another contradiction of Jesus' teaching. His own life and death, his call to discipleship and his letters to the churches in Smyrna and Laodicea (Rev 2.9; 3.17) all forcefully impugn any affirmation that the faithful enjoy economic prosperity and that poverty is an evidence of disobedience. This "gospel" must be recognized for what it is--an attempt to manipulate the things of God in order to acquire the things of humanity. Self-centeredness is the antithesis of discipleship.

• We do Jesus--and ourselves--serious injustice if we try to accommodate his teaching to our way of thinking and our lifestyles. Jesus means for his teaching to be taken seriously, to change our lives. As Williamson (188) warns, "if this message does not take our breath away, if we are not shocked, appalled, grieved, or amazed, we have either not yet heard it or heard it so often that we do not really hear it any more."

10.28-31 - Still mulling over Jesus' command to the rich man (v 21), Peter (speaking for the Twelve) calls Jesus' attention to their sacrificial obedience: "We have decisively left (aorist tense) all to follow (perfect tense) you permanently." As a matter of record, the Twelve stand out in sharp contrast to the rich young man. They have left family and property (cf 1.16-20). They persist in following Jesus on the way to Jerusalem. They are experiencing something of God doing the impossible.

In the midst of all the pressures upon them, they naturally wonder what they will gain. Without disputing Peter's claim, Jesus reassures them that God provides for his servants, now and in the future. Through his reference to family, home and fields (basic to fellowship, security and economic livelihood in Palestine), Jesus widens the scope of obedience beyond those fundamental loyalties to include all things highly treasured. His promise, however, is conditional: Jesus and the gospel must be the reason behind their actions. Moreover, the blessings include suffering persecutions (cf Ro 5.3-4).

Jesus goes on to say that, in the present age, his followers will receive much more than they have left. The disciples have already experienced a foretaste of this in their mission in Galilee (6.8-9). The early church shared with one another (Acts 2.42-47; 4.32-37) as members of the new family of God (3.30-35). In the present age, we enter upon discipleship alone; however, we do not remain alone: we find fulfillment in the fellowship of the church. In the age to come, our reward will be to live in fellowship beyond measure with God himself. When the Son of Man comes in the Father's glory (8.38), he will bring his reward with him (Rev 22.12). As Schweizer (214) said, "Discipleship to Jesus does not lead to poverty and deprivation, but to wholeness--to the experience of real life" now and in the age to come.

Verse 31 also indicates that the coming judgment by God will bring reversals in earthly status. Those who think they are worthy of God's favor will not find it; God's favor is freely offered to all who acknowledge their unworthiness. While Jesus promises rewards, they are entirely of grace, never of merit.

v. 29 - The Decalogue commanded (10.19), "Don't steal (another's property);" Jesus tells his disciples, "Leave your own property" (cf Barnabas, Acts 4.36-37). To follow Jesus also involves a relationship that even surpasses family blood ties. To marry, a man leaves his father and mother (10.7); to follow Jesus, a person may be called upon to leave all his relatives.
• "For me and the gospel" (cf 8.35) calls attention to one's incentives. Leaving family and possessions must be motivated by the determination to follow Jesus and share in the proclamation of the gospel. To leave in order to receive is contrary to the whole thrust of Jesus' teachings (cf 1Co 13.1-3). He denounces those who seek him for material gain (cf Jn 6.26).
• From the accounts of Paul's ministry, we know about some of his new family relationships (e.g., "children," 1Co 4.15; "sons," Tit 1.3 and Phm 10; "a mother to me," Ro 16.13). It is not hard to imagine that in his years of itinerant ministry, Paul received much more than he gave, even though he suffered much persecution (e.g., 2Co 6.4-10; cf. Jesus' promises in 4.17 and 13.9f).
v. 30 - Although followers may be called upon to leave their fathers, they are not promised new fathers, for God himself is the Father of this new family. Mark does not mention "wives" since his list is limited to blood relatives and to say "receive wives" would lead to misunderstandings.

C. THE RIGHT TO RULE IN THE KINGDOM, 10.32-52

Beginning and closing with references to "the way," this third tension-filled unit brings to a climax Mark's central division with its teaching on the relationships between Christology and discipleship. Building on his previous pronouncements, Jesus foretells more about his passion and resurrection, prior to making his first declaration of why he will suffer and die.

In sharp contrast to the Twelve, a blind beggar exemplifies true discipleship. With this illustration, Mark closes his recounting of the journey from Caesarea Philippi to Jerusalem, bringing the narrative to the threshold of the passion itself.

1. The Son of Man in the Hands of Gentiles, 10.32-34

In his description of their way up to Jerusalem, Mark makes three points. First, Jesus does not waiver in his determination to fulfill God's will that includes his death in Jerusalem. Second, he continues to lead the way, as others follow him. Third, emotions run high. Jesus presses forward with a sense of urgency. Though afraid, the disciples follow him. They are torn by conflicting hopes and fears. Tension fills the air. Nevertheless, they continue following Jesus.

Jesus gradually enlarges upon the subject of his death and resurrection (8.31; 9.31; cf 9.9-13). He realizes that his disciples are unable to grasp these thoughts, as they contradict deep-seated convictions about the victorious role of the Messiah.

For the first time, Jesus stipulates where he will die. "We are going up to Jerusalem"--there he will suffer the derision and humiliation of being mocked and spat on (14.65; 15.15-20). He will be flogged and tortured as a criminal prior to suffering a violent death (15.20-39).

We know from 9.31 that he will be handed over to unspecified men. Now he reveals the complicity of high Jewish religious authorities with the Roman authorities (cf 3.6) who alone had authority to inflict the death sentence. After condemning Jesus to death, the chief priests and scribes "will hand him over to the Gentiles" (15.1,10), an act designed to lead all Israel to disdain Jesus and his Kingdom. How could anyone who is mocked, flogged and killed by the Gentiles, the embodiment of evil, be the awaited Messiah who would deliver the Jewish people from the despised Gentiles?

This announcement stressing his suffering and death is Jesus' climactic thrust to prepare his disciples for his rejection in Jerusalem. Each detail will be fulfilled (cf 15.15-20), for what Jesus predicts, happens. After announcing such a shameful future, he concludes again with the promise that he will rise after three days.

Jesus' declaration adds to our understanding of "who he is" and "where he is going." In verse 45, Jesus himself will reveal why is he going to die.

v. 32 - The "way up to Jerusalem" reflects the steep ascent to Jerusalem in the central mountains. From Jericho, located below sea level in the Jordan River valley, the road ascends over 3000 feet in 15 miles.

• Some scholars understand that "the disciples were amazed; others (a larger group, probably including the women of 15.41) who followed were afraid." Others say "the disciples (one group only) were astonished and afraid as they followed." Some think that "Jesus was in deep distress and those who followed were afraid."

2. Jesus, Servant of All, 10.35-45

This passion-resurrection pronouncement is also followed by a story that demonstrates the depth of the disciples' misunderstanding. Jesus responds by giving additional teaching about the Messiah and discipleship.

10.35-40 - The disciples are certain that Jesus will soon establish the Messianic Kingdom, possibly upon arriving in Jerusalem (cf Acts 1.6). In response to James and John's childish request for "anything we ask," Jesus graciously asks, "What do you want me to do for you?" (cf 10.51). They want to sit at Jesus' right and left hand in his glory. In other words, they seek the positions of highest honor and authority next to his royal throne (cf 12.36; 1Ki 2.19). They never imagine that before long two robbers will occupy crosses at the right and left of the Messiah (15.27).

Jesus demonstrates extreme patience with them. He has repeatedly emphasized that he is on the way to suffering and death in Jerusalem. In this light, their request (v 37) is cruel. It must have hurt him deeply. Yet he answers gently, "You don't know what you are asking." The sons of Zebedee have confused his teaching, hearing only what they want to hear. Before dealing with their desire to rule over others (vv 42ff) Jesus tries again to open their eyes to the missing element in their thinking about the Messianic Kingdom: the Son of Man *must* suffer and die first, before there can be any resurrection and glory. So he asks, "Can you drink the cup I drink or be baptized with the baptism I am baptized with?" Possibly remembering their meals together and John's baptism (1.4-5), they affirm with self-confidence, "We can." Jesus does not dispute their claim (cf 10.28) but instructs them anew about what comes before his triumph. His words call each of us to reaffirm our own understanding of and obedience to Jesus' teaching.

In his own baptism, Jesus identified himself with sinners; now with the imagery of baptism he reaffirms his solidarity with sinful people. "To share someone's cup was a recognized expression for sharing his fate. In the Old Testament the cup of wine is a common metaphor for the wrath of God's judgment upon human sin and rebellion" (Lane 380). Employing these two metaphors, Jesus declares that he will voluntarily bear God's judgment in the place of the guilty (cf Isa 53.5). Glory is not the next step in God's plan, as James and John imply in their request. To the contrary, Jesus will die a shameful death as the substitute for sinners. This is his messianic vocation; this will be his cup and baptism that no one else can share.

Yet, in another sense, Jesus' cup and baptism are to be shared (v 39a; cf 1Pe 4.13). Whoever follows the Suffering Servant is to pour out his or her life for others, serving others above seeking personal well being. Jesus closes this dialogue (v 45), by calling attention to his own example: if the Son of Man came to serve, how much more ought his disciples to be servants.

Jesus confirms his future glory (v 40). At the same time, he affirms his submission to the Father's will as top priority. The sovereign God alone has authority to designate that will occupy places of honor; he will give them to those whom he has prepared. Neither working for rewards nor lobbying for advantages will determine God's decision.

v. 35 - The three disciples who were given special opportunities to learn (Peter, James and John; 5.37; 9.2) are the ones who present strong objections to Jesus' teachings (9.33 and here). In presenting Jesus with their request, James and John exemplify followers who, having begun with humility, later seek special privileges. Barriers to the gospel come from within the community as well as from outside (cf Ac 20.29-30).

v. 38 - Jesus was not speaking primarily of the cup and baptism of the ordinances given to his church, for he had not yet celebrated the Passover feast with his disciples (14.23ff). To share Jesus' cup and baptism means that all disciples are called upon to pour out their lives for others. James did this, suffering a violent death (Ac 12.2). After a long life of faithful service, John was exiled on Patmos (Rev 1.9).

• For cup as a synonym for suffering, see 14.36; Ps 75.8; Isa 51.17-22; Jer 25.15; Eze 23.31-34. Baptism symbolizes calamity, as in "immersed in troubles;" cf Ps 42.7; 69.2,15; Lk 12.50.

10.41-44 - The other disciples become indignant with the sons of Zebedee for preempting their own desires for special privileges. Having answered the brothers about positions of authority in the age to come, Jesus calls all his disciples together to teach them about the proper exercise of authority in this present age.

Jesus begins with a negative example: among the nations, those who are regarded as rulers abuse authority and exploit others. Lording it over people is the foundation upon which structures of domination are built. All too frequently rule is exercised in the interest of those who rule.

Jesus, however, measures greatness by service rather than domination. In the community of disciples, a new type of relationship is to prevail: his followers are to be servants (**diakonos**) of one another and slaves (**doulos**) to all. His humility is frequently presented as the pattern for believers' attitudes and relationships with others (9.35-37; Php 2.5-11).

In this pericope, however, Jesus presents his own servanthood as the norm for the proper exercise of authority in the church. Rather than insisting on his own rights, he exercises his authority in the interests of others, even to the point of being a slave who gives his life for others (v 45). By his "not so with you," Jesus declares that, in the church, only the servant is qualified to govern. Anyone who introduces the structures of secular society into the community of God's people dishonors the character of the church as the body of Christ.

v. 42 - In contrast to "they exercise authority," Jesus describes the role of the disciple as "servant" (engaged in humiliating service) and "slave" (without status). Jesus accepts for himself the ignoble rank of a slave. "You" (v 43) applies to all Christians.

v. 43 - James and John seek to turn their relationship with Jesus into personal advantage. Jesus, on the other hand, refuses to use his filial relationship with the Father for his own benefit. He expresses "his filial unity and obedience by taking on the role of a **doulos**, 'hidden in the shadow of God's hand' (Is 49.2), allowing God to glorify himself and accomplish his purpose through a humble, powerless servant" (Edwards 55n54).

10.45 - The cross, however, is more than an example of servanthood; it is also the foundation of our hope as sinners. Jesus now forcefully declares the reason for his crucifixion: "the Son of Man came to give his life as a ransom for many." This **lutron** ("ransom") is necessary, for humankind is in captivity to an alien power, with no means of bringing about its own liberation. Jesus willingly sacrificed himself in order to deliver us from this hopeless slavery by paying the purchase price of freedom. The price he paid was his own life. The benefit we receive is release from the domination of sin in order to enjoy communion with God (Tit 2.14; 1Pe 1.18).

This ransom is made on behalf of **polloi**. Although it is often translated "many," the word **polloi** is used here in the inclusive sense of "all." It appears five times in Isaiah's prophecy on the Suffering Servant. By drawing upon Isaiah 53, Jesus identifies himself as that Servant of God who gives his life as a ransom for sinners of all nations. On the eve of his crucifixion (14.24), Jesus again speaks of **polloi** with allusions to Isaiah 53.

Jesus' death is substitutionary. The sinless One voluntarily takes the place of sinners, in order that all humanity might gain what it could not earn for itself. The benefits of his vicarious death are available to each person who accepts God's offer of redemption. Ultimately, his cross is more than a symbol of suffering and death. It is the offer of redemption and a new life under God's rule. Verse 45 presents the key to understanding Jesus, for it focuses on Jesus' suffering and death on the behalf of all.

We have reached the climax of the central division of Mark (8.27-10.52) with its emphasis upon Christology and discipleship. In keeping with his literary style (cf 1.40-45; 6.1-6a), Mark closes this unit with a positive illustration of what it means to be a true disciple (10.46-52).

v. 45 - Marshall (40) explains that Jesus' declaration "teaches a universally available atonement, for 'many' is a Hebrew way of saying 'all'." Cf 1Ti 2.6: "gave himself a ransom for *all*." Because "the many" (Isa 53; Da 12.2,10) has a long history as a term for the covenant people, Mann (415f) translates **polloi** as "the community." See our comments on Mk 14.24.

• **Lutron** means "redemption," as seen in Israel's release from bondage in Egypt. In the Bible, there is no connotation of God as mercenary, demanding recompense, as in a literal ransom.

• Jesus employs two metaphors to describe giving himself as an offering to God for humanity's sake. As a "ransom," his death effects deliverance from sin and from judgment. As "the blood of the covenant" (14.24), his death ratifies a covenant bond between God and humanity, "a relationship of fellowship and obedience, which is based upon his gift of forgiveness, redemption and reconciliation" (Taylor 124f).

• God does not insult humanity by pretending that sin does not matter. Rather, he himself bears the full cost of forgiving it. Through his unique death, Jesus brought God's offer of redemption for sinners to ultimate fulfillment.

• As Best (Following 127) points out, "For Mark Christianity is not the imitation of Jesus...but redemption through Christ, and it is only on the basis of this redemption that imitation becomes possible." While disciples are called upon to follow Jesus' example in serving and laying down their lives for others (cf 1Jn 3.16), the distinction between Master and servant is absolute. "The servant is never summoned to give his life as a ransom for others in the way the Master has given his. And indeed it is only because the Master has given his life that the servant is able to offer service to others" (Best Story 89).

3. Bartimaeus, An Authentic Disciple, 10.46-52

Mark has woven many threads together in this division (8.27-10.52), producing a tapestry that is beautiful as an integrated work of art and amazing as a portrayal of life. He emphasizes the requirements for the Messiah and for disciples as they journey together "in the way" (**en te hodos**), the phrase which brackets the division. The question of Jesus' identity is woven through this division which begins with the title "Messiah" and closes with "Son of David." Two miracles of sight (8.22ff; 10.46ff) bind together this section which does not stress miracles.

The last healing narrative in Mark (but not the last miracle) centers on Bartimaeus whose attitudes and actions serve as a model and encouragement to all. This man knew what he wanted most and knew what to do with it when he got it.

10.46-52 - The journey from Caesarea Philippi will soon be over, for Jesus and his disciples have arrived in Jericho, the eastern gateway to Jerusalem. They are on the way to Jerusalem where Jesus will be crucified. Their astonishment and fear (cf 10.32) mix with the high expectations of the pilgrims their way to the Feast in Jerusalem.

Sitting by the roadside begging, blind Bartimaeus begins to shout in order to get Jesus' attention. Many try to stop him (cf 10.13), possibly thinking that Jesus is too busy or preoccupied to pay any attention to a destitute person. But Bartimaeus shouts all the more, "Son of David, have mercy on me!"

We do not know what Bartimaeus understands by the title, "Son of David." We know from his persistence, however, that he is convinced that God's mercy is abundantly available through Jesus. Knowing that he has nothing to merit Jesus' attention, Bartimaeus cries out, "Have mercy on me!" (cf 5.19).

Although he is urgently pressing on to Jerusalem, Jesus stops and says, "Call him." With these words, he rebukes those who would reject a "nobody." They call out to Bartimaeus, "Cheer up! (cf 6.50; Isa 35.4,5). He's calling for you." The beggar throws his cloak aside; what may have been his only possession is no longer important. With complete abandon, the blind man jumps to his feet and hurries to Jesus.

Jesus gives Bartimaeus an opportunity to articulate his desires by asking him, "What do you want me to do for you?" His answer is simple and straightforward: "I want to see." He is confident that Jesus can give him sight. "Go," Jesus tells the blind man, "your faith has healed you." Immediately Bartimaeus receives his sight and follows Jesus "in the way" (v 52).

Bartimaeus demonstrates the meaning of discipleship. He overcomes all obstacles in order to reach the One who is able to help him. He knows he merits no favors; he appeals only to God's mercy. Bartimaeus asks Jesus to give him sight, a request that stands in marked contrast to James' and John's response to Jesus' identical question (10.36). Furthermore, when he gets his request, he demonstrates his gratitude by following Jesus, the compassionate one who heard when he called and resolved his deepest need. He had discovered that (in Bernard of Clairvaux's words) "to those who seek him, God is good; to those who find him, he is all in all."

The first miracle of giving sight to a blind man (8.22-26) prepared the reader for this division on the meaning of Messiah and of discipleship, two themes inseparable from the cross. By stating that Bartimaeus followed Jesus "in the way" (10.52), the second miracle of giving sight leads us directly to Jerusalem and the cross itself. Having seen Jesus' personal care for the new community expressed in the word "serve" (10.45), we will see the supreme manifestation of his care: his death.

v. 46 - Mark and Mt 20.29 refer to leaving Jericho, while Luke 18.35 says Jesus was approaching Jericho, probably Herod's luxurious winter palace southwest of the old city of Jericho. R.C.H. Lenski (468) harmonizes the accounts in a different way: Jesus was leaving Jericho when he received an invitation from Zacchaeus (omitted by both Matthew and Mark) to spend the night at his home (Lk 19.1). As he reenters the city, he encounters Bartimaeus.

Matthew speaks of two blind men. Mark and Luke narrate only the story of Bartimaeus, perhaps because the original readers knew him.

• This story centers on the attitude and action of Bartimaeus, a fitting conclusion to this division's emphasis on discipleship. The word "call" (cf 1.16-20; 2.13-14) is repeated 3 times in this short story. The act of healing is not described.

v. 47 - Many of the Jewish people referred to David as "our father" (i.e., ancestor, as in 11.10; Ac 4.25); his name embodied the aspirations of the people of Israel. "Son of David" as a messianic title was taught in the Old Testament (e.g., 2Sa 7.12ff; Ps 89.3f, 19-37; Isa 11.1-5; Jer 23.5f; Eze 34.23f), by the scribes (12.35) and in Qumran documents.

Jesus is called the "Son of David" only here in Mark. The title is introduced abruptly, with no explanation. See Jesus' claim in 12.35-37. The theme of Christology continues to be unveiled in the title "Son of David" while maintaining some of its hiddenness.

v. 50 - The cloak was used as a bedroll at night. During the day a beggar would spread out this outer garment as a mat for receiving alms.

v. 51 - For both Mark and Isaiah, the recovery of sight was a sign of God's purposes being fulfilled through the Messiah; cf Isa 29.18; 35.5; 42.7,16.

• **Anablepo** ("recover sight") may imply that at one time Bartimaeus had been able to see.

v. 52 - "The Greek word **sozein** has the double connotation 'save, heal.' Thus 10.52 and 5.34 might as easily be translated 'your faith has saved you.'...Faith and salvation go together; thus many of the healing miracles speak of the saving power of God through Christ; like Jairus' daughter, those dead in sin are raised to new life (Eph. 2.5f)" (Best Disciples 187-188).

- PART 6 -
JESUS AND THE TEMPLE
11.1 - 13.37

In the previous division, Mark relates Jesus' predictions of the way he will go. These next three chapters present Jesus' public and private ministries in and near Jerusalem. Since they lead to the cross, scenes in this section compose a prelude to the passion and resurrection narratives in chapters 14-16.

While attention is focused on Jesus himself, the disciples are not out of the picture. They no longer express their opposition to Jesus' death or their desire for glory. What they lack in understanding is overshadowed by their resolve to be faithful even unto death.

The opposition leaders return in force, after being absent from most of the previous division (8.27-10.52). For the first time in Mark's narrative, Jesus arrives in Jerusalem. His first and last visits to the Temple (11.11; 12.41) are low drama but highly significant: he looks around and leaves, apparently an outsider there. His dramatic rejection of the Temple provokes strong reaction (as seen in a new section of five controversy stories, 11.27-12.44) which leads to his pronouncements about its future (chapter 13). As chapter 14 opens, the Temple authorities solidify their rejection of Jesus by laying plans to kill him.

• The chronology from Jesus' entry into Jerusalem (11.1) to the crucifixion constitutes a difficult problem in Mark. These events have traditionally been understood to have occurred within one week, and, from the fourth century on, have been celebrated liturgically as beginning with the Sunday before Easter. Since Mark does not refer to the Passover before 14.1, it is very difficult to determine whether he means that everything following 11.1 occurs within a single week.

The five debates in Jerusalem (11.27-12.37) parallel the five stories of conflict in Galilee (2.1-3.6). Some of the debates may belong to an earlier period in Jesus' ministry (they lack precise temporal links such as exist between the several sections of 11.1-26). By limiting his account of Jesus' ministry in Jerusalem to one visit recorded in the final chapters of his Gospel, Mark dramatically emphasizes the crucifixion and resurrection as the purpose of Jesus' life and ministry.

It seems appropriate to consider the events of 11.1-26 as taking place in sequence, Sunday to Tuesday, with 11.27-12.44 as a thematic collection set in the context of the third day; and chapter 13 sometime between the Feast of Tabernacles and the Passover.

A. THE PRESENT TEMPLE, 11.1 - 12.44

After much preparation, Jesus arrives in Jerusalem, the city David captured and made his capital. While it is not the center of the regional Roman government, Herod's magnificent Palace and the large military installations leave no doubt about Jerusalem as a center of power. The Temple is far more important, however, for that is where sacrifices are offered daily to the God of Abraham, Isaac and Jacob.

The joy of approaching God in his Temple is mixed with apprehensions, for those who accompany Jesus are troubled by his predictions about what lies ahead for him in Jerusalem.

• Each of the Evangelists gives a distinct emphasis to Jesus' entry into Jerusalem. As Williamson (204-5) points out, for John (12.12-19), the entry is triumphant; Matthew (21.5) stresses its humility; Luke (19.41-44) foretells the destruction of the city. While Mark does not omit Jesus' prophetic role, he continues the paradoxical interplay between hiddenness and revelation.

• From the time of David, Jerusalem was the capital of the Jewish nation but it never was the capital when a Gentile power dominated Palestine. Caesarea, by the Mediterranean Sea, was the capital of the Roman province during Jesus' time (cf Ac 23.23ff). Jerusalem became the capital of modern Israel in 1948.

1. Jesus Challenges the Temple Authorities, 11.1-26

From Jericho, upon reaching the brow of the Mount of Olives, travelers enjoy a spectacular view of the huge Temple complex dominating the city of David. Near the outlying villages of Bethphage and Bethany, Jesus, the King of glory (cf Ps 24) prepares for his entrance into the royal city of Jerusalem.

The story abounds with royal imagery. Old Testament prophecies are interwoven with Jewish expectations anticipating a restoration of the Davidic Kingdom.

JESUS ENTERS JERUSALEM AND INSPECTS THE TEMPLE, 11.1-11

11.1-7 - Jesus takes the initiative and plans his entrance into the city according to his purposes. He will not walk, as was his custom, but will ride on a colt to symbolize his peaceful mission. It is also of symbolic importance that the colt not have been used previously for secular purposes, this being a sacred mission. Jesus sends two of his disciples (cf 6.7) to the village with a specific directive regarding the colt: "The Lord needs it." His requisition of the colt includes due acknowledgement of the rights of the owner and the promise to send it back right away.

The two do as Jesus says and find that every step occurs through divine foreknowledge and according to his plan. Mark describes Jesus' commands and their fulfillment in almost identical terms in order to encourage readers to trust in Jesus' ability to foretell the future.

11.8-10 - As Jesus rides toward the city, some pilgrims spread garments and branches in the way before him, as for a royal procession leading to enthronement (2Ki 9.13). Believing that Jesus had come to Jerusalem in fulfillment of prophecy, they burst forth in antiphonal singing of the Hallel Psalms (Ps 113-118), a tradition of pilgrims approaching the Temple in both the Passover and Tabernacles Feasts.

"Hosanna!" is a transliteration of their spontaneous expression of homage, meaning "O, save!" (Ps 118.25,26). The second line ("May God bless him who comes") was originally a blessing pronounced on the pilgrims. It has a deeper meaning on this occasion, however; the parallel structure in verses 9 and 10 ("he who comes" and "the Kingdom that comes") identifies their singing as an acclamation of the King. The final Hosanna ("Save now, Lord, save now") explicitly ties the coming of Jesus to the dawning of the Kingdom and appeals to God to inaugurate the era of salvation.

11.11 - Mark's colorful report fades with his lackluster statement, "Jesus entered Jerusalem." No mention is made of the festive crowd; nothing is said about the reaction of the civil and religious authorities. No mention of prayer or worship or teaching, no indication that Jesus is recognized. Jesus does not go to the governmental palaces. Rather, he goes to the Temple (with the disciples, we presume) and inspects everything. Then he returns to Bethany.

Although Jesus himself initiated and planned his entry, his only words are directed to the disciples before the procession. He does not respond to the pilgrim's welcome or take advantage of their support. In the Temple itself, he acts like an outsider. The ironic contrast of verse 11 requires that we reconsider the scene.

In retrospect, we see that Mark treats the entrance with definite reserve. He does not cite Zechariah 9.9 when mentioning the colt (as in Mt 21.5; Jn 12.15; cf Isa 62.11). He carefully avoids any explicit reference to Jesus as King or Son of David. Yet we remember that Jesus is God's royal Son who proclaims the dawning of God's Kingdom (1.11,15). We also recall that Bartimaeus addressed Jesus as the "Son of David" (10.47). We remember the prophets' declarations that one day, a new King David will rule with justice and righteousness forever (Isa 9.1-7; 11.1-3; Jer 23.5f; Eze 34.23f; 37.24f).

Jesus, however, does not restore anything; he looks around and leaves for Bethany. We conclude that Mark does not picture this as a "triumphal entry." Paradoxically, Jesus' authority is being revealed in weakness, his Kingdom in hiddenness. The people are correct in hailing the King but wrong in expecting the Kingdom prematurely; first, Jesus must suffer and die, as he told the disciples repeatedly. The King will assume his throne on the other side of Jerusalem, on a hill called Golgotha (15.22).

With "messianic assertion and restraint" (Lane 393), by riding upon a donkey Jesus shows the disciples and the crowd that he is not the military Messiah they hoped for. Puzzled now, the crowd will later turn against him. Mark intends for us to understand that Jesus planned his entry just this way.

"Since it was already late, he went out to Bethany with the Twelve," as he would the following nights. There he has time alone with his disciples, far from the tensions encountered throughout the day and with little danger of being arrested. It seems to be a quiet ending to an exciting day, but it is the quiet before the storm.

v. 1 - Known for the succinctness of his accounts, Mark dedicates disproportionate space to the stories of the colt and (in 14.13ff) the room for the Passover. As Anderson (261) points out, "a pre-arrangement with someone in the city...is quite foreign to the spirit of the story." Rather, Jesus is presented as the one with the knowledge and power to make things happen. The recognition of Jesus' prophetic role prepares Jesus' disciples and Mark's first readers for facing his other predictions (e.g., 13.9ff).

v. 9 - "Those who went ahead" may mean they preceded Jesus physically. It could also mean they were impatient to see the arrival of his Kingdom. Normally Jesus went ahead and others followed.

v. 11 - The Temple (**hieron**) refers to the physical structures of the Temple. **Naos** (only in 14.58; 15.29,38) is the sanctuary including the Holy of Holies. From the time of the Monarchy, the Temple "symbolized the people's aspirations for spiritual grandeur and the incipient apostasy of the people" (Swartley Structure 223).

• Minear (107) observes that each of Jesus' entrances was "the entrance of the true King and Shepherd, for whom the very gates must lift up their heads (Ps 24.7). Each exit conveyed a sense of the departure of God's glory," the Lord rejecting those who rejected him. There was no place for him there.

• "Looked around;" cf 3.5,34; 5.32; 9.8; 10.23; 12.41; cf Jer 7.11c.

THE FIG TREE AND THE TEMPLE, 11.12-26

In sharp contrast to the "Hosannas" (11.10) but in harmony with what Jesus observed in the Temple (11.11), this new pericope presents Jesus in the distinctive role of the One who comes in the name of the Lord to exercise judgment. Jesus dramatically points to the termination of Temple rituals and foretells the establishment of worship accessible to all peoples (11.17).

The significance of Jesus' radical stance is made clear by Mark's organization of this passage. The dramatized parable of the fig tree (divided into prediction, vv 12-14, and confirmation, vv 20-21) brackets Jesus' direct action in the Temple (vv 15-19). Each of these two narratives throws light on the other; together they demonstrate Jesus' stand against a sterile religion and its leaders.

In contrast, the second part (vv 22-25) relates some of Jesus' teachings on faith, prayer and forgiveness as essential characteristics of authentic worship.

The Fig Tree, A Dramatized Parable, 11.12-14, 20-21

As Jesus is returning to the Temple the next morning, he sees in the distance a fig tree in leaf. Some figs appear prior to the normal harvest time. Since the early figs appear before the leaves, this tree appears to have some fruit. Being hungry, Jesus goes to the tree. Upon closer inspection, however, he finds nothing but leaves--evidence that the tree will produce no fruit. In the light of the tree's deceptive promise of fruit, Jesus says to the tree, "May no one ever eat fruit from you again."

Jesus intends for his disciples to overhear his words to the tree (an actor's "aside" is appropriate in a dramatized parable). In this way, he enables them to draw the correct lesson from the barren fig tree. As they pass this spot the next morning, Peter confirms Jesus' prediction. The tree is withered from the roots (vv 20-21).

These experiences with the fig tree bracket and interpret Jesus' action in the Temple. The fig tree is an integral part of Jesus' symbolic acts in Jerusalem in which he portrays God's judgment on the sterile religious life in Israel. God acts in judgment because he takes sin seriously, including sin committed in the name of piety.

v. 13 - In Palestine, fig trees bear fruit ten months of the year. Figs do not normally appear at Passover time. J. A. Motyer (NIDNTT I 724) explains that **kairos** ("time" or "season") here indicates the time of harvest, as in 12.2. The presence of leaves indicates that the tree ought to have fruit, for the harvest time is near. Therefore Jesus went to find out if it had any fruit even though "it was not the season for figs" to be harvested.

Others interpret "the time for figs" as a religious (not botanical) expression denoting the time of the Kingdom of God (as in 1.15). Thinking it was the time for supplanting Roman rule with a political messiah, many cried "Hosanna" (11.19). Jesus, however, shows that this is not that time.

• In the Old Testament, the fig tree symbolizes the fruitfulness of Israel (Dt 8.8), while its destruction is a picture of judgment (Hos 2.12; Isa 34.4; Jer 5.17; 8.13; Joel 1.2-12). Jesus is primarily concerned about the spiritual state of Israel (cf Micah 7.1-6).
v. 14 - Jesus' only miracle of destruction and his only violent action were not (as some say) "impulsive acts of ill temper" but deliberate action parables designed to proclaim a vital message about God's judgment against the subversion of his commands. Jesus was zealous for the Temple (cf Ps 69.9; Jn 2.17) because of his concern for God's holy name (cf Eze 36.21). Pruning cannot be perpetuated without limit, as Luke 13.6-9 teaches (cf Mk 12.9). Luke 19.41-44 makes it clear that Jesus laments the defilement of his nation; God's judgment inevitably follows. The God of love and mercy invites us to approach him in reverent and awe-filled worship, while, at the same time, reminding us that "our God is a consuming fire" (Heb 12.28-29). Jesus' actions give insight into the "wrath of the Lamb" (Rev 6.16) and express God's active opposition against all evil. This divine attribute is often overlooked. The destruction of an unfruitful tree and the disruption of the commercialization of an area designated for prayer are a small price to pay if Jesus' followers learn the lesson dramatized by these acts.
v. 21 - Peter said that Jesus "spoke against" the tree. In black magic, a curse is motivated by anger or jealousy to bring harm upon someone. Jesus' authority is not magical but based on his trust in God (11.22ff), enabling him to say that no one will ever again eat from that fig tree (11.14).

Jesus Disrupts Temple Activities, 11.15-19

11.15-16 - Jesus proceeds to the Temple, the heart of Jerusalem and the center of spiritual life for Israel. As in the case of the fig tree, the outward glory of the Temple, one of the greatest sanctuaries of antiquity, promised fruit; upon closer inspection the previous evening (11.11), however, Jesus had found none.

The vast Temple Mount provided many different atriums, rooms, etc. necessary for its various functions. Prominent among these areas was the large Court of the Gentiles, with majestic porticos facing an elaborate basilica. Similar to a public market, its shops served the thousands of worshippers who gathered from all over the world for the great feasts of Israel. Some exchanged regular coins for the shekels (coined without images, cf 12.16) required for payment of the Temple tax (Ex 30.13-16). Others sold animals certified for sacrifice after inspection by the authorities. Some shops specialized in the oil, wine and salt necessary for the sacrifices.

While merchants operated legally within an area considered semi-sacred, they charged the people exorbitant rates of exchange. The poor who bought pigeons because they could not afford larger animals for sacrifices (cf Lev 12.6; 14.22; 15.14,29) were victimized by the proprietors' greed. Religious authorities received a cut from these activities; the deceitfulness of wealth (4.19) had taken root among leaders of the Temple. Gentiles who came to inquire about the God of Israel were being squeezed out of the only area open to them by its prevalent bazaar-like atmosphere. The Court of the Gentiles was even used as a short cut between suburbs of Jerusalem.

All such activities hindered the Temple from fulfilling its purpose. By driving out the merchants and overturning their tables of wares, Jesus brings the religious activities to a halt. Without shekels, the treasury will fail; without animals, sacrifices cannot be offered; without cultic objects, the religious practices will cease. By his actions, Jesus declares symbolically that the Temple has ceased to function as God intended.

Just as the prophets in the Old Testament dramatized their messages (e.g., Isa 20.1-6; Jer 13.1-11; 19.1-13; Eze 4.1-15), Jesus performs this action-parable. The fig tree symbolizes the Temple that appears to bear fruit for God, while in reality it is barren, like the fig tree. Both the "sign-act" of the fig tree and the disruption of Temple functions portray the end of the Temple which was considered eternal by Jews of that day. After the crucifixion, there will be no further need for that Temple or its sacrifices.

11.17 - Jesus declares "Is it not written: 'My house will be called a house of prayer for all nations'? But you have made it 'a den of robbers'." With his quotation from Isaiah 56.7, Jesus claims the Lord's house as his own and thereby implies his oneness with the Father. He is personally inviting people of all nations to come to him. Jesus himself is the Temple where men and women of all ethnic groups meet God.

God's covenant with Abraham envisioned blessings for all nations, although his descendants had apparently forgotten this design. Jesus renews God's original purpose by establishing "a house of prayer for all nations." Contrary to the expectation of some that the Messiah would cleanse Jerusalem *from* the Gentiles, Jesus wants it cleansed *for* the Gentiles. The Lord of the Temple declares that in his house, foreigners and those forbidden by Jewish ceremonial laws (Isa 56.3) are welcome. Jesus already sought out Gentiles (7.24-30; 8.1-9; cf 5.1ff) and continues this emphasis in his teaching (13.27; 14.9,28; 16.7). He is the Messiah for all Nations. In Mark, the first human to confess Jesus as Son of God was the Gentile centurion (15.39). Oppression and exclusivism are out; the wall of separation (Eph 2.14ff) has been removed so that all who desire may enter.

Changing Jeremiah's (7.11) question into an affirmation, Jesus condemns the abuses committed in the Temple. It had become a "den of robbers," a place of retreat where people felt safe from punishment after doing detestable things (Jer 7.9-15), only to "go out again and again on new sorties. They had changed God's call to celebrate his glory into a profitable business. In so doing they commit something frightful: they put God at the service of sin" (Jeremias Theology 145). This judgment was not based on hearsay; as the Lord said in Jeremiah 7.11b, Jesus could also say, "I have been watching" (11.11; 12.41).

Like his actions earlier (11.14-16), Jesus' words pronounce judgment on Israel's barrenness and predict the Temple's destruction. Each of the following controversy stories (11.27-12.37) presents additional failures on the part of the religious establishment. Further prophecies of judgment follow (chapter 13).

Jesus has demonstrated his authority over the two most sacred institutions of Israel: he is Lord of the Sabbath (2.28) and High Priest over the Temple. With these words and actions in Jerusalem, Jesus exhorts God's people to authentic worship. His authority over the church is also indisputable; it is his, ransomed with his own blood (10.45; 14.24). Today's churches and their leaders are also subject to his on-sight inspection (cf Rev 1.12-3.22), for Christ is Judge over his people (cf Ro 11.21; 14.10; 2Co 5.10; 2Ti 4.1; 1Pe 4.17). In churches as well as in the Temple, avarice, spiritual sterility and "some flourishing programs stand condemned and therefore doomed by the word of Jesus Christ" (quoting Williamson 210).

By recording Jesus' words, Mark challenges Jewish religious leaders hostile to the Gospel to heed prophetic admonitions about false worship and turn to the One who fulfills messianic predictions. He urges every Christian congregation to welcome into its fellowship all believers, regardless of their social, ethnic and economic status.

11.18-19 - The chief priests and the scribes know Jesus has accused them of obstructing God's purposes and thus they fear him. Neither the words of the ancient prophets nor denunciation by this "intruder," however, leads them to repentance, for "the priestly leadership [is] far more interested in revenue from the merchants than in reverence for God" (Hurtado 170). Consequently they seek a way to kill the one who exposes their sinful practices. Although they have lost the true sense of communion with God that the Temple symbolizes, they are nevertheless willing to kill in order to maintain power. They must proceed carefully, however, for the crowd's reaction is unpredictable.

Following his dramatized message, Jesus withdraws to Bethany for the night.

v. 15 - The Court of the Gentiles, the largest of the outer courts, surrounded the Temple proper (inner courts) which was marked off by a stone wall about 5 feet high bearing inscriptions in Greek and Latin. Archaeologists have found two of these inscriptions bearing this message: No foreigner is allowed within the area encompassed by this balustrade. Whoever is caught will be personally responsible for his ensuing death.

Porticos enclosed the whole Temple area, providing ample space for scribes to instruct their disciples. In the central area of the Royal Portico along the southern end of the courts, Herod built a great basilica as a gathering place for large assemblies. One section served as the seat of the Sanhedrin.

• "These shops apparently belonged to the high-priestly family.... The Temple was said to be going to rack and ruin because of avarice and mutual hatred" (Jeremias Jerusalem 49). "The true Messiah's mission is to purge the temple of avarice, not the country of Romans" (Moule 90).

• None of the Evangelists uses the term "cleansing" in regard to Jesus' action which is more appropriately described as "disruption" and "condemnation" of its rituals. There is no thought of purifying it in order that it might function authentically, just as there is no hope of recovery for a tree withered from the roots up.

v. 17 - Jesus "taught continually," implying that his action in 11.12-16 and his encounters in 11.27-12.44 were a part of his teaching based on God's purposes as revealed in Scripture.
• "My house" (i.e., the church, the people of God and not their buildings) uniquely belongs to Jesus (cf "my church" in Mt 16.18). He is the Son over God's house (Heb 3.6). The risen Christ is the capstone in the new Temple (12.10).

Although the word "church" (**ekklesia**) appears in the Gospels only in Matthew 16.18 and 18.17, Mark presents Jesus' instruction on the nature and mission of the communities of believers by references to "his disciples," "his brothers and sisters" (3.35; i.e., "the family of God") and "my house" (11.17). In the New Testament, a great variety of metaphors speak of the multiple roles and the glory of the church.
• God's covenant with Israel welcomed all nations (or "peoples," **ethnos**): Ge 12.3; 22.18; 26.4; Isa 49.6; Zec 8.22; Ac 3.25; Gal 3.8; cf Rev 7.9.
• The practice of joining various Old Testament texts (as in verse 17) is found frequently in Mark (e.g., 1.2-3,11; 9.7; 13.24). Kee (47) points out that the meaning derived "is far more than a simple addition of the meanings of their components."
v. 18 - The high priest was the most important member of the priesthood and the most eminent person in the nation. His office was the very symbol of the Jewish religion. He was the only human privileged to enter the Holy of Holies, and that was restricted to the Day of Atonement. During the first century, his importance was greatly enhanced, for he represented the Jewish people in all dealings with Rome. When Herod the Great arbitrarily appointed a high priest, the office ceased to be life-long and hereditary and became wholly dependent upon political authority. The reigning high priest and the retired ones, along with scribes and elders, were counted among the 72 members of the Sanhedrin, the highest governing body in Judaism. In addition to their political power, the priestly aristocracy administered the Temple finances. The "chief priests" (mentioned 14 times in Mark) were those who wielded the power. The local priests scattered across the country (1.41) had little in common with the social, financial and political prestige of the priestly nobility in Jerusalem.
• The population within the walls of Jerusalem rose from 40,000 (ca 4 B.C.) to 80,000 before its destruction (ca 66 A.D.). During the feasts in Jesus' time, the population, swelled by pilgrims, rose to five times normal, or around 250,000.
• "Amazed" (**ekplessomai**) is Mark's characteristic way of expressing the reaction of uncommitted onlookers to Jesus' teaching. Cf 1.22.

Life In The New House Of Prayer, 11.22-25 (26)

The Temple has ceased to function as the place where humankind approaches God. How, then, are men and women to come to God in authentic worship? Jesus now provides the answer. Faith, prayer and forgiveness are essential for all who seek a true relationship with God.

First of all, Jesus calls women and men from all nations to "Have faith in God" (cf 1.15; 5.34; 9.23; 10.52). True faith rests in God himself. It is not tied to the Temple, for authentic worship is not dependent upon a location (cf Jn 4.19-24). Faith is our response to God's faithfulness to his promises and brings freedom from the bonds of legalism and ritualism. Those who have faith in God rely upon him (cf 12.42-44).

Just as Jesus is the archetypal person of the Spirit (1.9-11), he is also the archetypal person of faith. His faith is directed toward reality and is deeply involved in the act of living. He lives and works on the basis of faith expressed in obedience to and dependence upon God.

He calls upon us to express our faith in God through prayer, like he did. We can trust God to do what we cannot do, even during Jesus' absence. Such faith is not a matter of assuming "a positive mental attitude." Nor is it resignation to circumstances as inevitable, as though they were determined by fate, by impersonal forces or by horoscopes. Rather, in prayer we address the living God who responds personally to our requests. He may provide what is lacking or correct what is wrong; he may do the impossible (cf 9.23), such as removing a mountainous obstacle.

This promise regarding the power of prayer was not given to believers as "the secret for destroying fig trees; but the secret for so living that [we] should not be destroyed as the fig tree had been destroyed" (G. Campbell Morgan 257). Through believing prayer, this new community of faith is enabled to fulfill God's purpose of bearing much fruit in its mission to all nations.

Verse 24 is not a promise of prosperity for all Christians who pray in faith. Such claims contradict the whole thrust of Jesus' call to "die in order to live" (cf 8.34f; 10.24,29f). The measure of the disciple is "give," not "gain." Jesus warned (4.19) that "the deceitfulness of riches and the desires for other things" choke the word and make it unfruitful. Disaster frequently begins when people get what they want, for greed (which means "the desire to have") is evil (7.22). After denouncing the avarice of

Temple authorities, it would be most contradictory for Jesus to promise anything and everything that his followers might ask. God gives good gifts to his children (Lk 11.11-13), not those things that destroy.

Jesus promises believers what they need in order to do what he desires. In the immediate context, Jesus' promise centers on enabling his followers to become his "house of prayer for all nations." Believing prayer concentrates on making God's concerns a reality. To quote Cole (180), "Prayer is not simply asking God for the pleasant things we desire, but an earnest yearning for, and entering into, the will of God, for ourselves and others, be it sweet or bitter." This desire characterizes Jesus' action here and his prayer in Gethsemane (14.35-36). To be, to do and to pray for what he desires should also be the concern of those who follow him. In answering the question about the most important commandment, Jesus makes it plain that our greatest concern should be to love God and to love others (12.29-31).

The words "believe that you have received it, and it will be yours" (v 24) do not mean that a person can manipulate God. Rather, as Wilcock (57) stresses, "To pray in faith is to align ourselves with what Scripture tells us is God's purpose and plan." When God's desires as revealed in Scripture (rather than our own desires) determine our request, God gives us faith to believe that he has granted our petition. The assurance comes even while we are asking (1Jn 5.14-15); the fulfillment comes in due time. The first requirement, then, is to pray with faith that rests in God himself and desires what he desires.

Jesus lays down another requirement for authentic prayer: we must freely forgive our fellow-beings (cf Mt 5.23-24; 6.12; Lk 11.3-4; Col 3.13; 1Co 11.28-32). Forgiving one another is not optional in God's family that exists as a result of his costly forgiveness of our sins. The all-embracing, unconditional forgiveness of others demanded by Jesus ("If you hold *anything* against *anyone*, forgive him") is the clearest expression of gratitude any person can make to God for forgiving his or her sins. The freely forgiven freely forgive (Col 3.13). Prayer by one who does not forgive others freely "is *an unholy sham and a perverse caricature*, which deserves not to be heard" (Martin Action 109, italics his). A fruitful relationship with God requires reconciliation with our fellow-beings.

Life in the new house of prayer includes not only one's personal relationship to God (expressed, for example, by faith and prayer) but also one's human relationships. All who enjoy a new relationship with God and know him as Father (11.25) are enjoined to accept others in God's family as brothers and sisters (3.35). Mark may stress Jesus' teaching on forgiving one another because of the conflicts that arose between Jewish and Gentile believers in the early church. Frequently churches today resist or reject believers from other cultures, social or ethnic groups. Discrimination is contrary to God's purposes in his house for all nations (cf Gal 3.28).

Faith is manifested in love that forswears grudges, hate and vengeance. To forgive and to pray with love for enemies of the Gospel (cf Lk 23.34) is also required of us, for God loved us while we were his enemies (Ro 5.8-10). The true measure of the church is determined by the quality of its love, life and ministry in its daily experiences in the world.

Jesus exemplified authentic worship in his daily life as well as in his relationship to God. He calls the believer and the church to live, in this present evil age, the life of the age to come. By following Jesus' teaching, we demonstrate that the Kingdom of God is actually present, transforming lives. Our fellowship overcomes ill will and animosity. Those who are unwilling to forgive others, however, deny the reality of God's forgiveness in their own lives.

v. 23 - Jesus draws upon a rabbinic metaphor about overcoming difficulties. Paul's words in 1Co 13.2 may be reminiscent of Jesus' words here. If Jesus is alluding to the leveling of the land in the eschatological Day of the Lord (Zec 4.7; 14.4,5,10), "The prayer in question is then specifically a Passover prayer for God to establish his reign" (Lane 410). From the Mount of Olives, the deep rift of the Dead Sea (1312 feet below sea level) is visible in the distance beyond the Judean Desert.

• Worship is now related to Jesus, not the Temple. It is not dependent upon stained-glass windows, icons, pipe organs or images.

v. 24 - "It was the duty of the priests to give guidance to the people (on) the way to pray" (Benjamin Mazar Mountain 106). Mark presents Jesus' teaching on prayer here and in 9.29; 11.17; 12.40; 13.18,33;14.38, and his personal practice of prayer in 1.35; 6.46; 14.32ff.

v. 25 - "The heart of the Kingdom of God was Jesus' inner experience of God as Father. His mission was to share this experience with men" (Ladd Presence 173).

• "Mark's position is very similar to 1Co 13.2, which clearly declares that faith is manifested in love, rather than the extraordinary miracles accomplished by faith" (Schweizer 235).
• To pray standing up was a common posture (1Ki 8.14,22; Mt 6.5; Lk 18.11,13), although kneeling was also practiced (1Ki 8.54; Da 6.10; Ac 7.60; 20.36;21.5; Eph 3.14).
• To withhold forgiveness "shows that we have no consciousness of the grace that we ourselves have received, and thus that we are expecting to be heard on our own merits;" it is "a denial of the great principle of justification by faith" (Cole 181).
v. 26 - This verse is omitted because it is not a part of the original text. Cf. Mt 6.14-15.

2. Temple Authorities Challenge Jesus, 11.27 - 12.37a

The response of the religious authorities to the Temple episode is not long in coming. A delegation of representatives from the major groups that comprise the Sanhedrin interrogates Jesus: "What right have you to do these things?" This confrontation revolves around the subject of religious authority. The ensuing series of five closely articulated stories shows the reaction of the entire spectrum of those who oppose his thoughts and actions. Jesus' responses fortify their conviction that he must be eliminated in order to preserve the Temple. Sworn to obey God's word, the leaders of Israel do not repent when reminded of the words of Isaiah and Jeremiah; instead, they resolve to reject this prophet (11.17-18) in Jerusalem. From the standpoint of his followers, however, Jesus' answers provide further evidence of the religious establishment's inadequacy, vindicating his judgment on the Temple as barren.

During these encounters, Jesus addresses popular issues such as taxes, resurrection and the commandments. Instead of the previous concern over religious practices (2.1-3.6), these controversies deal with basic theological and ethical issues. The dominant theme of Jesus' identity underlies these discussions and is especially evident in the first and fifth stories.

Jesus does not use his authority to compel belief or acceptance. By participating in these debates, however, he confronts his hearers with the necessity of making personal decisions. Mark's style also challenges his readers to respond. While the issues raised in this series were of special importance to the church in its formative years, they continue relevant to this day.

Upon concluding Jesus' analysis of the Jerusalem Temple (ch 11-12), Mark relates his prophetic word about its future (ch 13).

• Opinion is divided as to the chronology of (11.27-13.37). As traditionally understood, these discussions all took place on the third day of Passion Week, in the courts of the Temple. Some writers (who may never have attended marathon seminars) claim it would be impossible to crowd all this into one day. While we do not deny the possibility of these discussions taking place within the one day, after 11.27 the references to time, place and circumstance in the text itself are either vague or absent.

A further comparison with the first series of controversies offers a possible solution to the question of chronology during this week in Jerusalem. As noted, Mark 2.1-3.6 begins with an event in line with the general chronological sequence of chapter 1; it continues thematically, however, disregarding chronology. Similarly, this section begins in temporal sequence; from 12.13 on, however, Mark apparently gathers stories which have thematic continuity with the passage. It follows that 11.27 probably occurred on Tuesday; 12.13-13.37 is not defined chronologically; and 14.1 resumes the chronological sequence.
• Here, as in the previous series (2.1-3.6), the religious authorities question Jesus in the first four stories; he takes the initiative in the fifth encounter. In the first series, their responses to Jesus progress from silence to plotting his death. Here, the progression begins with their hostility (12.12) and moves to amazement (12.17), silence (12.27) and admiration (12.32). When a scribe appears to be open to the possibility of becoming a disciple (12.34), no one dares to question Jesus further. This series closes with a pair of illustrations in which the authenticity of a widow's faith (12.41-44) stands in sharp contrast to the religiosity of the scribes (12.38-40).

These series of debates indicate that Jesus' presence and teaching provoke a series of conflicts with the religious establishment culminating in his being condemned to die. Although his accusers know the Scriptures, they fail to understand or live by them. Jesus relies upon the Scriptures as trustworthy and ministers in accord with them, but he freely contradicts the traditions.
• Robbins (165f) points out that in these encounters Jesus provides his disciples with an opportunity to accept some of the basic principles of his value system that they previously resisted.

THE QUESTION OF AUTHORITY, 11.27-12.11

The guardians of Israel interpret Jesus' most recent action (11.15-17) as a damaging offense against the Temple and an affront to their authority. They feel duty-bound to act before further damage can be done. Members of the major groups of the Sanhedrin probably formulate a strategy to arrest him and legitimize putting him to death (11.18). They choose a delegation composed of chief priests, scribes and elders (8.31; cf 14.43,53; 15.1) to wait in the porticos of the outer court so that they can approach him casually without provoking public enmity. This is the first of the five encounters in the Temple reported by Mark.

"By What Authority?" 11.27-33

11.27-30 - As Jesus is walking by, the representatives of the Sanhedrin approach him according to their plan. In a characteristically Jewish form of dialogue, they pose two questions: "By what authority are you doing these things (i.e., disrupting the Temple)?" Their second question moves from the abstract to the personal: "Who gave you authority to do these things?" Their questions are another way of asking "Who do you think you are, Jesus?"

Jesus does not answer them directly. Rather, following a rabbinic custom, he poses a question of his own (as in 2.9,19,25; 3.4,23; 10.3): "John's baptism--was it from heaven (i.e., from God), or from men?" This is not an evasive tactic but a counter-question designed to lead them to the truth through inductive reasoning. If they remember John's call to repentance and his announcement of the Coming One (1.4-8), they will conclude that John the Baptist was a genuine prophet sent by God. Then they will see that the One who authorized John's baptism has also authorized Jesus to inaugurate the Reign of God with all its attendant signs. Their judgment about John will thus determine their decision about Jesus.

In his counter-question, Jesus makes a veiled claim to be the Messiah, challenging them to decide for themselves and give a straightforward reply (as opposed to the endless debate of rabbinic discussion). By including Jesus' repeated demand, "Answer me!" Mark confronts the reader with the necessity of making a personal decision about the authority of Jesus.

11.31-33 - The authorities, of all people, should be able to answer, for Jesus' question was in the area of their competence and responsibilities. Rather than give a direct answer, however, they bypass the question, "What is true?" in favor of "What is a safe answer?" because they fear the people (11.32a; cf 11.18; 12.12). They fear to take a stand for the truth, for any acknowledgement of John's God-given authority "would expose themselves to the charge of unbelief. More, however, is involved than this; they would also be compelled to admit that the **exousia** (authority) of Jesus was from God" (Taylor 471).

In an effort to save face, they answer, "We don't know." (Ironically, the scribes prided themselves on their knowledge). Unwittingly, they vindicate Jesus' condemnation of the Temple, for in the midst of its richness, these members of the Sanhedrin, the highest Jewish court, demonstrate the moral poverty of its leadership. Their indecision results, not from ignorance, but from the lack of moral courage, as Jesus infers in his reply, "Neither will I tell you by what authority I am doing these things" (cf Jn 2.26).

Thus the source of Jesus' authority remains partially veiled. In the parable that follows, however, Jesus answers their question inferentially, confirming what Mark relates in 1.1,11 and 9.7: Jesus' authority is that of the Son of God (12.6-8).

v. 27 - Jesus was walking in the **hieron** (the general term for the whole temple complex), probably in one of the porticos, where the scribes taught their disciples. He never entered the **naos**, for the sanctuary was restricted to the priests. Presumably, this occurred on the same day (Tuesday) that Jesus disrupted Temple activities (11.15-17).

v. 28 - **Exousia** ("authority," 1.22,27; 2.10; 3.15; 6.7; 13.34) normally means divine authority, in contrast to **dunamis** ("power"). Here, however, it probably means a combination of right and power.

• Lane (413) claims that their question proves "that Jesus had never said openly that he was the Messiah." Throughout these debates, Jesus unveils his identity little by little, leading up to full disclosure during his trials (14.60-62; 15.2-5).

A Parable About Authentic And Usurped Authority, 12.1-12

Continuing the discussion about the source of his authority (11.27-33), Jesus tells two metaphors to this same delegation. The first is a parable that presents a realistic picture of life in first century Palestine. The second seems unrelated; it is a quotation about a building. Together, however, the two quotes present a panorama of redemptive history. Against the backdrop of God's salvific acts in Israel's history, the identity of Jesus becomes apparent to anyone with ears to hear.

12.1-5 - Jesus, master of narrative, tells of a man who planted a vineyard and took all the measures necessary for it to produce a harvest. He built a wall with stones cleared from that rocky land, dug a dual-level pit for treading the grapes and collecting the juice, and built a tower for watchmen to protect the fruit from animals and robbers. By the time Jesus describes in detail the owner's efforts to establish a complete vineyard, his hearers (well versed in the Scriptures) probably realize that Jesus is drawing upon Isaiah 5.1-7, a prophecy of judgment on Israel.

At this point, however, Jesus departs from Isaiah: "The owner rented the vineyard to some farmers and went away on a journey." In keeping with the agreement, the owner sent a servant to the vineyard at harvest time to collect some of the wines. The tenants, however, beat the servant cruelly and sent him away. The owner sent many other servants; the tenants beat some and killed others.

12.6-8 - In the face of such persistent rejection of his servants, the owner sends his sole heir, a son whom he loves (cf Ge 22.2,12,16). Rather than receive the son with respect, the tenants assume that the owner is dead and that his sole heir has come to claim his inheritance. So they kill him, planning to take possession of the property without an owner. As a final insult, they cast his body out of the vineyard (cf Heb 13.12).

12.9-12 - Jesus challenges his listeners to reflection by asking, "What then will the owner of the vineyard do?" Then he answers his own question, leaving no doubt as to the two-fold conclusion. First: judgment of the tenants is sure to follow. The subversion of God's purposes and the abuse of his authority are subject to his judgment, for God will not be an ally to sin. Second: the vineyard will be given to others. God will form a new covenant people (14.24; cf Ro 11.17-24), calling men and women from all nations to perform the purposes he had for Israel (Ge 12.3; Mk 11.17; 13.10, 27; 14.9).

This parable recalls events following the establishment of God's alliance with Israel. God sent his servants "to claim on God's behalf the loyalty and obedience owed to him by his people" (Cranfield 367). The prophets were ill-treated and even killed by those entrusted with authority over "the vineyard of the Lord Almighty, the house of Israel" (Isa 5.7). By Jesus' day, the appointed leaders have not only administered the Temple poorly, they have made it a source of personal gain (11.17). They have rejected the owner and are engaged in active opposition to Jesus (cf 3.28-29; 4.15). As a result, Israel itself bears no fruit to give its owner (cf 11.13; 4.7f).

After many demonstrations of love and mercy, God sends his beloved Son who is rejected by those to whom God has entrusted authority over Israel (cf 8.31). Now in this parable, Jesus informs those who reject him that he knows what they intend to do (11.12; 12.12).

Also in this parable, Jesus answers the question posed by the chief priests, teachers of the law and elders (11.28): God gave me authority to do these things, for I am his beloved Son. Gradually Jesus is giving those who oppose him clearer glimpses of his identity, although Mark does not say how much they understand at the time. Mark's readers understand clearly, however, that the beloved Son is Jesus, for they remember the Father's words in 1.11 and 9.7.

To reinforce the parable's reference to rejection, Jesus challenges those leaders, trained in Scripture, to recall part of the Hallel (Psalms 113-118) sung during their Passover meal. Psalm 118.22 refers to a stone that became the capstone although it had been rejected by the builders. Correctly understood, this Scripture would help them to recognize that the Son, rejected by those in authority over the Temple, will become the keystone of God's new Temple. By this shift in metaphor, Jesus looks beyond his death as the rejected Son to his vindication in his resurrection and to the building of his house for all nations.

The authorities latch onto the judgment of the tenants as the point of the story. They know Jesus is speaking the parable against them (v 12), just as he accused them earlier in the Temple (11.17). Through it, Jesus warns them against their plan and its consequences. Nevertheless, they are not about to repent of abusing their authority. Restrained by their fear of the crowd (cf 11.18; 12.37b; 14.1), they withdraw (v 12), determined to kill him, as their ancestors had killed previous prophets sent by God.

From the juxtaposition of these two metaphors and their setting in chapters 11 and 12, it becomes apparent that God is in the process of building a new worshipping community composed of those who meet him in the new Temple (i.e., in his Son Jesus) and produce fruit for him. As the body of Christ indwelt by the Holy Spirit, the church is also called the temple which God is building (1Co 3.16; Eph 2.21), of which Jesus is the capstone (12.10). The "house of prayer for all nations" (11.17) is the new covenant people (14.24), composed of believing Jews and Gentiles, with the responsibility of taking to the whole world God's offer of salvation ("repent and believe the good news," 1.15). Every believer has a responsibility in this mission.

The leaders of the new community of believers, however, bear special responsibility to avoid falling into the errors of those leaders. Moreover, this parable calls the church to repentance and warns especially its leaders about attempts to build one's own empire, forgetting that the vineyard belongs to God.

v. 1 - Although parable may contain elements of allegory, it is not an allegory in the strictest sense. It is "a dramatic presentation of a life situation which invites a judgment from the hearers" (Lane 416f).

• The parable is beautifully contextualized with descriptions of the economic situation of those days, for a large part of the Galilean uplands bore the character of latifundia. "Squatters' rights" (v 7) are based on ancient Jewish laws (Jeremias Parables 70f; Jerusalem 328).

v. 3 - Jesus' audience may wonder if he is siding with Galilean tenant-farmers protesting against the foreign landlords whose large estates they cultivate when he mentions the tenants' uprising.

v. 4 - Prophets were frequently called "God's servants;" e.g., Jer 7.25; 25.4; Am 3.7; Zec 1.6.

v. 5 -1Ki 18.13; 22.27; 2Ch 24.20ff; 36.15ff; Ne 9.26, etc., report the violent deaths of God's servants.

v. 7 - It is precisely because they recognize him as the son that they slay him. Based on this passage, Ladd (Theology 167) notes that "sonship is differentiated from messiahship" and that Jesus' "sonship is quite independent and anterior to his mission."

v. 9 - In the Greek, **kurios** ("owner") often means "Lord" as a title for God (cf 11.3).

• Although Jesus seldom answers his own questions, he does here, just as the questions asked in Isaiah's "song of the vineyard" (5.1-7) are followed by answers.

• The parable is not spoken against the nation as a whole (the vineyard) but against the leaders (tenants) who have failed to fulfill their part of the contract.

Paul cites his own salvation as evidence that God did not reject his people (Ro 11.1). Mark concludes this section with another example of a true believer in Israel, the poor widow of 12.41-44. A remnant of Israel joins those from every nation (cf 13.10,27) who respond to God's call.

• This is the first clear presentation in Mark of the theme of punishment, although there are hints of it in 3.29, 9.42ff and 11.12-21. God does not compel anyone to recognize his authority, but his patient efforts to lead women and men to repentance will some day cease and judgment will follow.

v. 10 - Psalm 118 is one of the passages most frequently quoted in the New Testament. Verse 22 was already being interpreted messianically by the rabbis.

• Scholars disagree as to the imagery of the stone. According to Richard N. Longenecker (50ff), **kephale gonias** (based on Ps 118.22 and employed in Ac 4.11 and 1Pe 2.4,7) is generally understood as "keystone": the rejected stone has become the "capstone" which culminates all building activities and stands supreme over the whole structure. In 1Co 3.11; Eph 2.20 and 1Pe 2.5f (based on Isa 28.16), the theme of "foundational cornerstone" is added, and in Ro 9.33, Lk 20.18 and 1Pe 2.8 (based on Isa 8.14), "the stone of stumbling and rock of offence." All three images are included in 1Pe 2.4-8, but the "rejected stone--capstone" motif is dominant. Whatever its imagery, the stone is essential to the building; so also Jesus is essential to the new community and is its center.

v. 12 - Jesus' house of prayer includes Gentiles without excluding Jews. The gospel leaves no room for anti-Jewish sentiments (cf Ro 11.17-24).

ON PAYING TAXES, 12.13-17

As a part of its broad attack on Jesus, the Sanhedrin sends another delegation composed of two groups representative of other segments of society. The Pharisees and Herodians seek to trap him on the burning question of taxes, a subject of the highest religious and practical importance at the time. This is the second of the five encounters reported by Mark.

Many pious Jews resent Rome because its leaders are corrupt religiously and morally (cf Ro 1.21-32). The Zealots (3.18) refuse to pay any taxes to their foreign captors.

The Herodians support the tax, for they are allied with Herod Antipas who is backed by the Emperor. A general refusal to pay taxes on their part would lead to the loss of both their political position and their livelihood. Although the Pharisees dislike the tax, they go along with it grudgingly, while debating the legal aspects of paying taxes to a foreign power. As the Pharisees in Galilee had done earlier (3.6, cf 8.15) these in Jerusalem join forces with Herodians in their determination to trap Jesus.

12.13-16 - Baiting their trap with flattery, the delegation addresses Jesus as "teacher" (a proper title for those responsible for interpreting the law). "Is it right to pay taxes to Caesar? Should we pay or shouldn't we?" An affirmative answer to this skillfully devised question will turn the crowds against Jesus as siding with the idolatrous Roman system. If he says, "No, don't pay," the Herodians will rush to the Roman authorities, denouncing him for sedition (cf Lk 23.2). "Yes" or "No" will attach a partisan label to the Kingdom he proclaims (as done before Pilate, 15.2ff). The delegation is convinced that Jesus cannot escape from its foolproof trap.

Jesus knows that they have little interest in finding a resolution to this sensitive issue that is dividing the nation. Thus he gives them an opportunity to reflect upon the hypocrisy (7.6) of their question by asking, "Why are you trying to test me?" Then he commands, "Bring me a denarius," this being the only coin acceptable for payment of the tax. Taking the role of prosecutor in this trumped-up trial, he holds up the coin as an exhibit and asks, "Whose image (**epigraphe**, cf 15.26) is this? And whose inscription?"

"Caesar's," they reply, referring to the emperor who minted the coin and whose image it bore. All coins bearing the inscription "Tiberius, Caesar, son of the divine Augustus" were considered property of the emperor.

12.17 - "Give back to Caesar what is Caesar's" was the first part of Jesus' response. He does not answer their question, "Shall we pay (**didomi**)?" Rather, he commands, "Repay (**apodidomi**, implying that the tribute is a debt) what is due." While this is not equivalent to saying, "Yes, pay the head tax," it does recognize that the emperor has rights and that the citizen has obligations to the government in exchange for the benefits received (e.g., the Jews benefited from the *pax romana*). In short, he is saying that whatever bears the imprint of Caesar is Caesar's due. This means that citizens owe loyalty and support to the state in return for its labor in the service of the common good.

"Give back to God what is his," Jesus says, completing his answer. No doubt he intends to remind the Pharisees that "God created man in his own image" (Ge 1.26). Whatever bears the image of God belongs to God, the sustainer of life and the source of every good thing (Ro 14.7-12; Jas 1.17), and is accountable to him. In addition to these rights based upon creation, through his work of redemption God enhances his rightful claim on our whole being (2Co 5.15).

The members of the delegation are amazed at Jesus. Their skillfully-set trap has failed; they can neither accuse him of sedition nor of bowing to Rome. Yet he has emphatically affirmed that divine honors belong to God alone and has rejected all attempts to deify the state or to ascribe divinity to any person. In addition, he has challenged those who have no reservations about using coins with Caesar's image to examine themselves as to possible compromise with idolatry and the imperial cult. His words are a rebuke both to those who desire to establish God's rule by force (like the Zealots) and to those who claim neither interest in nor responsibility to human government. He makes it clear that his program has political implications in spite of not being political.

While Jesus does not explicitly tell us what we ought to do, he gives guidelines for thinking through our decisions. As might be expected, his hearers continue to disagree as to what is owed to Caesar. Traditionally, many of Jesus' followers have seen "render to Caesar" and "render to God" as parallels, with responsibilities to Caesar subordinate to but not separate from those to God.

Others see Caesar as antithetical to God, not unlike the antitheses of "God/men" and "owner/tenants" in the preceding controversy. As such, these pericopes (11.27ff; 12.1ff; 12.13ff) indicate that Jesus rejects both the presence of colonial Rome and any revolt against it. According to Ched Myers (374), Mark's account both rejects any option of political cooperation with Rome and repudiates Caesar's authority and money.

In a more moderate stance, Vernard Eller (83) sees the tax question posed to Jesus as based on the false assumption that one must either absolutize the state (i.e., support the establishment as a god) or absolutize it as a satan (and join the revolution). "Jesus asks us to absolutize God alone and let the state and all other (powers) be the human relativities they are, at once relatively good and relatively evil--even as you and I are."

As the Christian community faces complex relationships with the changing demands of social and political structures, not all Christians will reach the same conclusions. There are no easy answers. Careful consideration of what Jesus does and does not say, in its historical context, provides invaluable guidelines. Discussion must also draw upon all of Scripture (including, e.g., the view of the state presented in Revelation, chapters 13 and 18) and remember the lessons of history.

v. 13 - The Zealots especially hoped for a worldly Messiah who would drive out the foreigners.

v. 14 - The head tax, added to the already oppressive burden of taxes, eventually contributed to the revolt of A.D. 66-70 that ended with the Roman armies crushing the Jewish and destroying the Temple.

v. 17 - In these few words, Jesus puts forth principles that his followers need in order to face issues which challenge the church throughout the centuries. These vital issues are frequently addressed by the writers of the Epistles (cf Ro 13.1-7, 1Pe 2.13-17; 1Ti 2.1-4; Tit 3.1f) in response to those who, like the Baptist (6.17ff) and Jesus (ch 15), obey God and therefore experience persecution and death (13.9ff).

• In Taylor's (478) words, Jesus' words have "deeply influenced all subsequent discussion of the complex relationships of Church and State." While their implications may be especially poignant for Christians in totalitarian states, they are frequently ignored in nations where church and state are allies. Jesus' instructions need to be given careful consideration by both advocates of civil religion (who see their nation and its culture as an extension of God) and by proponents of civil disobedience (who oppose, for example, paying taxes that support the arms race or unjust governments). Jesus' example should caution churches and pastors to avoid identifying themselves with partisan politics, thereby shutting out people of opposing political convictions and hindering the church from becoming a "house of prayer for all nations."

• After centuries of tragic experiences of the *union* of church and state (with either dominating the other), the *separation* of church and state came into focus (partly as a result of Jesus' teaching here), bringing with it a degree of religious and political liberty. "Separation" has been misunderstood to mean exclusive or isolated functions. In Lane's (425) analysis, "the duties toward God and Caesar, though distinct, are not completely separate, but are united and ruled by the higher principle of accomplishing in all things the will of God."

RESURRECTION AND THE GOD OF THE LIVING, 12.18-27

As a part of the overall strategy of finding a way to arrest Jesus, a delegation of Sadducees hopes that a theological question might succeed where a political snare has failed (13-17). This is the third of the five encounters reported by Mark.

12.18-23 - The Sadducees occupy high places in the Sanhedrin and the high priests come from among them. This priestly aristocracy has collaborated with the Roman authorities and, in the process, has become wealthy and proud of their worldly positions. Contrary to the Pharisees, who accept both the written and oral law, they hold only to the Pentateuch and deny the oral traditions, the resurrection and the existence of angels and spirits (Ac 23.6-8). They are threatened by Jesus' actions in the Temple, for their power and wealth depend on it.

After telling of a woman who was married consecutively to seven brothers, all in keeping with the law of levirate marriage, the Sadducees ask Jesus, "At the resurrection, whose wife will she be, since the seven were married to her?" They reason that the existence of this law proves that Moses would have foreseen the absurd consequences of such a law and not prescribed it, had he believed in the resurrection of the dead. Their story (possibly a well-known joke) is designed to ridicule Jesus, who is known to have taught about the resurrection.

For the sake of argument, the Sadducees are willing to assume that the resurrection is a fact and to support the popular notion that present conditions such as marriage will continue in an exalted form in the after-life. Jesus first deals with this premise (v 25) before dealing with the basic issue of the resurrection of the body (vv 26-27). He begins each reply with a counter-question in order to provoke them to reexamine their presuppositions. Then, so as to leave no doubt about his teaching, he closes each with a clear affirmation.

12.24-27 - The root of the Sadducee's error was their failure to understand either the Scriptures or the power of God. The Scriptures reveal the power of God to overcome death and grant to the righteous a superior quality of life on a higher plain. The exclusive loyalty of husband and wife (in this life) may be a preview of a relationship (in the future life) wider and deeper than that known in the best of marriages. God's power will grant to the resurrected a life like that of the angels.

Jesus makes it clear that death cannot abolish the life that he gives. Resurrection means deliverance from mortality and the perfection of fellowship with God, the essence of the Christian life now. In the consummation of the Kingdom, God will live with his people (Rev 21.3-4). While encouraging hope, the Bible discourages speculation, preserving the mystery about the "how" of the resurrection and the life of the resurrected.

The Sadducees know some of the contents of Scriptures (e.g., the levirate marriage passage), but they do not see any evidence of the resurrection of the dead in the books of Moses. In his reply, Jesus quotes God's self-revelation in the narrative of the burning bush, as recorded in Exodus 3.6 (one of the books they accept), to show that, "properly understood, the Old Testament testifies eloquently to the truth of the resurrection" (Cranfield 374).

God covenanted to bless Abraham, Isaac and Jacob and be their savior and provider (e.g., Ge 12.1-3; 15.1-18; 17.1-8). Centuries after the three patriarchs had died, God said to Moses, "I am the God of Abraham, the God of Isaac, and the God of Jacob." By this, God meant that their passing from this life did not break their relationship with him. They were very much alive in Moses' day; and they are still alive with God (cf Lk 23.43; 16.19-31; Php 1.23). God has not forgotten his relationship with them; he continues to care for them. We may be confident that God will also raise up their bodies and that they and the rest of the righteous dead will dwell with him forever.

As in the previous debate, Jesus concludes with a clear-cut affirmation: God is the God of the living; he cannot be relegated to the past. The patriarchs are alive, not because of "the nature of their experience of God, but the nature of the God whom they experienced. He is the *God of the living* because he is the living God himself" (Cole 191). Jesus' victorious reply prepares the reader for Jesus' death and resurrection, the historical fact upon which Christianity is founded. It gives hope to those who (literally or figuratively) take up their cross and follow him (8.34) and assures them that their God cares personally for his own in life and death.

Jesus categorically rejects the position of the Sadducees, for it is contrary to Scripture and the attributes of God. He began with a question about their position; now he concludes, "You are badly mistaken." They used the Bible to prove their points, instead of submitting their thoughts and programs to the authority of the word of God.

"The moral elevation of Jesus, the spirituality of his outlook, and the force of his personality" are, in Taylor's (480) words, "unobtrusive, but clearly discernible" in this further unveiling of his person. As Williamson (223) says, "Our hope is not only in the teaching, but in the Teacher."

v. 18 - This is Mark's only reference to the Sadducees. They are mentioned in Mt 3.7; 16.1-12; Ac 4.1; 5.17; 23.6-8, as well as in Matthew and Luke's parallels to this debate. The Sadducees' privileged position in this life may have reinforced their disinterest in life after death.

v. 19 - The name "levirate marriage" comes from the Latin **levir**, meaning brother-in-law. The concept is taught in Dt 25.5-10 (cf Ge 38.8; Ru 4.5). It was practiced by other nations prior to Moses and there are evidences that it was followed in Jerusalem in Jesus' time. The levirate law was given in order that the name of the deceased might not be blotted out (Dt 25.6). Anonymity is equivalent to non-being; to cut off the name means to annihilate. The law also provided economically for the widow, a necessity if she were to escape prostitution. It may have been used to exploit women by preserving wealth within the family, but that was not God's purpose.

v. 24 - Jesus' word ("Know the Scriptures;" cf Ezr 7.10) continues as an admonition for all believers and a warning for their leaders. Only those who know both God's word and power are qualified for leadership among God's people. This must be moral and experiential knowledge, rather than purely intellectual.

v. 25 - With the exception of "messenger" in 1.2, the word **aggelos** in Mark always refers to celestial beings in God's service (1.13; 8.38; 13.27).

v. 26 - While Jesus was answering the Sadducees' contention that death means extinction, his words also contradict death as a step in reincarnation. Quoting Minear (113), "Resurrection is not to be confused with reincarnation, nor is life in heaven to be confused with life on earth. · Resurrection means transformation" (cf 1Co 15.35-37). Death involves a radical change from a body designed for this earth to another designed for life in God's presence. "When men become 'like angels in heaven' (v 25), their whole being will be transfigured (9.2-3; Rev 7.9-17)."

• Just as the New Testament reports the bodily resurrection of Jesus, it teaches that the dead in Christ will be raised in radically changed bodies (Ro 8.10-11; 1Co 6.13-20; 15.36-38).

• "I am the God of Abraham, the God of Isaac, and the God of Jacob" expresses, "with unsurpassable brevity,.. that faith in God includes the certainty of conquering death" (Jeremias Theology 184).

• Compare the expression "I am" with "the Lord God, who is, who was, and who is to come" (Rev 1.4, etc.).

• In his comments on Exodus 3.6, Sarna (Exodus 42) states that, "by recalling the three Patriarchs, God implicitly evokes the promises of redemption he had made to them." This "I am..." functions "to emphasize effectively the unimpeachable authority behind the ensuing declaration." It also serves "to establish an unbroken historic continuity;" the same God was about to fulfill for Moses those promises made to the patriarchs. He adds (44) that "This title undoubtedly expresses special intimacy between the devotee and the deity who is his patron, protector, and benefactor."

• The Sadducees deny the resurrection (cf Ac 23.6-8), alleging that it was absent from the books of Moses, the only part of the Old Testament they accepted. Jesus bases his answer on those same books.

• While "the dead shall rise" is not one of its major themes, the Old Testament presents the God who lives and fulfills what he promises. Psalm 73.23ff is a confession that the believer will share in the life of the Sovereign God. The resurrection is taught or implied in Isa 25.8, 26.19; 38.18; Da 12.2; Job 19.25f; Ps 23.6. Taylor (484) claims that the idea of fellowship with God is what "the OT emphasizes in its nearest approaches to a doctrine of immortality."

• God said "I--the God of Abraham" (Ex 3.6). There is no verb in the Hebrew text, as is normal in such a statement. "Jesus implies that a present tense 'am' must be supplied" (Marshall 45).

Brevard S. Childs maintains that Jesus shares many features of first-century Judaic exegetical tradition on Exodus 3. "The entire witness of Genesis (17.4ff; 28.13f; 31.42) focuses on the continuity of God's promise and his covenant which extend to the children of the fathers. Indeed, the fathers continue to live in their sons (Isa 51.2)." (The Book of Exodus. Philadelphia: Westminster Press, 1974; p 82).

THE GREATEST COMMANDMENT, 12.28-34

Impressed by Jesus' answer to the Sadducees, one of the scribes takes the opportunity to ask a question about the Law. They distrusted Jesus' fidelity to this, the first and greatest tenet of Judaism. Jesus affirms his orthodoxy with an answer that was, to quote Bailey (Eyes 37), "pure genius as a summary of duty to God and people." This is the fourth of the five encounters in Jerusalem reported by Mark.

12.28 - The Temple is the seat of learning, where scholars expound the Law and encourage the laity to inquire. In the eyes of most teachers of the Law, however, there is little to learn from lay persons, especially from one such as Jesus who is interpreting the Law contrary to their traditions. Yet one of these professional theologians notices that Jesus has given a good answer. Skipping his colleagues' honeyed introductions (12.13f; 19ff), this scribe goes directly to the subject. By asking "which is the most important commandment?" he wants Jesus to define the one that explains all the others.

Debating the relative importance of the 613 commandments was a frequent scribal activity. This scribe's question presumes that piety is a matter of personal achievement. Unlike the others, however, he is setting no trap; rather, he wants to hear for himself the essential thrust of Jesus' teaching.

12.29-30 - Jesus begins his answer by going back to the roots of God's covenant with Israel, quoting the opening words of the **Shema** (Hebrew for "Hear!" Dt 6.5; cf Mk 4.3). By reciting this each morning and evening, the pious Jews recalled that God had spoken to Israel and that he is to be heard. The expressions "The Lord (**YHWH**) our God, the Lord is one" identify the unity and uniqueness of God's being, his character and his relationship with humanity. He is **YHWH**, the personal God who revealed himself as compassionate, gracious, merciful and just (Ex 34.5-7). In love, he established a covenant with his people and sealed it with his name.

Love (**agape**) for God is an obligation arising out of the fact that the Lord is the One and only God; all other gods are false. Moreover, love for God is the personal, grateful response to the God who loves, cares for and responds to all those who call upon him. He embraces the whole person and claims one's whole being for himself. As indicated by the repeated "all," God is to be loved with the totality of one's being. Jesus demands that men and women seek God "for his own sake, to have pleasure in him and to strive impulsively after him" (Lane 432).

12.31 - "The second commandment is this: 'Love your neighbor as yourself'." Jesus brings together two principles which form an indissoluble unity: love for people arises out of love for God (cf 1Jn 4.21). In answering the scribe, Jesus addresses every individual in this two-in-one commandment. By repeating in an urban setting two commandments spoken originally in a wilderness centuries earlier, he gives them universal validity; there is no situation ethics here. Together, they sum up human duty. The first commandment is essential for one to approach God; the second, to become like God.

As Cranfield (379) clearly explains, "The command to love one's neighbor as oneself does not in any way legitimize self-love (as has sometimes been thought); but in it God addresses us as the people that we actually are, sinners who love ourselves, and claims us *as such* for love to our neighbors." It means forgiving others (Mk 11.25), making excuses for them and desiring the best for them just as we do for ourselves. Love is expressed not merely in feelings and words, but also in action. A person who loves others in this way becomes very vulnerable. This is the way of the cross; this is the way Jesus loves.

Opinions vary as to whether these two commandments had been previously combined. One thing is undebatable, however: Jesus lived what he taught. His life and death flowed out from his love for God and for others. His life and ministry clarify, in living experiences, what these two commandments mean. His love for God and for others is convincing evidence of his divine Sonship.

The Qumran community taught: "love all the sons of light" (i.e., the members of the community) and "hate all the sons of darkness" (outsiders). "Love your neighbor" was taught in Judaism (Lev 19.18), but the concept of "neighbor" was only extended to their kindred (see comments on 14.24). Admonitions not to mistreat aliens (Ex 22.21; 23.9) were often ignored. However, God's love embraces all persons (Lk 6.32-36; Jn 3.16) and Jesus' house of prayer is open to all peoples (11.17). The command to "love your neighbor" requires that we treat all others as God treats us. God's children are his agents of reconciliation.

Jesus' words lead each of us to acknowledge: "I am self-centered. Often I don't even want to love others as myself. When I attempt it, I find that I can't. My only hope is to appeal to the Source of such love." Foreseeing our need, God gave his Spirit to indwell each believer. "The fruit of the Spirit is love (**agape**)...." (Gal 5.22). Love is the law of life for all those who follow him. His church should be a loving, caring community (cf Jn 13.34f).

"The double commandment constitutes the article of faith for the new fellowship in the Kingdom" (Kelber Story 64). It is the foundation of Christian ethical conduct. When in doubt as to what to do, the Christian must choose that which demonstrates love for God and for others.

12.32-34 - "Well said, teacher," the scribe replies, adding that love for God and for others "is more important than all burnt offerings and sacrifices." He wisely perceives the errors of the scribal emphasis upon ritualism and legalism. Having evaluated the one who came to evaluate him, Jesus says, "You are not far from the Kingdom of God." In contrast to the Sadducees who were moving away from the Scriptures and the power of God (12.24), this scribe is moving toward God's Kingdom. Will he follow Jesus?

There is no record of whether this scribe ever enters the Kingdom, although many teachers of the law were converted, especially after the resurrection (cf Jn 7.48; 12.42; Ac 6.7). He may have entered at that moment, for God's redemptive rule had already begun in Jesus. To enter the future Kingdom, one must follow Jesus now; it is not enough to agree with his teaching or to appreciate him objectively and intellectually. Jesus' words to the scribe should lead each reader to ask, "Am I *in* or only *near* the Kingdom of God?"

This is the fourth question directed to Jesus by the religious leaders. Even though no one dares ask him any more questions, the authorities do not desist from their plans to arrest and kill Jesus (14.1). In the next pericope, Jesus himself poses a question to his accusers (as he did in the fifth controversy in 2.1-3.6), a question centered on his own identity. These two pericopes form the climax of this series of debates and present truths foundational to Christianity.

v. 29 - **YHWH** (as it is written consonantally in Hebrew, the ineffable Name "Yahweh" having been replaced in Jewish tradition by **Adonai**, "my Lord") became the dominant name by which the God of Israel revealed himself as Redeemer and Judge. It is a personal name, standing for intimacy with God himself made possible through the covenant which he initiated (Sarna Exodus 45).

• By stating that "the Lord our God the Lord is One," Jesus stresses the unity of the one true God in solidarity with the Old Testament. The oneness of God implies that he serves the needs of all peoples (Jews and Gentiles alike), something the Temple had failed to do (cf Ro 3.29-20; 1Co 8.6; 12.5-6; Eph 4.5-6; 1Ti 2.5).

God is one, yet he reveals himself in Scripture as Father, Son and Holy Spirit, the triune God (cf 1.10-11). The three Persons of the Godhead possess the identical, undivided essence of the one Divine Being. They are not three gods or three parts of God. Jewish and Islamic accusations that Christianity espouses polytheism arise from misunderstanding the doctrine of the Trinity. Sharing Israel's monotheism, Jesus' disciples were reluctant to accept him as being more than a prophet. Only after his crucifixion did they acknowledge Jesus as the Son of God. Christians today may negate the doctrine of the Trinity by disproportionately emphasizing Christ or the Holy Spirit.

• God's self-revelation to Abraham and Moses led to Israel's insistence upon the exclusive worship of one God. As Sarna (Exodus 150) points out, "The gradual, evolutionary progression from polytheism to true ethical monotheism simply cannot be documented."

v. 30 - In everyday usage, "love" expresses an emotion (e.g., "a person falls in love"). As such, it is not controllable, predictable or enduring. Ego satisfaction is its principle motivation. The Greek word **eros** (which does not appear in the New Testament) includes this concept of love as well as sexual love in general. In the New Testament, the predominant word for love is **agape.** It demands the exercise of the whole person, including the mind and the will. It is self-giving and self-denying (cf 8.34) but not self-pleasing. It is the power to love one's enemies contrary to one's natural inclinations (1Co 13). Emotional satisfaction follows rather than determines Christian love. Those who love God with their whole being find the deepest of satisfaction, for their delight is in the Lord (Ps 37.4; 40.8; cf Mk 1.11).

• The "force" and the impersonal gods espoused by many religions are incapable of giving or receiving love.

• The Bible speaks of the heart (**kardia**; cf 7.21) as the seat of a person's inner life and the center of her or his actions. "Man's thoughts, his intellectual activity, the cognitive, conative, and affective aspects of his personality, are all regarded as issuing from the heart. The state of the heart defines, then, the essential character of person" (Sarna Exodus 64).

The soul (**psuche**) refers to the essence of life in terms of thinking, willing and feeling.

The mind (**dianoias**) is not mentioned in Dt 6.5. Its inclusion here may be to emphasize that one must use the mind in order to love the one true God and to distinguish between right and wrong. **Dianoias** (only here in Mark) is equivalent to "understanding" (**sunesis**) in v 33 (cf 4.12; 6.52; 7.14; 8.17,21). Instead of the mental passivity and esoteric trances of occult religions, one's mental facilities are maximized in Christianity ("the renewing of the mind, " Ro 12.2-3).

Ischuos ("strength") here is synonymous with **dunamis**.

Taylor (486) says these terms are not used to distinguish between human faculties, but "to insist on a complete response."

v. 31 - The Decalogue is also divided into a person's relationship to God, followed by one's relationship to humans. In both cases, the verbs are in the second person singular.

• Like others in the Holiness Code of Leviticus 19, "the love command in 19.18 has as its sole sanction the nature of God Himself: 'I am Yahweh'." By bringing together these two precepts, Jesus offers "a non-legal ground for obeying the commandment," placing ethical responsibility where legal norms previously defined the obedient person (Kee 158).

• Subsequent apostolic teaching emphasized love for fellow disciples as the beginning of obedience to this command (1Pe 1.22; Heb 13.1; Ro 12.10; 1Th 4.9. At the same time, it did not forget the universality of Christian love for all persons (Ro 13.8-10; Gal 5.14; 1Co 13; Jas 2.8; 1Jn 3.23).

• Although the two commandments (v 29-31) are interrelated, they are not identical. Love for God and love for neighbor are not one and the same thing. The God of Scripture is not an enlargement of the human image. God is a person; he invites--he demands--humans to enter into a personal relationship with him.

The first commandment opposes anthropocentrism, which finds expression in declarations such as "I keep the golden rule" or "I care for my family; that is my religion." Contrary to pantheism, God is "outside of and wholly apart from nature;" he "created nature and is sovereign over it." (Sarna Exodus 40). He is active within nature without being confused with it.

The only true foundation for life is theocentric; not nature or humanity or the human ego is the center. God alone is worthy of all our love and adoration.

v. 33 - "It is love that gives meaning to ritual, not the reverse" (Senior 26).

• The scribe recognizes that Jesus accepts the Law as a revelation of God and knows what is most important in it, i.e., humankind's relationship to the one God is based on love. Both Judaism and Christianity hold these basic tenets. Both acknowledge the oneness of God; both affirm loyalty to his commandments. Orthodoxy in teaching (monotheism) and in practice (love for God and for others) is essential for understanding between Christians and Jews.

JESUS ASKS THE SUPREME QUESTION CONCERNING HIS OWN PERSON, 12.35-37

Having reported Jesus' statement on love as the basic relationship between God and humanity, Mark now discloses how Jesus "takes the same crucial matter one step further, to the means by which that relationship is made possible: he re-focuses attention on himself as Messiah and Redeemer" (Wilcock 61).

Jesus' challenges the Jewish religious leaders to examine the Scriptural teaching on the "son of David." They give him no answers, for they have already rejected him. With this, Jesus concludes his public teaching ministry. Soon (13.1) he will leave the Temple, never to return.

12.35-37a - Religious leaders have posed four questions to Jesus. Now, as a crowd surrounds him in the Temple courts, Jesus initiates questions regarding the identity of the Messiah and his relationship to David.

God had revealed to David that he would establish his throne through David's offspring (2Sa 7.11-16). In Psalm 110, King David himself pays homage to this victorious priest-king whose reign has no end. Subsequent prophecies picture David's descendant as one whose devotion to God and prosperous reign would recall David's. By Jesus' time, "in all branches of Jewish opinion there was a settled conviction that the Messiah would be a descendant of David; even born in Bethlehem, the city of David" (Longenecker 109).

Against this background, Jesus asks, "How is it the scribes say that the Christ is the son of David?" He is not rejecting their conviction. Rather, he is asking what they mean when they say that.

Jesus then quotes David's words in Psalm 110.1. He attributes the psalmist's words to the Holy Spirit, thereby establishing them as fully authoritative and true, worthy of their undivided attention.

In the Hebrew text, the beginning of this Psalm reads: "The Lord (**YHWH**) said to my Lord (**Adonai**)." David's son Solomon was the Lord's anointed ("messiah") to rule in the place of his father (1Ch 29.23). He filled the personal relationship implied in the expression "my Lord."

As head of the dynasty, however, David would not have broken custom by addressing his son as "Lord." Significantly, in this Psalm God invites the one designated as "my Lord" to sit--not on the throne in Jerusalem--at his right hand and promises him victory over his enemies. Since no human can share heavenly honor with Yahweh himself, this exalted position must be reserved for "someone infinitely higher than any 'second David' could be" (Martin Foundations I 195).

From David's own words, speaking by the Holy Spirit, we conclude that "my Lord" does not refer to a human messiah but to a divine Messiah worthy to share God's glory without reservation. That Person could be none other than Jesus Christ, the Son of God. The New Testament writers understood this, for they consistently applied Psalm 110 to Jesus Christ. As Herbert Bateman IV (453) says, Jesus is "the unique fulfillment of God's promise to David. There is no other Davidic king like Jesus Christ. He is the anointed Messiah, the son of David." He alone dwells at God's right hand and exercises authority over all (Eph 1.20-21; Col 1.15-20; 2.9-10; 2Pe 3.22).

Using a rabbinical form of questioning, Jesus asks his listeners to reconcile two statements in Scripture: how can the Messiah be David's son (a fact attested by Scripture) and also David's Lord (also attested by Scripture)? The contradiction is only apparent, however, as the Messiah is more than David's son: he is also David's Lord.

Drawing upon Psalm 110, Jesus is unveiling the supernatural nature of the Messiah, while still avoiding the term because of the wrong connotations associated with it. As Kee (129) observes, this involves "subtly bringing together three strands: Son of God, Son of David, Lord (**kurios**), all of which connote for Mark the kingly role for which Jesus is destined, not in simple fulfillment of Jewish expectations, but in transformation of them." Jesus is consciously revealing his identity to those who listen carefully.

The religious leaders among his listeners know that this is no theoretical inquiry; it concerns the supreme question about Jesus' own person. Their concept of the Messiah is too small; their political-nationalistic kingdom is too selfish. They have turned a deaf ear to the witness of Scripture and to its source, the Holy Spirit (v 35). Their failure to respond positively to this challenge marks the point of no return. Since they cannot arrest Jesus for asking questions, they keep looking for a better opportunity (14.1). Later, the high priest demands that Jesus give a clear-cut answer to the related question, "Are you the Christ?" (14.61-62). In his reply, Jesus answers his own question about David's Son.

With the question "Whose Son is the Messiah?" ringing in their ears, Jesus concludes his public ministry. By closing the narrative so abruptly, Mark challenges each reader to answer the question, "Who is Jesus?"

12.37b - In summarizing these debates, Mark calls attention to the response of the people. As in Galilee, crowds in Jerusalem seek Jesus (6.34). They understand enough of Jesus' posture in the Temple to side with him against the religious leaders. Mark's vocabulary, however, alerts the reader to the crowd's inadequate response. The people hear Jesus "with delight," just as Herod did (the same phrase is used in 6.20). Their understanding is superficial; they are vulnerable to manipulative leaders (cf 15.11-15) and "quickly fall away" (4.16-17).

v. 35 - Cf these prophecies: Isa 9.6-7; 11.1ff; 16.5; Jer 23.5; 30.8-9; Eze 34.23-24; 37.24; Amos 9.11.
• Earlier, Jesus questioned his disciples about his identity (8.29). Now he calls attention to it again shortly before his suffering and death. He looks beyond the conflict to his exaltation, fully confident in the vindication promised in Psalm 110.1.
• This is a climactic encounter, giving additional insights into several themes introduced earlier. The series of five controversies began (11.27) with a question about the source of Jesus' authority; this, the last of the series, covertly answers: Jesus is the "my Lord" of Ps 110; his authority is that of the very Son of God.
• The Davidic descent of the Messiah is repeatedly prophesied in the Old Testament and Jesus affirms it here. Quoting Taylor (491-493), "The conviction that Jesus is the Son of God exalted to God's right hand rings out as with the tones of a bell" in

this and various other passages in the New Testament. The early church also believed and taught this truth; many Christians gave their lives rather than deny it.

Jesus' legal sonship from David's line is recorded in Mt 1.1; his natural sonship, in Lk 3.23. Jesus refers to himself as "Christ" in 9.41; 12.35; 13.21f; others refer to him as Christ in 1.1; 8.29; 14.61; 15.32.

v. 36 - Although the Davidic authorship of Psalm 110 is emphatically attested in Scripture, some writers have claimed that it was written during the Maccabean period (142-63 B.C), hundreds of years after David died (about 970 B.C.). This opinion is "now disproved by a recovery of a complete Psalter from Qumran which has been dated in the third century B.C" (Lane 436n64).

• In a manner consistent with Jesus' attitude toward the Old Testament, the New Testament bears uniform testimony to the divine origin of the Old Testament (cf Acts 1.16; 4.25; 28.25; 2Ti 3.16; Heb 3.7; 9.8; 10.15; 2Pe 1.21).

• Derek Kidner (391f) understands that in Psalm 110, King David speaks "as the prophet who declaims the enthronement oracle to the Messianic King, corresponding to the oracle given to other kings at their anointing or crowning (cf 1Sa 10.1f; 2Ki 11.12)."

• David, a vehicle of the Holy Spirit, was serving others by declaring God's prophetic word regardless of how much he understood of this Psalm (cf 1Pe 1.10-12).

• The Hebrew text reads, "The Lord **YHWH** said to my Lord **Adonai**." The Greek uses its only word for "Lord" (**kurios**) in both places. Mark designates Jesus as Lord (**kurios**) in 1.3. Now Jesus identifies himself as Lord in his discussion of Ps 110. The acclamation of Jesus as Lord is a confirmation of monotheism (1Co 8.6; Eph 4.5; Php 2.11).

• This victory is expressed in terms of the ancient practice of victors placing their feet on the necks of their defeated enemies (cf Jos 10.24; Ps 8.6).

• In light of Jesus' redemptive work on the cross, on the day of Pentecost Peter proclaimed Jesus' exaltation to the right hand of God as an accomplished fact (Ac 2.24-35; cf 5.31; 7.55-56). There (Php 2.9; Col 3.1), the exalted Christ already exercises the role of the Melchizedekian King-Priest (Ps 110.4; Heb 2.17; 4.14-15; 5.10; 6.20). The consummation of his kingdom awaits a future conquest over his enemies as also affirmed in Psalm 110.5-7 (cf At 3.21; 1Co 15.25; Heb 2.8-9). Then all enemies will be conquered and Jesus will be glorified with the glory he had with the Father before the world was (Jn 17.5).

v. 37 - Interpreters disagree as to which of David's offspring is indicated by the expression, "coming from his own body" (2Sa 7.12). According to Herbert W. Bateman IV (452), the promise may be applicable to succeeding Davidic kings as well as to Solomon. Of the ten or more historical settings proposed for Psalm 110, he accepts as reasonable the occasion of "Solomon's second coronation in 971 B.C. when David abdicated his throne to his son Solomon" (1Ki 1,32-35, 43-45).

• Mark reports that Jesus' emphasis upon Psalm 110 made a deep impression upon those present. Jesus' discussion also confirms the disciples' confession (8.29) and strengthens the biblical stance of the early church in its relationship to Judaism. Several passages (e.g., Ac 2.29-34; 13.23-39; Heb 1.5-13) point out the resurrection and exaltation of Jesus Christ, David's Greater Son, as fulfillment of this Messianic Psalm. This same Christology is taught in Ro 1.3f; Php 2.9-11; 2Ti 2.8.

FALSE AND TRUE PIETY, 12.38-44

Mark frequently concludes his literary units with an example of what has been discussed. This time, however, he presents two case studies, the first negative (12.38-40), the second positive (12.41-44). After showing the theological misconceptions and errors of the various groups of religious leaders, Jesus warns about hypocrisy. Then, in contrast to those who "devoured widow's houses" because of their greed and self-centeredness, Jesus praises a widow because of her unselfish love for God. Even in the midst of pretentious religious practices, there are some who are faithful. These two pericopes serve as a *warning* against false piety and as *encouragement* to radical commitment to God.

12.38-40 - The teachers of the law were held in high esteem by the people, for they, above all others, were responsible to know, obey and teach the high ethical standards of the Old Testament. Unfortunately, many of them failed to model the Law in their lifestyles and religious practices and thereby disqualified themselves as worthy of esteem.

Following in the tradition of Old Testament prophets (cf Mal 3.5), Jesus denounces these false leaders, warning the people, "Watch out (8.15; 13.5) for the teachers of the law." Although some were seriously seeking the truth (cf 12.28-34), unethical conduct was sufficiently widespread as to warrant a general warning. As might be expected, the ungodliness of the highest officials was also repeated among the ranks.

Jesus describes some of the ways in which such scribes showed their self-centeredness. They paraded through public places dressed in long white linen robes (normally restricted to certain scribal functions), requiring people to rise and bow to them and address them by such titles as "Rabbi," "Master" and "Father." In the synagogues, they sat facing the people, occupying the bench before the ark containing the sacred rolls. At banquets, they insisted on being seated in places of honor next to the host (e.g., Lk 14.7).

In addition, the scribes were opportunists, blinded by "the deceitfulness of wealth and the desires for other things" (4.18) in their pursuit of personal prestige and political power. They used their public reputation as pious people to gain the legal right to administer properties, and, in the process, took a percentage of the transactions. Their knowledge of the law facilitated their exploitation of the defenseless. The houses and belongings of widows were special prizes sought by corrupt scribes. Their long prayers impressed some; Jesus, however, exposed them as shams (Mt 6.7; cf Lk 18.10-14). God is not deceived by these unfaithful tenants of the vineyard (12.9; Gal 5.10; 6.7f). While others act out of ignorance, these trained religious leaders have broken the sacred trust of a high and honorable calling. On the Day of Judgment, "such men will be punished most severely" (v 40).

God requires that those who participate in his Kingdom live according to the highest of ethical standards. Its leaders are to be servants, like Jesus. They must exalt the Lord, not themselves (cf Pr 25.6f). Out of love for God and for others, they are to care for widows and orphans (cf Ex 22.22; Isa 1.17,23; 10.2; Jas 1.27; 1Ti 5.3ff). Their prayers are not to be a show of piety and the babbling of religious jargon but the expression of dependent children who, in faith (11.24f), invoke their loving Father.

Out of pastoral concern for his readers. Mark records Jesus' words as a warning against unethical conduct that might arise in the church. Unfortunately, the pursuit of personal power and prestige are often found among church leaders who are more zealous for self than for God. Cheap grace once led to the sale of indulgences; in this materialistic world, costly discipleship is easily forgotten. The high calling of spiritual leadership is sometimes sold to the highest bidder. Preachers present religion as the key to self-advancement and promise the life-style of contemporary society to their followers. Outward expressions of piety mask avarice and egotism. In light of the authoritative word of the Lord of the new Temple, will God's condemnation be any less severe on those who, in today's church, seek fame and fortune at the expense of integrity?

12.41-44 - Jesus sits down where he can observe the people placing their offerings in the 13 receptacles (called "trumpets" because of their shape) lining the walls of the Court of Women. Several rich persons ostentatiously put large amounts of money into the Temple treasury.

A poor widow approaches one of the receptacles. She has nothing but two copper coins. Instead of keeping one of the coins for herself, she gives them both.

Calling his disciples to him, Jesus contrasts the widow's action with that of the rich. Out of their riches, they have given a part; out of her poverty, she gives "everything--all she has to live on." He reckons "the sacrifice as great or small not by the amount given, but by the amount withheld for ourselves" (Cole 166). Jesus' system of values absolutely reverses concepts such as "bigger is better" and "give in order to receive."

Although women were exempt from studying the Law, this one practiced it, expressing love to God and neighbor as Jesus taught (12.30-31), in contrast to the scribes (12.38-40) and the rich man (10.17-22). Her generosity flowed from her commitment to God and trust in him.

Jesus commends this woman who honors "God *as God*, as the one to whom we belong wholly and who is able to care for us" (Cranfield 387). She exemplifies Jesus' prior teaching on the nature of his Kingdom and of discipleship. Jesus calls every disciple to give her/his life, even suffering the loss of all things for the sake of taking the gospel to all nations.

Once again, Mark holds up before us the example of a nameless woman (cf 7.24ff; 14.3ff). The scribe came near to the Kingdom (12.28-34). She, however, is totally committed to it. By calling attention to this woman, Jesus encourages all to radical discipleship, even those who are powerless socially and politically and those who are poor economically. Rather than succumb to all-male power structures, his disciples must rise above the old in forming his new community characterized by God's attributes of love, mercy and justice.

The exalted Lord continues to keep diligent watch over his churches, to encourage and bless, to correct and reprove (Rev 2-3). Even though many reject God's rule, there are individual exceptions, like this widow and the seven thousand who did not bow the knee to Baal (1Ki 19.18). In the remnant of the faithful, the seeds sown among the crowds take root and produce many times over. This story should encourage Christian workers who see "only a few poor widows" as a result of their ministries. They are reminded that their livelihood comes from people who give sacrificially.

This section began and closed with Jesus observing Temple activities (11.11; 12.41). He then leaves the Temple (13.1), never to return.

v. 41 - Three gates led from the Court of the Gentiles into the Court of Women, a large square measuring about 230 by 230 feet. Women could not pass through the fourth gate, as it led to the Court of Israel. Receptacles in the form of horns were placed in the Court of Women for the silver shekels contributed to maintain the service and build up the treasury of the Temple.
• We believe this pericope narrates an authentic, historically true account (and not, as some allege, a parable taken over by Jesus). It is in full harmony with the rest of Jesus' teaching and with the context of his encounters in the Temple. Jesus did not have to be told about the widow. As a keen observer of people and local customs, he could have appraised her situation from her manner, her clothing, etc.
v. 42 - Two Greek words are translated as "a poor person." The person called **penes** has nothing superfluous; the **ptochos**, nothing at all. Mark uses the latter term in describing this widow. Her coins (**lepton**) were the smallest ones in circulation, worth only one sixty-fourth of a denarius, the daily wage of a laborer. Mark uses the equivalent, **quadrans**, for the benefit of his first readers.

In contemporary society, there are many counterparts to the widows of Jesus' day--those who are alone, without means of support, vulnerable to exploitation and fraud. Was this widow one who had been robbed by scribes (12.40)?
v. 43 - "Calling the disciples" is Mark's indication of teaching directed explicitly to the church; the **amen** (3.28) that follows increases the emphasis.

B. THE FUTURE OF THE TEMPLE, 13.1-37

The great and beautiful Temple dominated the city of Jerusalem from its hilltop location. The magnificent Herodian palace never competed with it as the center of Israel's life, for the Temple was the symbol of God's relationship to the nation. On his first visit there (as recorded in Mark, 11.11), Jesus looked around and withdrew himself from the Temple. In subsequent visits, he disrupted its activities (11.12-25), defined and defended his own authority as over that of the Temple (11.27-12.44). Now as he leaves the Temple for the last time (13.1), Jesus prepares his followers for its destruction while encouraging them to fulfill their God-given mission until the consummation of his Kingdom.

The theme of Christology underlies the whole discourse (vv 6,9,13,21-27,32-36). This chapter climaxes Jesus' visits to the Temple as well as his deeds and words in chapters 11 and 12. It also gives eschatological significance to his passion. Both the way of the cross (8.34-9.1) and this discourse call for perseverance in trials and offer eschatological hope.

• "Apocalyptic" (from the Greek **apocalypsis**, meaning disclosure, revelation) is a technical term for writings about the end of the age which were produced between 200 B.C. and 100 A.D. Apocalyptic descriptions are dramatic; apocalyptic symbolism is often fantastic. The word is used to describe a genre of literature that is found especially in the Book of the Revelation and in sections of Ezekiel and Daniel.

The "little apocalypse" theory alleges that Mark 13 is not a trustworthy report of Jesus' teachings but was based on Jewish messianic documents. Attempts to attribute much of it to non-Markan origins have failed, however. Recent studies of word-frequency and grammar demonstrate that the whole chapter is thoroughly Markan in character. In fact, apocalyptic features are not found in chapter 13.

Jesus' teaching is distinctly prophetic rather than apocalyptic. This distinction is very important for the study of the Olivet Discourse. For example, Jesus, like the prophets, held history and eschatology in dynamic tension. But "this bond was broken in the apocalypses. (For them), eschatology stood in the future, unrelated to present historical events. The God of eschatology was no longer the God of history." (Ladd Presence 316).

The term "eschatology" means "last things" (death, judgment, heaven and hell). In modern biblical theology, it refers to a decisive manifestation of God's presence and power in an historical event in which he establishes his rule at the end of the present age.

1. The Setting of the Olivet Discourse, 13.1-4

During those days spent in the exceptional splendor of the Temple, the disciples no doubt came to concur with the popular saying that "no one has seen a truly beautiful building unless he has seen the Temple." As they leave, one of the disciples calls Jesus' attention to the Temple's grandeur. Jesus replies, "Not one stone here will be left on another; every stone will be thrown down." Through his words to the fig tree and his disruption of Temple rituals (11.12-21), Jesus has already sought to prepare his disciples for God's judgment upon the Temple. In his teaching in chapter 13, he prepares them to look beyond that traumatic event.

Jesus' words would have shocked any Jew, for the people did not believe God would allow the Temple's destruction. Worship there could not be interrupted, not even for one day. In reality, they had lost the true sense of communion with God. They imagined that as long as they kept up the rituals, they could sin in security. In rejecting the Son of the owner, they rejected God and his judgment becomes inevitable, as Jesus said (12.1-9). The destruction of the Temple, the symbol of God's presence in the midst of his people, will terminate his covenant relationship with them.

The western slope of the Mount of Olives offers an unobstructed view of the Temple mount across the Kidron valley. As Jesus is sitting there, Peter, James, John and Andrew (1.16-20) request in private an explanation (cf 4.10; 7.17; 9.28) of his announcement about the Temple (v 2). Jesus' reply is more concerned with the perseverance of his followers in troubled times during his absence than with supplying details of future events.

With deep concern because of their confidence in Jesus' word, the four disciples pose two questions: "When will these things (**tauta**) happen? And what will be the sign that all these things (**tauta panta**) are about to be fulfilled?" (v 4). As G. R. Beasley-Murray (Kingdom 324f) points out, their first question "reflects a belief that the ruin of the temple could not occur as a solitary event but would have to take place in conjunction with other significant happenings." Parallel to this but going beyond it, the second question is based on the popular belief that "the ruin of the Temple will occur as part of the end-time events (the language echoes Daniel 12.6-7)."

v. 1 - The Temple in Jerusalem was one of the greatest sanctuaries of antiquity. Its building complex formed the center of Judaism. Built of white marble decorated with gold, its dazzling beauty and location dominated the city. Its many functions required vast installations above and below the expansive pavements of the court area that totaled 57 acres (172,000 square yards) and occupied one-sixth of the total area of the city within the walls.

Jesus' prophecy was fulfilled in 70 A.D., when the Roman legions under Titus destroyed the city and the buildings of the Temple were leveled after being ravaged by fire. Its tremendous retaining walls whose foundations lay on bedrock still stand but the buildings were all destroyed.

v. 2 - "The true prophetic message has two sides that belong indissolubly together: it is proclamation of salvation and proclamation of condemnation. There are profound reasons for this: grace and judgment belong together" (Jeremias Theology 122).

• This discourse would convince the early church that the destruction of the Temple was not simply the Roman army crushing Jewish insurrection but a judgment of God upon his rebellious people. Political, economic, military, etc. interpretations of the world have their legitimate role. Jesus, however, is fulfilling the role of the biblical prophet: he is interpreting events from God's point of view.

2. A Description of the Events Up To and Including the Coming of the Son of Man, 13.5-27

The Olivet Discourse is the longest unbroken discourse passage in Mark. It is divided into two parts. The first is a description of events leading up to and including the second coming of the Son of Man

OVERVIEW
of
MARK 13

<table>
<tr><th rowspan="3">The
SETTING
of the
OLIVET
DISCOURSE

13.1</th><th colspan="3">A
DESCRIPTION OF EVENTS
up to
the COMING of
the SON OF MAN</th><th rowspan="3">The
COMING
of the
SON OF MAN

24

THE END OF
THE AGE</th><th colspan="2">The
TIMING
of these
EVENTS</th></tr>
<tr><td colspan="3">5

WHAT MUST HAPPEN BEFORE THE END
(implicit: Jesus is absent)</td><td>28

THE
KNOWN</td><td>37
32
THE
UNKNOWN</td></tr>
<tr><td>5
Sufferings
common
to All</td><td>9
Persecutions
of Jesus'
Followers</td><td>14
The
Desolating
Sacrilege</td><td>2 x "know"

"these
things"

parable of
the fig tree</td><td>3x"don't know"

"that day"
"that hour"

parable of the
absent owner</td></tr>
</table>

"Watch out"

"Keep awake"

(verses 5-27). It begins by spelling out three things that must happen prior to the end (5-23). The end of this age and the parousia (i.e., the coming) of the Son of Man (24-27) complete this first part.

The second part concentrates on the timing of these events (verse 28-37). It is divided into the "known" (i.e., the time of the events prior to the end, 28-31) and the "unknown" (i.e., the day or hour of the parousia, 32-37).

Jesus' purpose is not to impart esoteric information but to provide instruction and consolation for his followers during his absence. Mark's account preserves Jesus' pastoral intent, directing it to the needs of his readers who were facing persecution with the threat of impending further persecution. It prepares believers to continue their witness in the midst of travail just as Jesus fulfilled his mission while suffering in Jerusalem.

WHAT MUST HAPPEN BEFORE THE END, 13.5-23

Three units are clearly discernible in verses 5-23:

1. The appearance of deceivers and of sufferings common to all, 5-8.
2. The persecution of Jesus' followers, 9-13.
3. The desolating sacrilege and terrible distress, 14-23.

These units describe three things that must happen before the end of this age and the coming of the Son of Man, which in turn are described in verses 24-27.

The Sufferings Common to All, 13.5-8

Jesus does not promise that the days of King David are just around the corner, nor does he give a detailed calendar of future events. The opening word, **blepete** ("Watch out") sets the tone that is maintained through all that follows. The final word expresses a similar exhortation: **gregoreite** ("keep awake," v 37). Traumatic experiences are imminent. Disciples must face the future with caution and wisdom; their lives and expectations must be controlled by the word of the Lord rather than by circumstances or fear.

The most urgent need to "be on guard" arises because false religions excel in their capacity to deceive. In Jesus' absence (implicit in verses 5-23), many pretenders will claim to be the Messiah. They will try to deceive the disciples (v 5b), they will succeed in deceiving many (v 6b), and they will especially target the elect (v 22). Jesus' triple warning underscores the seriousness of this danger.

Wars, natural disasters and famines will occur. However, "the end is not yet." To a mother in labor, the beginning of birth pains (cf 1Th 5.3) mean sufferings with more intense pain to follow (cf Hab 1.2-6; Rev 6.11). Nevertheless these pains promise her that her long wait is almost over. In like manner, followers of Jesus persevere in the midst of painful realities, for they remember God's promises of eschatological liberation (Cf Ro 8.18-25).

Calamities in nature and civil strife must (**dei**, cf 8.31; 13.10) take place. They are indispensable before the end comes; they are not really signs of the end but signs that the end is detained. These disasters are characteristics of the historical interval between the resurrection and the parousia. They are signs of God's presence as judge in history that is moving to the end he has purposed. They are not, however, the sign the disciples requested (v 4).

Jesus evaluated and rejected false religious; his followers are to do the same (cf 2Ti 4.2-4). Especially in times of turmoil and instability, "charismatic" leaders and charlatans deceive many with their claims to have deciphered successfully the "signs of the times." Apocalyptic speculation should not sway Jesus' followers, for they have his word of warning. These signs indicate the advance of God's plan, not its consummation. He describes the sign of the end in verses 24-27: "At that time men will see the Son of Man coming in the clouds with great power and glory." This cosmic event will not be subject to misinterpretation.

Christians are not exempt from these calamities which befall humanity. They are, however, the specific targets of the trials described in vv 9-13.

v. 5 - This discourse presents material selected from authentic sayings of Jesus and accurately represents his mind.
• "The primary function of ch 13 is...to promote faith and obedience in a time of distress and upheaval." The discourse's exhortations are expressed in nineteen imperatives, with consolation expressed in the indicatives (Lane 446).
• Jesus' watchfulness in Gethsemane (14.34-38) leads to his triumph over death. His followers who are watchful will also share in his subsequent triumphs.
• The warning against deceivers begins and closes the section on signs (5-23), thereby emphasizing their prevalence and the damage they can produce. The Deceiver (Jn 8.44; Rev 12.9) is implicated in this work. Rev 13 details his skill as the arch-deceiver.
v. 7 - "The end." In contrast to a world understood in terms of eternal, cyclical movements, Jesus taught that the world began with creation (13.18; 10.6) and is moving toward the end (**to telos**) of this present age (**aion**). This is determined and controlled by God who is sovereign over all. The end is not a final cessation; rather, it precedes the final salvation and marks the beginning of the "age to come." Although in Jesus Christ the blessings of the future age have entered into this present age, the consummation of God's Kingdom awaits the coming of the Son of Man with great power and glory (13.26). His reign will be eternal (Lk 1.33), in contrast to the kingdom of Satan.

The Persecution of Jesus' Followers, 13.9-13

Having foretold of sufferings common to all humanity before the end, Jesus underlines the sufferings that his followers must expect in fulfilling their mission: "Be aware of the danger to which *you* will be exposed." All that follows in verses 9-13 are not signs of the end but are a part of "the beginning of birth pains" which befall Christians "on Jesus' account" (v 9) throughout the church age.

It is not implied that these troubles follow chronologically the wars, etc., just described. Apparently verses 5-23 present several "overlapping descriptions" of the period before the end, while presenting history as moving "from a situation where 'the end is not yet' to a situation where we know that 'he is near'" (David Wenham 128f).

Just as Jesus and John are "handed over" (**paradidomi**), those who follow him will be "handed over" to religious and political authorities. Local councils (sanhedrins) of Jewish authorities in synagogues located in Palestine and abroad will flog (Mk 14.65; 15.15; 2Co 11.24; cf Dt 25.1-3) them as apostate Jews. Christians will be brought to trial before governors (i.e., Roman authorities) and kings (Jewish magistrates in Israel).

They are persecuted because of their faithful witness. Every trial also provides an opportunity for a witness to the authorities and others (cf Paul in Acts 22-26). Such hardships should cause no one to desist, for "the gospel must (**dei**) first be preached to all nations" (v 10). This is a responsibility no disciple can side-step. As Jesus taught earlier (4.26-29), sowing is a prerequisite to the harvest (cf 13.27). It cannot be delegated to missionaries; all believers must share in this. This is a divine priority no church can second-rate, for the consummation cannot occur until all nations have first had the opportunity to accept the good news (cf Mt 24.25). The church must give priority to being "a house of prayer for all nations" (11.17). First, through human proclamation, the gospel will be preached throughout the world (cf 14.9); only then, through angelic activity, will the redeemed be gathered from every tribe and tongue (13.27). The eschatological is linked to the historical.

With the spread of the gospel among the nations, persecution will continue (v 11). While present with his disciples, Jesus came to their defense (e.g., 2.18,25; 7.5). He also made provision for them in his absence, sending the Holy Spirit as promised in Mark 1.8. By the power of the Spirit (Acts 1.8), the disciples are to continue the work Jesus began. Lest persecuted disciples imagine they have been abandoned, Jesus gives them extra assurance. The Holy Spirit is present with them in the hour of trial, enabling them to be faithful witnesses.

There is no hint of the gospel conquering the world. On the contrary, faithful disciples will even be betrayed to death by rebellious children (v 12; cf Mic 7.6f). Like Jesus himself (3.21ff; 6.1ff), they will be rejected by their closest relatives and betrayed by some within the family of his followers (14.10f, 44f). Hatred, conflict, and war will continue to characterize this age until the coming of the Son of Man (cf Rev 13). While this hatred is vented against the disciples, it is really rebellion against "the Lord and his

Anointed One" (Ps 2.1-3). As Minear (117) says, "nothing could make clearer the absolute antithesis between this world order and the Kingdom in which the love of God redeems all for his own sake."

These calamities and persecution do not mean that the end has come; they offer opportunities for the indispensable witness to the nations prior to the end. Jesus encourages his followers to stand firm to the end, confident that cross-bearing and evangelism are the will of God that must be fulfilled before the parousia. They endure to the end because the Holy Spirit (v 11) sustains them.

These warnings were timely for Mark's first readers, for deceivers and evil persons filled with hatred against Jesus and his followers appeared early in apostolic times (cf 2Th 2).

• Radical discipleship (8.34-37) may lead to these experiences. Life lost "for Jesus and the gospel" is true life gained. His promise of glory in 8.38 dovetails with 13.26-27.

v. 9 - **blepete** ("watch") is repeated from v 2; the personal pronoun is emphatic.

• The verb **paradidomi** ("to deliver up" to judgment and death; 1.14; 9.31) is used 10 times in Mark 14-15 in reference to Jesus' passion. Just as Jesus was handed over "for our benefit," his disciples are handed over "on his account" (8.35; 10.29) for the benefit of those to whom they bear witness of the gospel. The passive verb suggests that, behind human schemes, God is fulfilling his purposes (cf Isa 53.4-12; Ro 4.25, 8.32).

v. 10 - In classical Greek, **dei** denoted the compulsive force of Fate which impersonally determined the necessities of life, a force to which even the gods were subject. In contrast to "fate," the Biblical God is personally and powerfully active in history, lovingly seeking to redeem men and women from all nations. Mark uses **dei** to define what must take place in order to accomplish this: the passion (8.31); divine judgments in history (13.7); the worldwide proclamation of the gospel (13.10). These are not matters of some unalterable fate but are events determined by God's will as revealed in Scripture (cf Ac 1.16).

v. 11 - In a hedonistic world, suffering is to be avoided at all costs. Trouble turns some people away from God (cf 4.17). The gospel, however, presents suffering in a positive light. As disciples understand something of God's purposes in the suffering and death of his beloved Son, they gain insight into why Jesus' followers must pass through affliction and tribulations. Neither suffering the loss of life is the real issue (cf 8.35). Somehow, within God's purposes, these are necessary and never purposeless. They are related to the worldwide proclamation of the gospel and the consummation of God's Kingdom. Suffering produces perseverance, character and hope (Ro 5.3f; 8.28-29). Beyond suffering and death is the glory of the ultimate triumph of the Son that he will share with the elect (13.26-27).

The Desolating Sacrilege and Terrible Distress, 13.14-23

Jesus proceeds to announce another affliction so intense that it dwarfs the trials already mentioned.

13.14-18 - In his visions of the end time when Jerusalem and the Temple would be destroyed by an invading army, Daniel speaks of "the abomination that causes desolation" (also translated "the awful horror" and "the desolating sacrilege." Da 9.27; 11.31; 12.11) Among the Jews, this phrase signified an idolatrous object that causes religious havoc. The term itself does not indicate the nature of the profanation. The complete clause, "When you see the abomination of desolation usurping a place which is not *his*," however, suggests that a *person* creates desolation. This is in harmony with Paul's description of "the man of lawlessness" (2Th 2.3ff). This person who is identified as the Antichrist, is actively at work through other evil persons such as the many "antichrists" (cf 1Jn 2.18,22; 4.3) and "false Christs" (Mk 13.22).

This is Jesus' answer to the disciples' question regarding when the destruction of the Temple would occur (vv 2,4). The appearance "where he does not belong" of "the one who creates desolation" is the requested sign. Jesus' declaration suggests an historic event, a point in time and space. As he explains later (v 30), this was to be expected within a generation.

This event stands in contrast to the troubles mentioned earlier (vv 5-13). Civil strife and natural calamities (vv 7-8) and the persecution of believers carrying out their God-given mission (vv 9-13) are, by their very nature, spread over time and space. These are not signs of the end (vv 7-8); on the contrary, they characterize the interval between the destruction of the Temple and the end. In Wilcock's words (66), "they are simply constantly-recurring features of the church age." The time of the end (i.e., the establishment of the Kingdom of God and the abolishment of evil), however, has not been revealed (v 32).

According to 1 Maccabees 1.54ff, the Seleucid ruler Antiochus IV Epiphanes set up in the Temple of Jerusalem an idol representing Zeus and sacrificed a swine on the altar. He also destroyed part of the Temple rebuilt by Zerrubbabel (520-515 B.C., recorded in Ezra; 1Mac 1.39; 3.45; 4.38,48). Such acts which occurred in 168 B.C. were interpreted as "a sacrilege that desolates" the Temple. The memory of this was perpetuated annually in the Feast of Dedication (attended by Jesus in John 10.22-29).

Daniel's prophecy was regarded as already fulfilled. However, Jesus uses the phrase the abomination that causes desolation" in reference to the future, implying that the prophecy was not exhausted by the events of the Maccabean times. In verses 14-18, this crisis is described in the context of Judea. Jesus commands flight from Jerusalem, implying that the normal place of refuge, the Temple, would itself be destroyed. With compassion, he cautions about circumstances that would make flight difficult or impossible. Urgency is paramount (vv 15-16). He counsels prayer in their hour of affliction, just as he himself prayed (cf 1.35; 6.46; and especially 14.32-38). In contrast to those who claim that the future is fatalistically fixed, he knew that God answers prayer (cf Jas 5.17f).

By June, 69 A.D., in its determination to crush Jewish insurgence, Rome had subjected all of Palestine except Jerusalem itself and the fortresses of Herodion, Masada and Machaerus. After five months of siege, they conquered Jerusalem with terrible loss of Jewish lives. They destroyed the city and burned down the Temple. By the end of September in the year 70, Rome was the unquestioned ruler of Jerusalem.

Both Jewish Zealots and Romans had desecrated the Herodian Temple. The Zealots allowed criminals to roam about freely in the Holy of Holies. The Romans erected in the Temple a Roman standard with idolatrous images of the emperor affixed to invoke worship. These impious acts qualify as an "appalling sacrilege," committed by evil persons directed by the Antichrist. The events surrounding the fall of Jerusalem in 66-70 A.D. are a fulfillment of Jesus' words (Lk 21.20-24).

Recalling this part of the discourse, Mark's first readers would understand the destruction of the Temple as a judgment of God upon disobedience rather than as simply the political-military action of Rome in crushing Jewish nationalism. Institutionalized religion had taken over the Temple from God (12.1-9); the events of 66-70 A.D. confirmed that the glory of the Lord had departed from it (cf 1Sa 4.21). A new covenant people (14.24) was being formed among all nations, based on following Jesus.

v. 14 - The impersonal, neuter noun ("abomination") is modified by the masculine participle ("usurping").
• The clause "let the reader understand" is an insertion by Mark (cf 3.30; 7.3-4), calling upon the reader (and those assembled to hear the reading) to "pay close attention." Anderson (296) says this is "probably Mark's signal that a larger than life symbol is involved, namely the 'man of lawlessness' or the Antichrist (cf 2Th 2.1-12) who would war with God at the end."
• Daniel's prophecy was regarded as fulfilled in the desecration of the Temple in 168 B.C. Now Jesus speaks about the "desolating sacrilege" as though the prophecy contained significance previously unperceived. The destruction of the Temple in 70 A.D. is regarded as the historical fulfillment of Jesus' prophecy. However, was it limited to that, or did Jesus follow the pattern of Old Testament prophecy and joined near-at-hand events with distant ones in which the "fuller meaning" would be realized?

As we understand it, the discourse is both historical and eschatological. It appears that Mark 13.14-20 (in keeping with Da 12.1-2; Rev 3.10; 7.14; 13.5-10; 2Th 2.1-12) foresees in the immediate historical event the eschatological tribulation which will immediately precede the end. Believers will be severely tested and many will be martyred. The wrath of God, however, will not afflict his people (cf Ro 5.9; 8.1); it is directed toward the unbelieving world. The Day of the Lord "will not come until the rebellion occurs and the man of lawlessness is revealed" (2Th 2.3). Many evangelical writers understand that what the Jewish people ("this generation," 13.30) experienced in the destruction of the Temple foreshadows the final "desolating sacrilege." This blending of near-at-hand and distant events was the perspective of Old Testament prophets (Ladd Theology 198).
• The details of this discourse clearly indicate a period of history between the resurrection and the parousia. There are no hints of the consummation of the Kingdom in a brief period of time. The mission to all nations would require time. Fleeing from Jerusalem would be useless if verse 14 indicated the end. When the end comes, the elect will not flee but will be gathered together (v 27). For the ungodly, flight will be useless (cf Rev 6.15-17).

• Over the centuries, caves in the Judean hills were used by Jewish refugees. The church historian Eusebius (ca 300 A.D.) reported that, in response to the exhortation to "flee to the mountains," Christians fled to Pella, a town east of the Jordan River, and were thus saved from the devastation of Jerusalem. They possibly sought refuge first in less-frequented areas east of the Jordan, settling later in Pella.
• Scholars are not in agreement about whether Mark's Gospel was written shortly before or after the destruction of Jerusalem. In either case, the early Christians would have understood the fall of Jerusalem as at least partial fulfillment of the Olivet discourse.

13.19-20 - "Those will be days of distress unequaled from the beginning" is a quotation from Daniel 12.1. Some writers understand that Daniel is referring to the same historical situation portrayed in vv. 14-18.

On the other hand, the description in vv 19-20 seems so emphatic that it appears to suggest something more than the destruction of Jerusalem. The distress is so severe that "if the Lord had not cut short those days, no one would survive" (v 20). As D. Wenham (132) says, this description "sounds like something drawn out and also like something universal." This echoes Daniel 12.11f, where "the setting up of the desolating sacrilege marks the inauguration of a substantial period of suffering and apostasy. It is a period when patient endurance is called for." A remnant of believers survives because the Lord has shortened the days of the unparalleled tribulation from which they apparently would be unable to flee (in contrast to the command to flee, in verse 14c). This language is eschatological, envisioning the end of the world.

In the New Testament, the word **thlipsis** ("distress," "tribulation," "affliction;" 4.17; 13.19,24) is used in reference to afflictions which are "normal" in this age (13.6-13) and were experienced by the early church (e.g., Ac 11.19; 2Co 1.4, 8.2; 1Th 1.6; 3.3). History continues to be the scene of conflict until the eschatological consummation. The days of **thlipsis** spoken of here, however, are unequaled by previous or subsequent events. In the context of the quotations from Daniel, this "abnormal" tribulation belongs to the period of extreme catastrophes before the final salvation. It is called the "great tribulation" in the Olivet Discourse in Matthew 24.21 as well as in Revelation 7.14.

This passage is neither exclusively historical nor exclusively eschatological: the two mingle in dynamic tension with each other. As Hurtado (205) says, the historical judgment upon the Temple "is not the time of the end, and the disciples must be on their guard against false hopes and deceptive claims (21-23)." It foreshadows more divine judgments to come throughout the period it inaugurates while, simultaneously, it points to the eschatological great tribulation that is the immediate prelude to the end. For the modern reader, then, the fulfillment of these verses is past, present and future.

The whole period of history following the judgment upon the Temple is characterized by stress for humanity in general (13.5-8) and by the persecution of the church as it fulfills its mission among all nations (13.9-13). The ruin of Jerusalem portends other divine judgments to come upon sins in the church and upon false prophets and false Christs. The Antichrist will again and again embody himself in proud and sacrilegious persons. The people of God must face these trials with patient endurance (13.33-37; cf Da 12.13).

These judgments are rehearsals of the last judgment, when Satan makes his final attempt to destroy the people of God by political, economic, and religious means (cf 2Th 2.4; 1Ti 4.1-3; 2Ti 3.1-9; 4.3f; Rev 13). In his mercy, however, God will not allow his people to be wiped out. For the sake of the faithful remnant, the "elect whom he has chosen," God will shorten the agonies of those days. "The Kingdom of God will abolish evil only in the Age to Come. *But God has not abandoned this age to evil*" (Ladd Theology 203, italics his). He is sovereign over history.

13.21-23 - False messiahs and false prophets will exploit people's desire to escape from trouble by promising security. They will set their words and visible signs against Jesus' word and refusal to provide a sign (8.11f; 15.32). They will claim that Christ is already present (in contrast to the description of his appearance, given in 13.24-27). They will aim their deceit especially at the elect (13.5-6).

This part of the discourse (vv 5-23) draws to a close with verse 23. It closes as it opened: "Watch out!" (**blepete**, "be on your guard"). In answer to the disciples' question about "all things" (v 4), Jesus adds, "I have told you all things ahead of time."

But what exactly has been disclosed? The purpose of the discourse has been made clear. Throughout, Jesus exhorts his followers to be alert because of the prevalence of deceivers. He encourages believers to prevail in the midst of the most adverse circumstances. He assures them that God is fulfilling his purposes and demands that they fulfill their mission to all nations.

As to what to expect, Jesus indicates that the ruin of the Temple would take place in conjunction with other significant happenings, namely, the overlapping events in verses 5-13 and 19-23. He also makes it clear that the desolating sacrilege inaugurates the final lap before the Second Coming.

Jesus has answered the practical while avoiding the speculative. In verses 24-27, he will tell about the real climax of this age. His instructions about the "timing" of these events will bring the discourse to a close (vv 28-37).

These afflictions were already a reality among Mark's first readers, for the world that crucified their Lord was pursuing his church with the same hostility (e.g., Ac 7.54ff; 12.1f). Also in recent years, countless thousands have died because of their faithful witness. Jesus' words continue to be very relevant, for they describe what those who follow him can expect as they run the last lap before the Son of Man comes in power and glory.

v. 19 - Daniel 12.1 goes on to give assurance that God will mercifully deliver a faithful remnant of his people in the days of his judgment.

v. 20 - "No one would be saved" (the verb is **sozo**, v 20) means "no one would survive." In 13.13, however, **sozo** refers to the life of believers saved by losing it for Jesus' sake, as in 8.35.

• In the Old Testament, the elect were the people of the Covenant (cf 1Ch 7.16; Ps 105.43; Isa 65.9); here, "the elect (**eklektos**, 13.20,22,27; cf 3.13f), whom he had chosen" is applied to the people of the New Covenant (14.24; Ro 8.33; Col 3.12; 2Ti 2.10; 1Pe 1.1; 2.9).

• "To judge from various passages, e.g., Mt 24.37-42 (cf Lk 17.26-35), Luke 21.34-36 (cf 1Th 5.3), the final time of tribulation is not going to be a period of total, unmitigated disaster for everyone" (D. Wenham 137).

v. 22 - False prophets and false miracles are consistently denounced in Scripture, from Dt 13.1-5 through Rev 13. They are collaborators of Satan, the great Imitator (cf 1Jn 4.1ff; 2Th 2.1-12).

THE SECOND COMING OF THE SON OF MAN, 13.24-27

Having revealed the things that must precede the end of this age (5-23), the discourse now turns to the subject of the end of time as we know it (24-27).

13.24-25 - Jesus taught that God is the creator and sustainer of the universe, as revealed in the Old Testament. His disciples knew that the disruption of the orderly processes of the planets was beyond human ability. If such an event should happen, it would be God himself at work, interrupting the normal course of history to do something absolutely unique.

Drawing upon Old Testament imagery, Jesus said,

"the sun will be darkened,
and the moon will not give its light;
the stars will fall from the sky,
and the heavenly bodies will be shaken."

The significance of an upheaval of such magnitude must be extraordinary. The prophets employed similar expressions to indicate God's acts of judgment and blessing. Jesus uses them to signify the culmination of the judgments spoken of in 13.6-23, ushering in the blessing identified in verses 26-27.

13.26-27 - Having suffered the consequences of humanity's rebellion against God, the universe painfully awaits its Liberator (Ro 8.19-22). Suddenly, in contrast to all the deceitful claims about Christ's presence (13.21-12), the sun, moon and stars seem to cry out, "Look, here is the Christ!" On his ascent to heaven, a cloud hid Jesus from his disciples (Ac 1.9-11). The glory of the despised Servant (Isa 53.3) will be hidden no longer. The Son of Man will be seen by humanity as he comes in his chariot, the clouds (Ps 104.3). He is the King of the universe who has received sovereign power from the Ancient of Days (Da 7.13f). All the divine attributes now shine forth from the Son of Man, for his glory is that of the one and only Son of God (cf Jn 1.14).

Prior to his departure, Jesus charged his followers with the responsibility of proclaiming the gospel to all peoples (13.10; 14.9; cf 11.17). In responsive hearts throughout the world, the gospel has born much fruit (4.20, 31f) and the harvest has come (4.29). The Shepherd sends out his angels to gather his own from the ends of the earth (cf 8.38; 1Th 4.17). As in the days of his discipling ministry (1.16-20; 3.13), Jesus gathers them to himself. The consummation of God's rule, like its beginning, is centered in the person of Jesus.

In striking terms, Jesus describes the consummation of God's redemptive purposes as he portrays the coming of the Son of Man to establish God's rule among men and women from all races and lands. We are unable to describe in scientific terms exactly what will happen. Through these poetic expressions, however, we gain insight into the overwhelming theological significance of this event. This matchless coming of the Son of Man marks the arrival of God's new Kingdom in all its glory. "The kingdom of the world has become the Kingdom of our Lord and of his Christ, and he will reign for ever and ever" (Rev 11.15).

Jesus enhances the promised regathering of the dispersed Jews (Dt 30.4; Isa 11.12; 27.12-13) to include the elect of all nations. Their common bond is the person of Jesus Christ. Even though God's judgment fell upon Jerusalem and the Temple, the elect includes the faithful remnant of Israel. God's new people includes both Jews and Gentiles. The focal point is no longer the Temple, the visible symbol of national unity (cf Ac 2.9ff). The Son of Man himself brings the full realization of the Kingdom of God.

The sum of these declarations leaves no doubt as to the person of Jesus, the Son of Man: he is the Son of God. Throughout his earthly ministry, his self-revelation to his disciples has been progressively clearer. Within a very short time, in similar terms (14.62), Jesus will reveal his identity to the religious authorities who will judge him to be a false witness and will do with him everything they wish (cf 9.13).

Mark reports three other occasions (cf 8.38; 9.7; 14.62) in which Jesus foretells his return in power and glory. Without these references to his parousia, it would be impossible to obtain an adequate understanding of who Jesus is. With them, we are given a proleptic glimpse of the greatness and splendor of the Son of Man before seeing his humiliation portrayed in Mark 14-15.

v. 24 - The shift in time and space from the previous section is forcefully emphasized. The Greek conjunction translated "but" expresses a strong contrast, setting this visible, supernatural event over against the misleading words of false messiahs (vv 21-23). The next phrase, "in those days," was commonly used in reference to the last days, but without defining any specific time (e.g., Jer 3.16ff; 5.18; 31.29; 33.15-16; Joel 2.29; 3.1; Zec 8.23). The last temporal phrase ["after (following) that tribulation"] makes it clear that what follows does not take place "within those days" of the historical desecration of Jerusalem. The question of "how long after those days?" is addressed in verses 32-36.

"In those days after that tribulation" does not rule out the possibility of an eschatological great tribulation ushering in the end. The phrase bears a close verbal link with verse 19 ("in those days will be tribulation"). As noted in comments on 13.19-20, the tension between vv 14-18 and vv 19-20 seems to indicate a final tribulation with a future antichrist. (According to 2Th 2.1-12, "the coming of the lawless one," empowered by Satan and "authenticated" with signs and wonders, will take place before the coming of Christ.) These and other considerations seem to confirm a "deeper meaning," namely that there will be an eschatological great tribulation as the immediate prelude to the end. D. Wenham (136n13), for example, finds in the Gospels "an expectation of two distinct judgments, one to fall on Jerusalem and the Jewish people (e.g., Lk 19.41-44), probably in (their) near future, and the other to be universal and unexpected (e.g., Lk 17.22-37)."

• Although nothing more is said about "the abomination that causes desolation" (v 14), the Discourse implies that Satan's evil reign is finished (cf Rev 19.11-20.15).

v. 24-25 - Isaiah 13.10 and 34.4 are combined in this statement. The first three parallel statements are summed up in the fourth. In Rev 6.12-17, similar cosmic disturbances result in great distress for humanity.

• God created the world (10.6; 13.19) and controls the sun, moon and stars. They are not deities; they neither control nor influence the world and its people. They are subject to God's purposes and powers, contrary to astrology, horoscopes, worship of the stars, etc. (cf Dt 4.19; Isa 47.13; Jer 8.2; Am 5.26).

v. 26 - "At that time" (**tote**, v 26) is a "final eschatological 'then'" (Cranfield 406). The sudden, open appearance of the Messiah comes in almost instantaneous succession to the cosmic disturbance.

• Much of this imagery is drawn from the Old Testament. The invisible God made his presence known in theophanies (Ex 19.9; 34.5; Lev 16.2; Ps 104.3). These visible acts revealed his glory (Ex 16.10; 24.16). Glory also has an eschatological concept (e.g., Isa 60.1-3; 66.18). "One like a son of man, coming with the clouds of heaven" is drawn from Daniel's theophanic vision (7.13-14). "In the New Testament, **doxa** (glory) is primarily an eschatological concept, referring to the visible manifestation of God at the end of the age to establish his Kingdom (Mk 8.38; 10.37; 13.26)" (Ladd Theology 275).

Clouds are associated with the glory of God revealed in theophanies and with the power of God in judgment (cf Isa 19.1; Ps 97.2f; 104.3). The forces of nature respond to the action of their supreme Commander (cf Joel 2.10; Isa 13.10; 34.4; Eze 32.7-8; Am 8.9).

The Son of Man sends out angels as his messengers, and, like God in the Old Testament, he gathers the chosen people (Dt 30.3; Isa 43.6; 66.18-21; Jer 32.37; Eze 34.11-16; 36.24; Zec 2.6,10).

The poetic expressions, "the four winds" (e.g., Eze 37.9; Dan 7.2; 8.8; 11.4; Zec 2.6) and "the ends of the earth to the ends of heaven" (e.g., Dt 4.32; Jer 12.12) indicate the worldwide dimension of the church at the end of the age (cf Mk 11.17; 13.10; 14.9).

• The use of symbolic language does not necessarily imply unreality or fiction. A symbolic expression can present a real event with greater impact than literal speech, as in "the fire devoured the forest."

• Generally the verb **horao** means to see with one's own eyes. It is also used of spiritual insight in present experience (15.39; 16.7) and in eschatological perspective. Here and in 14.62 it refers to the parousia, at which time that which was manifested privately at the Transfiguration (9.2-8) will be revealed publicly.

The shift from the second person plural in vv 5-23 to the impersonal third person ("they will see") may point to a lapse of time beyond the life of that generation. The verb suggests that his coming will be a universal event.

• The "coming of the Son of Man" is not a metaphor for individual salvation. Such as interpretation does grave injustice to Jesus' eschatological teaching and questions the historical character of the gospel. Like the first, the Second Coming of Jesus will take place within human history. The future divine intervention terminates the present evil age and inaugurates a new world in which God's purposes for both the individual and humanity reach their fulfillment.

3. The Timing of These Events, 13.28-37

Up to this point, Jesus has described both the things that must happen before the Second Coming of the Son of Man (13.5-23) and the event itself (13.24-27). Now he focuses on the timing of these events. First he speaks about the events reported in verses 5-23, then the eschatological drama depicted in verses 24-27.

The discourse concludes with two contrasting declarations, each with its own parable. In verses 28-31, "know" is repeated twice (**ginosko**, vv 28,29). Verse 32 changes the topic from "these things" and "all these things" (vv 29,30) to "that day or that hour," discussing the latter under a triple "do not know" (**oida**, vv 32,33,35). The switch to this synonymous verb emphasizes the contrast. The "known" and the "not known" clearly distinguish these two units.

Jesus is not interested in satisfying curiosity about the future. He opens and closes the two-part conclusion with exhortations: "learn" and "watch!"

THE "KNOWN" TIME, 13.28-31

Calamities and trials characterize the whole period of the church age, bringing suffering to humankind in general and persecution to God's people (vv 5-23). They are not the end. They point to the coming of the Son of Man. God has not lost control of history; rather, he is bringing history to the culmination he predetermined. We know that the end of this age is near.

13.28-29 - Unlike most trees in Palestine, the fig tree loses it leaves in the winter, giving the appearance of being dead. But "as soon as the twigs get tender and its leaves come out, you know that summer is near." By this parable, Jesus is teaching that, when you see "these things" happening (i.e., the troubles that his followers are to experience, 5-23), you can be certain that the consummation (24-27) is coming. That is as certain as spring buds signaling the coming of summer.

By the year 70 A.D., the generation of Jesus' contemporaries had experienced many of the troubles Jesus was referring to. For Israel, the destruction of the Temple was, in a sense, "the Day of the Lord," for God had acted in judgment. While such a fulfillment of Jesus' prophecies indicates that the Lord is "near, right at the door," they do not indicate how long the period of afflictions will last.

Nor is the prophecy limited to the calamities experienced then. In the framework of the Old Testament prophets, an act of God in history was understood as an anticipation of the eschatological Day of the Lord. In the same way, Jesus' prophecy of judgment upon Jerusalem was the starting point, foreshadowing the eschatological judgment at the end of this age. The historical and the future events are held in dynamic tension (as explained earlier, 13.19-20). As Ladd (Presence 323f) says, "The historical is described in terms of the eschatological and the eschatological in terms of the historical."

13.30-31 - The generation of Jesus' contemporaries did not pass away until it experienced the historical judgment, but this does not exhaust the prophecy. "Generation" has an eschatological meaning as well as an historical point of reference. This generation (8.12,38; 9.19) continues to inhabit the earth and, at the end of this age, will experience the abomination that causes desolation, completing the fulfillment of this prophecy.

From the biblical perspective, God's redemptive acts in Jesus Christ--from the incarnation to the parousia--are essentially one event. Ever since the incarnation, people have been living in the last days.

Jesus confirms (30a) and reconfirms (31) the veracity of his words. The prophets' authority depended upon their transmitting "thus says the Lord." Jesus, however, claims sovereign personal authority with his **amen lego humin** ("truly, I tell you;" see 3.28). "My words will never pass away" (v 31) is a christological affirmation: Jesus is claiming for his words what is said of God's words in the Old Testament: they "stand forever" (Isa 40.8).

v. 28 - The Greek word "parable" ("lesson") is used here for the last time in Mark. The parables here and in verses 34ff are "straightforward," given to disciples for their learning. The verb "learn" (**mathete**) in verse 28 is a cognate of "disciple" used throughout Mark.

v. 29 - The Greek **eggus estin** can mean either "he (the Son of Man) is near" or "it is near," i.e., "his coming" or possibly "the Kingdom of God," as in Luke 21.31.

• After almost two thousand years, the Son of Man has not yet come in the clouds. This delay does not seem like "nearness." The relationship between nearness (or imminence) and delay is a part of the tension between the historical and eschatological.

• The discourse does not picture the fall of Jerusalem "as coming immediately before the end, but as inaugurating a period of 'desolation' and great 'tribulation'" followed by the end. "The end is 'near' after AD 70, in that we are in the final lap of the end-times; but how long that lap will last is not specified" (D. Wenham 132).

v. 29-30 - The terms **panta** ("these things," v 29, reappears from vv 4a, 23) and **tauta panta** ("all these things," v 30, from v 4b) refer to the events described in 13.5-23 as signs that lead up to the end, in answer to the question posed in verse 4. For "these things" to refer to verses 24-27 would be redundant: "when you see the Son of Man coming in the clouds, he is near." Furthermore, verses 24-27 portray the end, the day or hour of which is known only to the Father (v 32). The "day and hour" in verse 32 relates to a distinctly different event, namely, the parousia (vv 24-27). The failure to make this distinction contributes to the false assertion that Jesus mistakenly thought the end would come within that first generation.

v. 30 - In Mark, the word **genea** ("generation") is used only by Jesus in reference to a kind of people he describes as critically asking for signs (8.12), "adulterous and sinful" (8.38) and "faithless" (9.19), recalling Dt 32.5,20. In 13.30, "this generation" refers primarily to Jesus' contemporaries as undergoing the judgments described in 13.5-23. This does not, however, preclude God's judgment on humanity in general, considering the prophetic language of the passage as a whole. Since the emphasis of "this generation" falls on the class of people, the temporal element seems to be of secondary importance.

Moreover, in contrast to other parables where judgment comes suddenly and without advanced warning (13.15-18), this parable (with Mt 24, 2Th 2, etc.) speaks of knowledge of the nearness of the end. The whole period between the two advents is characterized by troubles and by people with a spirit similar to Jesus' contemporaries.

• The delay led people to question if Jesus would ever come. Jas 5.7f and 2Pe 1.16; 3.4ff exhort believers to go on expecting his coming, despite ridicule on the part of others. However, God mercifully delays the end in order to give women and men opportunity for repentance and faith (cf 2Pe 3.9).

• The prophecy of "the abomination that causes desolation" is often explained as "trifocal," with fulfillment in 167 B.C., in 70 A.D., and at the end of this age.

v. 31 - As Beasley-Murray (Kingdom 334) observes, "my words" refers to "Jesus' entire proclamation of the Kingdom of God and his relation to it."

THE "UNKNOWN" TIME, 13.32-37

In this pericope, the "known" (13.28-31) becomes the "unknown" (13.32-37); "these things" (which happen prior to the end of this age) switches to "that day." "That day" is Old Testament terminology for the end of this age, the Day of the Lord's coming in judgment and blessing. While the nature of the parousia has been manifested (vv 24-27), its precise time is not revealed. It is a secret of God the Father.

After indicating several of the Son of Man's divine prerogatives (cf vv 24-27, 30-31), Jesus now declares one of his truly human attributes: he shares humankind's limitations of knowledge. This limitation reveals some of the glory of the incarnation rather than detracting from Jesus' superior authority. At the same time, he affirms his close filial relationship: as Son, he consistently submitted every detail of his life and ministry to his Father's purposes (cf 8.31; 10.40; 14.32-42). He knew the parousia as a fact ordained by God; he left its timing with his Father. As representative man, the Son of Man lived by faith.

By means of a parable, Jesus calls upon us to follow his example of confidence in God's merciful timing. Exhortations to watchfulness (vv 33,37) bracket his encouragement to hope and faithfulness in the midst of uncertainties. The Olivet Discourse reaches its climax and conclusion in the clear teaching of this parable.

In preparing his disciples for his absence, Jesus reminds them of a familiar scene. Prior to leaving on a journey, the owner of a house assigns responsibilities to each of his servants. Their lack of knowledge about when the master will return is no excuse for failing to do their duty.

Jesus has assigned tasks to his followers in terms of dedication (e.g., 8.34-36), personal relationships (9.33-10.45), life-style (10.29-31) and mission (13.10). During his absence (i.e., the church age), the disciples are put in charge of Jesus' house of prayer. Rather than spend their time speculating about the hour of his return, they are to keep at their tasks, with patience and persistence. Since they do not know when the owner will return, they will be tempted to sleep on the job.

At the end of the parable (and at the end of Mark's Gospel), the Master of the house has yet to return. Even now, "the time of the appearing of the Son of Man in glory is unknown, but the fact that he will come is certain. The church is called to live vigilantly in the certainty of that coming" (Lane 484). The tension between the imminence and the delay is deliberately designed to make it impossible to know the time of Jesus' coming, while demanding readiness for a sudden event. For his followers in every age, caught in this tension, Jesus' final instruction should prevail: "I say to everyone: 'Watch!'"

With these words, Mark closes another major division of his Gospel (chapters 11-13) in which he showed how the leadership of the Temple in Jerusalem was irreverent in ritual (11.15-16), confused in theology (11.27-12.37) and corrupt in ethics (12.38-40). Its rejection of the Son of the Owner (12.1-12) required the destruction of the Temple, symbol of God's presence. The new people of God have the responsibility of preaching the gospel to all nations, regardless of the cost (11.17; 13.10,32-37). With this, Jesus closes his formal teaching to his disciples as reported by Mark.

In the midst of debates over chapter 13 (and eschatology in general), let us not lose sight of this great truth: "The Son of Man will come with great power and glory" (13.26). His coming is certain, settled in the Father's counsels and assured by the Son's promise. May we keep our inquiries about "When?" in their proper place (cf Ac 1.6-9). While "we wait for the blessed hope of the glorious appearing of our great God and Savior, Jesus Christ," let us remember that he redeemed us "from all wickedness and to purify for himself a people that are his very own, eager to do what is good" (Titus 2.12-14; cf 2Th 1.7; 1Pe 1.7; 4.13).

The following chapters (14-16) relate how the religious authorities do what they planned (11.18; 12.9,12; 14.1) and Jesus had foretold (8.31f; 9.31;10.33ff). His death and resurrection guarantee the return of the Son of Man in great power and glory.

v. 32 - "You do not know" in verses 33 and 35 is linked to "no one knows that day" in this verse.
• Jesus finally answers the question about when the end will come. However, as Hurtado (212) says, "his answer is likely to be disappointing to anyone wishing to be able to calculate the end, as is the fashion of some ancient and modern so-called prophecy experts." Jesus insists that God alone knows the time of the end.
• To know the length of this period would require knowledge of both the beginning and the end. We know the beginning but (as Jesus said here) only God knows the end.
• "That day or that hour" (32), "that time" or "critical moment" (33) and "when the owner returns" (35) are used synonymously, recalling the Old Testament conception of "the Day of the Lord" (e.g., Am 5.18ff; Isa 2.12; Zec 14.7). Here it indicates the day of the coming of the Son of Man (e.g., Amos 9.11; Mic 4.6; 7.11; Zep 3.11,16f; Joel 3.18; Zec 9.16). In the New Testament, "the day of the Lord" is often used with reference to Christ (e.g., 1Co 1.8; 5.5; 1Th 5.2f; 2Th 2.1f; 2Pe 3.10; Php 1.6,10; 2.16).
• "The impression of Jesus which the gospels give is not that he was wholly bereft of divine knowledge and power, but that he drew on both intermittently, while being content for much of the time not to do so. The impression, in other words, is not so much one of deity reduced as of divine capacities restrained... The God-man did not know independently, any more than he acted independently.... His knowing was bounded by his Father's will" (Packer Knowing God 54f)
v. 33 - As Minear (117) points out, "Concern for dating the end must be replaced by concern for enduring to the end (v 13)."
v. 35 - The Roman military's four night watches were more familiar to Mark's readers (cf 6.48).
v. 36 - "To sleep" is the antithesis of "to watch." The servant who "watches" performs his assigned task patiently, even in the midst of adverse circumstances. His constant prayer is "Come, Lord Jesus" (Rev 22.20; cf "your Kingdom come," Mt 6.10; Rev 6.10). Yet he is neither anxious about fixing dates nor discouraged by difficulties which arise as he obeys his yet-absent Lord. He fulfills his mission, confident that Jesus will return. Elsewhere, the call to watch is associated with prayer and resistance to the powers of this world (e.g., 1Th 5.6-8; 1Pe 4.7; 5.8-9; Ro 13.11-13; Rev 3.3).

- PART 7 -
JESUS' SUFFERING, DEATH AND RESURRECTION
14.1 - 16.8

Pilgrims have traveled far to celebrate the Passover and the Feast of Unleavened Bread in Jerusalem. The vivid re-enactment of the historical deliverance from Egypt stimulates messianic expectations. Some nationalists see this as an opportunity to provoke a popular insurrection against contemporary oppressors. The Roman authorities bring in occupation forces from Caesarea prepared to crush any uprising. Tension runs high in Jerusalem.

The religious authorities' determination to kill Jesus is fomented by his action and debates in the Temple (ch 11-12). Their plot against him unfolds parallel to Jesus' own preparation for his death and resurrection. Jesus even provides his accusers with the evidence they need to condemn him.

The disciples apparently forget Jesus' admonition to "Watch!" (13.37). In spite of his efforts, they are not prepared for his death. Others fulfill the roles they abandon.

Mark identifies these historical events as fulfillment of Jesus' predictions. He stresses their theological significance and establishes the connection between Jesus' passion and the Feast of the Passover. The events unfold according to God's purposes as revealed in the Old Testament (with special emphasis upon Isaiah 53 and Psalms 22 and 69). In his death, Jesus is revealed and recognized as the Son of God.

The resurrection is emphasized as an inseparable part of the passion and of the gospel. However, the narrative does not end with the resurrection; it looks beyond. As Jesus fulfills his earthly messianic role, his followers are commanded to fulfill their role as disciples. The unity of Mark's Gospel is demonstrated as the major themes culminate in its closing chapters.

The author weaves the various episodes into a single, swiftly-moving narrative. In Minear's words (119), "The struggle steadily becomes more intense. Each word and deed becomes more heavily weighted with meaning, each unit becomes a solemn summary of what happened earlier as well as a pregnant forecast of what will happen thereafter."

A. PREPARATIONS FOR JESUS' DEATH, 14.1-42

The Jewish religious authorities realize that their conflict with Jesus has reached a point of no return. Jesus must be killed if they are to preserve the Temple and its rituals. Their personal prestige and all they are sworn to uphold is at stake. When and how Jesus will be killed becomes top priority.

Against the background of the Passover, Jesus seeks to alert his disciples to his coming betrayal, death and resurrection; the results, however, are discouraging. With his Father, he finalizes his personal preparations for his passion. Even while emphasizing his coming death, Jesus repeatedly speaks of what he plans to do after his crucifixion.

1. Preparations by Enemies and by a Friend, 14.1-11

The religious authorities seek to kill Jesus, the common people favor him, an unnamed woman anoints him, and one of the Twelve betrays him. By giving this short résumé of various responses to Jesus, Mark confronts the reader with the necessity of taking a stand; no one can be neutral about Jesus.

PRIESTS PLOT TO SEIZE JESUS, 14.1-2

The countdown begins as the chief priests and the teachers of the law seek a way to seize Jesus by deceit and put him to death. If he were arrested in the Temple during the feast days, the people might riot, for Jesus' influence is widespread (cf 12.37b).

v. 1 - By Jesus' time, the Passover and the Feast of Unleavened Bread had merged into the seven-day "Feast of the Passover." Leaven (yeast) was usually obtained from a piece of yesterday's dough, providing continuity from one baking to another. To go without leaven during the Feast of Unleavened Bread symbolized a break with the past and a fresh start.

• The execution of a false prophet had to take place during the feast in order to deter others from this crime (Dt 18.20; 7.13). However, the authorities awaited an opportunity to arrest Jesus when no crowd was present (Lk 22.6).

A WOMAN ANOINTS JESUS, 14.3-9

Jesus enjoys table fellowship in Bethany (11.1,11f). His host is Simon the Leper, a man who knew rejection but had found in Jesus a friend of social outcasts (e.g., 1.40ff; 2.13-16). The tranquility of this dinner is shattered as a woman approaches Jesus, breaks the long neck of an alabaster jar and pours its expensive perfume on his head.

Some of those present remonstrate with their companions, "Why this waste?" Others declare that gifts to the poor are much more expedient; in fact, they are a sacred obligation, especially during the Passover (cf Jn 13.29). Sensing general accord in condemning her act, they direct their indignation at the woman herself.

Jesus, however, comes to her defense, saying, "She has done a beautifully fitting thing to me." Although she could have kept this perfume as a family heirloom, she chooses to do what she could for Jesus. She does not measure the cost of this act of loving devotion to her Lord. She gives the best that she has to him who is about to give his life for her. She knew the second commandment (12.31) is transcended by her primary responsibility (12.30). Concern for the needy is only a part of what it means to love God.

The text does not explain why she chooses this way to express her devotion to Jesus. The anointing of the head was an ordinary courtesy (Lk 7.46; cf Ps 23.5; 141.5). Prophets anointed the kings of Israel (1Ki 19.16, 2Ki 9.6). David was anointed "in the presence of his brothers" (1Sa 16.13; cf Ps 45.7; 89.20). Previously anointed by the Spirit at his baptism (1.10), Jesus is now anointed by a woman in the home of a social outcast. Does she perceive that he is the Messiah?

While the woman's conscious intention is not stated, Jesus affirms that this is a timely act that will be remembered. Jesus will not always be in their midst. Her action actually serves as preparation for his burial, for Jesus will soon die by violent hands and be buried unceremoniously and without anointing.

Her dedication to Jesus serves as an example of authentic discipleship to those who worry about other things (e.g., 9.34; 10.37). "Her deed springs from a personal love for Jesus which, on occasion, breaks all patterns, defies common sense, and simply gives. Spontaneous, selfless, and timely, her gift calls us to love Jesus in this way too and not to judge the way others express their love for him" (Williamson 249).

With his typical solemn vow (**amen**; 3.28), Jesus declares that wherever the gospel is preached throughout the world her act will be remembered. Jesus sees beyond his burial to his resurrection and the global spread of the gospel, beginning with these imperfect disciples.

By defending this woman who apparently intruded on a banquet of men, Jesus again sets forth, in a world dominated by men, the inherent worth of women. Mark frequently presents women as examples of the insight and devotion lacking in the male disciples (e.g., 1.31; 7.24-30; 12.41-44; 15.40; 15.47-16.1). By leaving her nameless, countless other unheralded heroines of the faith can more easily identify with her.

v. 3 - It is probable that Simon was cured, but the stigma of leprosy remained in his nickname.

• Nard is an aromatic oil extracted from a root native to India used to perfume the head and hair (SS 1.12; 4.13f) and to anoint the dead (16.1). Its value (equal to a year's wages for a day laborer; cf 6.37) indicates that it may have been a family heirloom, passed from mother to daughter.

• Unfortunately, Jesus' statement about the continuing presence of the poor has been twisted into a pretext for indifference to economic injustices. This occasion presented a once-for-all opportunity to honor Jesus. On the other hand, Deuteronomy 15.11 (alluded to by Jesus) commands generosity to "your brothers" and to all the poor (cf Gal 6.10) as a continuing responsibility.

A DISCIPLE CONSPIRES AGAINST JESUS, 14.10-11

The chief priests receive some unexpected help in their plans to arrest and kill Jesus (14.1f), possibly in response to their appeal for information (Jn 11.57). Judas Iscariot, one of the Twelve, provides the opportunity the authorities were seeking. They need not wait until the feast is over (cf 14.2)

Both Judas and the chief priests exercise their free will; they are responsible for their actions. At the same time, God foresaw this and is governing the timing and coordinating all according to his purposes. As suggested by the passive form of the verb, it is ultimately God who "hands over" Jesus to death.

v. 12 - Mark writes with a pastoral concern for his readers who were betrayed by family members (13.12f). They find comfort in remembering that Jesus was betrayed by "one of the Twelve" (3.19; 14.10,13).

v. 13 - Judas put a price tag on his loyalty (cf Zec 11.12f; Mt 26.15). Jesus, however, calls our attention to two women (12.42-44; 14.3), each of whom expressed devotion regardless of the cost.

2. The Passover Meal, 14.12-26

While "outsiders" prepare for Jesus' death (14.1-11), Jesus and his disciples prepare for the Passover meal. Jesus gives new meaning to this traditional feast that dramatized Israel's past and future. It now portrays the significance of his vicarious death that ratified the new covenant. This act of table-fellowship hosted by Jesus is bracketed by predictions of his betrayal and desertion by his closest followers.

Even as Jesus' arrest and crucifixion draw closer with each passing minute, bright rays of sunshine break through the storm clouds. With numerous appeals to the Old Testament, Jesus explains the purpose of his death and looks beyond to his resurrection and the consummation of God's Kingdom.

PREPARATIONS FOR THE PASSOVER, 14.12-16

One of four major annual festivals in Israel, the Passover looks forward to God's redemption while recalling his gracious liberation of Israel from Egyptian bondage. Mark carefully links these events with the Passover meal that begins the weeklong festival (vv 1,12,14,16). It is a family celebration, requiring days of careful preparation (Ex 12.1-27; Dt 16.1-8). The house is thoroughly cleaned to remove any leaven; couches are provided; food, herbs and wine are obtained beforehand. On the afternoon prior to the meal itself, the Passover lamb is killed and roasted and the meal itself prepared.

Normally, disciples are responsible to make preparations for their rabbi to observe the Passover. Jesus' disciples place themselves at his disposal. He then sends two of them (cf 6.7; 11.1) into the city with specific instructions. The owner of the house where they will commemorate the feast has much already prepared (v 15). The two disciples put on the finishing touches (v 16).

v. 12 - Mark does not record all that takes place in the Passover Meal. Jesus doesn't follow every detail of its traditional observance; he adds new elements (cf 2.22) which give emphases to the new covenant.

On the first day of the Feast of Unleavened Bread, a lamb is sacrificed in preparation for the Passover meal. While Mark does not elaborate upon the theme of Jesus as the Passover Lamb (as John's Gospel and Revelation do), it is implicit in the new interpretation Jesus gives to the Last Supper.

vs. 13-16 - Jesus' instructions here, as in 11.2-6, offer his disciples almost immediate confirmation of the reliability of his assertions as encouragement to trust in his word. He may have made prior arrangements with the owner of the upper room in order to escape detection by those seeking to arrest him.

v. 13 - Normally a man would carry water in a leather bottle and a woman would carry it in a pitcher.

v. 15 - This large upper room is often identified with Acts 1.13 and 12.12.

PREDICTION OF BETRAYAL, 14.17-21

As sunlight fades from the Jerusalem sky, ushering in the Jewish Friday, Jesus celebrates the Passover with his disciples. This is the principal act of table fellowship in the Jewish year. Jesus is host, for he is the head of the new family (3.34f). In this, his final gathering with the Twelve, Jesus previews some aspects of the next twenty-four hours in which he will be crucified and buried, after his resurrection (v 28) and after his absence (v 25).

The participants normally begin the festive evening with an inaugural blessing and prayer, followed by a dish of bitter herbs and sauce and the first cup of wine. Next, they recount the institution of the Passover, praise God for the salvation wrought in Egypt, sing the first part (Ps 113-114) of the Hallel (the new song of future redemption) and drink a second cup of wine. These are preliminary to the meal itself (14.22).

Jesus probably follows this general pattern of observance, with two distinct variations. First, Jesus foretells his betrayal by one of the Twelve (vv 18-21), and during the meal itself, gives new significance to the bread and wine (vv 22-25). He begins and concludes these pronouncements with **amen** sayings ("I tell you the truth;" vv 17,25), his solemn guarantee of the certainty of these words (cf 3.28; 14.30).

Previously (9.31; 10.33), Jesus predicted that he would be betrayed. Now he declares specifically that he will be betrayed *by a friend.* The air of tranquility and mutual acceptance that characterize sharing a meal (cf 2.15) is disrupted by his words. The traitor is not named; instead, the emphasis is on his participation in the fellowship as one of the Twelve. Shaken and saddened by the thought, they are too bewildered to accuse their companions. Each disciple disavows the accusation as it concerns himself. One by one they ask, "Surely not I?" Their self-confidence has been shaken.

Jesus, however, knows that these events are by divine appointment: "the Son of Man will go as it is written about him" (v 21). He is keenly aware of the mission he has freely chosen. He is confident of God's faithfulness.

The traitor also participates in fulfilling God's plan. He does so as a free agent, not a robot. Nevertheless, Jesus warns him that he will be judged for his act. Divine sovereignty does not diminish human responsibility. By sharing the meal as though he intends no harm to Jesus, the traitor aggravates his offence.

v. 17 - Gerhard Lohfink (91) affirms that "the absence of women from the Twelve and from the Last Supper has absolutely no implications for the role which Jesus attributed to women in the people of God." The Twelve represented the tribes of Israel; but in the Near East at that time, women could not represent tribes. "Jesus integrated women among his students with an astonishing freedom and without regard for the expectations of contemporary Judaism."

v. 18 - The Passover was originally eaten in haste, while standing (Ex 12.11). Now, by custom, even the poorest recline during the festive meal as a sign of freedom from slavery.

vs. 18-20 - Various phrases indicate Jesus' close relationship with the traitor: "one of you," "eating with me," "dips into the bowl with me" and "one of the Twelve." Cf Jn 13.18 with Ps 41.9. Jesus, however, does not name his betrayer. Marshall (52) says "the identification in Mt 26.25 was probably made in quiet reply to Judas himself, or else he might have been lynched on the spot: Peter had a sword!"

vs. 18-22 - These events are not necessarily narrated in chronological order. In Luke, the prediction of the betrayal (22.21f) follows the institution of the Last Supper (22.14-20).

v. 19 - By relating the disciples' "surely not I!" Mark calls upon each reader to examine himself as to the possibility of betrayal, denial or falling away, even after eating at the Lord's table. In his teaching on the Lord's Supper, Paul also calls for self-examination (1Co 11.28ff). Character weaknesses should be corrected early, lest they reappear with multiplied negative consequences.

v. 20 - To dip the flat unleavened bread (used as an eating utensil) into the same dish was a token of intimacy (cf Ruth 2.14). To break table-fellowship was a very detestable act. From Qumran documents, the phrase "one who dips bread into the bowl *with me*" would indicate that Judas deliberately denied Jesus' leadership by not waiting his turn as required by custom. Mark gives no hint as to when Judas leaves the upper room; John 13.30 says Judas leaves immediately after receiving the morsel.

v. 21 - The words "as it is written" (as in 9.12) may not refer to any one passage but "simply mean that the sufferings of the Son of Man are a part of God's plan and are indicated in a variety of passages, such as Isa 53.1-6; Ps 41.9-13" (Hurtado 225). Cf Acts 2.23.

• Jesus' declaration, "woe to the betrayer," is neither a curse nor a threat; it is a cry of sorrow and anguish derived from the death wail. Cf 9.42.

• There is no suggestion of fatalism here. Jesus exercises the highest expression of free will, which is voluntary submission to God's will (cf Php 2.8). Judas also exercises his free will, casting aside all Jesus has taught. Neither psychological determinism nor concepts of predestination, fate and destiny exempt men and women from giving account to God. "The Divine necessity for the Passion was no excuse for the free agent who brought it about" (Swete 334).

THE COVENANT MEAL, 14.22-26

After the inaugural activities described above (14.17), the Passover meal itself normally consists of another blessing followed by eating roast lamb with unleavened bread and bitter herbs. Jesus transforms two aspects of the meal (the bread and the wine) into symbols of his life and ministry. "This scene is one of the most vibrant theological crescendos in Mark's Gospel. Here Jesus will interpret the ultimate significance of his death" (Senior 53). Moreover, he looks beyond his death, confident of the consummation of God's Kingdom, notwithstanding betrayal and desertion by the disciples (vv 18-21; 27-31).

14.22 - As usual, Mark does not fill in the details. Most likely Jesus sits up from his reclining position and, as the head of the family, recites the usual Jewish prayer: "Blessed be the Lord, our God, the King of the universe, who has caused bread to spring out of the earth." The disciples answer, "Amen," declaring their oneness with the blessing.

Over the centuries, faithful Jews partook of the "bread of affliction" (Dt 16.3) as a symbolic act by which they remembered their forefathers, shared personally in deliverance from bondage in Egypt and participated in the national liberation. Custom (based on Exodus 12.26ff and 13.8 and practiced even today) prescribed that the head of the household break the bread, offer it to his family and explain the various aspects of the meal in the light of Israel's historical redemption.

In this same tradition, Jesus breaks the bread and offers it to his "family." However, he gives it a new significance, saying, "Take it; this is my body" (v 23). He does not look backward to Egypt but forward to his own death only a few hours away and declares, "I am giving myself to you." He invites his followers to receive ("Take it") a share in all the benefits which he will secure through his sacrifice for the people of the new covenant.

v. 22 - Our task here is to understand Mark's account of the Last Supper. The Synoptics and Paul all manifest agreement in significant areas, although each author concentrates on features especially significant to his first readers. Attempts to reconstruct the whole evening are inconclusive. This should frustrate any tendency to create a fixed ecclesiastical ritual. Remembering Jesus' denunciation of ritualistic practices, churches should seek to avoid meaningless repetition of this ordinance of the Lord.

• **Eulogeo** (v 22) and **eucharisteo** (v 23) are used interchangeably in the Gospels and are translated as either to bless (i.e., praise) God or to give thanks to God in prayer. Following Jewish custom, Jesus probably blesses God for the bread and gives thanks for the wine. The term "eucharist" comes from **eucharisto** (to give thanks) and implies that the Lord's Supper is a joyous celebration.

• Lenski (620) claims that breaking the bread does not symbolize Jesus' death by violent action; rather, it was essential for distributing the bread.

• Since the bread Jesus offers here symbolizes his very self which he is about to "give as a ransom for many" (10.45), the command to give bread (6.37) takes on the deeper meaning of "Give them Jesus."

14.23-24 - Following the Passover meal itself, the host exhorts those present to praise God. Then, with the third cup of red wine mixed with water in his right hand, he offers thanks and all affirm their gratitude to God with their "Amen." Also the common cup is passed for all to drink.

Mark relates such a procedure in brief (v 23) but concentrates on the magnitude of its meaning as expressed in Jesus' words, "This is my blood of the covenant which is poured out for many" (v 24). On the historic Passover night, God's redemption of his people from slavery was symbolized by the Passover blood (Ex 12.21-28), leading to his covenant with Israel at Sinai which was ratified with blood (Ex 24.8). Jesus announces *a new covenant* to be sealed with blood. It is not, however, confirmed with the blood of animals; it is made effective through Jesus' own blood (cf Heb 9.15,20; 10.29; 13.20).

Since the blood is the life, he declares that he is *giving himself*. Moreover, his blood will be "poured out," meaning he will die a violent death.

By offering the cup to them, he is *giving himself to them*. In concept and in the vocabulary used, this phrase recalls Jesus' previous affirmation about giving his life as a ransom for many (10.45). In both passages, Jesus clearly identifies himself as the Suffering Servant of Isaiah 52.13-53.12. He surrenders himself in a substitutionary, atoning death. Jesus himself is the sacrifice.

The new covenant that God promised through Jeremiah (31.31) is about to be established. Jesus defines his own crucial role in it. Now, as in 10.45, he affirms that his death is "on behalf of many." "The many" is the redeemed community which has experienced the remission of its sins through Jesus' sacrifice and so is enabled to participate in the salvation provided under the new covenant. The rabbis taught that there is atonement for all sins and sinners, but there is no ransom for the nations. Jesus, however, dies vicariously for all. His death offers the benefits of this covenant to the breadth of humanity, for "he bore the sins of many" (Isa 53.12; cf Heb 9.28).

In his statements about the bread/wine (body/blood), Jesus' emphasis is the same: he is *giving himself*. Each phrase has its distinctive contribution, but all dramatize his vicarious offering of himself. On this new and enduring basis, he offers a share in his death. Each one who partakes of this covenant fellowship is thereby committing him- or her-self to follow Jesus in the giving of self (cf 8.34ff).

He also offers his followers a share in his resurrected life, for the bread and wine of table-fellowship are a pledge of his abiding presence with them. As God was with his people in ancient times (e.g. Ex 3.12; Jos 1.5; Isa 41.10), Jesus promises to be with the people of the new covenant throughout the period in which he is separated physically from them (16.7; cf Mt 28.20). The reader responds by living with confidence and responsibility.

Jesus has only one thing to offer: himself. The sooner the church learns it has *nothing to offer save Jesus Christ and him crucified*, the greater will be its contribution to its contemporaries. If the church does not offer Jesus Christ, no one else will. This must be the priority of every church and every believer.

v. 23 - In the Old Testament, "to drink the cup" symbolizes either to undergo God's judgment or to participate in his salvation. Jesus underwent God's judgment (emphasized in 10.38; 14.36; 15.34ff) in order that we might receive the benefits of salvation (emphasized here).

v. 24 - Blood was identified in the Old Testament with vitality and was regarded as constituting the very essence of life. The daubing of the blood on the door frames (Ex 12.7) indicated both the identity of the occupants as Israelites and the preservation of their lives. The New Testament sees in the blood of Christ (i.e., his death) the ultimate significance and guarantee of the Old Testament typology.

• Cf Ge 9.4; Lev 17.11; Dt 12.23. Body, blood and "poured out" are all sacrificial terms.

• Some insist that a God of love forgives without any need of a sacrificial death. The New Testament, however, presents God as *holy* love. "Since God is love, he provides forgiveness for the sins of men (and women); and since he is holy love, he provides that forgiveness through the medium of the sacrificial, atoning death of Christ" (Ladd Theology 190).

• A covenant is a treaty or agreement between two parties, such as the one established at Mt. Sinai by God with Israel's representative, Moses. The sacrifice of animals was necessary to seal the agreement on Sinai (Ex 24.1-8); "the blood of the covenant" (i.e., the death of Jesus) is the sacrifice by which the new covenant is made effective (cf 1Co 11.25; 2Co 3). The superiority of the new covenant is explained in Hebrews 8-10. In essence, it is highly personal, like a marriage alliance. Its primary benefit is God's pledge: "I will be their God (Ge 17.7-8)."

• "Many" (**polloi**) is a Semitic expression meaning an immense number or all (see comments on 10.45). In the Old Testament, it often connotes non-Israelite peoples. Like Jesus' house of prayer (11.17), the new covenant is extensive to all nations (cf 7.26ff; 13.10,27; 14.9; Isa 56.6), in contrast to the restrictive practices in the Temple. The reign of God is freed from a purely national context, for it is open to all nations while implying the gathering of Israel.

• God chose Israel to be the "people of his inheritance" (Dt 4.10)--his kindred and established with them a covenant sealed with the blood of animals. In it he defined the rights and obligations, as well as the status and privileges of those who were "of one flesh" (i.e., the descendants of Abraham). Jesus offers to people of all nations a kinship relationship with God by establishing--through his own blood--a new covenant. Through this covenant of grace kinship relationships are extended--and expanded--to the "many". It defines our privileges and duties to God and substantiates his commitments to us.

vs. 22-24 - The bread and the cup obviously were not the literal body and blood of Jesus, for he was present physically with his disciples when he spoke these words. "My blood which is poured out" is a Semitic way of describing violent death (cf Ge 9.6; Dt 19.10; Mt 23.35). This saying is neither a mystical nor a magical formula for changing the wine into blood. There is no implication here that he altered the elements in any way. The very thought of eating flesh or drinking blood would have been repulsive to the disciples (cf Lk 17.12; Ac 15.20,29). Consumption of blood was forbidden on pain of death (Lev 3.17; 7.26f; 17.10, 14; 1Sa 14.32ff).

The Passover feast was a parabolic action. Jesus does not change it to literalism; rather, he maintains its symbolic spirit. The Supper looked forward to his approaching death; its elements become new object lessons to explain the new covenant. He declares the eschatological meaning of the ancient typology. So, by giving the bread and the cup, Jesus speaks of giving himself in death on behalf of others as the sacrifice that institutes a new covenant. To partake of these elements is to declare dramatically, "I am also included in the 'many' for whom Jesus died." Those who share in this table-fellowship dramatize their close union with Jesus and with others in all of life and mission.

vs. 23-24 - The "Last Supper" became the "Lord's Supper" (1Co 11.20), for Jesus explicitly ordained (Lk 22.19; 1Co 11.24f) its celebration by the church. He is spiritually present, as host of *his* Supper. It is especially a fellowship with Jesus. To partake of the bread (which Jesus identified as "my body," meaning "my person") means one is joined to Jesus.

As believers today partake of the two elements, they contemplate the past, present and future. They look back at the reality of Jesus' gift of himself in establishing the new covenant. They declare their personal inclusion in that covenant, resulting in reconciliation to God and in fellowship with the people of the covenant. They look forward to Jesus' return (14.25; "until he comes," 1Co 11.26). They accept the responsibility of working out in everyday life the meaning of entering into a covenant with God.

Family discussion is a fundamental part of Israelite education (cf Dt 6.7ff, 20ff). In response to questions about the Passover, the family head recounts the biblical account and explains the meaning of each part of the meal. Those who desire to restore meaning to their observance of the Lord's Supper may find enrichment through discussion.

14.25 - Normally the Passover meal was unhurried and involved much discussion, concluding with a fourth cup of wine and the singing of Psalms 114-118, the last part of the Hallel. Mark proceeds directly to the conclusion of the Supper.

Devout Jews interpreted the four cups of wine in terms of the four-fold promise of redemption set forth in Exodus 6.6-7: "I will bring you out...I will rid you of their bondage...I will redeem you...I will take you for my people and I will be your God." While fulfilling the first three promises, Jesus abstains from the concluding cup on this occasion and vows with a solemn "amen-saying" that he will complete the unfinished meal when he celebrates the messianic banquet which inaugurates the age to come.

During the Supper, Jesus employs the metaphors of the bread and wine to picture the restoration of communion between God and sinners. At its conclusion, Jesus adds the metaphor of the royal wedding feast that symbolizes table-fellowship with God and the final union of the triumphant Christ with his bride. On "that day," when the Kingdom is fully consummated, Jesus will again gather his family, break bread and pass the cup of blessing to his people.

With his words "no more," Jesus declares "that his decision to submit to the will of God in vicarious suffering is irrevocable" (Lane 508). With equal conviction, he knows his death is not the end. His absence is only "until that day." For Jesus, this phrase envisions his triumphant return (13.24-27, 32). For the believer, this "stunning prediction of hope and victory planted in a story that rushes toward death" (Senior 61) guarantees a new relationship with Jesus beyond death.

vs. 24 -25 - Probably some or all of John 14-17 occurred between these two verses.

v. 25 - During Jesus' absence, many will come claiming "I am he" (13.6). His followers should not be misled, for Jesus adds this to his previous warning: he will not be seen until he comes in the clouds (13.24-27) and then he will drink the cup anew with them (14.25).

• The word "until" appears in all the Gospel accounts of the Supper and in Paul's phrase, "until he comes" in 1Co 11.26). It contains a promise which "fills the celebration with joyous hope of the fulfillment in the Kingdom of God and transforms the present moment with all its risks and challenges...by placing it in the light of that future" (Anderson 315).

• This promise, made to his disciples who disowned him within a few hours, constitutes a promise of their restoration as a result of God's forgiveness (emphasized in the new covenant, Jer 31.34).

• According to Jewish tradition, a righteous man would intercede for Israel on the hour of his martyrdom (cf At 7.60; Mt 5.44). Jesus' solemn avowal of abstinence from drinking the fourth cup with his disciples may possibly have preceded his intercessory

prayer recorded in John 17. This would imply that he is the Servant (Isa 53.12) who "bore the sins of the many and made intercession for the guilty."
• The meal in the Upper Room meant "a sacrifice in which (the disciples) had a share; a covenant making them beneficiaries, though they did not deserve it; and a reunion promised with Jesus face-to-face in a joyous fellowship beyond death." These pledges can be ours today. (Martin Action 129).
• On this feast, see Isa 25.6-8; Mt 8.11; 24.1-14; 25.1-12; Lk 14.15-24; 22.29f; Rev 19.9.

14.26 - The table-fellowship was normally concluded by singing the second half of the Hallel Psalms antiphonally, one chanting the text and the others responding with "Hallelujah." Jesus makes the words of these Psalms his own prayer of thanksgiving and praise. He will fulfill his vows in the presence of all the people (Ps 116.12-19); he extols the Gentiles to praise God (Ps 117); he declares his steadfast confidence in his ultimate triumph: "I will not die, but live, and will proclaim what the Lord has done" (Ps 118.17). He sees his own death and exaltation in the prophecy of the rejected stone (Ps 118.22; Mk 12.10). He is assured of God's guidance as he passes through distress and suffering to glory.

With his disciples, Jesus leaves the old, walled city, crosses the deep Kidron valley and ascends the slopes of the Mount of Olives.

3. Prophecies And Denials Of Abandonment, 14.27-31

Earlier, Jesus made several attempts to awaken his disciples to the dangers that lay ahead. He taught that some who receive the word with joy quickly regress when trouble or persecution comes (4.16f). He had exhorted them to make every effort to avoid hindering one's own self or others (cf 9.43-47).

14.27-28 - Now Jesus makes his last attempt to prepare them, announcing that "You will all fall away." This prophecy is supported by an appeal to Zechariah 13.1-9, which describes God's judgment on the nation, leading to cleansing from sin (v 1) and to the creation of a new covenant people (v 9). In the process, the shepherd, "the man who stands next to" the Lord (v 7), will be struck down and the sheep scattered. Only a remnant will survive severe trials before sharing in the blessings of God's people.

Jesus identifies himself as "My shepherd" of Zechariah's prophecy. This shepherd is no ordinary leader; as Joyce G. Baldwin points out (Haggai, Zechariah, Malachi, 197-198), he is "the Lord's gift to his people, one who dwells side by side with the Lord, his equal." Jesus again declares that he will die under the judgment of God (see 10.38ff and 14.36) as he gives his life as a ransom for others (10.45). His death is according to the will of the Lord (Isa 53.10), a part of the "divine necessity" (8.31; 14.21).

As a shepherd concerned for his sheep, Jesus also applies Zechariah's prophecy to his disciples. He reminds them of their vulnerability, telling them that they, like sheep, will scatter in panic when their Shepherd is killed. They fail to stand firm under trial (4.17); within a few hours they fall away (14.43-50,66-72). However, their failure will not thwart God's purposes.

Jesus hastens to add that neither his death nor their flight is final. He will rise from the dead and will precede them to Galilee (8.31; 9.9,31; 10.34; 16.7.). The risen Lord will regather his disciples who have been refined in trials and will lead them in their mission to all nations.

v. 27 - Zechariah's phrase, "the 'shepherd-king' will be struck" (i.e., killed) becomes, in Jesus' words, "I will strike the shepherd." Jesus' self-designation as shepherd appears in all the Gospels and in 1Pe 2.25; 5.4; Heb 13.20; Rev 7.17. Zechariah 13.7 (cf Mic 5.4; Eze 34.23) describes the promised Messiah as shepherd over God's people. His position next to the Lord recalls Mk 12.36 and Ps 110.1.
• In the Old Testament, the image of sheep is used of Israel; in the New Testament, the flock is a symbol of the church (Jn 10.1ff; 21.16; Ac 20.28f; Eph 4.11; Rev 12.5; 19.15). Peter understands here that Jesus is applying Zec 13.7 to himself and his disciples. Pastoral ministry includes forewarning believers as to dangers that lead to failures (cf Jesus in 4.15ff; Paul in Ac 20.29), as well as feeding and leading the flock.
• "Scattering" and "gathering" are terms widely used in the Old Testament. They describes the dispersion of Israel as an act of God's judgment (Jer 17.1-4; Eze 12.15) and its gathering as an act of mercy designed to bring all nations to himself (Isa 40-

66). While this promise of gathering was fulfilled historically after the resurrection, it may imply an eschatological regathering of Israel.

• The Qumran community understood the shepherd of Zec 13.7 to be an eschatological figure. Martin (Foundations I 201) claims that "they will be scattered" is a technical term which points to the parousia, indicating a time of tribulation before the end of the age. Kee (110) writes that the quotation from Zechariah "is far more than a vivid metaphor for a leaderless people; it depicts the eschatological community enduring persecution and suffering in expectation of God's vindication of them in the time of the end. Mark makes this explicit when he joins to this quotation a prediction of the renewal of the community under Jesus' leadership following his resurrection from the dead (14.28)."

14.29-31 - Peter does not pay any attention to Jesus' promise of resurrection and reunion. He protests the implied affront to his loyalty. He considers himself to be an exception; he will not fall away.

Jesus' strong response begins with **amen** ("I tell you the truth;" 3.28). He speaks directly to Peter: "Today--yes, tonight--you yourself (emphatic) will disown me three times before the rooster crows twice" (cf 14.72). The others will fall away; Peter's offence, however, is greater. In his resistance to denying himself (8.34), he will persist in denying Jesus. In Schweizer (308) words, "He who feels secure and considers himself to be different from all others will fall the farthest."

Peter had previously (8.32) rejected the idea of Jesus' suffering; now he accepts death as a possibility not only for Jesus but also for himself. But he rejects vehemently (cf 14.71) the idea of disowning Jesus. The other disciples all side with Peter, contradicting Jesus as though they knew themselves and the future better than he did. Jesus' forewarnings are drowned out by their self-confidence (cf 10.39). In the last analysis, they are not ready to lose their lives (8.35). Beyond all else he suffered, Jesus bears additional pain inflicted by those nearest to him.

This scene demonstrates that the disciples' faithful ministries after Jesus' crucifixion are not the result of their own abilities or virtues. Hurtado (229) adds, "The life and mission of the church rests upon Christ alone, not upon human leadership." God still takes failure-prone lives and transforms them into his fruitful servants.

4. Gethsemane, 14.32-42

Preparations for Jesus' death dominate the passion narrative in which Mark carefully weaves together the various historical and theological threads introduced in previous chapters. Having focused on outsiders and on the disciples, Mark now turns the spotlight on Jesus himself. Bracketed by the prophecy of abandonment and its fulfillment, the Gethsemane scene pictures Jesus facing this hour of crisis alone.

In deep distress, Jesus prays, for his personal preparation flows from communion with his **Abba** (Father). We walk on holy ground as we contemplate Father and Son and gain new insights into their persons and purposes.

14.32-36 - Jesus and his disciples climb the slopes of the Mount of Olives to a regular meeting place called Gethsemane. He comes to pray, for his whole life is directed Godward. He has instructed his followers on prayer (9.28f; 11.23ff; 12.40; 13.18). Mark, however, focuses on three occasions (1.35; 6.46 and here) in which Jesus prays in solitude, at night, in a critical moment in his ministry. These are fundamental events for understanding Jesus and his mission.

Mark's third account of Jesus praying is distinct, for he describes Jesus' stressful state and narrates the substance of his prayer. In this way, he accentuates the supreme importance of Jesus' time alone with his Father on this Passover night.

Jesus takes only Peter, James and John with him. These three had earlier witnessed Jesus' power over death (5.37-43) and a preview of his glory (9.2-8). Now they see Jesus distinctly different from all previous experiences. In Mark's emphatic words, Jesus begins "to be greatly distressed and troubled." Moreover, Jesus himself confesses the struggle of his soul: "My heart is breaking; it almost kills me."

As he faces extreme horror and suffering, Jesus identifies himself with those who pour out their emotions, complaints and even recriminations to God with raw honesty in "prayers of lament." He tells of his pain by echoing the prayers of his people in their moments of deep anguish. Jesus' humanity is very evident as, with transparency of heart, he tells his disciples of the deep affliction that is shattering his soul.

Jesus does not turn to these disciples for comfort and support, even though Peter (14.29) and James and John (10.35-39; 14.31) had declared their readiness to face anything with him. They have not demonstrated ability to help Jesus nor do they intercede for him.

Jesus himself is keeping vigil as he faces the cross. Out of concern for them, he says, "Stay here and keep watch." They also need to be alert as spiritual and physical dangers arise. However, they fall asleep; and since they do not face Jesus' unparalleled crisis, they are unprepared for their own trials (e.g., 8.34-38; 10.38f; 13.9-13; 14.27-31).

In the intensity of his anguish, Jesus turns to God in prayer. He knows this conflict is not a charade but a life-and-death struggle. The temptations that began in the desert (1.12-13) continue, testing him deeply. We gain further insight into the depths of his humanity as we see him proceed alone and prostrate himself in supplication to God. Mark prepares the reader for the full impact of Jesus' trial by stating the essence of his prayer: "if possible the hour might pass from him" (v 35).

"**Abba**," Jesus says, using the diminutive form of the Aramaic term for Father to express the heart of his relationship to God. He speaks to God "as a child to its father: confidently and securely, and yet at the same time reverently and obediently" (Jeremias Theology 67). Overwhelmed by his own weakness, he entrusts his life to his Father as the Sovereign God with whom "everything is possible." During this extreme trial of his faith, when the Kingdom itself is at stake, Jesus is an example to those whom he encourages (in nearly identical language) to trust God, with whom "everything is possible" (9.23; 10.27).

Jesus does not shrink from the prospect of death by crucifixion. Rather, he staggers at the thought of being alienated from his Father (cf 15.34) as divine judgment falls upon him, the Sinless One who bears the sins of others. "The awesome concept of himself as sin bearer...must have been for Jesus indeed *full of dread*." He realizes that all of his conflicts with evil are "now coming to a single, inexorable point. He (is) face to face at this *hour* with the power of evil manifested in the sharpest way," as Mann says (591-592, italics his).

Contemplating this cup of wrath, Jesus experiences the inner struggle of his will, for he is human. Rather than hide his repulsion from his **Abba**, he prays, "Take this cup from me." This is not, however, a demand; it is a request based on the condition, "if possible." Then Jesus declares his unnegotiable loyalty to God's will: "Yet not what I will, but what you will." This is true prayer, a pattern for all who are committed to live under God's dominion.

"God made him who had no sin to be sin for us" (2Co 5.21). Although Jesus dies under divine judgment on sin, he is not the personal object of God's wrath. His suffering is "on behalf of many" (10.45; 14.22-24). His vicarious death means that he came to pay a debt he did not owe, because we owed a debt we could not pay.

v. 34 - The night following the first Passover was also a night for the Lord and all Israel to keep vigil (Ex 12.42). The need for disciples to "keep watch" at all times (13.35-37) has already begun: "in the evening," 14.17f; through the midnight hours, 37-42; "when the cock crows," 66-72; and "at dawn," 15.1.

v. 35 - Jews normally stood in prayer. Here, however, Jesus falls to the ground, defenseless before God in supplication and reverent submission (cf Ge 17.3,17). Prayer (as L. Doohan says, 75) is "one of the clearest indications of creatureliness."

• The "hour" refers to Jesus' suffering at the hands of sinners (v 41), with emphasis upon his final agony on the cross. In theological terms, this is a soteriological hour, with eschatological consequences. "The hour" and "this cup" are synonymous expressions for the significance of his passion.

• Jesus is unique in addressing God with the intimate, homey "**Abba.**" "*We do not have a single example* of God being addressed as **Abba** in Judaism, but Jesus *always* addressed God in this way in his prayers. The only exception is the cry from the cross (Mk 15.34 and parallels), and the reason for that is its character as a quotation" (Jeremias Theology 66, italics his). Nowhere does Jesus include others with him by the expression "our Father" (cf Jn 20.17; Mt 6.9 is not "the Lord's prayer" but the prayer Jesus taught his disciples), for he is uniquely God's Son by nature (cf 1.1,11; 9.7; 12.6,35.ff). We are children by adoption. This is the only time **Abba** is used in Mark, for Jesus uses it only in direct address and not in his references to "Father" (8.38; 13.32). Because of Jesus, the Holy Spirit enables a child of God to approach God as **Abba**, Father (Ro 8.15-17; Gal 4.6).

v. 36 - Jesus' prayer in Gethsemane recalls the laments which comprise approximately one third of the Psalms, the Prayer Book of the Jewish people. Unlike the sanitized product often heard in churches (or cited in Lk 18.11f), prayer is openness before God.

• The outpouring of God's wrath is described in the OT as "the cup of staggering" (e.g. Ps 60.3; Isa 51.17,22). This cup which Jesus is about to take symbolizes more than suffering and death; it means "redemptive suffering which involves the bearing of sin" (Taylor 554). Jesus drains this "cup of God's wrath" on behalf of sinners (cf 15.34; Isa 51.17,22) as God himself strikes the shepherd (as Jesus said earlier, 14.27). In 10.45 and 14.22-24, Jesus made it clear that he bears the judgment of God as the Suffering Servant and Sin-bearer of Isaiah 53.

Unlike the wrath of humans, God's wrath is free from sin. It is his constant attitude toward sin. Without it, God would cease to be fully righteous and his love would degenerate into sentimentality.

• Both pronouns are emphatic in Jesus' words, "not what **I** will but what **you** will."

• As Lane (522) says, "Just as rebellion in the garden brought Death's reign over man (Ge 3.1-19), submission in Gethsemane reversed that pattern of rebellion and sets in motion a sequence of events which defeated Death itself (cf Heb 5.7-10)."

• Jesus is not the unwitting victim of fate, arbitrarily imposed by an omnipotent Deity. He struggles as a man enduring deep internal tension; but he chooses God's will. Jesus' humanity is real, complete and permanent. He is subject to all the conditions of human existence; but he never ceases to be God. His human and divine natures are united in one person and remain without change, each fulfilling its part. His humanity is universal and not individual, including all that belongs to the essence of humans.

14.37-40 - Returning to the three disciples, Jesus finds them sleeping. In reproving them, he first singles out Peter, possibly in view of his confident boast (v 31). "Simon," he says, "could you (singular) not watch one hour?" Then (changing to the plural imperative) he admonishes all: "Watch and pray, so that you will not fall into temptation." God offers them a way to escape falling into temptation (cf 1Co 10.13). Satan, however, seeks their downfall.

Jesus has repeatedly resisted Satan's attempts (1.12-13; cf Heb 4.15) to turn him aside from his appointed way. Now Satan concentrates all his efforts to win a decisive victory. As the hour of his vicarious death approaches, Jesus is the object of vicious satanic temptations. In addition, as he bore our sin, Jesus is the object of the holy wrath of God. He accepts these two burdens in his commitment to making God's reign a reality. These account for his being overwhelmed with sorrow.

In the midst of his own unparalleled trial, Jesus is concerned about his disciples. They need to "watch and pray," for they, too, are being tempted. Jesus teaches them (and his church through them) that reliance upon frail and finite human nature (**sarx**, "the flesh" means all that humans are spiritually without God) leads to failure, in spite of one's best intentions. Dependence upon God's willing Holy Spirit, however, enables one to "watch and pray," overcome human weakness and resist the demonic. Jesus knows the frailty of human nature, for he is fully human. He also knows the enabling power of the Spirit, for he is Spirit-filled (1.10).

Twice more, Jesus prays the same thing. He steadfastly persists, consciously and deliberately confirming his commitment to obey his Father. Twice more the Shepherd (v 27) looks after his three vulnerable sheep. With heavy eyes, they sleep rather than pray. They seem unable to perceive what is going on. Even in the midst of his own unparalleled agony, Jesus continues to instruct them on watchfulness, prayer, and the Spirit as essential aspects of true discipleship. Through his honest lament and fierce commitment to God's will, Jesus provides the model for the church, exposed to temptation. Watchfulness becomes a key exhortation for the early church not to forget the weakness of the flesh, whether in facing martyrdom or in far less demanding circumstances (e.g., Ro 13.11-14; 1Th 5.6,10; 1Pe 5.8; Rev 3.2f).

v. 37 - By addressing him as "Simon" (3.16), Jesus warns Peter that he is reverting to his life prior to becoming a disciple.

vs. 37-38 - The command to vigilance in 13.33-37 had primary reference to the unknown hour (13.32,35) of the return of the owner (i.e., the parousia), whereas the command here refers to "the hour" well known to the Son (the hour of his suffering and death).

v. 38 - Some understand "spirit and flesh" here as distinct and antithetical elements of human nature. However, these terms present "the common Old Testament distinction...between man as dependent upon the Spirit of God and man as a frail creature subject to the limitations of his earthly nature" (Taylor 555). "The flesh is weak" is verified in the disciples' failures. Cf the flesh and the Spirit in Ro 7.14-8.17.

• "The spirit is willing" draws upon Psalm 51.10-12, where the reference to the "Holy Spirit" is bracketed by "steadfast spirit" and "willing spirit." The meaning here, therefore, is that God has given his steadfast Holy Spirit to dwell continuously in the believer, willingly preparing and sustaining each one in crises. Cf. Mark's references to the gift of the Holy Spirit (1.8) who aids in times of need (13.11; also Romans 8.26: "the Spirit helps in our weaknesses," including that of not knowing "what we ought to pray."

• Itioka (182) reports that evil spirits can hinder prayer and Bible reading by causing uncontrollable sleep.

• Probably the resurrected Lord himself told the disciples about his prayer in Gethsemane (cf Lk 24.27f).

14.41-42 - Returning the third time, Jesus awakens them, saying, "Enough! The hour has come." This is the hour when he will drink "the cup." Then he adds, "Look, the Son of Man is handed over into the hands of sinners." The climax of his ministry is upon him.

Even before Judas appears, Jesus says to his disciples, "Rise! Let us go forward to meet the one who betrays me!" Jesus unhesitatingly goes forward to the cross; his prayer was heard, as Hebrews 5.7 confirms. With firm resolution, he will drink the cup and experience the horror that he dreaded at Gethsemane. This is his Father's will, and to do God's will is his unnegotiable commitment (v 36).

Jesus will speak no more of his suffering; henceforth, he undergoes suffering itself in a silence broken only by two Messianic confessions (14.62; 15.2) and two cries from the cross (15.34,37). The preparation for Jesus' suffering and death is concluded; the passion itself begins.

vs. 41-42 - These verses are subject to differences in translation. Is the word about sleeping a command, statement or question? We have sought to understand the details in the light of the whole.

v. 42 - These are the last words Jesus personally addresses to his disciples in Mark; in 16.7, his last message to them.

B. JESUS IS CONDEMNED AND CRUCIFIED, 14.43-15.47

With Judas' cooperation, the religious leaders have finalized their plans to arrest Jesus. Through time alone with his Father, Jesus has completed his preparation for his death. Only the disciples are not prepared as the armed band places Jesus under arrest. They flee as he is led off to be tried.

Mark records three "trials" that take place between Jesus' arrest and his crucifixion. Religious and political leaders interrogate Jesus in the first and third trials. Though disdainful of each other, the Jewish and Roman authorities form a coalition that results in Jesus' condemnation to death by crucifixion. Although each trial is a miscarriage of justice, Mark's allusions to the Old Testament make it clear that Jesus is giving himself as a ransom for many, in accord with God's will.

These two interrogations frame Peter's informal "trial." Unprepared to resist temptation, he disowns Jesus in contradiction to his own affirmations while unwittingly fulfilling Jesus' prophecies. Mark presents the three "trials" in such a way that each complements and interprets the others.

Jesus' suffering as the "man of sorrows" (Isa 53.3) intensifies after he is condemned to be crucified. He is flogged and mocked as king by the whole company of soldiers before reaching Golgotha. During the hours in which he hangs on the cross, he is subjected to cruel derision as truths about his person and purpose are unintentionally expressed by his tormentors.

As Senior (117) points out, this is "one of Mark's most skillful narratives, catching up the major motifs of Christology and discipleship that have run throughout the Gospel and bringing them to their final expression." Paradoxically, the great themes of the gospel reach their zenith in the apparent nadir of the cross. In the crucifixion, the revelation of who Jesus is and where he is going takes a giant step forward.

1. Jesus is Arrested, 14.43-52

Quickly, the scene in Gethsemane changes from Jesus' lonely struggle to his arrest by an armed crowd and his betrayal into the hands of sinners. Both his arrest and the flight of his disciples are presented as additional evidence of the truth of Jesus' predictions.

14.43-50 - Judas appears. The betrayer has been making arrangements to deliver Jesus over to the Jewish authorities. The chief priests, the teachers of the law and the elders see no further need for delay until after the feast (cf 14.2), as Judas provides the choice opportunity they need. So to make the arrest, Judas leads a small contingent of Temple police along with servants of the high priest (v 47). Jesus must be taken without causing a popular uprising.

According to custom, no disciple greets his teacher first, for this would imply equality. Judas, however, calls out, "Rabbi!" thereby openly repudiating Jesus' authority. Then, with a kiss, a friendly gesture of respect, Judas completes his arrangements for handing over Jesus. In the process, Judas identifies himself as a hypocrite who (in Senior's words, 81) transforms "a sign of love into a signal for death" and a traitor from among the Twelve. His rejection of Jesus is complete, and he has handed himself over to evil.

So the armed men arrest Jesus. A bystander strikes out, cutting off the ear of the High Priest's servant. In marked contrast to his armed attackers and the self-appointed defender, Jesus answers them with dignity, armed only with his word. He who submitted himself to God does not resist being delivered into their hands, for this is God's will for him (cf v 36; 9.31). In his own betrayal and arrest, Jesus serves as an example to Christians persecuted on his account (13.9-13).

Jesus calls attention to the irony of taking such drastic measures against him. Is he an outlaw (like those in 15.27) or a political subversive, as their methods imply? With this rhetorical question, Jesus replies to Judas' affront, reaffirming his role as a teacher. He reminds them that he had been ministering openly in the Temple (as he had in Galilee, cf 6:14), with nothing to hide.

Nowhere--not even here--does Jesus protest against any indignity done to him. He accepts their actions in the light of Scripture, for they point to God's purposes and identify him as the suffering Servant" (Isa 53.3,12) and the stricken Shepherd (Zec 13.7).

With the first strike against Jesus, made by "a friend who shared his bread" (Ps 41.9), all the sheep scatter (as he had warned them, 14.27,29). They are unable to accept suffering as a requisite for Messiahship and for discipleship (8.31-34). Their very human resistance against the idea of suffering has been building up since Jesus' first pronouncement of his suffering (8.31). Refusing to deny themselves (8.34), they now desert Jesus and flee.

v. 43 - Mark names the three groups that composed the Sanhedrin (cf 8.31; 11.27; 14.53,55).

v. 45 - Custom dictated that social equals kiss each other on the cheek; that a disciple kiss the hand of a rabbi; a servant, his master's hand; a son, his parent's hand (Bailey Eyes 16).

v. 49 - Jesus' words, "Every day I was with you, teaching in the Temple courts," suggest a longer ministry in Jerusalem than the week of the crucifixion.

v. 50 - Although Peter's denial is reported (14.54, 66-72), this is the last appearance of the other ten disciples in Mark's Gospel. However, Jesus promises to regather and give them authority to minister (14.28; 16.7).

14.51-52 - As Jesus is being led away, a young man who followed Jesus flees in panic as he is about to be seized by the soldiers, leaving his garment behind. In this way, Mark (who alone records this incident) emphasizes that Jesus was abandoned by all and calls upon his readers to reexamine the depth of their commitment to "follow Jesus," regardless of the cost.

Most likely, this incident is a modest signature of the author's personal involvement in this historical event. Mark does not supply the details we might desire. However (not unlike Alfred Hitchcock who appears for a few seconds in each film he directed), Mark sketches a small picture of himself in his work. As Wilcock (71) suggests, "commentators find it very hard to account for verses 51,52 if the young man was *not* Mark, risen from bed in his home in Jerusalem, perhaps the very house where the supper had just taken place (14.15; Ac 1.13; 12.12), and throwing a sheet or loose garment around himself to follow Jesus and the eleven. 'I was no more courageous than the rest,' he says, 'but at least I saw it happen.'"

v. 51 - The verb **akoloutheo** probably means "follow as a disciple" (Bratcher and Nida 41).

vs. 51f - Writers present many different proposals for the inclusion of these verses in Mark. Among them are: these verses are inspired by Ge 39.12 or Am 2.16; nakedness symbolizes laying aside clothes (as in the burial of Jesus or the baptism of followers, cf Ro 6.3-5) and rising again with white robes (cf Rev 3.5). Mann (187) claims the Passion account is framed by references to a young man (14.51 and 16.5).

• The text does not clarify whether the young man had been wearing nothing but a fine linen outer garment or whether he was wearing it over his under-garment.

2. On Trial, 14.53 - 15.20a

Jesus is subjected to two interrogations, the first based on religious accusations, the second on political questions. The Jewish authorities reject as blasphemous Jesus' claim of being God's special agent and mock him as a false prophet. After trying Jesus as a political pretender, Pilate condemns Jesus to death and the Romans cruelly deride him as a pathetic king. Taken together, we understand that Jesus was rejected by the principalities and powers of this world working through the religious and the political/military establishments of that day.

Between these two accounts, Mark reports Peter being interrogated about his relationship to Jesus. While Jesus is giving a piercingly clear confession of his identity (14.62), Peter is disavowing his own identity as a follower of Jesus (14.68-71).

Mark records these three "trials" in such a way that each interprets and compliments the other. The first and third form a pair, with parallel features. Both the high priest and Pilate ask Jesus about his identity, both react to his silence and each receives an answer that facilitates his case against Jesus. Each of his judges unintentionally calls attention to who Jesus really is.

Mark challenges the reader to reconcile Jesus' claims to be God's Anointed King with the multiplied indignities he endures. He says almost nothing about Jesus' responses to all the questioning, accusations, shouting and torture. By portraying the defenseless silence of Jesus, however, Mark drives home the point that Jesus suffers deliberately and willingly, fully convinced that God's will is being done. In these trials, Jesus' own words and the ironic declarations of the other participants serve to reveal with greater clarity who he is. The Sanhedrin's and Pilate's interrogations appear to be the human race judging Jesus, the Son of God. In reality, however, *humanity itself is on trial.*

These trials also prepare the readers for understanding the crucifixion and accepting Jesus' death as a ransom offered for them personally (10.45; 14.22-24). Mark's first readers experienced the same kinds of testings Jesus and Peter underwent. With Peter, each believer is confronted with his/her own choice to deny self or to disavow Jesus.

JESUS' CONFESSION BEFORE THE SANHEDRIN, 14.53-65

In the beginning of his report on the Sanhedrin's interrogation of Jesus, Mark informs his readers that Jesus' interrogators seek not the truth but evidence against him. When the false witnesses fail to present a coherent case, the high priest goes directly to the subject of who Jesus is. For the first and only time in Mark's Gospel, Jesus openly proclaims his identity as God's Messiah destined to power and glory. By weaving together several strands of messianic expectation, Jesus provides the Sanhedrin with all the evidence it seeks to judge him as worthy of death.

14.53-54 - The arresting officers take Jesus to the great hall on the second floor of the high priest's palace for a hastily called session of the Sanhedrin, the Jewish Supreme Court. Although he fled when

Jesus was seized (v 50), Peter does not disappear completely. He follows at a distance, enters the courtyard and mingles with those warming themselves by the fire. Nights in Jerusalem can be cold.

Having mentioned Peter's proximity, Mark focuses on the interrogation of Jesus before returning to Peter (vv 66-72). The two scenes occur simultaneously and each sheds light on the other.

v. 53 - Originally an appointment for life, the high priesthood fell under political control. The governor of Syria removed the high priest Annas (Jn 18.13) from office. However, he succeeded in getting five of his sons and his son-in-law, Caiaphas, appointed to the high priesthood and continued to exercise much power. Identified by name in Mt 26.3,57, Caiaphas held office from 18 to 36 A.D., which includes the time of these proceedings. See 11.18 for an additional word on the priesthood.

In 1990, the Caiaphas family tomb was discovered in a Jerusalem necropolis. A magnificently decorated ossuary inscribed with the name "Joseph bar Caiaphas" contained the bones of a 60-year old man, alleged to be the mortal remains of this same high priest who was referred to by Josephus as "Joseph who was called Caiaphas."

v. 54 - How could Mark know what happened in the high priest's palace and in Pilate's presence when no follower of Jesus was present? Probably Jesus told his disciples after the resurrection. Also, the news of Jesus' condemnation spread through Jerusalem like wildfire. "Knowledge of what happened (in the Sanhedrin) can have been given by members of the Sanhedrin (Joseph of Arimathea or Nicodemus) or obtained through discussions between Jews and Christians" (Taylor 565) and through reports of those present in Pilate's court.

14.55-61a - The first witnesses disqualify themselves, for their stories do not agree (cf Dt 17.6; 19.15; Nu 35.30). Others accuse Jesus, saying they had heard him say, "I will destroy this man-made temple and in three days will build another, not made by man." Jewish tradition claimed that the Messiah would both destroy the Temple because of the sins of the people and rebuild it. The leaders want to know if Jesus' teachings about the Temple are a veiled claim to Messiahship (2Sa 7.13; Zec 6.12f).

Mark, however, labels these charges as "false testimony" (14.57-58) because Jesus never said *he* would destroy the Temple in Jerusalem (11.12-21; cf 13.2,14ff) nor did he include any reference to "three days." Each of his three pronouncements about his suffering and death, however, include a prediction of his resurrection in three days (8.31; 9.31; 10.34). While the allegations of the false witnesses and the mockers (15.29) are false, the accusers do speak a truth they do not intend. Suffering and death will destroy Jesus' body, but in three days he will rise again (cf Jn 2.21). The resurrected Jesus is the new temple, offering to all--Jews and Gentiles--access to the Most Holy Place (Heb 10.19; Eph 2.18) through the new covenant (14.24). When the Temple was destroyed, this truth was a source of great comfort to Jewish believers.

Although the High Priest demands an answer to these accusations, Jesus remains silent (cf Isa 53.7).

v. 56 - They probably accused Jesus of lacking regard for the Sabbath (2.18-3.6) and the oral traditions (7.1-5), he ate with sinners (2.15) and disrupted Temple activities (11.15ff).

v. 58 - This is Mark's first use of **naos**, the sanctuary; it is used again in 15.29,38. In contrast, **hieron** refers to the entire Temple complex (cf 11.11). Cf charges at the crucifixion (15.29). When asked about rebuilding the Temple in Jerusalem, some modern Israelis reply, "Messiah will rebuild it."

• "It is not surprising to find true words on the lips of false witnesses" (Best <u>Following</u> 214). Ironically, the leaders readily lay aside the law against false witnesses in their attempt to preserve the Law.

• Jesus is the temple not made by humans (see comments on 15.38). In the Epistles, the metaphor of temple is extended to the church, as the community which exists in Jesus' name and in which God dwells by his Spirit (cf 1Co 3.16; 2Co 6.16; Eph 2.20-22). In Mark's Gospel, the term "church" does not appear. Jesus' "house of prayer for all nations" (11.15-25) is the church, of which he is the cornerstone (12.10-11; 1Pe 2.5-8).

14.61b-62 - The chief priests and scribes still suspect that Jesus regards himself as the Messiah. They are convinced that he lacks some messianic qualifications. Even though he poses a threat to Israel, they have failed to find ostensible grounds for condemning him to death. Consequently, in desperation Caiaphas desists from diplomacy and derisively asks the decisive question: "Are you the Christ, the Son of the Blessed One?"

After maintaining silence during the inquiry, Jesus answers the High Priest's question. In fact, he goes beyond what is asked, stating openly who he is and (looking beyond his death) where he is going. He breaks through the veil of secrecy held throughout his public ministry.

"I am," Jesus replies. With his "I am" (**ego eimi**), however, Jesus is saying much more. He is identifying himself with the revered name that God uses to describe himself in the Old Testament (e.g. Exodus 3.14). By deliberately using this same expression, Jesus solemnly affirms his presence as a theophany, a revelation of the divine presence.

"Son of Man" is Jesus' self-designation for both revealing and hiding his identity. In response to Peter's confession, "You are the Christ," Jesus defined his ministry in terms of the Son of Man (8.31). Now, in answering the high priest's question, "Are you the Christ?" Jesus links his identity as the Christ to the description of the son of man in Daniel 7.13-14. During the time his identity was veiled, Jesus used the title "Son of Man" primarily to indicate his suffering. Now that he has been delivered into human hands (9.31), Jesus uses the title openly to emphasize his triumph as the Messiah.

In his answer, Jesus goes beyond a simple affirmation of his Messiahship as a descendent of David. By combining the messianic descriptions given by the psalmist (110.1) and the prophet (Da 7.13-14), Jesus assigns a deeper meaning to his Messiahship than that seen in the individual texts.

The question about Psalm 110, presented by Jesus in the Temple debates (12.35-37) but left unanswered by the teachers of the law, now reappears, with Jesus himself giving the answer. He clearly identifies himself as the One addressed by the Lord (**YHWH**). He is more than David's son. He is also David's Lord, and by divine determination, he will be exalted above his enemies to judge and rule "at the right hand of the Mighty One." Furthermore, he is the Son of Man to whom (as Daniel 7.13-14 says) God gives authority, glory and sovereign power. All peoples shall worship him in his Kingdom that will not pass away.

Jesus, this humiliated itinerant teacher who stands before members of the highest Jewish authority, unabashedly foretells that one day the present situation will be reversed. Those who judge him now as a pretender to David's earthly throne will see him, David's Lord (12.36), sitting at the right hand of God as their judge. He will come on the clouds of heaven, for God has given him dominion over his eternal Kingdom. Here, for the first time, Jesus openly declares his identity as the true Messiah. He claims for himself the glorious destiny that belongs to the Messiah, David's Lord, the King who will judge and rule with divine sovereignty. By giving this self-revelation at this time, Jesus guarantees his crucifixion. He voluntarily gives his life as a ransom for many (10.45).

v. 61b - The high priest's question "Are you the Christ?" concerns who Jesus really is. He avoids a direct reference to God by saying "the Son of the Blessed One." Here, as in 8.29 and15.2, Jesus accepts the appellations given, but with reservations.
• Recent research reveals that the expression "Son of God" was understood to be a messianic title in pre-Christian Judaism.
• From the beginning of Mark's Gospel, Jesus is consistently (though reservedly) identified as Messiah. His role as David's royal heir is suggested (10.44f; 11.10; 12.35ff) but left in suspension. At that time, both titles were so wedded to nationalistic concepts that he had to change their connotations in order to communicate his message. Mark's readers need a clear understanding of Messiah and his mission in order for the church to fulfill its mission in the world.

v. 62 - If Jesus had not replied, it would have been construed as a confession of guilt (cf Lev 5.1; 1Ki 22.16). Mark records only three times in which Jesus speaks after being taken prisoner (14.62; 15.2, 34).
• Jewish scholar Sarna (Exodus 42f) points out that "I am" was characteristic of God's self-manifestations in the Old Testament. The Sanhedrin understands that "I am" is theophanic, for (as Williamson points out, 265) "a messianic claim would not in and of itself have been considered blasphemous." **he dunamis** ("the Almighty" or "the Mighty One") is another reverential synonym for God; see "I am" in 6.50.
• Beyond Jesus' three major pronouncements about the suffering, death and resurrection of the Son of Man (8.31; 9.31; 10.33f), he also makes three awesome affirmations about the glorious manifestation of the Son of Man (8.38; 13.26; here). All three draw heavily on Daniel 7.13-14 and include the terms "Son of Man," "come," "power," and "see" (**horao**, Mark's distinctive term for eschatological insight; cf Daniel's "I saw one like a son of man"). While this is the language of visions, the prophecies refer to an objective and definitive unveiling of what God has kept concealed. Here, as in 13.25, Jesus refers to the parousia. Both his prophecies of death and of exaltation are essential to an understanding of the gospel.

"You will see" does not mean the parousia would take place in the lifetime of his hearers but rather that Jesus will someday judge those judging him.

• By determining the time and place of confessing openly his identity, Jesus, not the authorities, determines his death. He "controls when his opponents will win the indictment, as well as the specific charge they level against him. Only the claim of who he is, which they judge to be blasphemy, provides the grounds for his conviction" (Rhoads and Michie 88).

14.63-65 - The high priest immediately understands that Jesus claims to be the divine "Son of the Blessed One." He tears his clothes in a show of indignation (cf 2Ki 18.37; 19.1,4) and denounces as blasphemy Jesus' virtual identification with God.

By itself, a claim to be the Messiah would not have been considered blasphemous. Jesus, however, declares before the Sanhedrin that he is not a human messiah but the Lord (12.37), the sovereign Ruler and Judge of Israel, God's beloved Son. He claims the divine prerogatives of the "I am." No more witnesses are necessary: Jesus has volunteered information that, in the eyes of the Sanhedrin, justifies putting him to death.

Although Rome forbids the Sanhedrin from exercising the death penalty, its members can take out their anger against Jesus. Some spit on him; others hit him. Some mock him in a game of "blind man's bluff," demanding that he prophesy. The guards beat him. Ironically, their actions only confirm Jesus' prophetic role and messiahship by fulfilling his previous predictions (8.31; 10.33-34).

v. 64 - Previously, the scribes had rejected as blasphemous Jesus' claim to forgive sin, but they held those thoughts to themselves (2.6-10). Now in consensus with the chief priests and elders, they reject Jesus' claim as outrageous blasphemy and openly condemn him as worthy of death. In reality, they are the blasphemers, for they commit transgression against God by rejecting his Anointed (cf 3.28-29).

• Both the Jewish and Roman legal systems were exceptionally just, but officials throughout history have placed themselves above the laws they are sworn to uphold. Mark makes it clear that neither the Sanhedrin nor Pilate were primarily concerned about proper legal procedures. The religious leaders were not seeking to ascertain the truth; rather, they were "looking for evidence against Jesus so that they could put him to death" (14.55; cf 3.6; 11.18; 12.12; 14.1). Pilate no doubt followed Roman legal procedures as far as feasible; as pressures multiplied, however, he abandoned any desire for justice and chose political expediency. The staccato rhythm of Mark's narrative accurately reflects a court scene marked by turmoil.

In bearing testimony to the gospel, many Christians experience similar injustices, from arrest under the cover of darkness to condemnation resulting from trumped up charges and from ambitious judges interested in their own political well-being. Jesus models how believers should act under trial.

PETER'S DENIAL, 14.66-72

Mark narrates three trials. The two in which Jewish and Roman authorities interrogate Jesus bracket the one in which commoners question Peter. Jesus patiently submits to two harsh trials before hostile judges. He courageously reveals his identity. Peter, on the other hand, is tested under gentle pressure by curious bystanders and denies his identity as one who follows Jesus. When he recalls Jesus' words, he breaks down and weeps.

14.66-71 - While Jesus is suffering physical and psychological abuse, not far away, in the courtyard of the palace, Peter is warming himself at the fire. A maid who works for the high priest scornfully accuses him, "You also were with that Nazarene, Jesus." "I don't know or understand what you're talking about," Peter retorts. Previously, Mark states that the disciples' did not "know" or "understand" Jesus (4.12-13; 6.52; 8.17f; 9.6,32). Now the reader realizes that, ironically, Peter (like the other false witnesses) doesn't really know Jesus.

Peter moves out into the entryway. No, the fire is not too hot. He had distanced himself from Jesus (v 54); now he tries unsuccessfully to get out of range of further accusations. The same girl says to those standing around, "This fellow is one of them." In denying this, Peter's Galilean accent (cf Mt 26.73) may have led bystanders to voice their conclusion: "Surely you are one of them, for you are a Galilean." As the charges become more specific, "Peter's apostasy flares up like a smoldering fire bursting into flame" (Senior 102). He begins to curse and swear, invoking God to punish falsehood and to bear witness for the truth. He swears he does not know Jesus. Simultaneously, in the courtyard and in the great hall, Jesus' prophecies are being fulfilled (14.30).

14.72 - Rather than deny himself (8.34f), Peter disowns Jesus. He had been ashamed of Jesus' words (8.32f); now he is ashamed of Jesus himself (cf 8.38). Upon hearing the rooster crow, Peter remembers Jesus' words spoken in response to his boast (14.30). He breaks down and weeps. This is the beginning of his repentance.

Peter had imagined himself prepared to die with Jesus (14.31), but he failed in a small trial, as we often do. Peter never spoke a word against Jesus. Nevertheless, he denied him in three ways: he pled ignorance, he denied being a part of the Christian community, and he finally denied any relationship to Jesus. Peter is still thinking like humans (8.33; see also Lk 22.31). However, by not persisting in his error, he gives proof of being a disciple.

Unlike Judas, Peter and the other disciples do not try to destroy Jesus in order to save themselves. "They are not against Jesus. They fail at being for him," as Rhoads and Michie (128) point out. Peter does not reappear in Mark, but he does not drop out of the picture. He is restored to fellowship and ministry (implied in 16.7 and stated in John 21.15-17). Peter' experience illustrates the heart of the gospel: God gave Jesus up for us, but he does not give up on us. When his children fall, he lifts them up to follow in the way. For several decades, Peter obediently fulfills Jesus' words, "when you have turned back, strengthen your brothers" (Lk 22.32).

We see ourselves in this story of a disciple who has failed to prepare for the trials that befall believers. We also learn that leadership in the church is the result of God's grace, rather than personal merit (cf 2Co 4.7). Jesus builds the church with such unlikely material as Peter.

v. 71 - The verb "curse" is left without a direct object. Some writers suggest "May I be accursed if I'm lying" or "Curse you for accusing me." Others claim Peter cursed Jesus to escape persecution (similar to Christians who escaped death by cursing him). It may be an intended ambiguity. There is, however, no suggestion of vulgarity or profanity in the expression.

v. 72 - Some say the phrase "rooster crow" does not indicate the shrill cry of a fowl, but refers instead to the Roman bugle call denoting the end of the third (midnight to 3 a.m.) of four night watches (13.35). The bugle call would be heard throughout the city. However, given 14.30, 72, the words are probably to be taken literally as a cock crowing.

• The restoration of those who fail under pressure is painful, especially when the "faithful" make reconciliation difficult for those who have "collaborated" with the enemy. Such conflicts would particularly disrupt fellowship in the small "house churches" of Mark's early readers.

JESUS' CONDEMNATION BY THE ROMAN AUTHORITY, 15.1-20a

In his role as an official of the Roman Empire, Pilate investigates the Sanhedrin's charge that Jesus is a revolutionary. Although he finds Jesus innocent of any crime, Pilate succumbs to pressure and hands Jesus over to be crucified. As the title of "king" is applied to Jesus for the first time and repeated in mockery, the reader is confronted with the paradox of God's Anointed, destined to heavenly power and glory, being subject to mockery and devastating torture at the hands of sinners (9.31; 10.33-34).

This trial complements the interrogation by the Sanhedrin, adding the condemnation by political authorities to that of the religious establishment. The popular demand for Barabbas' release leads to Jesus' crucifixion, in dramatic demonstration of the Son of Man's giving his life in ransom for others.

15.1 - As soon as it is morning, the whole Sanhedrin holds a consultation to plan their strategy. In their interrogation of Jesus (14.55-64), they concluded that he was worthy of death for he had committed blasphemy. Under the jurisdiction of Roman rule, however, they could not condemn him to death or execute him. The actual sentence could only come from Roman authorities. Since Pilate would consider the charge of blasphemy to be insignificant, the Sanhedrin must charge Jesus with an offense that will ensure his death.

They reach their decision: Jesus will be accused of leading a covert civil rebellion against Rome. Confident that this charge will get Pilate's immediate attention, they bind Jesus and hand him over to the Gentiles (as Jesus foretold, 10.32).

v. 1 - Pontius Pilate is introduced without any description for he was well known to Mark's first readers, having been the Roman prefect of Judea from 26-36 A.D. His official residence was in the coastal city of Caesarea, a marvelous example of Herod the Great's urban planning. He was in Jerusalem to keep order during the Passover.

Though known as inflexible, merciless and obstinate, Pilate was also an astute politician. He was loyal to Rome and had not forgotten how the Jewish leaders humiliated him in protesting his use of the Temple treasury to finance aqueducts for Jerusalem. Above all else, he sought to save his own skin. Although his decision was made under great pressure, he (like everyone else) was responsible for his acts. Also, before Roman law, he bore the sole responsibility of judgment in a Roman tribunal.

• Opinions are divided as where the trial took place. Uncertainty about the historic sights results in part from the early church's emphasis upon worshipping a risen Savior (cf 11.17; Jn 4.23). Efforts to identify historical places came later.

• See note on 3.6 as to conspiracies between religious leaders and secular authorities.

15.2-5 - Mark limits his report on Jesus' trial by the Roman magistrate to essential details. Pilate knows that he must crush any seditious activity in Jerusalem. At the same time, he wonders why the Jewish religious leaders would cooperate with him. Determined to waste neither time nor words, he asks the accused, "Are you the king of the Jews?" He probably directs his scorn at the chief priests as well.

Jesus' answer, "You said it" (or "that statement is yours") seems evasive. The problem is, what kind of king does Pilate envision? If Jesus gave a straight affirmative answer (as he gave the high priest, 14.62), Pilate would assume that Jesus had political pretensions and posed a threat to Roman law. On the other hand, he could not say straightforwardly "No, I am not," for he was anointed by God to be head of the Kingdom (1.11; 12.35-37). This was not the occasion to explain his non-militaristic, apolitical messiahship.

The title "King" now begins to stand out, having been used initially by Gentiles (15.2-26) and later, scornfully, by Jewish leaders (15.32). To avoid wrong or inadequate connotations, Jesus does not use this title.

Fearing that Jesus might escape their trap, the chief priests pile up accusations against him (e.g., "he opposes payment of taxes to Caesar," Lk 23.2) in an effort to bolster their denunciation. Jesus, however, says nothing. Pilate then challenges Jesus to defend himself, for he knows that some of the charges are trumped-up. "But Jesus still makes no reply" (v 5; cf 14.61a; Isa 53.7).

Pilate is amazed. He has witnessed many struggles for power, many life-and-death trials. However, he has never seen anyone like Jesus; the accused is in full command of the whole procedure. As Peter wrote later, "When they hurled their insults at him, he did not retaliate; when he suffered, he made no threats. Instead, he entrusted himself to him who judges justly" (1Pe 2.21-23. cf 1Ti 6.13-14). The way Jesus faced suffering is an example for all those persecuted because of him (13.9-13).

v. 2 - "King" becomes a predominant term in chapter 15. Although explicit attribution of kingship to Jesus is absent, it is implicit all through the gospel of the Kingdom. Jesus is anointed by God (1.11) for David's Son (12.36) will become Lord over God's Kingdom. Like David, Jesus is enthroned years after his anointing. Pilate and the taunters are ironically speaking the truth: Jesus is the King.

"King of the Jews" is changed by the religious leaders to "King of Israel" (v 32). The former designated nationality; the latter refers to the Jews in the sense of God's chosen people.

15.6-11 - During the Passover festivities it was customary to grant amnesty to a prisoner chosen by the people. This may have been a concession on the part of the Roman administration of Judea because the Passover was a celebration of liberation.

Barabbas is in prison with other insurrectionists who had committed murder in one of the frequent revolts against foreign rule (e.g., Lk 13.1). A crowd stages a mass demonstration in favor of his release. As they are about to make their request, Pilate cuts them off with a contemptuous question, "Do you want me to release the king of the Jews?" Pilate perceives the malicious intent (envy) of the clergy. He knows that their accusations against Jesus are meant to protect the religious establishment, not Caesar's throne. To release Jesus under these circumstances would be good for him politically. On the other hand, he has no desire to liberate the rebel Barabbas.

The chief priests, however, are not about to be out-flanked. They know the crowd hates Roman imperialism and is predisposed to reject anything Pilate might favor. The people are disappointed in the passive Jesus; Barabbas, on the other hand, is a hero, for he fought back against the oppressor. The priests probably spread word of the Sanhedrin's decision regarding Jesus. They successfully stir up the crowd to demand Barabbas' release.

v. 6 - Local Roman governors often granted amnesty according to their own discretion.
v. 8 - This crowd likely came as partisans of Barabbas interested in his release and indifferent to Jesus' fate. Those who welcomed Jesus' entry into Jerusalem (11.8) may have been Galilean pilgrims. If some of the large crowd that listened to Jesus with delight (12.37) were present now, they may have changed their attitude after hearing of the Sanhedrin's accusation against Jesus. A few vocal priests in the midst could "stir up" (v 11) swift changes in the crowd's attitude.

15.12-15 - Torn between the demands of angry demonstrators and a clerical power block on one hand, and his loyalty to Rome and personal sense of justice on the other, Pilate is deeply frustrated. With disdain, he asks the crowd what they want him to do with Jesus. They shout back, "Crucify him!"

Seeking to awaken their lost sense of justice, Pilate protests: "Why? What harm has he done?" This is the third time Pilate indicates a willingness to release Jesus (15.9, 12, 14).

The crowd's frenzied shouting, "Crucify him!" drowns out all reason. The astute politician fears what could happen if he refuses their clamor. Justice gives way to expediency, revealing his lack of firm moral values. Drawing upon Roman experience in placating restive mobs, Pilate sets Barabbas free and condemns Jesus to death. Ironically, Pilate's decision portrays the gospel message: sinners are set free because the Sinless One gives his life as a substitutionary ransom for others (10.45).

After Pilate gives the order for Jesus to be flogged, he hands Jesus over (**paradidomai**) to be crucified. Unknowingly, he fulfills Jesus' prediction ("the Gentiles will flog him," 10.33-34) and Isaiah's prophecy (God delivered up his Servant for our sins, 53.4-6). After the resurrection, the disciples finally understand that Jesus' death was according to "God's set purpose and foreknowledge" (Ac 2.23).

v. 13 - Only Romans used crucifixion, and only for three classes of non-Roman offenders: slaves who had committed serious offenses against life and property, habitual criminals, and conspirators against Roman rule. Jesus was crucified as an enemy of the State, sentenced by Romans who reserved for themselves the right of execution. According to Dt 21.23, "anyone who is hung on a tree is under God's curse." Capital punishment under Jewish law was by stoning. The crowd took the law into their own hands when they stoned Stephen (Ac 7.58).
v. 15 - Flogging (scourging) was never inflicted on Roman citizens. Those who were condemned to death were often bound to a pillar, beaten with leather whips laced with bone or metal until the victim's flesh and entrails were laid bare. Some died under the whips, for no limit was placed on the number of blows administered by several guards experienced in the art of cruelty.

15.16-20a - Rather then take Jesus directly to the place where he will be crucified, soldiers under Pilate enact a parody in honor of this pathetic self-styled king from Galilee. Like a palatial guard, they escort the king into the palace where, in the presence of the whole detachment, he receives the "honors" due such a dignitary. They dress him up as befitting majesty: a purple robe for royalty, and a crown (of thorns) as a sign of his claim to divinity.

With feigned respect, they salute him: "Hail, king of the Jews!" They heap indignities upon Jesus. Repeatedly, soldiers lampoon the idea of royal authority by flailing the king on the head with his "royal staff" (a reed). Instead of the kiss of homage, they spit on him. On bent knees they worship him, mocking him as a pretender to Caesar's throne. Jesus of Nazareth, who had demonstrated his power over sickness and storm, is now subject to all that sinners want to do to him.

When they had finished their sarcastic "king for a day" skit, "they took off the purple robe and put his own clothes on him." They led him out of the palace and took him to the cross.

In spite of their mockery, the soldiers were declaring the truth, for in fact, that humiliated person is the true "King of Israel." They were unknowingly fulfilling Old Testament prophecies (e.g., Is 50.6; 53.3,5; Ps 22.6) and Jesus' own predictions about his suffering and death (8.31; 9.31; 10.33f).

Following the Sanhedrin's conclusion that Jesus was worthy of death, he was beaten, spat upon and ridiculed (14.65). Following Pilate's decision, Jesus was subjected to more brutality by the Romans: he was ruthlessly flogged (v 15) and then maliciously humiliated by a detachment of soldiers bent on mercilessly taunting their already bruised and bloody prisoner. As Hurtado declares (249), "The Roman practice of crucifixion involved more than simply hanging a person upon a cross to die; it involved the complete degradation of a person and unrestrained torture, so as to make the punishment the most feared of all in the ancient world."

Remembering Jesus' suffering brings solace to those who endure travesties of justice, brutalization and death as a result of following Jesus, just as he promised (13.9-13).

v. 16 - The whole detachment is probably an auxiliary company of between 200 and 600 non-Jewish troops from Palestine which accompanied Pilate from Caesarea to Jerusalem to maintain order.

v. 17 Jesus was stripped for the flogging; in the palace, he was wrapped in a purple robe. Now they put his own clothes back on him. Normally the condemned man was led naked to the place of execution and scourged on the way. Jesus, however, was not flogged again (since he had already been scourged, most likely he would have died by flagellation, contrary to his prediction of death by crucifixion). Prior to his crucifixion, he was stripped again and his clothes divided among the executioners (v 24).

• These scenes also offer insights into human nature and the nature of authority. The propensity towards violent solutions did not end with the first century. Humanity's revolt against God is evident in domestic violence as well as in police and military brutality. Human authority is coercive (cf 10.44-45), whereas, as Williamson (274) says, "Jesus exercises power though weakness and authority through love."

v. 19 - In the NT, "on their knees" is often associated with prayer (Lk 22.41; Ac 7.60; 9.40; 10.36; 21.5).

3. Jesus is Crucified and Buried, 15.20b-47

Mark describes the rejection of Jesus with stark simplicity, calling upon the reader to understand this event in the light of antecedent themes and through his numerous quotations and allusions to the Old Testament. While mercilessly mocking Jesus, even his enemies ironically reveal the significance of the crucifixion.

The details harmonize with what is known of the extreme cruelty of crucifixion procedures and confront the reader with the reality of the brutal humiliation of Jesus and his apparent helplessness.

Years after God anointed his Son (1.10-11), Jesus is finally hailed--in mockery--as king. Royal honors are bestowed on him. His throne is a cross and those whom he would govern kill him. The results of his reign begin to appear immediately, however, as the way into the presence of God is opened to those previously excluded.

THE CRUCIFIXION OF JESUS, 15.20b-32

An execution squad of four soldiers (Jn 19.23) leads Jesus out to crucify him. Normally, the condemned man carried the horizontal beam of the cross. Because of intense activity during that week, followed by a night of interrogations, ridicule and brutal flogging, Jesus is physically unable to carry the beam. He is truly man, suffering from rejection and weakened by torture.

15.20b-24 - In the absence of disciples or any volunteer to assist Jesus, the soldiers coerce a bystander, Simon from Cyrene, to carry the cross. Upon arriving at Golgotha, the soldiers offer Jesus wine mixed with myrrh, known for its effect of dulling the excruciating pain of crucifixion (cf Ps 69.21; Pr 31.6). Jesus does not take it, however, for in his dedication to God's will, he will consciously and deliberately drink another cup (14.36).

Since the executioners are entitled to the victim's clothes, they determine by a game of chance with dice what portion each will get of Jesus' last remaining possession (cf 2Co 8.9). Mark reminds us again of the fulfillment of Scripture by quoting Psalm 22.18 ("they divide my garments among them and cast lots for my clothing"). The soldiers are indifferent to Jesus' suffering, interested only in personal gain and hedonistic pleasure.

Moreover, Mark introduces this Psalm because of its portrayal of the suffering of a righteous man. He will make further allusions to it (in verses 29 and 34), for Psalm 22 vividly confronts the reader with the crucifixion.

Mark's readers were well acquainted with execution by crucifixion, for tens of thousands of people had been crucified by the Roman Empire. Based upon ancient literary sources and the remains of a Jewish victim found in Jerusalem in 1968, the usual procedure has been well documented. After being stripped and flogged (cf 15.15), the criminal was tied or nailed to the cross beam which was then lifted up and fastened to the vertical beam. His feet were then nailed to the upright stake. A small seat of wood was fastened to the upright of the cross, preventing the contorted body from complete collapse while also prolonging the victim's agony. Death came from suffocation, exhaustion or bleeding to death.

Such was the intense physical agony and deep humiliation that Jesus experienced. Mark does not dwell on these aspects of Jesus' death, however; with utmost constraint, he says, "they crucified him" (v 24). His emphasis falls upon the significance of Jesus' death.

v. 21 - Simon, from the North African district of Cyrenaica, may have come to Jerusalem for the feast. His sons, Alexander and Rufus, are probably named because they were known by Mark's first readers and could vouch for the story (cf Rufus in Ro 16.13). Perhaps this experience led to their conversion. Simon's carrying the cross reminds us of the cost of discipleship (8.34). The failure of the disciples, however, has reached its nadir (14.27).

v. 22 - Golgotha is a transliteration of the Aramaic word for skull (the Latin for which is Calvary). Based on their skull-like appearance and proximity to a tomb, General Charles Gordon proposed as the historical site of the crucifixion the caves outside the present northern wall of Jerusalem. "Gordon's Calvary" and the nearby "Garden Tomb," however, are not supported by historical and archaeological evidence. The more probable site is near the Church of the Holy Sepulcher. A later wall enclosed this location within the city. Both Jewish and Roman law required executions to be held outside the city (cf Lev 24.14; Ac 7.58).

15.25-32 - Mark's account of the first period of three hours (from 9 a.m. till noon) emphasizes the scandal of the cross. Following his terse understatement of the act of crucifixion, Mark presents a scene of uninterrupted mockery in which each class of accusers viciously upbraids Jesus in terms of a major issue of the Gospel itself. Although designed to ridicule Jesus as a hypocrite and a complete failure, each charge testifies indirectly to Jesus' claims (as in 14.58, 15.2, etc.).

According to custom, a tablet informed the public as to the crime for which the person was being executed and served as a warning for anyone who might be thinking about defying Rome. The inscription, "the King of the Jews," officially charges Jesus with sedition; he is ostensibly executed for claiming to be a kingly pretender in defiance of Rome. Also Pilate insults the Jews, implying that the pathetically helpless Jesus was the kind of king they deserved. In the deepest sense, however, this is the authentic title, occupying the most appropriate place, for the gospel of the Kingdom is centered in the cross.

Abandoned by his chosen aides, the king is given two robbers for his royal court, one on his right and one on his left. Contrary to all protocol, these attendants heap insults on him, even though they, too, are dying.

The proclamation of a king calls for a celebration. Those who pass by, however, hurl insults at Jesus. They "shake their heads" in derision, mocking the one who supposedly set himself up as God's choice for rebuilding the temple (14.57ff). If he were so righteous and powerful, he would save himself from death by coming down from the cross. They assume that Jesus is principally concerned with saving his own life (although he never performed a miracle to benefit himself, only others). These accusations imply that Jesus deceived himself as well as others. In Hurtado's words (255), "Their mockery "reveals their distorted notion about what truly constitutes the work of God's servant, the Messiah, and points to the very heart of what Jesus' work is."

The chief priests and scribes joke with one another at the sight of that ignominious figure on the cross, reveling in his disgrace. While mocking his powerlessness to save himself, they inadvertently admit that he has saved others. These taunters also unwittingly speak elements of truth.

With cruel sarcasm, they scoff at the claims Jesus made before the Sanhedrin (14.61-62) and before Pilate (15.2): "Let this Christ, this King of Israel, come down now from the cross, that we may see and believe." Drunk with their own sense of power, they manifest their inability to conceive of a Servant-King. Jesus, that man of action who saved others, now submits in weakness and silence to all that people would do to him. He undergoes torture, humiliation and mockery, knowing that he is dying in obedience to God, his Father who loves him (1.11; 9.7; 12.6).

They unknowingly state the very truth of the crucifixion: Jesus gives himself as a ransom for others (10.45). In order to save others he must not and cannot save himself. The soldiers mocked Jesus out of ignorance (vv 15-20), but the chief priests act out of unbelief. They demand proof before faith. Such evidence cannot be forthcoming (cf 8.11-12): the external evidence they demand would have made true faith impossible. They are rejecting the only true sign, the cross. They only see the crucifixion as a scandal; by the power and wisdom of God, however, the cross is a revelation of who Jesus really is (1Co 1.22-24).

Who is Jesus? The high priest once asked if he were the Christ (14.61). Pilate focused on "the king of the Jews" in his interrogation (15.2). These great themes--messiahship and kingship--now come together (v 32). Unwittingly, what they ascribe to him in derision is the truth.

Moreover, the chief priests and scribes do not say "king of the Jews," but "King of Israel" (15.32), a designation for **YHWH** (Zep 3.15; Isa 44.6) that is never used for human royalty. Jesus' deity underlies this contention. This means their mockery is actually blasphemy, for Jesus is the Son of God. The Pharisees thought Jesus was blaspheming (2.7), and the high priest denounced him for blasphemy (14.64). In reality, those who hurled insults at Jesus (v 29) and the religious leaders at the cross (v 31f) are committing blasphemy. The very accusation made against Jesus has come full circle (cf 3.28f).

v. 25 - Minear (129) writes that "Mark's account of this event is somber and glorious. Perhaps we should read it in the way we listen to great music, like the *Passions* of Bach. We should listen not to the separate words but to the recurring cadences and rhythms. We should sense the contrapuntal movement which weaves together the strident shrieks of the mob and the quiet deep voice of God."

• Mark divides the crucifixion scene into three periods of three hours each (vv 25,33,34), adopting the Jewish method of calculating time (in contrast to his previous use of the Roman method, e.g., 13.35).

Mark states that "it was the third hour (i.e., 9 a.m.) when they crucified Jesus," while John 19.14 says that Pilate began his judgment of Jesus "about the sixth hour" (i.e., noon, by the same mode). While Romans, Greeks and Jews counted their hours from sunrise, the Romans reckoned their civil days from midnight. John stated the time according to the practice of his first readers. Thus Mark and John are in agreement: the Sanhedrin reached its decision "very early in the morning" (Mk 15.1), took Jesus to Pilate who began judgment "about 6 a.m." (stated by John on "local time") and the crucifixion at 9 a.m.

v. 26 - The inscription declares Caesar's claims to authority over Jesus who commanded that we give ourselves wholly to God (12.17, 30). Jesus gave himself to Caesar in order that we who are dominated by Caesar might be free to give ourselves wholly to God. Through his death, the King of the Jews becomes the King of kings (Rev 11.15; 19.16).

v. 27 - The verbal similarity of 10.40 and 15.27 reminds us that the robbers occupy the places of honor requested by James and John. Jesus promised those disciples a share in his sufferings (10.39). As Isaiah 53.12 foretold, the servant of God is rejected and numbered with the transgressors.

• The term Mark uses could mean either robbers or insurrectionists.

v. 28 - Some versions include "and the scripture was fulfilled which says, 'He was counted with the lawless ones'" as verse 28. Since the better attested manuscripts do not include this reference to Isa 53.12, it is omitted in modern versions of Mark. It is, however, quoted in Luke 22.37.

v. 29 - Mark affirms that Jesus is the Just One of Israel by drawing these words from Psalm 22.7; see below on 15.34.

v. 31 - The verb **sozein** describes Jesus' purpose to "save life" (cf 3.4), recalling those liberated by his power (cf 5.23,28; 6.56; 10.52).

v. 32 - In his suffering and death, Jesus exemplifies all he taught about total faith in and obedience to God, about denying self and suffering as the least of all. He gave his life, refusing to save himself, and thereby saved many. He fulfilled the two greatest commandments: he loved God with his whole being and he loved us more than himself.

THE DEATH OF JESUS, 15.33-41

15.33-36 - At twelve o'clock darkness covered the whole land and lasted until the moment of Jesus' death at three o'clock in the afternoon. The precise statement seems to vouch for a literal darkness (although its nature is undefined). As portrayed in Scripture, darkness frequently has cosmic and eschatological significance (cf Jn 1.5; 8.12). Mark's words recall the plague of darkness in Egypt (Ex 10.21-22) as God judged Pharaoh prior to his deliverance of Israel.

The dialectic of God's judgment is held in tension with his impending deliverance. By submitting to the powers he came to expel, Jesus shows his greater strength. In dying for humanity, he defeats the world rulers of darkness and rescues women and men from their dominion (Eph 6.12; Col 1.13). The darkness announces that God's implacable, definitive justice is at hand.

The darkness is expressed first visibly, then audibly, as Jesus cries out in a loud voice, "My God, my God, why have you forsaken me?" This is the only saying from the cross recorded by Mark, and from earliest times interpretations have varied. Certainly the cry of desolation is quoted with the intention of providing more than just psychological insights into Jesus' subjective experience. Admittedly, the full sense of these words is beyond human comprehension. Who can fathom the depths of the intimate relationship between the Father and his much loved only Son? Jesus' quotation from Psalm 22 must be understood as the inevitable effect of the horror he experienced in Gethsemane. The prayer on Jesus' dying lips wails out from the agony of the cross as he sacrifices his life for others, including those who crucify him.

Psalm 22 is the prayer of a righteous man who, suffering from attacks by his enemies, laments the sense of being forsaken by God. His primary concern, however, is not to chastise God for his failure to provide deliverance, but rather to plead for God's presence in the midst of his suffering. He cries out, "Why?" as he wrestles with "the bitterest blow known to the religious man--the sense of having been let down by God" (Hooker 102). Yet he recognizes that God (v 15c) on whom he has always depended has placed him in this mortal predicament (cf. Job 13.15).

It is not surprising that Jesus prayed this classic prayer of the tormented Israelite, for he lived in and according to the Scriptures. As in Gethsemane, he again finds in the Psalms of lament an expression of his own struggle (cf 14.34).

Jesus is experiencing the desolation described by that lonely sufferer (Ps 22.1-21). By quoting Ps 22.1, Jesus reveals that he is the embodiment of the Righteous One facing death. In his baptism, Jesus identified himself with sinful humanity and was commended by his Father (1.9-11). Later, Jesus affirmed that his identification with sinners would be complete: he would die, suffering the consequences of sin (8.31). Once again his Father voiced his approval (9.7). From the time of his betrayal, Jesus has been suffering intensely in the hands of sinners (10.33; 14.41), yet God has not spoken. On the threshold of death, Jesus cries out--but God does not answer. In utter aloneness, Jesus feels the full brunt of evil. God's silence constitutes the ultimate depth of Jesus' suffering.

The "why?" of God's abandonment is left without an explicit answer here. On the other hand, throughout the gospel, even in its appeals to the Old Testament, we have been given bases for understanding why God temporarily turned aside from his Son. In giving his life as a ransom for sinners (10.45), Jesus drinks the cup of God's wrath (10.38f; 14.23f; cf Gal 3.13). As God's righteous servant, the sin-bearer (Isa 53.11-12), the sinless one is made to be sin (2Co 5.21; cf 1Pe 2.24) and is therefore cut off from God (Isa 59.2; cf Dt 21.23; Hab 1.13). Jesus stands outside the mercy of God because he bears the judgment of God. The darkness of Satan's domain surrounds the sinless One who bears the sins of humanity. As he penetrates into human lostness, he experiences, alone, the full horror of human sin and the vicious, all-out attacks of the evil one. The abandonment by his Father is not merely felt; it is real.

On the cross Jesus experiences the horror that he dreaded at Gethsemane. He cries out in anguish, for he is truly human. In all this horror of desolation, he has lost everything but his faith in God. His cry is not an accusation against God; it is an expression of faith in which he clings to his Father and still knows him as "my God, my God." He continues faithful to the commitment he made in Gethsemane:

"Not what I will, but what you will." His cry of dereliction both plumbs the depths of human doubts and scales the height of faith.

Some of those standing around hear Jesus' cry and think he is calling Elijah. Elijah was expected to appear in the last days, as forerunner of the Messiah (Mal 4.5; Mk 9.11-13). According to popular beliefs, Elijah befriended the helpless, protected the innocent and rescued the righteous. Someone hurriedly offers Jesus some cheap wine to drink, possibly thinking it will prolong his life long enough for Elijah to save him from the cross. If Elijah doesn't help him, they will have further proof that Jesus' claim to be the Messiah is false.

What a pathetic sight! Jesus hangs there on the cross, a criminal before Roman law, cursed by God in the eyes of the Jews. He has been stripped of everything. Nothing is left to him--not his body, not his modesty, not the least consideration of any kind--only death.

v. 33 - A solar eclipse is impossible at Passover time, for the moon is full. Some suggest that the "sun failed to give its light" (the meaning of Luke 23.45) because a sandstorm from the desert (sirocco) blocked out its light in that region.
• The prophets (Am 5.18; Isa 13.9ff; Jer 15.6-9) foretold that the Day of the Lord would be darkness, not light, as people wait in the shadow of death for their redemption (Isa 9.2; Mt 4.16). Darkness is also evident in prophecies of the end times (13.24-27; Rev 6.12-17). Jesus said to his enemies, "This is your hour, and the power of darkness" (Lk 22.53), darkness being a symbol of the power of Satan (Acts 26.18; Eph 6.12). At Calvary, the ruler of darkness marshals his maximum strength for a decisive battle.
v. 34 - Some understand that Jesus' cry was an intense expression in bitter anguish, that he only felt forsaken but did not experience utter abandonment by his Father. Quoting Martin (Mark 120), this interpretation is to be refused as "a minimizing exegesis." We take this cry of abandonment as utterly real. Paradoxically, however, the unity of the trinity is not broken. The Son is at this moment cut off from the Father in the sense that Isa 59.2 is fulfilled in 2Co 5.21 and Dt 21.23 is fulfilled in Gal 3.13.

As Jesus drank the cup of God's judgment, he stood outside the mercy of God. He bore our separation from God, in order than we might be united with him. Although believers may feel forsaken at times, they are never abandoned (Heb 13.5).
• Jesus uses **Abba** ("Father") in all his prayers except here, where he quotes Ps 22.1: "My God, my God." Mark translates this verse to benefit his non-Jewish readers. Jesus' prayer in Gethsemane (14.32-36) and his cry from Golgotha are so interrelated that neither can be understood alone.
• See also comments on "a loud cry" below (15.37).

15.37-39 - Death often stalked the crucified for days before claiming its victim. This is not a typical death by crucifixion, however. "With a loud cry"--not a faint gasp from a exhausted, dying man, but a loud cry--Jesus breaths his last. Any thought of defeat is drowned out by the surprising strength of Jesus' cry. The darkness ends at the moment Jesus dies. By his death he has broken the power of darkness (cf v 33).

By reciting the beginning of Psalm 22, Jesus makes the whole Psalm his prayer. In it, the suffering one's prayer for help is heard and his lament becomes (vv 22-31) a magnificent hymn of confidence, hope and thanksgiving in the congregation. Families from the ends of the earth join in worshipping the Sovereign Lord. The Psalm concludes with "He has done it." On the cross, Jesus claims for himself this triumph of the defeated. His loud cry is most likely the victorious "It is finished" of John 19.30, the equivalent of "He has done it."

The theme of the kingship of Jesus acquires prominence when Pilate refers to Jesus as king (15.2). In mockery, others hail Jesus as king, speaking and enacting the truth in ignorance, infamy and unbelief (v. 32). For them, the crucifixion belies his royalty. Far from contradicting his message of the Kingdom, however, Jesus' crucifixion is paradoxically the moment of his coronation. His Kingdom is as different from earthly realms as his crown of thorns contrasts to the Caesars' pomp and ceremony.

Likewise, the cross appears to say, "Jesus is *not* the Messiah." However, Jesus repeatedly declared that his suffering and death were indispensable requisites for messiahship. The cross now confirms the confession, "You are the Christ" (8.29,31). The full identity of Jesus--implicit in God's words to Jesus at his baptism but veiled from men and women throughout his ministry--is now made known through the apparent tragedy of the crucifixion. The Messiah-King is revealed in the death of the Suffering Servant.

The rending of the curtain of the temple (v 38) recalls Jesus' controversies with the temple authorities (ch 11-12). When Jesus dies, the thickly woven curtain is "torn in two from top to bottom," signifying that God himself is terminating the Temple order forever.

The Epistle to the Hebrews (6.19f; 9.3-8; 10.20) declares that, since Jesus entered the Most Holy Place on our behalf, believers can enter with confidence into the presence of God. This teaching contributes to the view that the inner veil was torn at the death of Christ.

Mark, however, appears to be referring to the outer curtain which hung in front of the doors at the entrance to the Temple. This gigantic, colorful tapestry portrayed a panorama of the entire heavens. At Jesus' baptism, the heavens were rent as God declared to Jesus, "You are my Son" (1.11). Now, at Jesus' death, God tears the heavens in two (Isa 64.1) as he reveals that Jesus is his Son.

Abruptly switching the narrative back to the scene of the crucifixion, Mark focuses attention on the Roman centurion in charge of the execution squad (v 39). As he stands in front of Jesus, hears his cry and sees how he dies, the centurion says of the one he just crucified, "Surely this man was the Son of God." Looking into the face of the dying Jesus, the centurion realizes he is standing in God's presence, seeing (as it were) the very "face of God." Jesus' hidden identity is now disclosed. The centurion sees clearly who Jesus really is. At Jesus' baptism in death, the centurion confesses publicly what God declared earlier (1.11; 9.7): Jesus is God's Son.

Golgotha reveals who Jesus is. By his baptism, Jesus formed a bond with sinners; by dying, he completes his identification with them by bearing the consequences of their sin, namely, death. Jesus gives "his life as a ransom for many" (10.45). These major emphases of the gospel converge and reach their climax at Golgotha. For the first time in Mark, a human declares who Jesus really is. Beyond that, the centurion is a Gentile. Ethnic restrictions in the Temple in Jerusalem no longer hold. The ransom paid by Jesus (10.45) is valid for Gentiles as well as Jews. Persons from all backgrounds are welcome in God's Kingdom (11.17; 13.27; 14.8). Jesus is the Messiah for all nations.

To affirm that Jesus was crucified does not require faith; that is a simple statement of historical fact. To affirm that Jesus died for my sins is a confession of faith in Jesus as God's Son who gave his life as a ransom and thereby enables men and women to stand in the presence of God. The gospel goes beyond a statement of God's acts among people; it appeals to you and to me to "follow Jesus." This is *a call to true worship*, for Jesus--not the Temple--is the true locus of God's presence! To "be with him" is equivalent to living in the presence of God (cf Ps 27.4).

v. 37 - On two occasions, demons cried out "in a loud voice" upon being driven out by Jesus (1.26; 5.7). The recurrence of this phrase in the crucifixion narrative (15.34) has been interpreted as depicting Jesus in a state of surrender to evil spirits (Kelber Story 81) or as the shout of demons upon being exorcised (Myers 462). This writer finds those explanations doubtful. In that decisive battle, the power of darkness probably attempted to possess Jesus. There is no indication, however, that it succeeded.

Mark identified Jesus' first cry "in a loud voice" as the cry of dereliction (v 34). In his second loud cry (v 37), Jesus, the "Spirit-filled Spirit bearer" (1.10), "gave up his spirit," as Matthew (27.50) and John (19.30) report. Mark says, "Jesus breathed his last." His loud cry was a voluntary act, at a moment of his own choosing when he lays down his life (Jn 10.17f) and gives up his spirit (Jn 19.30). His last words from the cross (Luke 23.46) are also triumphant: "Father, into your hands I commend my spirit."

• This whole scene is abhorrent to the Jewish mind, and Greeks are repelled by the idea of a divine figure undergoing physical suffering (cf 1Co 1.23). Some dismiss Jesus' death as a wasted or defeated life. Some early Christians misunderstood the gospel and denied the humanity of Jesus. How could the One who relieved suffering be so vulnerable? While men and women discredit Jesus because of the cursed cross, God credits him and it became the means by which Jesus triumphs. Jesus did not lose his life; he gave it on behalf of sinners. His resurrection and the preaching of the gospel throughout the world (14.8; 13.10,27) reveal Jesus as the embodiment of God's final triumph.

• The crucifixion is proof that God takes sin very seriously. He acted in righteous judgment and merciful love. Having borne our sins, Jesus becomes "our righteousness, holiness and redemption" (1Co 1.31). The crucifixion boldly expresses the reality of Jesus' humanity. His deity and humanity "are not contradictory but are harmoniously affirmed. In doing fully the will of his

Father, even unto suffering and death, Jesus was fully (perfectly) human and fully (perfectly) divine" (Swartley Mark: Way 187).

• Some preach health and wealth as a legal right of children of the King who suffered and died in ignominy. Is this not a denial of the humanity of Christians? Is the servant greater than the Master? Jesus' sufferings were a foretaste of the church's afflictions in the world (ch 13). Those who make healing paramount in the church's ministry and promise prosperity to the faithful overlook these realities.

Jesus is rightly perceived to be the Son of God through his faithful servanthood, suffering and dying, rather than through his miracles. His suffering and death enable Christians to face their own suffering and death. According to his sovereign will, God heals some and not others. Meanwhile, because of Jesus' victory through suffering and death, Christians know that "in all things God works for the good of those who love him," who are called "to be conformed to the likeness of His Son" (Ro 8.28-29). They join in creation's groaning while waiting for the full redemption yet to come (Ro 8.18-23).

v. 38 - According to Josephus, the beautifully designed outer veil (cf 2Ch 3.14) extended almost 80 feet in height. Ancient traditions speak of remarkable happenings at the outer entrance some forty years before the destruction of Jerusalem in A.D. 70, about the year that Jesus was crucified.

• Mark displays the structural unity of his narrative by bracketing it with the two events in which the heavens are torn, at the beginning (1.10) and here, near the end of Jesus' earthly ministry.

v. 39 - Obviously, this confession is not the result of what happened in the Temple, unseen from Golgotha. It arises as he stands "in front of Jesus." At Golgotha, God shows his "face" to the centurion. Simultaneously, in the Temple area, the God whose presence was veiled within the Most Holy Place, makes a public statement by rending the veil. His glory now shines forth.

• Harry L. Chronis (110) points out that "in front of" is an idiomatic expression for "standing in the presence" or "before the face of God." Cf Ex 27.21; 37.24; Lev 1.3; 4.7; Dt 12.18; 18.7; Ps 109.14,15. This christophany is a theophany, for the manifestation of Jesus' true identity is equivalent to God himself showing his face.

• Although the phrase lacks the definite article, rules for the use of the article in Greek show that "definite predicate nouns which precede the verb usually lack the article" while "a definite predicate nominative has the article when it follows the verb." Thus the correct translation is "the Son of God" (Lane 571n69). From the very beginning, Jesus is the Son of God in the fullest sense. The passion is the decisive revelation of his divine Sonship.

• Jesus is called "the Son of God" by the author (1.1) and by those unaffected by his redemptive ministry, i.e., God himself (1.11; 9.7) and evil spirits (1.24; 3.11; 5.7). Implicitly and explicitly, Jesus also refers to himself as God's Son (12.6,35-37; 13.32; 14.61-62).

• The centurion's confession places him in direct conflict with the worship of the emperor as a son of the gods, just as it did for many of Mark's early readers.

15.40-41 - Near Golgotha's hill, some disciples are watching all that takes place. They are among those who came with Jesus, following him and caring for his needs in Jerusalem as they had in Galilee. These women are fulfilling the requisites of a disciple--"following Jesus" and "serving" (1.18; 1.31; 10,45; cf 8.34-37). According to prevailing standards, women were second-class citizens; but Jesus accepts all "marginalized" persons as his disciples.

Among the many women disciples (cf Lk 8.1-3) who are there watching, Mark names three. By repeatedly citing the positive attitudes and actions of women, he quietly but persistently seeks to remove male prejudices and gain recognition for women as authentic disciples (cf Gal 3.28). Mark himself inverts the established practice of not accepting women as witnesses. As Lane says (577), he presents them as "eyewitnesses to the primary events proclaimed in the gospel, the death (v 40-41), burial (v 47) and resurrection (16.1)." By their presence at these locations, they serve as guarantors that the empty tomb is the same one in which the body of Jesus had been laid.

v. 41 - Jesus received support provided by his followers, a practice followed by the twelve (6.7-10).

• Jesus had released Mary of Magdala (a fishing village on the western shore of Lake Galilee) from demonic control. There is no basis for identifying her with the sinful woman of Lk 7.37. Little is known today about Mary, the mother of James and Joses, although Mark's first readers probably knew her. James the younger and James the son of Alphaeus (3.18) are probably two different individuals. Salome was the wife of Zebedee and the mother of James and John (cf 1.19; Mt. 27.56).

Excursus: Who Killed Jesus?

Some claim that Mark reflects a tendency in the early church to lay blame for the crucifixion on the Jews and to exonerate the Romans. This claim is said to arise from a desire to relieve pressure on Christians undergoing trial before Roman magistrates.

We see no evidence that Mark is seeking to pin Jesus' death on the Jewish people. By presenting in parallel form the two trials and the subsequent mockery, Mark draws attention to the responsibility of both religious and civil authorities for his death. The priests (15.1) and Pilate (15.15) "hand over" Jesus. Romans and Jews mock and beat Jesus. All share the responsibility of his crucifixion.

Jesus ministry began in conflict with Satan (1.12-13). His entrance into Satan's stronghold has *already* restricted demonic activity, but the adversary's power has *not yet* been destroyed (3.27). Satan continues his attempts to overthrow God's purposes, by direct attack (14.34-36), through nature (4.38ff) and by "the power of darkness" (15.33). As "the god of this world" (2Co 4.4), he worked through powerful religious and political institutions to crucify Jesus. As a result of satanic activity (Lk 22.3), "the rulers of this age...crucified the Lord of glory" (1Co 2.8).

Religious-political alliances fiercely opposed Israel (e.g., 1Ki 16.30-33). Although they competed with each other, these powers are aligned against Jesus and his followers. The worst attacks against the church arose through the collaboration of political and religious foes. In Revelation 13, the eschatological conflict is also pictured as a coalition of political and religious forces against the people of God.

Thus we conclude that Mark's portrays Jesus' condemnation as the work of Satan via human institutions, the "principalities and powers" visible at the two "trials." Mark seeks to alert the church to this two-pronged opposition that is repeated through the centuries. When Mark wrote, Christians were suffering similar rejection by the political and religious powers with the tacit consent of the general public blinded by its own immediate, self-centered interests.

One of the most tragic results of blaming the Jews and exonerating the Romans is the persecution of Jews as "Christ-killers." Although the Sanhedrin judged Jesus to deserve the death penalty, the actual sentence and execution were by Roman authorities. As 15.16-20 makes very clear, the Romans crucified Jesus with sadistic enthusiasm. (To be consistent, should not the descendants of the Romans be persecuted as "Christ-killers"?).

Mark (in harmony with the emphasis of all Scripture) lays emphasis upon the complicity of all humankind in Jesus' death. All the sons of Adam (and not just the sons of Abraham) are responsible. Jesus came to call sinners (2.17) to participate in his house of prayer for all, Jews as well as Gentiles (11.17). His message is one of forgiveness (2.10; 3.28; cf Lk 23.34). Hate arises from evil hearts (7.21-23) which are far from God (7.6). *Hatred, violence and vengeance in the name of Christ are contradictions in terms as well as disobedience to God's commandments (12.29-31).* Jesus commanded us to love one another. Christians have additional reasons to love Jews: they gave us two of our most precious possessions: the Old Testament and the very Jewish Jesus.

As related by Martin (Action 149), the British artist Stanley Spencer vividly portrayed the responsibility which all must share for Jesus' death. When the men and women from his village of Cookham saw his painting entitled "Christ Carrying the Cross," they observed that Spencer had used *their* faces in the crowd. *They* were a part of the mob crying, "Crucify him!" Williamson (269) emphasizes the same thought: in the condemnation and crucifixion of Jesus, "there are no spectators pure and simple. All are participants...even the reader."

THE BURIAL OF JESUS, 15.42-47

A group of women take over the role which male disciples normally fulfill. The women witness Jesus' death and burial; they confirm that the same tomb in which he was buried is empty. They are the first to hear that Jesus is risen and to receive the command to tell others.

15.42-47 - Friday was called "Preparation Day," for on that day people normally scurried about preparing everything for a work-free observance of the Sabbath. According to Dt 21.22-23, even the body of a criminal must be buried on the day of his execution lest the land be desecrated. Greater would be the shame if the body were left on the cross over the Sabbath. Jewish law forbade the burial of criminals in family tombs; their bodies were thrown in a ditch. Haste is necessary if Jesus' body is to be buried, for he died only a few hours before the Sabbath began (15.34).

By Roman law, on the other hand, those sentenced to death forfeit their property and even the right to burial. Sometimes relatives could gain permission to bury a criminal executed for lesser charges. Frequently, however, the bodies of those found guilty of treason were left to rot on the cross.

No relative comes to claim Jesus' body. John the Baptist's disciples "took his body and laid it in a tomb" (6.29), but Jesus' eleven fail to fulfill this, their duty. The women disciples (vv 41-42) stand no chance of approaching Pilate with such a request.

Joseph of Arimathea, a prominent member of the Sanhedrin, asks Pilate for Jesus' body. This is a bold move, for by honoring Jesus' body he could be censured as siding with a criminal. Nevertheless, Joseph did this as one who shared Jesus' expectation in the coming of God's Kingdom (v 43).

Pilate is surprised that Jesus was already dead, for many victims hung on the cross for two or three days before dying. Upon the centurion's verification of Jesus' death, Pilate grants the request to bury Jesus' body, thereby acknowledging that Jesus was no common criminal.

Even though it was the Passover, purchases necessary for a burial are allowed. With help (cf Jn 19.39-42), Joseph follows the Jewish burial customs and places the linen-wrapped body in a tomb cut out of rock. He then rolls the stone into place, covering the entrance to the tomb. He has done what he can (cf 14.8) to give Jesus' body an honorable burial.

Two of the women who witnessed the crucifixion (vv 40-41) watch where the body is laid (v 47) so that after the Sabbath, they can return to anoint the body as a final evidence of their care for him.

With the burial of Jesus, the passion predictions are fulfilled in all details except one. Jesus claimed that "after three days he will rise again" (e.g. 8.31).

v. 43 - Joseph of Arimathea probably came originally from Ramathim (1Sa 1.1), 30 miles NW of Jerusalem. Mark does not say he was a disciple but does point out that Joseph took great personal risk to do what Jesus' followers should have done. The combined witness of Mt 27.57, Jn 19.38 and Lk 23.50-51 indicate he was a secret disciple who had not consented to Jesus' death. Although Jesus rejected the spiritual bankruptcy of the religious leaders, the scattered seed grows (4.26) and Jesus' house of prayer is open to all, including Joseph of Arimathea, an influential (cf 1Co 1.26) member of the religious establishment that rejected Jesus. Marshall (61) sees no reason to suppose that Joseph was even awakened to attend the Sanhedrin's meeting. Within weeks after the resurrection, many priests were also converted (Ac 6.7).

v. 44 - Mark establishes the historicity of Jesus' death by providing factual details such as Jesus dying in Jerusalem, on a certain day, his death verified by authorities, the body buried in a certain place by a certain man and witnessed by certain persons. The repetition of such words as "body," "corpse," "died" and "dead" make it clear that Jesus was really dead.

These facts enabled the early church to answer allegations such as: Jesus had not died but had been nursed back to health from a coma; the women went to the wrong tomb on Sunday morning, an impostor appeared, claiming to be the resurrected Jesus. Of course, no one could present the body of Jesus in support of allegations that he had not risen from the dead.

v. 46 - Money could not change hands until after the festival (Mann 657). Certainly a prominent member of the Sanhedrin could buy on credit.

• The tombs of the wealthy (he was "with the rich in his death," Isa 53.9) were carved in limestone cliffs. Radiating out from the entrance chamber were the burial niches with rock shelves for the bodies of family members. Because of the impending Sabbath, the burial took place with the utmost speed. The tomb was new (Mt 27.60), i.e., as yet unused (Lk 23.53). For protection against animals and intruders, a large stone disk was placed in a stone channel, cut on a slope to facilitate rolling it into place to cover the entrance.

C. JESUS HAS RISEN FROM THE DEAD, 16.1-8

The resurrection of Jesus is neither an appendix nor an epilogue to the gospel; it is an integral part, explicitly and implicitly taught throughout the whole gospel. It is emphasized equally with the suffering and death in the passion predictions (8.31; 9.31; 10.34) and reinforced by Jesus' explicit promises in 9.9 and 14.28. By continuing his references to time and place, Mark makes it clear that the crucifixion and the resurrection are equally historical. He stresses that the risen Jesus is the one who was crucified. Without the resurrection Jesus' redemptive work on the cross is incomplete; a gospel without the resurrection is not the gospel of Jesus Christ. Without the resurrection, the "good news" would have terminated as bad news.

Friend and foe alike certified Jesus' death. His followers assumed his life has ended in defeat. The men who followed Jesus drop out of the picture after Jesus' arrest (14.50). The women disciples go to the tomb to pay their posthumous esteem. Hope in the dawning of God's rule among humankind seemingly dies with him.

The whole scene suddenly changes, however, with the evidence of the empty tomb and the announcement that Jesus has risen! By his death, he proves his obedience to the will of God. By his resurrection, God vindicates the crucified Son of Man, accepting his death as a ransom on behalf of many (10.45). By raising Jesus from the dead, God makes it clear that "Jesus *is* the Son of God," updating the centurion's declaration that Jesus "*was* God's Son" (15.39). All that Jesus promised in the passion pronouncements is now fulfilled and our confidence in the final victory of God's rule is strengthened.

Through God's messenger, the women learn of Jesus' resurrection and his promises. Will the women and men disciples fulfill their part? Mark closes his Gospel with this implied question as a springboard to confront his readers with their own response to the resurrected Son of God.

As Cranfield's (463) says, this straightforward narrative "reads like an eye-witness account, not a dramatization of a religious conviction."

16.1-3 - As the day dawns on the first day of the week (our Sunday), these same faithful women (15.40f) return to the tomb where they know Joseph of Arimathea had placed Jesus' body shortly before the Sabbath began (i.e., before sunset Friday). A proper burial requires the loving care of those who know the deceased. They are determined to serve Jesus in death as they had during his ministry. They plan to anoint the corpse with perfumed oils they probably purchased when the Sabbath was over (i.e., Saturday after 6 p.m.).

On the way, they ask each other about who would roll the very heavy stone disk away from the entrance to the tomb. As they draw near, however, they discover that it has already been rolled away. God has already taken care of what they could not do.

16.4-5 - Upon entering the tomb, they are utterly astonished by what they see. There is a person sitting on the right side of the tomb. His appearance is that of a young man; he is dressed in a white robe. Is he an angel? Mark simply relates what the women report. The identification of the person sitting in the tomb fades in importance as he speaks, for his words identify him as a messenger of the resurrected Jesus.

Like the two dejected persons on the road to Emmaus, these women had no doubt hoped that Jesus was the one would redeem Israel (Lk 24.13-21). His crucifixion, however, destroyed their high expectations in him. They went to the tomb to pay their last respects to their dead leader. Upon seeing the open tomb and then the young man, their emotions take another jolt.

v. 2 - The author marks the passage of time throughout the passion story: Thursday evening (14.17), "cockcrow" (14.72); Friday "dawn" (15.1), 9 a.m. (15.25), noon (15.53), 3 p.m. (15.34); and "very early on the first day of the week" (16.2), Sunday, the resurrection day. Jesus had said that he would arise "after three days," exactly what Matthew and Luke call "on the third day." We say "the day after tomorrow."

v. 4 - The stone had not been removed for Jesus to exit but for the women to enter and see the reality of the resurrection.

v. 5 - Mark says the women saw "a young man" (**neaniskos**). An angel (**aggelos**; Mt 28.5) may be either a human messenger of God or a heavenly being who appears in human form (cf Ge 18; Heb 13.2). Lk 24.4 says "two men" (**andres**). Later, Mary Magdalene saw two angels (**aggelos**) in the burial niches where the body had been laid (Jn 20.12). Some authors propose symbolic meanings for Mark's young man in a white robe. For example, he is seen as a symbol of Jesus himself, of baptismal rites, of the Markan community reborn in the resurrected Christ, or a symbol of a glorified martyr.

• Most interpreters understand that "a white robe" (cf Lk 24.4, Ac 1.10) implies the person was an angel. The same Greek term is used for the robe given to the returning prodigal (Lk 15.22) and for the garment worn by priests, scribes, and glorified believers (Mk 12.38; Rev 7.14).

16.6-8 - "Don't be alarmed," the young man says. With this phrase (5.36; 6.50), he identifies himself as Jesus' spokesperson on a mission of mercy, rather than judgment. He informs the women that he knows all about their reason for coming to the tomb. "You seek Jesus the Nazarene, who was crucified." They have made no mistake about the place or about the person whose body was laid there. They are mistaken, however, in their purpose: there is no corpse to anoint. Besides, an unnamed woman had already anointed his body for burial (14.8).

Then the messenger announces some of the most beautiful words ever heard by mortal women and men: "He has risen! He is not here! See the place where they laid him." Death does not have the last word.

"Go, tell his disciples and Peter," the young man commands. Jesus did not abandon those who had abandoned him (14.50), nor did he abandon Peter who had denied him (14.66-72). Through his emissary, Jesus takes the first step, freely offering to forgive (2.10) even sins against him and restore those who have stumbled. Failure need not be the last word in the life of a disciple. The message of the resurrection embodies acceptance by God as a result of the cross.

"Tell (them that) Jesus is going ahead of you into Galilee." The risen Shepherd will continue to lead (1.17) his disciples. He still acknowledges them as his disciples, in spite of their disloyalty and denial. The Lord goes before his people (cf Isa 42.16; 49.10) as he had in the wilderness (cf Ex 13.21). The promise made on the way to Gethsemane (14.28) was about to be fulfilled: the resurrected Jesus gathers his scattered sheep (14.27) and assembles his followers as God's flock. When he appears in the parousia, he will send his angels to gather his flock from among all nations (13.27; cf 13.10; 14.8). Then he will fulfill his promise to "drink the fruit of the vine in the Kingdom of God" (14.25).

To the women and men paralyzed by fear, the message is: "Go, and you will see him." Like Jesus' initial call, "Follow me," this promise is conditional: it demands a personal response. Only if they exercise faith by going will they see him.

The young man repeats Jesus' promise (14.28), stressing the fact that in Galilee the disciples will see him with their own eyes. Jesus' resurrected body still resembles the old one, yet it is fundamentally different, with new properties and powers. It has been lifted to a new level of existence.

But why did Jesus specify Galilee? The disciples expected that, without delay, the resurrected Christ would establish God's Kingdom (cf Ac 1.6-8) with Jerusalem as capital. Jesus, however, taught that the consummation of the Kingdom was not yet; it awaits worldwide evangelization (13.10, 27). He had first called his disciples, trained, taught and sent them out in Galilee. Returning there marks the beginning of their mission to all nations. Furthermore, Mark's readers in all ages are hereby warned against the church's tendency to turn inward and to centralize its ministry locally, forgetting that its mission is to all peoples.

We can only imagine the emotional impact this experience has on these women in the empty tomb. The reality of what they see and hear jars their whole being. Mark indicates by a variety of expressions that the women act both out of a deep sense of awe and out of anxious fear. This interpretation is also psychologically reasonable, for deep emotions spring from a number of sources and flood several areas of one's life.

In the Old Testament, some prophets were overcome with weakness upon receiving God's call; others responded to his presence with fear and flight. Silence was appropriate when God spoke. People wilted before him. In the gospel narrative, people have also reacted to God's action in Jesus with alarm, awe and amazement. Now in the empty tomb, when the presence of the living God is experienced as never before, the women are gripped by a wondrous sense of awe.

Besides that, the women have more than ample cause to be trembling with fear. Would they, as followers of Jesus, suffer as he had? Devout Jews expected God's judgment would follow the resurrection of the dead. Did they fear that Jesus' resurrection was a prelude to the day of God's wrath? The command to "Go and tell" contradicted society's refusal to accept women as witnesses. Who would believe them?

Unable to collect their thoughts or control themselves, they run out of the tomb and flee. *For the moment*, they say nothing to anyone, for they are afraid.

v. 6 - The passive form of the Greek verb means, "he has been raised." God struck the Shepherd (14.27) and then raised him from the dead (cf Eph 1.20).

v. 7 - "He is going ahead" (**proagei**;14.28; 10.32) is a technical term for a shepherd's work.

• The messenger's words may contain a gentle rebuke to the women for seeking to anoint Jesus' body instead of recalling his promise to rise again. In Mark, "seek" (v 6) is often used of misguided or hostile activity (3.22; 8.11; 11.18f; 12.12; 14.1,11,55).

• "Go, tell" parallels the missionary commission recorded in the other Gospels and in Acts 1.8. This command implies that Jesus forgives the disciples for their disobedience and cowardice. His promise to lead them implies that they will be reinstated in ministry. The other Evangelists report that Jesus commissioned them during his appearances in the regions of Jerusalem and Galilee (Mt 28.16-20; Lk 24.36-49; Jn 20.19-22; 21.1-19; cf 1Co 15.5-7)

Peter is singled out, not as an attack against his person or as indicating a superior position among the apostles. Mark's readers know of his failures. He is mentioned personally to assure that he will suffer no discrimination.

• The disciples had seen Jesus' mighty works, yet they are slow to understand (6.52; 8.17). As the first half of Mark's Gospel drew to a close (8.29-33), they saw Jesus as the Messiah, but rejected any thought of his passion. Like the blind man at Bethsaida (8.26), they needed a "second touch" to remove the blindness from their eyes. The crucifixion and resurrection of Jesus will open the eyes of their understanding and they, like the centurion, will see clearly who Jesus really is and proclaim, "This is the Son of God."

v. 8 - Mark expresses the range of the women's emotions with: tromos ("trembling"), **ekstasis** ("bewildered;" 5.42) and **phobeo** ("fear"); in vv 5-6 (cf. 9.15; 14.33), **exethambethesan** ("alarmed," "dumbfounded"). He uses **phobeo** sometimes to indicate the profound reverence with which humans respond to the awesomeness of God's power or revelation in Jesus (cf 4.41; 5.36; 6.50; 9.6) and other times to describe apprehensive fear (cf 5.15; 6.20; 9.32; 11.18,32; 12.12).

• All previous references to women in Mark's Gospel are positive; only here do they fail. According to the other Gospels, the women delivered the message (Mt 28.8-10,16; Lk 24.19; Jn 20.18) to the disciples, who told others. Jesus' appearances in Galilee are described in Mt 28.16; Jn 21; those in Jerusalem, in Lk 24-Ac 1. Many (if not most) scholars agree that those Evangelists knew Mark's Gospel.

(THE "LONG ENDING" - 16.9-20)

Before concluding our comments on verse 8, we will consider the verses that concluded Mark's Gospel in many versions of the New Testament. These verses (9-20) are known as "the long ending." The oldest, most reliable manuscripts, however, end with what we know as verse 8. The "long ending" was probably attached some time before the middle of the second century. The origin of the alternative "short ending" (between verses 8 and 9) is unknown. Both were likely written in an attempt to complete Mark's narrative, which (many claim) "ends too abruptly."

Internal evidence also indicates that Mark did not write these endings. Their language and style are unlike those of the preceding chapters. The positive emphasis upon signs (16.17, 20) is contrary to their questionable results in the previous chapters (e.g., 6.5; 8.11f). The longer ending appears to be an editorial compilation, possibly for catechetical use, with most of its contents drawn from the other Gospels. There is almost universal agreement that, in the light of both internal and external evidences, these endings were not a part of the original narrative. We concur with Cole (259): "It would be unwise to build any theological position upon these verses alone; and this no responsible Christian group has done."

The last phrase in the Greek text of verse 8 is **ephobounto gar** (literally "they were afraid because"). Many scholars argued that Mark did not conclude his narrative with such a highly ungrammatical statement: either Mark's conclusion was lost or destroyed, or he was unable to finish writing his Gospel. Recent studies, however, demonstrate that Mark habitually uses the conjunction **gar** as a part of his narrative techniques to denote an explanation for surprising or confusing events, precisely the way he uses it here.

With insights gained from analyzing this Gospel as a unified, integrated story, an increasing number of writers now contend that Mark deliberately ended his Gospel at 16.8. As Hooker (118) says, "there is no more because he did not write more, and he did not intend to write more." We, too, believe that this is the original and fully adequate ending. We conclude with an analysis of what he did say and why.

16.8 - Some readers fault Mark as incomplete because he did not include appearances of the resurrected Jesus as in the other Gospel accounts. Also they want a positive ending, with fear turned into joy and silence into proclamation. Mark feels no need to repeat what his first readers already know. Nor does he feel compelled to offer "see and believe" evidence (cf 15.32) of the resurrection. He must be accepted on his own terms. Mark does stress the fact that Jesus has risen. He simply does it in a way and for a purpose that many readers do not expect. His primary concern is about what his readers do with the historical reality of Jesus' death and resurrection.

Mark does not infer that the women failed to deliver the message. If their silence had been permanent, no one would have heard about their experience.

The author intended to close with 16.8 because he had completed what he set out to do. He revealed that Jesus is the Christ, the Son of God who entered Satan's domain and gave his life as a ransom for both Jews and Gentiles, thereby bringing near God's rule. He has given assurance that when Jesus returns, God will establish his rule in power and his victory will be complete. The messianic identity is no longer a secret, for the reader knows who Jesus is, where he went and where he is going.

With these last verses, the author portrays discipleship as following the risen Jesus who leads his disciples into an insecure world. Mark calls upon all his readers to "go and tell" boldly, even if they, like his first readers, face death as a result of proclaiming the gospel. By ending his narrative abruptly, he forces his readers to think about the tragic consequences if they fail to share the good news.

In the beginning of the gospel, Jesus' command to follow him (1.16-20) was accompanied by his promise: "I will make you fishers of men." That was the beginning of discipleship; 16.1-8 is the end of the beginning. Throughout his ministry, Jesus has been fishing for people, while modeling for his disciples what it means to "go and tell." Even now, disciples do not go alone, for Jesus goes before them (16.7).

Although Mark has completed his teaching, this is only the beginning of discipleship, not its fulfillment. The future of discipleship is left uncertain, for this depends upon whether men and women follow Jesus and continue the work begun.

Mark's organization of his narrative provides clues to its meaning. The first half of the Gospel closes with Jesus giving sight to a man physically blind (8.22-26). His "two-step cure" dramatizes the persistent dullness of the disciples (8.11-21) and prompts the disciples' confession of Jesus as Messiah. But their concept of the Messiah is still inadequate (8.29-31). Later, when Jesus is arrested, they all flee; for they still do not see things clearly. The second half of the Gospel closes with the promise, "you will see him." That "second touch" will give them insight and understanding, and they will begin to confess Jesus as the Son of God.

Mark 16.1-8 is not a conclusion but a transition designed *to lead the reader to follow the resurrected Christ into the world.* The first believers stayed close to Jerusalem, in spite of the risen Jesus' commandment to move out to the ends of the world (Ac 1.8). Only when great persecution broke out did they disperse and preach the word wherever they went (Ac 8.1,4). Mark makes it clear that God ordained that the gospel be preached to all nations. Jesus himself leads his disciples (16.7) in fulfilling that mission.

The command to follow Jesus has never been rescinded. The advance of God's rule among men and women is the responsibility of every believer. The messianic identity remains a secret for many people as long as Jesus' present disciples remain silent. By his abrupt ending, Mark challenges each reader to complete his/her part of the narrative in terms of proclaiming the resurrection to his/her contemporaries. To be silent is a danger greater than persecution and death. The gospel is good news only if shared.

Mark ends his narrative with **gar** ("because," "for") in order to emphasize that the gospel has begun but not ended. It did not end with Jesus' resurrection. It continues even today as his followers proclaim his death and resurrection. This is a good way to end the narrative of the beginning of the gospel.

v. 8 - When the women "came to themselves and began to realize the truth, joy mingled with their fear and predominated and their flight was changed into an eager haste to deliver their message" (Swete 399).

• A few days later, the same fearful disciples were so convinced of Jesus' resurrection that they proclaimed this fact in this same city in spite of the threat of persecution and death (e.g., Ac 2.32; 4.10).

• Mark did not inform his readers about Jesus' post-resurrection appearances, for that was common knowledge (cf 1Co 15.5-7). Jesus' resurrection was foremost in apostolic preaching (e.g., Ac 2.22-36; Ro 1.3-4). Mark does not always give an explicit account of a conclusion already well known to his readers (e.g., "the fulfillment of the promise that Jesus would baptize with the Holy Spirit is never recounted because the readers know it happened" Best Disciples 130). Furthermore, in Mark Jesus himself has already provided essential information of what lies beyond the crucifixion.

• The Greek **arche** ("beginning"), used in Mark's opening phrase, "carries the idea of the first model (as in archetype) as well as that of coming first temporally" (Swartley Mark: Way 196).

SUGGESTIONS FOR REFLECTION AND ACTION

Prologue - 1.1-13

1.1-8 Analyze each terms in Mark1.1 as to its significance for your daily life.
What is the role of a messenger of God? In what ways are you one?
Share with a non-Christian what repentance means in your experience.
In what ways did your baptism establish your identity?
Give thanks to God for his forgiveness and for the gift of the Holy Spirit.

1.9-13 Why do you think the Father and to the Holy Spirit participated in Jesus' baptism?
What does Jesus' baptism mean to you?
What were Satan's purposes in tempting Jesus? in tempting you?
Is the gospel for you principally a creed or a personal involvement with Jesus Christ?

Jesus' Authority Affirmed and Contested - 1.14-3.6

1.14-15 What does the presence of God's Kingdom mean to you in your daily life?
Describe your personal response to Jesus' commandment, "Repent and believe the Gospel."
What are the evidences that you live under God's kingly rule?
Identify areas of your life which are not under the rule of God. What do you plan to do about them?

1.16-20 How do you respond to Jesus' call?
Is his call limited to those "chosen for religious careers"?
How is your commitment to Jesus seen in your involvement with the people of God?

1.21-39 Describe Jesus as you see him in 1.21-39.
In what ways do you respond to Jesus' teaching?
How do you establish your priorities? What good things distract from them?

1.40-45 How do you respond to Jesus' authority?
What is your basic purpose in coming to Jesus?
What extenuating circumstances warrant your disobeying God's commands?
What other important principles for your life do you discover here?

2.1-12 Compare yourself to: 1) the paralytic; 2) his friends; 3) the scribes.
How does your faith help others get to Jesus?
What obstacles has your faith overcome lately?
What is the place and purpose of healing:1) in the ministry of Jesus? 2) in the church today?
Does healing always occur when sins are forgiven? Cf Trophimus, 2Ti 4.20; Paul, 2Co 12.7-10.
On what conditions have your sins been wiped out?

2.13-17 Identify the outcasts in your community. Take a careful look at your social prejudices.
How do you share the joy of knowing Jesus?
How can you use "table fellowship" to introduce people to Jesus?
In what ways do your religious convictions form a bridge or a barrier to your reaching out to others?
How have you risked your reputation for Jesus' sake?

2.18-22 What motives characterize your life under Jesus' rule? What roles do rituals play?
Analyze the good news as a restricting/liberating force in your life.
How do you handle conflicts between the new and the old in personal and church life today?
How do you avoid "throwing out the baby with the bath water"?

2.23-28 What rules dominate your life?
What hinders you/your church from helping people in need?
Discuss the values of persons and institutions. What relationships should exist between them?
How does the knowledge of Scripture help you resolve these questions?
How can you live under the lordship of Jesus rather than that of traditions and institutions?
How you can observe the Lord's day in the light of Jesus' teachings here?

3.1-6 Is Jesus Lord of your day of worship? of your whole week?
Intercede for fellow believers who face political-religious coalitions against the gospel.
From 2.1 to here, what constitutes a religious person: as seen in Jesus, as implied by his critics?
Which of these qualities characterize your life?
What do these paragraphs say to those whose religion is a matter of keeping rules?
As an aid to your discipling others, write down your observations on how Jesus made disciples.

The Source and Nature of Jesus' Authority - 3.7-6.6a

3.7-12 Look up the places mentioned on a map of Palestine in Jesus' time. Considering the distances and the transportation available, what does this mean about the people's desire to see Jesus?
What obstacles do you overcome to seek him? Why do you seek him?
How do you measure success in Christian ministry?

3.13-19 Define Jesus' calling to you.
How has following Jesus contributed to the formation of your character?
What does it mean to be set apart for Christian service?
Considering our weaknesses, what hope is there for the church today?
What are the positive/negative results of the heterogeneous composition of the local church?

3.20-30 How are attempts made to discredit Jesus' work today?
What does Mark 3.27 mean to you personally?
Meditate on the grace of God that forgives "all your sins."
How would you counsel one fearful of having committed the "unforgivable sin?"
What spirit controls your life?

3.31-35 What is the basis for belonging to God's family?
What does being a member of God's family mean to you?
How do you show that you belong?

4.1-9 How does this parable influence your understanding of God's activity in the world?
How do you respond when God does not work according to your expectations?

4.10-13 What is the general purpose of parables?
What is the teaching of vv. 11-12?
Explain relationships between vv. 11-12 and the parables narrated in this section.

4.14-20 What type of soil are you?
What are some other obstacles to the growth of God's word?
Identify areas in your life in which you are receptive/resistant to God's word?

4.21-25 How does this passage encourage you? warn you?
Test your "hearing." What is your score?

4.26-29 How do you react to the delay between planting and harvest?
How has the cry for immediate results influenced you?

4.30-32 What does this parable teach you about the kingdom?

4.33-34 How have these parables clarified your knowledge of God's activity in the world today?
How have they effected your role in it?

4.35-41 What place does reverential awe have in your worship of Jesus?
How does this story help when you ask, "God, don't you care?"
How does the failure of the twelve help you to overcome your fears and weaknesses?

5.1-20 Initiate reconciliation in a hostile environment.
In the light of this passage, pray for missionaries opening new frontiers for the gospel.
When is it more appropriate to tell how much the Lord has done for you than to preach?
How do you help others recently liberated by Christ?
What place does the desire for economic advantages play in your life?
Research biblical teaching on the "principalities and powers".

5.21-43 What are Mark's purposes in relating these events? Are they achieved in your life?
How do you handle doubts about Jesus' caring?
How does your faith grow? How do you relate Jesus' power to your faith/doubts? to your health?
How does Jesus relate to people? How do you?
Compare Jesus' care of the woman with the church's mission to isolated and alienated persons.

6.1-6a How can familiarity with the gospel become a barrier to those brought up in a church?
How can such barriers be overcome?
How do you handle rejection?

The Expansion of Jesus' Ministry - 6.6b-8.26

6.6b-13 How can you best carry out the principles prescribed for the disciples?
In what ways is the gospel hindered by the violation of these principles?
Are any of these missing in your life?

6.14-29 According to your contemporaries, who is Jesus?

Consider the place of repentance in your life/ in your ministry.
In the light of this passage, pray for all those in authority (1Ti 2.2).
Intercede for those who today face persecution and even death because they belong to Jesus.
6.30-44 How do you see today's multitudes?
What is the significance of this miracle for believers today?
What are your responsibilities in view of Jesus' command, "You give them something to eat"?
What are your favorite excuses?
What do you do when there is not sufficient for yourself?
How does this story help you face an impossible situation?
6.45-52 How do you respond to Jesus' commands?
Recall experiences that have strengthened your faith.
Thank God for not giving up on you.
Apply the truths of this pericope to your own life.
6.53-56 How do your past experiences influence your present service to others?
7.1-13 What place does the Bible have in your thoughts and actions?
What are you doing to enhance the role of Scripture in your life?
How do you resolve conflict between doing God's will and following religious rules?
Describe your own attempts to play off one commandment against another.
How does the enforcing of certain Christian practices today contribute to the neglect of others?
Identify the neglected ones. What can you do to bring them into balance?
Identify the elements in your lifestyle that are based on Scripture, those based on tradition and those based on selfishness.
How can you harmonize your lifestyle with what you profess?
7.14-23 What "do's" and "don'ts" (taboos) form a "spiritual elite" today?
How does this passage relate to the proclamation, "Repent and believe the good news"?
Evaluate your life in the light of vv. 21-22. What do you hunger and thirst after?
Pray "Create in me a pure heart" (Ps 51.10).
How does your life verify your dedication to moral purity?
What are you doing to curtail and get rid of things which defile your life?
7.24-30 Thank God for those through whom you "heard about Jesus."
Who "heard about Jesus" from you this week?
Discuss with others the results of trials of faith.
How do you/your church relate to "unqualified people"?
7.31-37 How is your "hearing"? your "speech"?
Why could Jesus visit the Decapolis now, after leaving "by popular request" previously (5.1-20)?
How can you avoid stereotyped communication of the gospel and fashion it according to the needs and understanding of each individual?
8.1-10 How has God shown his compassion in your life? How do you show compassion?
What lessons have you learned because God graciously gave you a second chance?
What can you learn from Jesus' inter-personal relationships here?
How does knowledge of the inclusive nature of God's Kingdom influence your life?
8.11-21 What does your faith depend upon signs, experiences, emotions or God's word?
Do you seek signs or do you seek God?
Search for and discard any "yeast" which diminishes your commitment to Jesus.
How can past experiences of God's grace help you face new and different ones?
8.22-26 Evaluate your "eye sight."
In the light of Mark 1.1 through 8.26, what does God want of you?
Summarize what you have learned in chapters 1-8 about Jesus; about discipleship.

On the Way to the Cross - 8.27-10.52

8.27-9.1 What is your answer to "Who is Jesus?"
Who are you in the light of who Jesus is?
How do you deny your self-centeredness? What helps/hinders you as a disciple?
Does following Jesus involve you in the brutal realities of life or is it an escape from them?
9.2-13 What is your abiding impression of the transfiguration? Why do you think it took place?
What difference do God's words here make in your life?
Have you allowed present trials to blot out the promise of future glory?

What do you do when Jesus' teachings contradict convictions you've held for years?

9.14-29 Describe this scene in terms of the human dilemma.
Imagine the thoughts and feelings of the disciples, of the father.
Analyze Jesus' words and actions.
Identify your recent failures. What have you learned from them?
What does this story teach you about faith? about prayer? about discipleship?

9.30-50 What constitutes greatness in modern society? in your church? for you personally?
How do the desires for individual/group superiority find expression in your life? in your church?
How can you show your appreciation for persons with ministries different from yours?
How can you help those new in faith? What stumbling blocks can you remove?
How do you avoid influencing others to sin? avoid sin in your own life?

10.1-12 In what ways do Jesus' teaching enrich your views on marriage?
What does this passage teach that will help your marriage?
Why is faithfulness in marriage emphasized and love not mentioned?
What is your attitude towards divorced people?
What do you think Jesus would say today about marriage and divorce?
What can you do to diminish the problem of divorce in contemporary society?

10.13-16 Identify the "insignificant" people in your culture. What is your attitude toward them?
How do you encourage children to come to Jesus?

10.17-31 What claim do riches have on you? What have you left for the sake of the gospel?
Make a list of what hinders your following Jesus.
Do you share your life and home with those who have left families and homes for Jesus' sake?
Have you diluted Jesus' teachings or changed your lifestyle?
How can you and your church follow these teachings more seriously?

10.32 -45 How do you seek greatness or exercise authority?
Whose slave are you? (cf Romans 6.16-18).
What are the requirements for leadership in your church?
How can you help people who insist on being first?
What does it mean to you to be ransomed? How do you help free people who are in captivity?

10.46-52 What does Bartimaeus' story tell you about himself? about Jesus?
What do you want above all else? How do you go about getting it? What would you do with it?
What have the nameless people in this division taught you through their encounters with Jesus?

Jesus and the Temple - 11.1-13.37

11.1-11 Retrace these events from the standpoint of the two disciples.
Are you withholding anything--self, son, daughter, time, resources--the Lord has need of?

11.12-26 What would Jesus overturn in your church?
How can worship become more authentic for you? for your church?
What pleases you even though it displeases God?
What insights do Jesus' teachings give about why prayers are not answered?
How can you learn to forgive as freely as you want to be forgiven?

11.27-12.12 Consider the responsibilities and dangers of religious authority.
What pressures influence your decisions? What do you value most, a true or a safe answer?
Contemplate God's most unusual response to rebellion (12.6).
Consider the roots and growth of violence in this parable.
What does this passage say about Jesus' identity and mission?
What does it suggest about Jesus' attitude towards Scripture?

12.13-17 How does Jesus' teaching here affect your attitudes towards paying taxes?
What in your life properly belongs to God? Does he control it?
What areas of life do you see as belonging exclusively to the state?
What is your understanding of the relationship between "Caesar" and God?
What demands does your society/government make beyond what is its due? What are your attitudes/courses of action?

12.18-27 Compare your view of the Scriptures with Jesus'. In what ways do you submit your beliefs and opinions to the Scriptures? How do they influence your view of life and death?
What does "he is the God of the living" mean to you?
What is the message of this pericope for those contemplating suicide?

12.28-34 What are the irreducible truths of Christianity?
How do you love God with your mind?
What gives meaning to your acts of worship? to your relationships with others?
What did you do today out of your love for God? for others?

12.35-37 What is the basis of your convictions?
Who is Jesus? What is he like? Where is he now? What is he doing?
How has your comprehension of biblical truth benefitted from these controversies? What difference does this perception make in your daily life?

12.38-44 What are the contemporary parallels of those practices censured by Jesus?
Does Jesus censure or commend your conduct?
What principles should govern your giving? Reevaluate your concepts of generosity.
How does the responsibility of proclaiming the gospel to all nations affect your giving and lifestyle as well as those of your church?

13.1-27 What does 13.10 mean to you personally? to your church?
How do the teachings of this discourse affect your view of the world? your life?
When is it right/wrong to flee from difficult situations?
What does it mean to you when Christians in another part of the world suffer deep distress?
How can you identify false prophets?
Share with someone the declaration that the Son of Man will come with great power and glory.

13.28-37 What task(s) has the Owner of the house assigned to you?
How do you "watch"? What tends to lull you/your church to sleep?
What is the overall impact of the Olivet Discourse on you? How does it help you face the future?

Jesus' Suffering, Death and Resurrection - 14.01-16.08

14.1-11 Describe the woman's feelings throughout this experience.
What ways do you have of showing your devotion to God?
What are the primary values in your life?
Does it hurt you to give?
Discuss how a gift of money might be a flight from personal involvement.
What do you learn about Jesus from this event?

14.12-21 How does Jesus' betrayal by a friend help you face interpersonal relationships?
How does Jesus' blending of the old and the new help you adapt to a changing world?

14.22-26 How can you celebrate the Lord's Supper with all the meaning Jesus intended?
How do you work out in life your covenant relationship with God?
How can you enrich your children's understanding of Christian things (cf Dt 6.6ff)?
What are you doing about those who are still outside the covenant?

14.27-31 What can you learn from the disciples' failures?
How has a personal failure affected your belief in who Jesus is?
How has Jesus proven to you that he is greater than any failure?

14.32-42 How does Jesus' experience in Gethsemane influence your sense of God as Father? the reality of temptation? the weakness of human nature? the availability of divine help? your responsibility as a disciple? the greatness of his sacrifice?
Do you care for others when you yourself are going through afflictions?
In the light of Jesus' prayer in Gethsemane, examine your prayer life as to transparency; persistence; your primary commitment.
In what situations do you hide your feelings from God? Why?
Explain how your loyalty to Jesus has been tested/demonstrated in daily experiences?
What are some indications of a watchful disciple? a watchful church?

14.43-52 Trace the steps that led to the disciples' flight.
What do you learn about yourself by observing the disciples here?
What do you learn from Jesus' action and words in this pericope?

14.53-65 Relive this whole procedure from the standpoint of each participant.
What do you learn from Jesus' composure? How do you account for it?
What does Jesus' confession tell you about who he is?
How do you react when false testimony or character assassination is used against you?

14.66-72 Trace the steps that led to Peter's denial.
What warnings/encouragement does this story bring?

What do your failures teach you? Are you willing to allow others to learn from your failures?
Compare/contrast Peter and Judas.

15.1-20a Identify the motives and emotions of each participant in these scenes.
Reread the passion narrative from the standpoint of a believer on trial for his faith.
Analyze the nature and use of authority in these trials.
What would be your role as a member of the crowd?
What do you mean when you talk and sing about Jesus as King?

15.20b-47 Read this division as though reading it for the first time. Identify yourself with each participant.
What does it teach you about God? Jesus? yourself? humankind? life and death? about sin?
What further messages does this have?
What does the centurion's experience teach you?
Relate this miscarriage of justice to God's sovereignty and to the offer of salvation.
How does Jesus' use of Ps 22 enhance its meaning for those who are lonely today?
How is Jesus' death more than a supreme example of martyrdom?

16.1-8 What are your responses to Jesus' resurrection?
What are your responsibilities in light of his resurrection?
How do you take the initiative in restoring disciples who have fallen along the way?

SELECTED BIBLIOGRAPHY

In the commentary, references to books and articles cited include the author's name (accompanied by an abbreviated title where more than one of his/her works is listed below) followed by the page number.

ACHTEMEIER, Paul J. Invitation to Mark. Garden City: Doubleday & Co., 1978.

-----. Mark. (Proclamation Commentaries). Philadelphia: Fortress Press, 1986.

ALTER, Robert. The Art of Biblical Narrative. New York: Basic Books, 1981.

ANDERSON, Hugh. The Gospel of Mark. (New Century Bible). London: Oliphants, 1976.

BAILEY, Kenneth. Poet & Peasant and Through Peasant Eyes. Grand Rapids: Eerdmans Publishing Company, 1983 (combined edition).

BARCLAY, William. New Testament Words. (Daily Study Bible). Philadelphia: Westminster Press, 1974.

-----. The Gospel of Mark, revised edition. (Daily Study Bible). Philadelphia: Westminster Press, 1975.

BEASLEY-MURRAY, G.R. Jesus and the Kingdom of God. Grand Rapids: Eerdmans, 1986.

BEST, Ernest. Disciples and Discipleship: Studies in the Gospel according to Mark. Edinburgh: T. & T. Clark, 1986.

-----. Following Jesus: Discipleship in the Gospel of Mark. Sheffield: JSOT Press, 1981.

-----. Mark: the Gospel as Story. Edinburgh: T. & T. Clark, 1983.

BONHOEFFER, Dietrich. The Cost of Discipleship New York: Macmillan, revised paperback edition, 1963.

BRATCHER, Robert G., and NIDA, Eugene A. A Translator's Handbook on the Gospel of Mark. Leiden: Brill, 1961.

COLE, R.A. Gospel according to Mark. London: Tyndale Press, 1961.

CRANFIELD, C.E.B. Gospel according to St. Mark, revised edition. (Cambridge Greek Testament Commentary). New York: Cambridge University Press, 1977.

DOOHAN, Leonard. Mark: Visionary of Early Christianity. Santa Fe: Bear & Co., 1986.

ELLER, Vernard. Christian Anarchy: Jesus' primacy over the powers. Grand Rapids:Eerdmans, 1987.

FOWLER, Robert M. Loaves and Fishes: The Function of the Feeding Stories in the Gospel of Mark. Chico: Scholars Press, 1981.

GOURGUES, Michel. Os Salmos e Jesus, Jesus e os Salmos. São Paulo: Edições Paulinas,1984.

HOOKER, Morna D. The Message of Mark. London: Epworth Press, 1983.

HURTADO, Larry W. Mark. (Good News Commentary). San Francisco: Harper & Row, 1983.

ITIOKA, Neusa. Os deuses de Umbanda. São Paulo: ABU Editora, 1987.

JEREMIAS, Joachim. Jerusalem in the Time of Jesus. Philadelphia: Fortress Press, 1977.

------ New Testament Theology. New York: Charles Scribner's Sons, 1971.

------ The Parables of Jesus. New York: Charles Scribner's Sons, 1972, second revised edition.

KEALY, Seán P. Mark's Gospel: A History of its Interpretation. New York: Paulist Press, 1982.

KEE, Howard Clark. Community of the New Age: Studies in Mark's Gospel. Philadelphia: Westminster Press, 1977.

KELBER, Werner H. Mark's Story of Jesus. Philadelphia: Fortress Press, 1979.

-----, editor. The Passion in Mark: Studies in Mark 14-16. Philadelphia: Fortress Press, 1975.

KIDNER, Derek. Psalms 73-150. Downers Grove: Inter-Varsity Press, 1975.

LADD, George Eldon. The Gospel of the Kingdom. Grand Rapids: Eerdmans, 1959.

-----. The New Testament and Criticism. Grand Rapids: Eerdmans, 1967.

-----. The Pattern of New Testament Truth. Grand Rapids: Eerdmans, 1968.

-----. The Presence of the Future. Grand Rapids: Eerdmans, 1974.

-----. Theology of the New Testament. Grand Rapids: Eerdmans, 1974.

LANE, William L. Gospel according to Mark. (New International Commentary on the New Testament). Grand Rapids: Eerdmans, 1974.

LENSKI, R. C. H. The Interpretation of St. Mark's Gospel. Minneapolis: Augsburg Publishing House, 1946.

LOHFINK, Gerhard. Jesus and Community. Philadelplhia: Fortress Press, 1982.

LONGENECKER, Richard N. The Christology of Early Jewish Christianity. Grand Rapids: Baker Book House, 1970.

MANSFIELD, M. Robert. "Spirit and Gospel" in Mark. Peabody: Hendrickson Publishers, 1987.

MARSHALL, I. Howard. Mark. (Bible Study Book). Philadelphia: A. J. Holman, 1978.

MARTIN, Ralph P. Mark - Evangelist and Theologian. Grand Rapids: Zondervan, 1972.

-----. New Testamento Foundations: A Guide for Christian Students, 2 volumes. Grand Rapids: Eerdmans, 1975.

-----. Where the Action Is (Biblical Commentary for Laymen). Glendale: Regal, 1977.

MAZAR, Benjamin. The Mountain of the Lord: Excavating in Jerusalem. Garden City: Doubleday and Co., 1975.

MANN, C. S. Mark. (Anchor Bible). Garden City: Doubleday & Co., 1986.

MINEAR, Paul S. Mark. (Layman's Bible Commentary). Atlanta: John Knox Press, 1982.

MORGAN, G. Campbell. The Gospel according to Mark. New York: Revell, 1927.

MOULE, C. F. D. The Gospel according to Mark. (Cambridge Bible Commentary on the New English Bible). Cambridge: University Press, 1965.

MYERS, Ched. O Evangelho de São Marcos São Paulo: Edições Paulinas , 1992. Translation by I.F.L. Ferreira of Binding the strong man: a political reading of Mark's story of Jesus (New York: Orbis Books, 1988).

NINEHAM, D. E. Saint Mark. (Pelican New Testament Commentaries). Middlesex: Pelican Books, 1963.

New International Dictionary of New Testament Theology, 3 volumes (**NIDNTT**). Colin Brown, general editor. Grand Rapids: Zondervan, 1975-1978.

PALLARES, José Cárdenas. A Poor Man Called Jesus. Maryknoll: Orbis Books, 1986. Translated from the Spanish by Robert R. Barr.

PERRIN, Norman. The Resurrection according to Matthew, Mark, and Luke. Philadelphia: Fortress Press, 1977.

PRONZATO, Alessandro. Un Cristiano Comienza a Ler El Evangelio de Marcos, 3 volumes. Salamanca: Ediciones Sígueme, 1982. Translated from the Italian by Germán González Domingo.

RAWLINSON, A. E. J. The Gospel according to Mark. (Westminster Commentaries). London: Methuen & Co., 1925.

RHOADS, David, and MICHIE, Donald. Mark as Story: an Introduction to the Narrative of a Gospel. Philadelphia: Fortress Press, 1982.

ROBBINS, Vernon K. Jesus the Teacher: a Socio-Rhetorical Interpretation of Mark. Philadelphia: Fortress Press, 1984.

SARNA, Nahum M. Exploring Exodus. New York: Schocken Books, 1987.

SCHWEIZER, Eduard. The Good News according to Mark. Atlanta: John Knox Press, 1970.

SENIOR, Donald. The Passion of Jesus in the Gospel of Mark. Collegeville: Liturgical Press, 1991.

STOCK, Augustine. Call to Discipleship: A Literary Study of Mark's Gospel. Wilmington: Michael Glazier, Inc., 1982.

-----. The Way in the Wilderness. Collegeville: Liturgical Press, 1969.

SWARTLEY, Willard Myers. "A Study in Markan Structure: the Influence of Israel's Holy History upon the Structure of the Gospel of Mark". Ann Arbor: University Microfilms, 1988.

-----. Mark: The Way for All Nations. Scottdale: Herald Press, 1979.

-----. "The Structural Function of the Term `Way' in Mark", in The New Way of Jesus, William Klassen, ed. Newton: Faith and Life Press, 1980.

SWETE, Henry Barclay. Commentary on Mark. Grand Rapids: Kregel Publications, 1913, reprinted in 1981.

TAYLOR, Vincent. The Gospel according to St. Mark, second edition. (Thornapple Commentaries). Grand Rapids: Baker, 1966.

TELFORD, William, editor. The Interpretation of Mark. Philadelphia: Fortress Press, 1985.

WENHAM, David. "'This Generation will not pass...' A Study of Jesus' Future Expectation in Mark 13," in Christ the Lord: Studies in Christology presented to Donald Guthrie. Harold H. Rowdon, editor. Downers Grove: InterVarsity Press, 1982.

WILCOCK, Michael. Mark. (Bible Study Commentary). London: Scripture Union, 1982.

WILLIAMSON Jr., Lamar. Mark. (Interpretation: A Bible Commentary for Teaching and Preaching). Atlanta: John Knox Press, 1983.

YODER, Perry. From Word to Life: a Guide to the Art of Bible Study. Scottdale: Herald Press, 1982.

ARTICLES IN JOURNALS

BATEMAN IV, Herbert W. "Psalm 110.1 and the New Testament", *Biblioteca Sacra*, Vol 149, no. 596 (Oct-Dec 1992).

BEASLEY-MURRAY, G.R. "Second Thoughts on the Composition of Mark 13." *New Testament Studies*, 29 (1983) pp 414-419.

BIBLICAL ARCHAEOLOGY REVIEW (**BAR**). Washington, D.D.: Biblical Archaeology Society.

CHRONIS, Harry L. "The Torn Veil: Cultus and Christology in Mark 15.37-39." *Journal of Biblical Literature*, 101/1 (1982) pp 97-114.

EDWARDS, James R. "The Baptism of Jesus according to the Gospel of Mark", *Journal of the Evangelical Theological Society*, 34/1 (March 1991), p. 43.

ULANSEY, David. "The Heavenly Veil Torn: Mark's Cosmic 'Inclusio'." Journal of Biblical Literature, 110/1 (1991), pp 123-125.